I0188825

CALIFORNIA HIGHWAY PATROL
3511
TRAFFIC OFFICER

The Zodiac Killer Cover-Up

AKA The Silenced Badge

LYNDON E. LAFFERTY

MANDAMUS
PUBLISHING
VALLEJO, CALIFORNIA

FIRST EDITION

Library of Congress Control Number: 2011927430

Lafferty, Lyndon E.

The Zodiac Killer Cover-Up AKA The Silenced Badge / Lyndon E. Lafferty

ISBN: 978-0-9829363-0-6

Published in the United States of America by:

Mandamus Publishing
PO Box 5268
Vallejo, CA 94591

AND

Outskirts Press, Inc.
10940 S Parker Road–515
Parker, CO 80134

www.outskirtspress.com/thezodiackillercoverup

Visit the Author's website at: www.thezodiackillercoverup.com

Jacket graphic designer: Stacy Forbes
Jacket design team: Lyndon, Yvonne, Carol, and Stacy

Interior images designer: Carol
Interior images design team: Lyndon, Yvonne, and Carol

PRINTED IN THE UNITED STATES OF AMERICA

AUTHOR RECEIVES ***SHOCKING*** MYSTERY LETTER

A WARNING OR DESPERATE PLEA?

Someone is scared to death, pleading for the author to stop the publication of this book.

To say my family and I are not intimidated, perhaps threatened, would *not* be a true statement.

As incredible as it may seem, just two days after the *Vallejo Times-Herald* printed a very nice article (November 1, 2010) about my book announcement party, I received a most disturbing letter.

The letter was also dated November 1, 2010. It was a full page, single-spaced typewritten letter, written by an extremely intelligent person with a detailed knowledge about the Zodiac. This person, who claimed they knew things about the killer and the case in general that nobody else knew, stated that if I printed my book—"Many innocent people could spend the rest of their lives in prison if the truth were told."

The anonymous person even included some physical evidence that would prove the true identity of the Zodiac. We could only wonder how this person obtained this "alleged evidence." The text and the wording of the letter was chilling, if not threatening. The address label was typed on a separate piece of heavy paper, cut off, pasted onto a regular envelope, and the letter was signed *"A Concerned Citizen."*

Two of my friends came over immediately and James

Dean took some photos.

I called a Special Agent with the Department of Justice in San Francisco and two Special Agents were at my house within an hour. The agents sealed everything and returned the next day to retrieve their sealed envelope after the Vallejo Police Department asked them to proceed with any investigation.

There is much more I could say about this bizarre letter.

My family members are very concerned, some suggesting I report it to the local media immediately. However, the coincidence is overwhelming and I feel certain there are those skeptics, who by nature and breeding, would find it most convenient to accuse me of creating a sensational fraud to promote sales of the book, and a few already have.

If the reader is asking the obvious question: “Do you think this letter is from the Zodiac?”

My answer is: It is quite possible.

The evidence enclosed with the letter is both suspicious and baffling. I do know that the Department of Justice is handling this matter as a serious incident.

ACKNOWLEDGMENTS

I dedicate this book to my loving wife Yvonne, for her patience, understanding, support, and great strength. She is my dearest and best friend, my seventh-grade sweetheart, and ever more.

To my children Lisa, and Curtis, who, even though I might not have always been there for them, they were always there for me.

To Carol, for her dedication, wit, creative brilliance, and my trusted typist who went on to review, edit, and proofread the final versions of my book. Carol was my personal collaborator and her suggestions were inspiring, giving my book a new luster. Thank you, Carol.

To my "Editor-in-Chief" Richard Hack, who helped turn a mass of writing into a comprehensible narrative. Richard is a true professional and with his guidance and support this story is now being told.

To the many detectives of several police departments, forensic specialists, members of the Department of Justice, FBI, OSI, and Naval Intelligence, I thank you for your cooperation and assistance in this lengthy investigation.

⋆ A special word of thanks to FBI Agent Floyd Barrus

(deceased) who provided information, which kept this case alive over these past 40 years, and it was my distinct honor to know Agent Barrus.

★ And to a special person, Homicide Detective Sergeant Leslie Lundblad Sr., who was forced to terminate his investigation. Ordered to destroy his file and notes on the suspect, the most significant case in his entire law enforcement career. He became sullen, withdrawn, and bitterly resentful. His inspiring words still echo from the grave: “Mr. Johnson, you tell Lyndon to never quit; he's got the right man.”

★ And most of all to my partner of 39 years, retired Naval Intelligence Agent Jerry Johnson, for his unwaivering dedication to our investigation.

To our task force psychologist Kate Riley, who met with us on several occasions. Kate provided a profound, excellent treatise on the psychological factors in the Zodiac serial killer. She is, indeed, a remarkable person who gave freely of her valuable time and professional expertise. We certainly thank you, Kate Riley.

To Edward T. Blake of Forensic Science Associates who ran our DNA, meeting with us on a few occasions, and Supervising Criminalist Paul Holes of the Contra Costa Sheriff's Department who has shared an ongoing and active interest in this investigation.

A special thanks to the affable and brilliant Marty Nemko, PhD, KGO radio talk show host and celebrity, who gave me the inspired name for my book. Thank you, Marty.

Also, I dedicate this book to my loyal and devoted task force, the Mandamus Seven. As a collective group, you provided the strength of endurance and a profound sense of justice to continue this incredible investigation. It was a great honor to know and associate with each and every one of you.

Lastly, I want to recognize the former presidents of the American Cryptogram Association, Edward Steinke, Henry Ephron, and William Sutton for their assistance. Independently, and each in their own way, gave me positive assessments of my code analysis. They motivated me to continue until I discovered Zodiac's methodology and his pattern in the last undeciphered 18 letters of his name. The pattern proves the name without question.

I would like to thank the senior staff member of the FBI Cryptology Unit in Quantico, VA who advised they had received a directive from President George W. Bush's office to appraise my code work. However, since they cannot prove my work is wrong, they will not say it is correct. Their reticence does little to nothing for the cause of justice, but considering the magnitude of the Zodiac case I can understand their delicate position in this matter. I would gladly testify under oath that my work is valid and would withstand the most critical examination. I would not expect them to do the same.

Respectfully,

Lyndon E. Lafferty

CONTENTS

PROLOGUE		I
I	GROWING UP IN VALLEJO • World War II	1
II	KOREAN WAR—JAPAN • Military Code School	5
III	CALIFORNIA HIGHWAY PATROL	11
IV	FACE-TO-FACE WITH THE ZODIAC • Staring Into the Face of a Psychotic Killer • His Next Victim?	19
V	SUSPECT CALLED IN	33
VI	OTHER AGENCIES • Federal Bureau of Investigation (FBI) • Criminal Identification and Investigation (CII) • Sheriff's Department • Naval Intelligence Services (NIS) • Office of Special Investigations (OSI)	43
VII	BACKGROUND ON SUSPECT	53

VIII	THREE SECRETS AND THREE OATHS	59
	• Destroy the Files	
	• Official Adultery and Blackmail	
	• National Security Agency Code Encryptions	
IX	ZODIAC CREATED	65
X	SIERRA CLUB INFAMY	71
	• Lake Tahoe	
	• Mysterious Disappearance of Donna Lass	
XI	SLEEPY HOLLOW	79
	• Voodoo, Black Magic, Hex Symbols	
	• The Two Witches	
	• Mount Diablo	
XII	SLIPPERY FOX	95
	• The Cops Are Busted	
	• Murder Same Night	
XIII	GENERAL INVESTIGATIONS	99
	• Interviews	
	• Meetings, Many Agencies, and Detectives	
XIV	SCHEMED SEDUCTION	107
XV	PERSONAL PROFILE	121
XVI	"ALL THE WORLD'S A STAGE"	135
	• The "Fish Bowl" Event	
	• Palm Prints	
XVII	THE CONFESSIONS	147
	• The Psychiatrist and The Grand Wizard	

XVIII THE LADY BLEW HER COVER! 157
- Mysterious Telephone Calls

XIX THE RAID 163

XX HANDWRITING AND OTHER EVIDENCE 169

XXI LES LUNDBLAD JR. AND MISCELLANEOUS 199
- Father, Sgt. Lundblad, and Zodiac

XXII MATHEMATICAL ANALYSIS 225
- Cal State University, Sacramento

XXIII LAKE BERRYESSA 237
- Sand Compaction Tests

XXIV I WATCH YOU A LOT 245

XXV RELATED INCIDENTS 253

XXVI THE LIBRARY! WHO, ME? 289
- Code Reference Book
- *The Mikado* Record

XXVII THE MOUNTAIN RETREAT 297
- Vicinity of Lake Tahoe
- Esoteric Society: Murder of Priest

XXVIII SAN FRANCISCO POLICE DEPARTMENT 309
- Tap Dance Kings
- Many Serious Problems
- Charges of Corruption

XXIX	ROBERT GRAYSMITH • Author of Two Books on Zodiac	327
XXX	PAMELA (SUENNEN) HUCKABY • Sister of Victim	335
XXXI	*AMERICA'S MOST WANTED* • John Walsh • Several Letters From Zodiac	353
XXXII	THE MANDAMUS SEVEN	357
XXXIII	CODE WORK	375
XXXIV	PSYCHOLOGICAL PROFILE • Psychological Profile by Clinical Psychologist (MFT) Over 20 Years Experience Specialty in Addictive Medicine Kaiser Permanente, San Francisco Bay Area and Private Practice	405
XXXV	CURRENT EVENTS	415
XXXVI	CONCLUSION • Letters ▪ State of CA Attorney General Bill Lockyer ▪ FBI ▪ President George Bush ▪ To - FBI Cryptographic Lab ▪ From - FBI Cryptographic Lab	429
DIARY NOTES		451

PROLOGUE

We know the true identity of the killer, Zodiac, and have known convincingly since March 15, 1971.

I was the first law enforcement officer to report a Zodiac suspect, and I am the only law enforcement officer to write a book about the case.

We ask now for a fair opportunity to be heard, and most importantly, a full and fair assessment of the evidence. For many years my partner and I have asked for nothing more. In light of the abundance of evidence, we would not settle for anything less. The obstacles have so far been insurmountable, and they are legion. For better or worse, circumstances very much beyond my control made me the heir to this investigation.

Who is the Zodiac? He is a pitiful, egocentric killer who hates women and young children, a sociopathic predator with virtually no self-esteem, who secretly wants to be arrested for his terrible acts of homicide. He is the most notorious, spine-chilling, and blood-curdling killer since Jack the Ripper.

Claiming 37 victims, the Zodiac's blood lust is supreme. The recently apprehended Gary Leon Ridgeway, the confessed Green River Killer of 48 victims in Washington and Oregon, is now regarded as the foremost serial killer in the nation. Like the Zodiac, Ridgeway had been a prime suspect for a long time, seventeen years. He was finally arrested on November 30, 2001. Ridgeway hated prostitutes, his primary targets, and young runaway girls. He was the classical opportunist, with sexual gratification his driving force.

Zodiac is another breed entirely. Revenge and a shattered ego were the compelling factors behind his need to kill. Zodiac was also empowered by taunting the police with his letters and codes, always bragging he would never be caught. With bravado he wrote to the police, notable personalities, and local newspapers in the San Francisco Bay Area and Riverside, California.

He is lonely and frustrated, and according to the Department of Justice (DOJ) profilers, a latent homosexual. Unlike typical serial killers, the Zodiac had a definite motive of revenge, to punish not solely his victims but society-at-large. His killings were a double-edged sword whereby he could brag he was better and smarter than all the judges and cops put together. By taunting them with his letters and codes, he executed his program of proving he was the killer. The murder of Paul Stine, the cab driver in San Francisco, was a plan carried out with detailed perfection. Zodiac needed physical evidence to prove to the world he was Stine's killer, so he cut off the major portion of the man's shirt. In subsequent letters, the Zodiac enclosed small remnants of the shirt, which were positively identified by the authorities.

The DOJ includes the killing of Cheri Jo Bates in their Zodiac profile. While the matter is still unresolved, the weight of the evidence tends to authenticate her murder by the Zodiac. This murder occurred just after midnight of October 30, 1966, on the UC Riverside campus. Zodiac had obviously stalked the young student. He disabled her Volkswagen, offered his assistance, and then slashed her throat. Here is the letter he sent shortly afterward:

THE ZODIAC'S LETTER TO THE PRESS-ENTERPRISE AND THE RIVERSIDE POLICE, 29 NOVEMBER 1966

(Diplomatic reproduction)

THE CONFESSION

BY ___________

SHE WAS YOUNG AND BEAUTIFUL. BUT NOW SHE IS BATTERED AND DEAD, SHE IS NOT THE FIRST VICTIM AND SHE WILL NOT BE THE LAST. I LAY AWAKE NIGHTS THINKING ABOUT MY NEXT VICTIM. MAYBE SHE WILL BE THE BEAUTIFUL BLOND THAT BABYSITS NEAR THE LITTLE STORE AND WALKS DOWN THE DARK ALLEY EACH EVENING ABOUT SEVEN. OR MAYBE SHE WILL BE THE SHAPELY BLUE EYED BROWNETT THAT SAID NO WHEN I ASKED HER FOR A DATE IN SCHOOL. BUT MAYBE IT WILL NOT BE EITHER. BUT I SHALL CUT OFF HER FEMALE PARTS AND DEPOSIT THEM FOR THE WHOLE CITY TO SEE. SO DON'T MAKE IT EASY FOR ME. KEEP YOUR SISTERS AND DAUGHTERS, AND WIVES OFF THE STREETS AND ALLEYS. MISS BATES WAS STUPID. SHE WENT TO HER SLAUGHTER LIKE A LAMB. SHE DID NOT PUT UP A STRUGGLE. BUT I DID. IT WAS A BALL. I FIRST PULLED THE MIDDLE WIRE FROM THE DISTRIBUTOR. THEN I WAITED FOR HER IN THE LIBRARY AND FOLLOWED HER OUT AFTER ABOUT TWO MINUTES. THE BATTERY MUST HAVE BEEN ABOUT DEAD BY THEN I THEN OFFERED TO HELP. SHE WAS THEN VERY WILLING TO TALK TO ME. I TOLD HER THAT MY CAR WAS DOWN THE STREET AND THAT I WOULD GIVE HER A LIFT HOME. WHEN WE WERE AWAY FROM THE LIBRARY WALKING, I SAID IT WAS ABOUT TIME. SHE ASKED ME "ABOUT TIME FOR WHAT." I SAID IT WAS ABOUT TIME FOR HER TO DIE. I GRABBED HER AROUND THE NECK WITH MY HAND OVER HER MOUTH AND MY OTHER HAND WITH A SMALL KNIFE AT HER THROAT. SHE WENT VERY WILLINGLY. HER BREAST FELT VERY WARM AND FIRM UNDER MY HANDS, BUT ONLY ONE THING WAS ON MY MIND. MAKING HER PAY FOR THE BRUSH OFFS THAT SHE HAD GIVEN ME DURING THE YEARS PRIOR. SHE DIED HARD. SHE SQUIRMED AND SHOOK AS I CHOAKED HER, AND HER LIPS TWITCHED. SHE LET OUT A SCREAM ONCE AND I KICKED HER HEAD TO SHUT HER UP. I PLUNGED THE KNIFE INTO HER AND IT BROKE. I THEN FINISHED THE JOB BY CUTTING HER THROAT. I AM NOT SICK. I AM INSANE. BUT THAT WILL NOT STOP THE GAME. THIS LETTER SHOULD BE PUBLISHED FOR ALL TO READ IT. IT JUST MIGHT SAVE THAT GIRL IN THE ALLEY. BUT THAT'S UP TO YOU. IT WILL BE ON YOUR CONSCIENCE. NOT MINE. YES I DID MAKE THAT CALL TO YOU ALSO. IT WAS JUST A WARNING. BEWARE...I AM STALKING YOUR GIRLS NOW.

CC. CHIEF OF POLICE
ENTERPRISE

(Diplomatic reproduction: an original version; no corrections made)

On the evening of December 20, 1968, a high school couple, David Faraday and Betty Lou Jensen, were sitting in their car late at night parked on a desolate road in a popular lovers' lane between Vallejo and Benicia, a town a few miles east. Then, they were stalked and shot to death with a small .22-caliber weapon. The Zodiac wrote another letter to the police, giving them exact and specific details to prove he was their killer.

On July 4, 1969, Darlene Ferrin (née Suennen) and Michael Mageau were attacked at midnight as they sat in Darlene's car at Blue Rock Springs Park in Vallejo, yet another popular hangout for young lovers. This time the assailant's weapon was a 9-mm automatic pistol. Darlene was dead on arrival at the hospital, but Michael Mageau survived. The Zodiac drove to a phone booth just two blocks from the sheriff's department and called the police department, claiming he had just killed two people at Blue Rock Springs Park.

Then, on September 27, 1969, Zodiac struck again at Lake Berryessa (a man-made lake in adjoining Napa County) just a short drive from Vallejo. Now wearing the infamous black Zodiac hood adorned with a bright white cross-hair symbol, he crept upon a young couple lying on the shore of Twin Oaks Cove. Standing suddenly in front of Cecelia Ann Shepard and her friend Bryan Hartnell was a large man holding a 9-mm automatic pistol or a .45-caliber weapon. A large bayonet-type knife was strapped to the hooded man's waist. He ordered Ms. Shepard to tie Hartnell's hands behind his back, and then proceeded to tie her hands behind her, also.

After a rather lengthy conversation, almost friendly at times, Zodiac said he would have to kill them. At Hartnell's request, Zodiac stabbed Hartnell a few times first, but then in an orgasmic frenzy stabbed young Cecelia Ann Shepard 24 times. Three of the stab wounds included one on each breast and one to the vaginal area. Hartnell survived, but Cecelia Ann Shepard died two days later from her critical stab wounds. As he did in

Vallejo, Zodiac called the Napa Police Department claiming he had just killed the young couple at Lake Berryessa. He also left a note on Bryan Hartnell's Karmann Ghia. Zodiac's writing on the car door stated the time as 6:30, and included the dates of the other two murders in Vallejo, 12-20-68 and 7-4-69.

Within a few days, letters and cryptic codes were sent to the *Vallejo Times-Herald*, the *San Francisco Chronicle*, and the *San Francisco Examiner*. The first cipher-code was in three parts, with one part sent to each of the respective newspapers.

On October 11, 1969, Paul Stine, a cab driver in San Francisco, was shot once in the head with a 9-mm automatic pistol. His passenger was the Zodiac. This was the first instance of any witnesses seeing the killer. There were kids across the street in a two-story apartment watching as the killer cut the shirt from the lifeless body of the driver, and then calmly used it to wipe the interior of the cab. There were even two San Francisco police officers that talked with Zodiac as he was walking away from the crime scene.

So it was, shocking and sudden—a mad-dog killer was on the loose, and apparently living nearby, very close indeed. This is when the composite sketch was made, and every police car in the entire Bay Area carried one on its car visor, including the CHP.

I am the only living person who can testify to the true and actual events, circumstances that made the case next-to-unsolvable. This 40-year-plus journey began when I stared into the quivering and snarling face of a sociopathic madman in November of 1970 from my parked Highway Patrol car. There is no doubt in my mind I was a target, his next victim. This experience, too, was mine and mine alone, one that haunts me to this day. He intended to shoot me just like he later shot a security guard and another young man, at different locations, on the same night in 1973, and both in their left eye. I am alive today due to an instinctive survival reflex. Any deliberation could have been fatal.

Proud and arrogant in their stupidity, the authorities in Solano County conspired to release a mad-dog killer and give him immunity from the law. This man, who had begun calling himself the Zodiac in August of 1969, went on to kill a total of 37 people, a number closely confirmed by the DOJ.

After several months of investigation another obstacle surfaced, which compounded the problem. Sergeant Lundblad told me, "Guess what, the Lake Herman Road killings are not ours. That small strip of land, the pull-out, is within the city limits of Benicia, and I have been ordered to turn everything I have over to them." He continued, "Can you believe this? I have given my word to several kids that I would never reveal their identity, and I will keep my word. They are getting absolutely nothing from me."

> *To this day, the Solano County Sheriff's Department has no official jurisdiction in the Zodiac case. For some unknown reason this information has never been made public.*

The crime scene evidence, bullet casings, photographs, etc., were all gathered and placed into evidence by the Solano County Sheriff's detectives. The sheriff's department also conducted witness statements and other interviews. Therefore, when the Benicia Police Department assumed official jurisdiction in the investigation several months after the fact, they were not enthused. Indeed, they maintained such a low profile in the Zodiac case the public-at-large continued to refer additional leads and information to the Solano County Sheriff's Dept. Lundblad told me, "They are not 'happy campers.'"

Detective Sergeant Leslie Lundblad was the lead homicide investigator for the Solano County Sheriff's Dept. and in charge of the Zodiac killings within their jurisdiction.

After I conducted a very preliminary investigation of this menacing madman, and discussed my findings with FBI Agent Floyd Barrus, Barrus ran a background check and advised me,

"He is a phony son-of-a-bitch."

"Floyd, what is the deal—what did he do?"

"Lyndon, I cannot tell you!"

When I told Sgt. Lundblad what Agent Barrus had discovered, Lundblad became very interested in this strange man. Unknown to his superiors Sgt. Lundblad sent two of his deputies to interview neighbors and others who knew this individual. The deputies reported that the neighbors said the man was really strange and he was away from home two or three nights a week. (Lundblad told me the entire story but later denied telling me.)

Nearly three months later Sgt. Lundblad decided to call Mr. Tucker in for questioning. When Tucker went home he called his wife immediately and this is when the shit hit-the-fan. Sgt. Lundblad was called by his boss and ordered to meet him in the judge's chambers in Fairfield. Lundblad could tell his boss was enraged.

Sitting in concert in the judge's chambers was Lundblad's boss (the Sheriff of Solano County), the most powerful and admired Judge Dennis Winston, and one other superior court judge. The dynamics of this meeting must have been totally surreal, as the judge had a terrible secret he could never share with any living soul. Shocked and dumbfounded he was undoubtedly speechless as Sgt. Lundblad related a false story of why he had called in Mr. Tucker. (He could not reveal the man was a Zodiac suspect.) It is not unlikely the judge might have suspected that he, himself, was the fly in the ointment, that he was perhaps under investigation being accused of committing adultery with Mr. Tucker's wife, and this was the real reason Tucker had been called in for questioning.

Whatever was said by whom, Judge Winston made it very clear Mr. Tucker was a fine man and unless he had killed someone he would not be investigated for anything. The sheriff obediently complied, assuring the prestigious judge he would take care of everything.

Alone with his boss after the embarrassing encounter, Lundblad told his boss the real story but was ordered to burn his files, destroy all of his notes and never mention the man's name again.

It was months later that Sgt. Lundblad discovered the judge was screwing the suspect's wife—Mrs. Tucker. He later told me the whole story, and then said, "You can never breathe a word of this to anyone."

Committed to a vow of secrecy on three critical factors, which could help solve the case, my personal life became a living hell. When Sgt. Lundblad died in October 1977 he took with him the terrible secrets, which had haunted him since that memorable date in 1971. For six-and-a-half years Sgt. Lundblad lived in a shadow of shame, embarrassed by his lifelong career in law enforcement. His conscience made him cringe every time I walked into his office. His personal secretary, wife, and family members all personally confided to me how the shattered man's life had been changed, the disgust and disdain that he felt for his boss and the judicial system, in general. He felt like he brought great dishonor to the badge he wore, in fact, like a knife had been plunged into the middle of his back. Yet, with Lundblad powerless to change events, the greatest shame was laid where it belonged—on the Superior Court judge, and Lundblad's boss.

Our suspect did not simply fall through the cracks. From March 1971 he was shielded and protected just like a foreign dignitary with diplomatic immunity. When Sgt. Lundblad was ordered to destroy his notes and his file and never mention the suspect's name again, this investigation received a death sentence. The corrupt and unscrupulous attitudes of a Superior Court judge and his obedient lackey, the sheriff, were outrageous. Conspiracy to commit a felony is entirely too mild a term to describe the crime for which they should be charged. Their actions enabled the insane killer to continue on his path, a vengeful blood lust. The judge was very aware that our suspect had every reason to hate him with an unbridled passion, and that our suspect had personal and intimate information, which could destroy his reputation and political career.

I have never been able to share my information with any police department. The authorities contacted have included the State of California Attorney General's Office and the Federal Bureau of Investigation (FBI). My partner became our primary spokesman, giving the police agencies just enough information to hopefully gain their support. This never happened, in spite of our continued efforts.

Early on, after I discovered several disclosures of sensitive information, which threatened the security and safety of my family, I became extremely guarded with my information. Sitting in the bleachers or creating a website of scurrilous and redundant information is one thing, but to be directly involved with your life on the line is another matter indeed. Those of you who have not been there will never understand, nor could I expect you to.

Other departments had little or no interest, as the man was not their suspect. Yes, Sgt. Lundblad's badge was silent until his death and for many other mitigating factors mine was, also.

Jerry Johnson, my dedicated partner from Naval Intelligence, has been the mover and shaker, a guiding light in this entire case. Jerry has taken the position that until our suspect is arrested we are in no position to write a book. However, my perspective is somewhat different. An arrest would be the crowning glory of our 40 years of investigation, but I am now convinced this will never happen. Our suspect may never be arrested or charged with the Zodiac killings because the conventional "smoking gun" does not exist.

Considering the facts of my own personal health, and that our suspect is 91 at this writing, time is running out. But there are other reasons to go to press, which are very germane. An FBI analysis of my code decryptions has been performed with very positive results. Considering the fact it was to me and me alone that Sgt. Lundblad revealed his shocking story, I am now a key and principal witness, the one who verified Lundblad's story.

There are still many problems. The suspect as well as the sheriff, who released him, are still very much alive. In the face of threatening lawsuits and possible elements of danger, I nonetheless feel compelled to tell this fascinating tale. In order to mitigate personal pain and embarrassment, the true names of four central players involved shall not be mentioned.

In this prologue I should state our suspect's name is now known by several people, including those with their own computer websites. His identity has leaked from other police departments and various incompetent and careless persons. Until this writing, Jerry and I will swear under oath that we have never revealed our suspect's identity or name to any person without official jurisdiction.

Unable to disclose the sensitive details, honoring my pledge of secrecy, we were, in effect, dismissed with prejudice during the early stages of this investigation. However, year after year, sources very close to this case advised, "Your man is still a strong suspect."

We have asked ourselves many times, "If our suspect had been cleared many years previously, why did Fred Shirasago of the DOJ want to hear our tape recording in 1985?" Additionally we ask, "Why do their handwriting experts ask us for additional writing and printing samples, especially after three separate examinations were performed over the years?"

One essential fact cannot be stressed enough. When our suspect was *cleared* by the Solano County Sheriff's Dept. (and the judge), how many times did they repeat this unprecedented sham to other agencies and homicide detectives throughout Northern California?

What police department would pursue a suspect when they had been advised: "We have checked out this man very carefully, and he is a highly respected citizen with no criminal record, and he most certainly is not the Zodiac."

As the Zodiac case has never been resolved, it is still an

"open" case officially; but unless the authorities receive new evidence, e.g. DNA, the investigation is, in reality, a closed matter. Furthermore, there are several detectives and at least two police departments who still sincerely believe the Zodiac case was solved when Arthur Leigh Allen died in October 1992. The Vallejo and San Francisco Police Departments admit that Allen was their strongest and best suspect.

Jim Lang, the Deputy District Attorney of Solano County, who was working with the Vallejo officials told them many times, "You have no evidence, and therefore no case, against Arthur Leigh Allen."

He also told them: "Their [our] suspect is much stronger and a better suspect than Allen, and you should focus your resources on him."

We are always amazed at comments such as these. It is simply tragic—if the suspect is not their own, they are blind, deaf, and dumb. Arthur Leigh Allen had already been cleared of suspicion in July 1971 and was again in 2002.

Given the suspect's advanced age and health problems, it is generally agreed by the professionals that he will not go on another killing spree. Those of us in law enforcement have learned that the professionals are often wrong. When the safety of your beloved family members is in doubt, then it is only prudent, and wise, to err on the side of caution. I have had a personal association with the killer that has created a living nightmare—and none of it within my means to prevent or change.

When we recall the travesty of the gross injustice in the OJ Simpson double-murder case, we can better understand how logic becomes an idiot's playground. Things happen that are not supposed to happen. As God is my witness, my partners and I (the Mandamus Seven) have always tried to share our material and our case with the proper authorities, but in the past 40 years the latter have ignored and stymied and stonewalled us again and again.

Many years ago I told my group, "Hey, no more—they can all go straight to hell."

My dilemma has been this: How can we reveal the facts and maintain the integrity of anonymity, protecting the rights and lives of all concerned? As Cicero, the Roman orator, said,

> "Any man may make a mistake,
> but none but a fool will continue in it."

If in all these years I have made a tragic mistake, then there is no bigger fool than I. Of course, there are several of us in this category, and we are all guilty if we are wrong. Compelled to follow the trail wherever it would lead, each turning twist revealed one fact leading to another—five, ten, twenty, a hundred and more. If you were with us, what would you say?

Time after time, year after year, I wished it were not real; that reasons, yet to be discovered, would answer all our nagging questions and the truth of his innocence would be revealed. My involvement has been a constant struggle, and I have prayed I would wake up from this terrible dream. Can somebody, please, tell me why this man is not the Zodiac, so I can get on with the rest of my life? There was absolutely no doubt in my mind we would find evidence to exonerate our suspect completely, but the exact opposite occurred, time after time.

My health and my marriage were nearly destroyed, and many times when my kids needed their dad, I was not there for them. My prayer today is:

> In some way, I can mend some broken hearts and be there whenever I am needed. I did not share the sacrifice alone.

A curse or a blessing? In my heart and soul I believe we have solved the Zodiac case, but the man, most likely, will never be charged. During all these years there have existed powerful and life-threatening reasons why I had to conceal my identity and my involvement in this investigation. I have had to lie to family and friends alike, and at times, strangers out of the blue.

Over lunch with the various authorities we contacted, it was never possible to relate the complete story of our suspect. When we parted company the detectives would ask, "What the hell does the schoolteacher have to do with the Zodiac case?" "Who are those guys anyhow?" "What agency are they with?" "Did you get their case number?"

The greatest problem we could never overcome was having no authority whatsoever while trying to convince an official agency to question and investigate our strong Zodiac suspect. We tried desperately to turn the man over to any department that would listen, with no success at all.

When our years of work fell into the unauthorized hands of another author, my partners and I were shocked, and I became enraged. St. Martin's Press was getting ready to print things, which could place my family members in a great deal of danger. We were dealing with a pure psycho, and they were getting ready to tell him who we were.

And this, my dear reader, was the caliber of people we were trying to work with. Do you think I am going to trust a bunch of badge-toting clowns with additional information? Not me—never again.

I asked, "How does one proceed in this impossible dilemma? How does one continue an investigation without any legal standing, and unable to trust one's investigative findings with careless officials who truly hope your suspect is not the real Zodiac anyhow?"

It is extremely difficult when a detective with jurisdiction must first clear the way by asking permission from the mighty and influential Superior Court judge—the same judge who created the insane Zodiac in the first place.

Caught between a rock and a hard spot, poor Sgt. Lundblad died a broken man. He had devoted his life to law enforcement and had an outstanding record. When he was ordered to terminate his Zodiac investigation and destroy the suspect's file, he was crushed. From that day on he was a very miserable person. However, and known only by his family members, he continued his own investigation on his days off. His son, Leslie Jr., confided to me, "I went with my father on more than one surveillance, and my father was convinced your suspect was the Zodiac killer."

This is not your typical crime story. This book is also a personal revelation of my attitudes to life, in general, and my cherished beliefs about man's relationship to God. Fundamentally, my concepts of morality and trust in my fellow man were stretched to my mental and physical capacity, and at times beyond.

This Zodiac investigation of our suspect should have died when the principal investigator and official authority was ordered to terminate his investigation and never mention the suspect's name again. But the self-reliance that took shape in my early youth, the experiences, and exposure in a conflicted society during World War II formed attitudes of bias, caution, suspicion, and self-preservation. Most significantly, I learned the value of patience and persistence. If a man has faith and believes in his goal, he will prevail.

In his last letter dated April 24, 1978, Zodiac said,

"I AM BACK WITH YOU."

In this letter he claimed 37 victims. The FBI is still attempting to authenticate other Zodiac letters, which have never been released to the public domain, and they are discussed in my book.

Perhaps in another day and time, pretending to be something I am not and forgetting the lessons of my youth, I would have relinquished my rights and rolled over to the authorities in a pusillanimous tremor.

In Japan during the Korean War, when I was denied

emergency leave to visit my mother on her deathbed, I swore an oath to myself:

> No man would ever again violate my God-given rights—and no man would terminate our Zodiac investigation. Unlike many cops, I had an attitude long before I ever wore a badge.

The Mandamus Seven were convinced beyond the shadow of any doubt that they knew the true identity of the serial killer, the infamous Zodiac. Shrouded in complete secrecy, this group of professionals continued their investigations until death took many of them, one by one. Today, of the original group, only four of the seven remain, and one or two new ones have stepped in.

Now, after more than forty-plus years of silence, the true story will be told for the very first time. The public will be stunned by the shocking and outrageous official corruption in this investigation on the one hand, and the license to kill that was issued on the other. The psychotic Zodiac is still alive, a respected member of his community, and living day-to-day. He is still laughing at the stupid police.

Profilers in the Zodiac case might have asked, "Would it be normal, rational, and indeed predictable behavior for the Zodiac to employ his code-writing talents as he terrorized the public-at-large?" While it was on their list (military code experience) it was just passed over without much concern. In any event, the Zodiac knew better than anyone else that any person with a code background was a critical and vital clue to his identity, a major factor in the Zodiac investigation.

As a side note, the errors made by Zodiac in his first three-part cipher did not receive a lot of publicity. These errors would not have been made if he had been a true expert. What this does tend to prove is giving weight to the premise he did use a reference source to assist him. He had lost track of his letter substitutes on a few letters, (i.e. HONGERTUE for

DANGEROUS). He also missed A or S a few times (i.e. ATOP for STOP).

One of my friends I worked with in Japan received a high commendation from our agency and accolades from the CIA, as he and another buddy had broken one of the Russian codes. When I saw him in Branson, MO at our convention recently, he told me all about it. One does not have to be a genius to solve a code. Dan told me, "We were determined and persistent, and we finally put it all together." He also said, "I never made rank so fast in my entire career." These are the guys copying letter perfect, Moscow and Peking Press at 60 to 90 words a minute, while they read a magazine. The transmissions of code are so unbelievably fast it sounds like radar.

Back in civilian life, just prior to the expiration of my security clearance, I received a letter from the National Security Agency asking if I wanted a job. Due to my mother's continued poor health, I had to decline.

Please refer to Chapter XXXIII for a detailed discussion of my personal decryptions of Zodiac's unsolved codes and ciphers. The Zodiac made a fatal mistake because he never thought he would ever be an official Zodiac suspect. Along with past presidents of the American Cryptographic Society, the FBI Cryptoanalysis Unit, to a degree, has also proffered a positive assessment. This is now critical evidence in the Zodiac case.

For the sake of brevity, omissions and deletions could have been made in the telling of my story. However, it is my opinion anything less than a detailed comprehensive report would be not only unwarranted, but also an act of irresponsible literary license. Armed with the totality of the facts, a prosecutor will welcome all the information he can find. In addition, 37 homicide victims and their families will settle for nothing less, and rightfully so. The principal role of the investigator, in fact, his sacred duty is to disclose every known fact. If the jury is expected to render a verdict, which is just and intelligent, they should know it all. The people are the final arbiters.

I

GROWING UP IN VALLEJO

I grew up in the city of Vallejo, California some 30 miles northeast of San Francisco, and about 60 miles southwest of Sacramento, the state capital. Strategically located on the Carquinez Straits near the northernmost reaches of San Francisco Bay, Vallejo is adjacent to the mouth of the Napa River at the west end of Solano County, and Mare Island Naval Shipyard, formerly a major shipbuilding center and naval base. To the east lies the great Delta of the Sacramento and San Joaquin Rivers, which provide fresh water to the fertile farmland of the Central Valley and many of the cities of Southern California.

Close to two major freeways and a number of state highways, Vallejo is nestled within a web of roads that can take you fast and far in any direction.

Zodiac's first three victims in Northern California lived in Vallejo, and eventually, over time, more would be added to his list. Over one-fifth of his claimed 37 victims were from Vallejo; lives he took on a killing spree that lasted eight years or more, perhaps much more.

It was here that I worked as an officer on the California Highway Patrol, devoting 28 years to law enforcement. I have lived here my entire life, with the exception of Japan, where I lived for two years during the Korean War.

It does not seem likely that any two psychologists would agree on the influence of environment in a child's formative years and the societal attitudes in the adult life, but they must be very real indeed. There is little doubt in my mind; my reaction to and attitudes toward life, in general, have been greatly influenced by the experiences in my youth. When the war ended in 1945 I was only 12 years old, and I had already experienced many things in life that should not be allowed. And I learned how to survive on the streets at a very young age.

Vallejo, during World War II, was a four-year Mardi Gras, which would make the French Quarter in New Orleans look like a tea party. With the gambling parlors on lower Georgia Street, the bars, prostitutes, penny arcades, Frank's It's Rich Café, Chinese restaurants, the Hanlon, Strand, Senator, Rio Del Mar, Rita, Studio and Victory theatres, Vallejo was a wild, frenetic town.

The underground Bozeman's pool and billiard parlor was a favorite hangout for all the punks. Secret doors and tunnels crossed from lower Georgia to Virginia Streets and some are still there. Organized crime owned all the pinball machines, while the notorious Baby Face Nelson had a contract to rent a house for two weeks a year, located across the street from the old Vallejo General Hospital on Tennessee Street. I know the family.

In the beginning of the war the government was building several housing tracts to accommodate the thousands of people they were importing to staff Mare Island Naval Shipyard. Thousands of others migrated to Vallejo and Hunters Point in San Francisco, all looking for work. Suddenly, Vallejo became a mixture of several diverse cultures, a shock to the established white community. The population swelled from 12,000 to 25,000 overnight with marines, sailors, and Filipino pachukos with their thick soles and gold chains. The Hell's Angels were also frequent visitors, 30 to 50 in a pack; they would literally take over the city. With the booze flowing like water, riots were not uncommon, especially on Friday and Saturday nights. Vallejo was not a happy resort town, and it seemed to mirror the depression and the hostility of the war itself.

This was also the environment of the popular Zodiac

suspect, Arthur Leigh Allen, with whom I went to school and knew fairly well. Lee, as he was called, was one-half semester behind me in school. He helped win many swimming events for the Vallejo High School Apaches and was a superb diver.

II

KOREAN WAR – JAPAN

On October 1, 1952, I joined the United States Air Force during the Korean War. The government was concerned with a failing of our communication intelligence and the National Security Agency was ordained, mandated in the same month and year. With code interception and code decryption, Communications Intelligence (COMINT) became a priority. After spending eight-and-a-half months in radio electronics and basic code schooling, I was offered an opportunity to join an elite top-secret branch under the chain of command of the National Security Agency, the USAF Security Service, which I accepted. Studying advanced and foreign codes, I spent another eight weeks in the sultry heat of Biloxi, Mississippi, and soon found myself in Moriyama, Nagoya, and Obu, Japan where I would live the next two years of my life.

"Lafferty, we couldn't believe the results of your final examination, so we pulled our master tape and discovered eight mistakes on our tape. Congratulations—you are the first person in the history of our school to pass the examination with a perfect score." The grizzled master sergeant, with hash marks covering most of his uniform, shook my hand and I left his office in a daze. He never explained how they discovered the eight mistakes, and I never asked.

A few days later I was called for an interview with the base commander, Major General Powell.

"Airman Lafferty, what do you want to do with the rest of your life?"

"Sir, I have absolutely no idea, sir."

"Well, we would like to offer you a job here at Keesler Air Force Base as a code instructor. What would you think about that? Promotions and making rank are especially good in our technical and teaching positions."

"Sir, I am speechless—I truly do not know what to say, sir."

"Well, you give it a lot of thought."

We continued to talk for about another twenty or thirty minutes, and I walked back to my barracks "on Cloud Nine." (His WAF secretary was absolutely beautiful—hmm.)

My Air Force specialty was as a code intercept operator and in this capacity I had considerable experience in working with a variety of domestic and foreign codes. If someone had told me that my code training would be instrumental in solving a serial killer's code some twenty years later, some maniac who called himself the "Zodiac," I would have called them crazy.

There were only seven of us with a priority flight status, and when we landed at Fukuoka Air Force Base in Japan we were totally exhausted. It was about 1:00 AM in the middle of December, the ground hard with snow and ice. The faint lights were barely visible through the freezing fog as we lugged our heavy duffel bags over our shoulders. As our boots crunched the snow, we were led through a maze of wooden-floored tents, the air thick with smoke from the oil-burning heaters.

"Ano-nay, koko benjo—benjo, benjo."

("Here is the bathroom—benjo.")

The old Japanese papa-san opened a door showing us the bathroom.

The only thing we removed were our boots when we slipped under the frozen sheets and two wool blankets. Papa-san fired up our stove and in ten minutes we fell asleep. Around 2:00 or 3:00 AM in the totally dark tent, I woke up with a splitting headache. My nostrils and throat were nearly clogged shut from an acid-like burning, and I jumped out of bed kicking open the two doors for fresh air. The tent was filled with toxic fumes, and I shook my buddies awake telling them to get out. Some were gagging and coughing, but in a minute we were all gasping for fresh air outside the tent. Within a few minutes several military police (MP's) were there and dozens of other GI's shivering in their shorts asking, "What the hell is going on?" Someone said, "Where did the rags come from?" It appeared that our heater vent had been stuffed with rags.

Later the same day we found ourselves aboard a "goony-bird" C-46, even after the pilot, a captain, told the terminal commander, a master sergeant, "Your plane will never leave the ground with the weight of seven men and their 100-pound duffel bags."

"These men have a priority flight clearance, and I am giving you an order to take them." (We were shocked.)

The plane was shaking violently, and with the lightning and hail we all thought we were surely going to die. The one crew member did not give us much hope when he had us put on bulky parachutes and showed us how to pull the ripcord. Some of the guys got sick and were barfing in coffee cans hanging from their necks.

The next night found us sleeping in the cellar of a beautiful hotel in Tokyo, only to be jarred awake by a strong earthquake. Welcome to Japan!

Japan was a wonderful experience, and during my two-year tour I swam the ocean in the Ise Peninsula, Lake Kawaguchi, and attended Nagoya University. I participated in Japanese-Christian youth groups, and danced with the Nagoya Ballet (Minoru Ochi) as a tap dancer and opened his recital with "An American in Paris."

My crowning glory was climbing Mt. Fujiyama (Fujisan). The Japanese have a saying:

> "He who climbs Fuji-san once, is wise.
> He who climbs Fuji-san twice, is a fool."

My buddy Scotty and I literally flew down the lava flow to catch our guide. He had stolen Scotty's new 35-MM camera with its telephoto and wide-angle lenses. He had a 30-minute lead on us, and we came down so fast we had to wait another 30 minutes before he arrived at station number five. We escorted him to the local police station, and we persuaded the officer to let him go without any charges. As hundreds of villagers looked on, we regretted the fact his humiliation could actually cost him his life—by his own hand. The sight was pitiful. The officer pointed down the dusty road giving him an order to leave. The crowd parted, and the poor man, with his head hung low in shame, walked away. Not one person spoke a word to break the eerie silence.

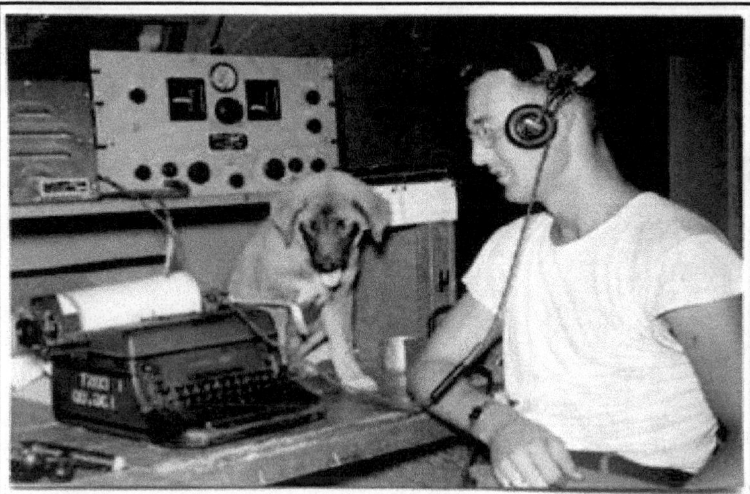

Donald Dickey and his radio mascot. A typical code intercept work station.

Converted barracks from horse stables, Moriyama, Japan.
In my room, me on right and good buddy Donald Dickey.

Myojin Torii, gate of purification on top of Mt. Fujiyama.
Me with hiking staff and guide.

Bottom of Mt. Fujiyama. Would never do it again.

III

CALIFORNIA HIGHWAY PATROL

It is just my opinion, but based on twenty-eight years of law enforcement and dealing with many agencies—FBI, Secret Service, Naval Intelligence, INS, and a host of detectives in numerous police departments—the California Highway Patrol is the finest law enforcement organization in the state, if not the entire country. In the 1960s and '70s, the CHP was making more felony arrests each year than the combined efforts of the five largest police departments in the entire state of California. I would guess the ratio today is still the same.

A good friend encouraged me to take the test. We had worked together at the Metropolitan Life Insurance Company, and he resigned to join the CHP. He told me later, "It was the best decision I ever made."

Passing 156th out of 6,000 who had taken the test, I found myself in the very next class, the Governor's class of January 1964. The last thing I wanted to do in life was pack a gun and wear a badge. However, like my good friend said it turned out to be one of the best decisions in my life, also. Much like the military, the regimen and discipline were tolerable, but the power of the badge created a few assholes you could not escape. As they rose to the level of their incompetence, they demonstrated the "Peter Principle" precisely. However, the vast majority of officers on the road were intelligent, dedicated, and courageous.

On a quiet Sunday morning about 9:30, we received a call to respond to an "11-80" (a very serious accident with no details). The location was eastbound Highway 24, just east of the Caldecott Tunnel, with bodies in the traffic lanes. Straddling the gravel divider and the fast lane, at 60 to 90 miles per hour is one thing, but when you are doing so on the wrong side of the freeway, that is something else. My break-in officer was giving me my first white-knuckle ride, and there were many more to follow.

Arriving on the right side of the freeway, we saw two persons lying in the center lane on the blind side of the curve as vehicles shot out of the tunnel at high rates of speed. The drivers were hitting their brakes, some fishtailing around the two helpless and unconscious people. We pulled between the bodies and the tunnel. I know, for a fact, that Officer Jim Cherry saved two lives as he literally pulled them out of the center of the traffic lanes. As he did this, I was running toward the tunnel throwing flares in the air as fast as I could light them. The two victims survived, and it was the knowledge and courage of Officer Cherry that saved them. In a situation like this, it is not a matter of if the persons would be hit, only when.

Over the years I made several felony arrests and had other memorable experiences, some of which I have tried to forget. The nightmares and the post-traumatic syndrome continue—unending. But there is something about the adrenaline rush, which is very euphoric.

"Officer," a motorist said in an excited tone, "there is a large group of cars coming down the freeway, forcing people off the road, throwing beer bottles at the cars, and some are actually stopping in the traffic lanes. And—oh God, here they come!"

This was my first meeting with the "Lower Den" car club of Oakland—Cougars, Mustangs, Plymouth Road Runners, Camaros, Coupe de Villes, and Dodge Chargers. Nearly every car had the skulls, dice, or panties hanging from their mirror, and after counting about twenty of them, I lost track. They had traffic backed up behind them for over a mile.

Turning east onto Highway 4 from Interstate 680, they

turned again onto Solano Way, which was a very narrow road through some swampy marshland. The Concord Police Department blocked their entrance into the city of Concord, and the group of cars began turning around. Parking at a 45-degree angle, I used the patrol car to block them from leaving. As one car slipped by, the driver hollered at me, "Hey boy, you better put down your telephone."

The situation was really heating up as about a dozen young black males began walking toward me. I was standing behind my open door with my right hand wrapped around the butt of my 12-gauge shotgun, which was resting on the seat just out of sight.

I told the group, "You have walked close enough," but they kept right on coming. I then pulled the shotgun into their line of sight and pumped a round into the magazine, telling them again, "You have come close enough."

As they began to dance and jive one of them said, "Shit man, he ain't gonna fuck with your black ass—he'll blow you away. Hey motherfucker, you use that?"

I replied, "You sure don't want to find out."

It seemed like forever, but I soon heard sirens in the distance. In about ten minutes every police vehicle and officer within a fifteen-mile radius had arrived. A couple of stolen vehicles were recovered, and several people were arrested for outstanding warrants and a variety of drug and weapons violations. I enjoyed every single minute of this event.

The next day my lieutenant asked me, "How many citations did you write?" I told him, "Not one."

After an armed robbery at the Safeway store on Interstate 80 and Georgia Street, Vallejo, the cops were searching for a black-over-yellow T-Bird, 1963 or '64 vintage, with three black males. Another vehicle with two more men was also reported, but they thought the vehicle had gone west across the Carquinez Bridge.

I had just finished having a cup of coffee with my

sergeant at the Black Oak Restaurant in Vacaville. The CHP had a patrol car at Interstate 680, one at North Texas Street in Fairfield, and the sergeant had positioned himself at Cherry Glen Road just south of Vacaville.

I pulled over onto the shoulder at Interstate 505, eastbound on Interstate 80. About five minutes passed and I observed a black-over-cream T-Bird go by in the center lane. It was actually traveling slightly slower than the rest of the traffic, but the only person visible was the driver, a black male adult. I called my sergeant and asked him, “Did you see that T-Bird?”

“That’s negative.”

“Well, he just drove right by you.”

Within a minute or two, two more heads popped up, and away we went at speeds in excess of 120 MPH. Turning sharply, hoping to lose me, the driver jumped over a raised divider at the off-ramp to Midway Road. He had slowed down to about 90 for this evasive turning maneuver, but then accelerated to 120 MPH down the narrow two-lane county road.

As we flew through the stop signs, my red light would not even stay in place. By the time another motorist would hear my siren I was already gone.

The dispatcher kept calling, “22-11 where are you?” But it is very awkward to drive at those speeds and talk on your radio at the same time.

“22-11, 22-11, do you read? 22-11, where are you? 22-11, what is your 10-20 (location)?”

The occupants of the T-Bird were throwing things from their car, still traveling 120 MPH. Then, after about 15 miles, I saw their brake lights and a huge cloud of dust just as I passed the “End of Road” sign. I hit my brakes and that big Dodge did not want to stop. As the dust cleared I saw the T-Bird on a dirt driveway with a sign that read “Private Duck Club.” The T-Bird was turning around, and I said to myself, *Showtime!*

“22-11, 22-11, what is your 10-20?”

As the T-Bird continued to turn, I backed into position

behind a small metal shed, loaded my shotgun, and jumped from the patrol car. For additional protection I had thrown open both doors. The dust was still flying, and even though my ignition was off the motor was still chugging away with the radiator boiling over.

"22-11, 22-11, what is your 10-20? Any unit near Midway Road come-in to Vallejo."

There was no doubt in my mind I would be another Gary Cooper in his famous movie *High Noon*. So I waited and waited, but they did not show. I walked from behind the shed and saw they had simply vanished. It occurred to me they were probably on foot, but the T-Bird was nowhere in sight. I called the dispatcher and tried to explain my location. I then drove down the private driveway and soon discovered the abandoned T-Bird stuck in a muddy ditch, but the occupants had simply disappeared.

In about thirty minutes we apprehended the three males as they were walking down a gravel road heading toward the small community of Rio Vista. The caretaker of the duck club had given them a ride on his tractor, oblivious to the facts or the danger he was in. The very next day, Vallejo police officers put on their wet suits and several canals were searched for the money and any weapons they might find. The officers found nothing. Even though I had told them the robbers were throwing things out of the windows, they never asked where. I am fairly certain the money they stole from Safeway is still where they stashed it, and I have a fairly good idea where it is located.

While these stories might seem fascinating, I can assure you that most CHP officers can tell you incredible tales of their own true-life experiences. Many CHP officers have given their lives in the line of duty, defending the honor and integrity of the badge they wore.

My epochal story of the Zodiac began in the late summer of 1970 and is still with me today.

GRADUATION PHOTO—CHP ACADEMY—CLASS OF JANUARY 1964
Lyndon Earl Lafferty—ID 3511

The California HIGHWAY PATROLMAN

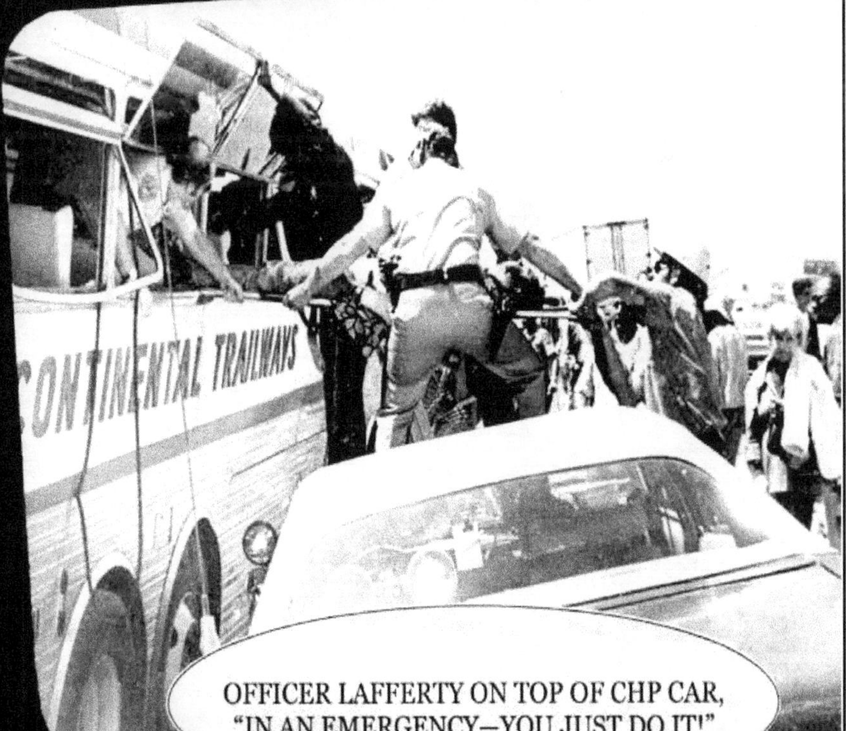

OFFICER LAFFERTY ON TOP OF CHP CAR, "IN AN EMERGENCY—YOU JUST DO IT!"

DECEMBER • 1976

75c PER COPY

IV

FACE-TO-FACE WITH THE ZODIAC

After more than 40 years of agonizing and frustrating investigation into one of the most baffling serial-killer cases, the Zodiac, I must tell this fascinating and unbelievable story.

At the time it all started, I never dreamed the Zodiac would boast and brag about shooting a cop while he sat in his car. As I recall that day, I truly believe I am a survivor by luck. It carved an indelible impression on me; one I shall never forget—when I turned to look directly into the face of a sociopathic maniac.

With his face quivering in spasms and an unflinching stare of hate, fixed and intense, I knew I was looking into the eyes of death. Never in my entire life had I experienced that feeling, a chill of fear that turned my blood to ice when I looked into his snarling face.

The suspect was first observed sitting in his white 1961 Chevrolet sedan on the eastbound side of Interstate 80, just north of the city of Vallejo in the pull-out area across from the Hunter Hill rest area. He was there mornings, day after day, possibly three or four days a week, and this routine continued for many weeks.

On fewer occasions I would see him in the westbound rest area directly opposite the eastbound side. He was always neatly dressed, sometimes wearing a tie. I began to suspect he was an undercover FBI agent, but whoever he was, he was becoming very conspicuous. I never thought he might be stalking me.

Later, after checking his license plate number and doing a preliminary background check, the FBI advised this man was a phony s.o.b., but either would not or could not elaborate at that time.

One day when I was parked in the westbound rest area on Hunter Hill, Interstate 80, a man pulled broadside to my patrol car, approximately five inches away. He was so close I could tell he was staring at me. After a few seconds I turned and looked into a snarling, quivering, spastic face. He did not drop his eyes or turn away, and I knew at once the man was a crazed psycho. Here was a man with a plan.

There was only one other vehicle in the entire parking lot, and it was parked at the far end approximately 200 feet away. There was nobody in sight, in or around this other vehicle, and it was most likely they were sleeping, which is quite common at this car and truck rest stop. In this rather remote and isolated setting, there were just me and one very strange and psychotic person. Yes, I say psychotic because, generally speaking, most people do not go out of their way to cause a confrontation with a police officer. Ninety-nine percent of the people do just the opposite.

I know many officers who would have tried to stare the man down, and others who would have gotten out of their patrol car, walked to the passenger side of the depraved man's vehicle and asked him if he was all right, but it is doubtful they would have used that specific language. It almost appeared the man was having an epileptic seizure.

Whether by a sixth sense, intuition, or pure fear, I shifted into reverse and backed away very quickly. It was my gut feeling that in another second I would be staring into the muzzle of a .45 semi-automatic pistol.

As I merged onto the freeway, it suddenly occurred to me this was the same man, and the same 1961 white Chevrolet car, which I had been observing for several weeks, off and on, parked first on one side of the freeway in the eastbound rest area, and then, at times, on the same day, in the westbound rest area.

But there was something else that chilled me to the bone. The man resembled the composite sketch of the Zodiac released by the San Francisco PD. The horn-rimmed glasses were very prominent as was the reddish tint of his hair. The general facial features were not exact, but very close indeed. The shape of his hair was nearly a perfect match.

Considering the frightening and bizarre encounter I had just experienced, and glancing at the Zodiac sketch carried in every patrol car, I accelerated to a very high speed, turned around at Highway 37, raced back to American Canyon overcrossing, and returned to the rest area. The man was gone. If he had stopped just to use the bathroom facilities, he still would have been there.

What were his intentions? Was he stalking me? Am I lucky to be alive? Did I have his license plate number? Did I find out who he was? I began looking into this guy, and before too long I found out his deadly secret.

It is a tragic state of affairs, and a severe indictment against law enforcement agencies, but we have known the identity of the serial killer Zodiac for decades. The authorities were never truly interested because he was not their suspect. They could never seem to understand that we had no official status and no legal standing to detain him in this investigation. We were advised many times, "Call him in; get his palm prints, and handwriting, etc."

They simply could not comprehend our involvement in the investigation. It is interesting to note that of the three suspects in Robert Graysmith's first book, ours was one. Jerry and I together, on our own time, have accomplished as much as or more than any police department with jurisdiction over the case. We have records and information other agencies do not have, information that might possibly be the work of the Zodiac. We have heard over the years, that if somebody was researching the case they should contact Lafferty and Johnson, and some have done just that.

While it is conveniently ignored by the officials, we can fill in the five critical elements in a crime—*who, where, when, what, and why*.

The amended drawing and age are very important. Initially, the age of the killer was given as 25 to 35. But thirteen months before my face-to-face encounter, after finally admitting they had talked with a man very close to the scene of the Paul Stine killing, the San Francisco PD provided more details. Updating the age from 35 to 45 most definitely put our man in the ballpark. Later, of course, San Francisco Police Inspector Dave Toschi told me, "The killer could have been as old as 50," and this matched our guy perfectly.

But there was more than the age. The amended drawing revealed a much thinner upper lip and a much fuller face, with a slight beefiness or puffiness to the lower right cheek. A 1969 photo of our suspect bears a striking resemblance to the amended drawing, including the distinguishing characteristics just mentioned.

As our relationship with the San Francisco PD became somewhat strained, we never bothered to confirm what we had heard, that every taxicab and police car in San Francisco was carrying a photo of our suspect on their visors. At that time, it did not seem important or relevant to know one way or the other; probably it was true.

Consider the following scenario: Two trained and experienced police officers are called by their dispatcher, who advises them a cab driver has just been shot. The cops are fairly close, and within a minute or two, when they are almost upon the scene, they spot a guy walking up the sidewalk and there is nobody else around. It is dark. They stop and ask him, "Have you seen anything or heard anything strange?"

The guy says, "Yeah, this guy just ran past me waving a gun."

Red flag? Say what? If the guy is telling the truth, in the

minds of the cops, he is at least a damn good witness.

So what do the cops do? They speed off, letting the Zodiac walk away, laughing.

What kind of a man can be so convincing? Apparently, the cops were not suspicious at all, and this in itself is a strong clue. Here is the kind of man who can convince innocent young women to get into his car without any hesitation whatsoever. First, he is a much older person than your common street criminal, is quite neat, and most of all very well spoken. In addition, he is composed, serene, and unruffled because he is a cold-blooded, psychotic professional and very intelligent.

It is true, the initial call broadcast by the dispatcher gave the wrong ID, saying the suspect was a black not a white male. However, experienced police officers are quite aware of such mistakes being made. You can never know the circumstances of a situation unless you are there. Many officers would have reacted automatically in another way, knowing this man was in the wrong place at the wrong time. If for no other reason than their own personal safety, knowing the suspect was armed, it seems the two should have handled the encounter much differently.

After my face-to-face encounter with the schizoid at the rest stop, I made the first disclosure of my investigative results to FBI Agent Floyd Barrus. After Barrus ran a background check on Mr. George Tucker he called me at home and advised, "The man is a phony s.o.b."

Barrus stated, "Lyndon, you have a very strong suspect here and you must definitely follow through."

My next disclosure was to my office commander, Captain Frank Bates, and he became very excited and placed a call to CHP headquarters. Within an hour a lieutenant with Internal Affairs arrived and we had a long discussion on how to proceed. At this time Capt. Bates made another phone call and received permission for me to assist the authorities in this investigation.

The very next day, a Mr. Mel Nicolai with California State

Criminal Identification and Investigation (CII) met me at my home to review the matter, and we then met with Sgt. Leslie Lundblad at his Vallejo office.

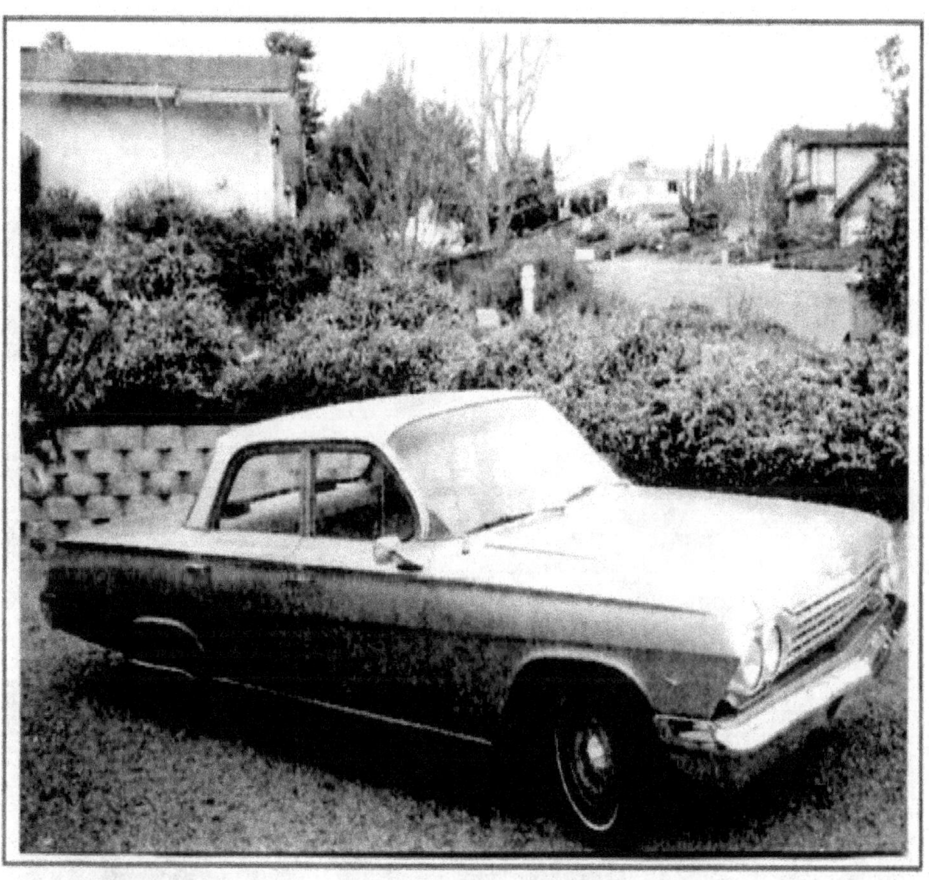

1961 – '62 Vintage Chevrolet Biscayne, four door, white: Suspect owned a vehicle matching this one, minus the skirts. Many witnesses described this vehicle at the Lake Herman Road killing site on December 20, 1968. Many other witnesses described this vehicle in association with Darlene (Suennen) Ferrin, shot to death on July 4, 1969 at Blue Rock Springs Park, Vallejo, California.

Suspect driving this vehicle when observed sitting in his vehicle watching the passing traffic on Interstate 80 on Hunter Hill rest area, both east and westbound. Suspect driving this vehicle when he confronted the CHP officer in his patrol car.

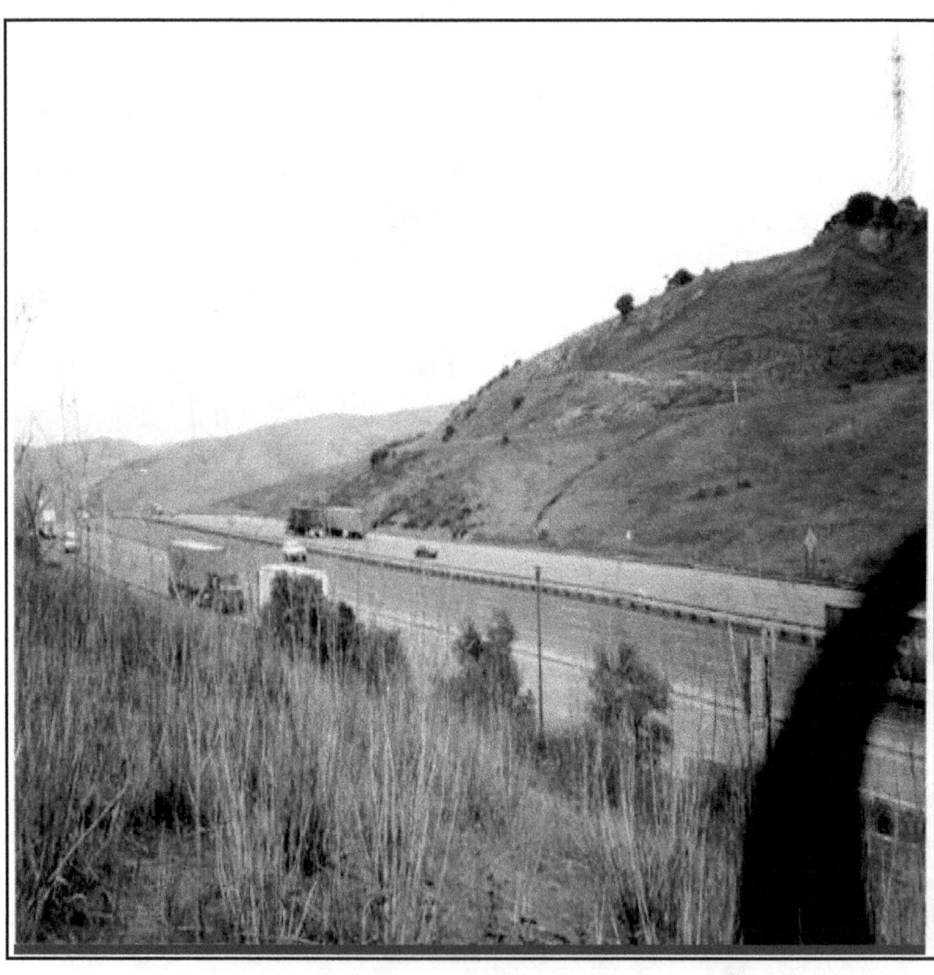

Photo taken 2002: In 1970 the far side of the freeway, eastbound Route 80, was not a designated rest area, but the truckers and other motorists routinely used this pull-out area. The locals call this Hunters Hill and it overlooks the city of Vallejo to the south about one mile away. This pullout was closed to traffic a few years later.

The suspect was first observed sitting in his white 1961 Chevrolet sedan on the eastbound side of Interstate 80 in the pullout area. He was there in the mornings day after day, possibly three or four days a week. This routine continued for several weeks. On fewer occasions I would see him in the westbound rest area directly opposite the eastbound side, always neatly dressed, sometimes wearing a tie. Whoever he was, he was becoming very conspicuous. I never thought he might be stalking me until several years later.

Later, after checking his license plate number and a preliminary background check, the FBI advised this man was a phony s.o.b., but either would not or could not elaborate.

Photo taken 2002: This is the westbound rest area on Hunter Hill, Interstate 80, overlooking the city of Vallejo. In 1970 the marked parking spaces did not exist. (See diagram next page.)

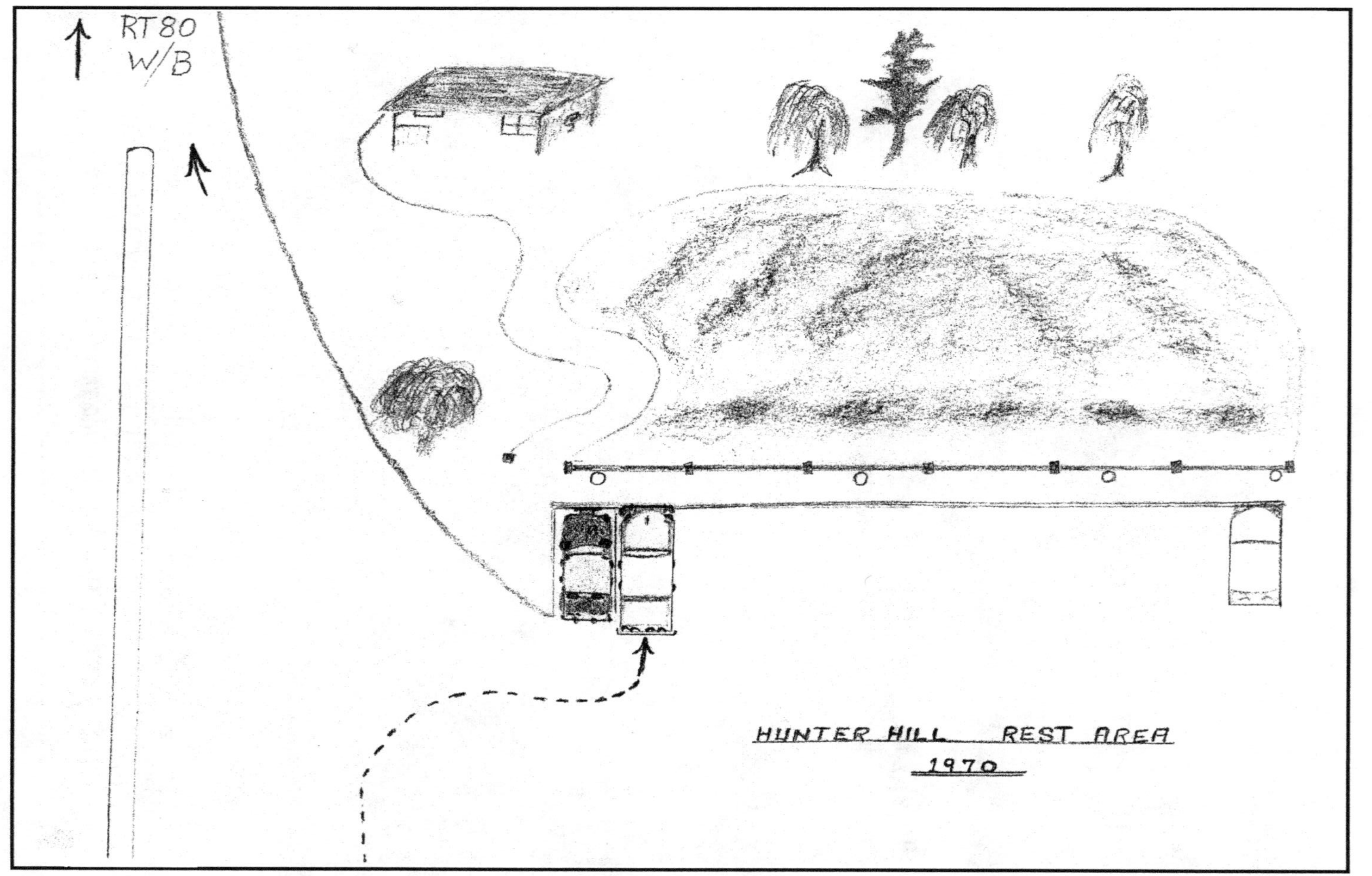
RT80
W/B
HUNTER HILL REST AREA
1970

WANTED

SAN FRANCISCO POLICE DEPARTMENT

NO. 87-69 OCTOBER 13, 1969

WANTED FOR MURDER AND ROBBERIES OF CAB DRIVERS

SUSPECT: WMA, 25-30 Years, 5'8" to 5'9"
Reddish Brown Hair - Crew Cut,
Heavy Rim Glasses,
Navy Blue or Black Jacket

M.O.: Suspect takes cab in downtown area at 9:30 P.M. and sits in front seat with driver. Tells driver destination is Washington and Laurel area or area near Park or Presidio. Upon reaching destination, suspect orders driver to continue on at gun-point into or near Park where he perpetrates robbery.
In one case victim was shot in head at contact. Victim's wallet and I.D. in the name of Paul L. Stine and Taxi Cab keys missing.

WEAPON: 9 mm Automatic

Suspect's latent lifts available for comparison.
Refer Homicide Case No. 696314
Robbery Cases No. 692895 and 687697

ANY INFORMATION:
Inspectors Armstrong/Toschi
Homicide Detail

THOMAS J. CAHILL
CHIEF OF POLICE

WANTED

SAN FRANCISCO POLICE DEPARTMENT

NO. 90-69 WANTED FOR MURDER OCTOBER 18, 1969

ORIGINAL DRAWING

AMENDED DRAWING

Supplementing our Bulletin 87-69 of October 13, 1969. Additional information has developed the above amended drawing of murder suspect known as "ZODIAC".

WMA, 35-45 Years, approximately 5'8", Heavy Build, Short Brown Hair, possibly with Red Tint, Wears Glasses. Armed with 9 MM Automatic.

Available for comparison: Slugs, Casings, Latents, Handwriting.

ANY INFORMATION:
Inspectors Armstrong & Toschi
Homicide Detail
CASE NO. 696314

THOMAS J. CAHILL
CHIEF OF POLICE

SAN FRANCISCO POLICE DEPARTMENT

NO. 90-69 | WANTED FOR MURDER | OCTOBER 18, 1969

ORIGINAL DRAWING AMENDED DRAWING

Supplementing our Bulletin 87-69 of October 13, 1969. Additional information has developed the above amended drawing of murder suspect known as "ZODIAC".

WMA, 35-45 Years, approximately 5'8", Heavy Build, Short Brown Hair, possibly with Red Tint, Wears Glasses. Armed with 9 MM Automatic.

Available for comparison: Slugs, Casings, Latents, Handwriting.

ANY INFORMATION:
Inspectors Armstrong & Toschi
Homicide Detail
CASE NO. 696314

THOMAS J. CAHILL
CHIEF OF POLICE

We had information that our George Tucker was a security guard in Marin County for a short period of time, but this was never verified.

But, when a security guard by the name of Gordon Swinford was shot to death as he was sitting in his locked car on September 24, 1973 while working for a truck leasing firm in Oakland, the fact that he lived in Vallejo, that he was shot one time in his left eye, we were mildly curious.

When, on the very same evening a young man, Kirk Hughes, walking down a residential street in Berkeley a short time after Swinford was killed, was also shot in his left eye, we believed there was most likely a connection. To confirm our suspicions, ballistics proved the same gun was used in both murders.

We believe that the security guard, Swinford, is the cop that Zodiac bragged about when he said, "I shot a cop as he sat in his car."

We ask, was Swinford an AA member also? We also discovered there is a huge fellowship of AA members on San Pablo Avenue, San Pablo, CA. This avenue is a major four-lane roadway linking Berkeley and Oakland in just a few minutes driving time.

We were also reminded of the George Pimental brutal murder when his index finger had been severed and forced in his left eye socket.

Local newspapers reported the shootings of Swinford and Hughes on September 26, 1973, yet another anniversary date—that of the Donna Lass disappearance from the Lake Tahoe casino on September 26, 1970.

V

SUSPECT CALLED IN

When Sgt. Lundblad called in our suspect, he needed a cover story so he would not unduly alarm him. So on March 15, 1971, George Russell Tucker drove down to Vallejo to meet with him. I truly wished Lundblad had told me in advance of his plans. I didn't hear about this interview until several weeks later.

Tucker was obviously miffed at the inconvenience, and he displayed a very arrogant and hostile attitude from the moment he stepped into Lundblad's office. Lundblad tried to make the interview casual and impersonal.

"What's this all about anyhow?" Tucker demanded to know.

"Well, it's nothing serious at all. We're calling in a lot of people, and this is why. As we are having a lot of muggings and robberies up at the rest areas, I have asked my deputies to make note of all the license numbers of people they see up there. If they are local, we call them in just to advise them they must be very careful because we have had some terrible assaults up there. And there are a lot of homosexuals that hang around up there, you know."

"So what's wrong with homosexual activity?" Tucker asked.

"Nothing at all, I suppose, as long as it's done in the privacy of one's home and not performed in public places. So this is just for your protection, you know, just to let you know to be careful."

Lundblad continued: "Now, just for the record, could I

have your date of birth and social security number—and your military identification number, if you have ever been in the service?"

I was shocked when he told me about the interview later. To my way of thinking, Lundblad was out in left field with the third question; it was not routine and should have never been asked.

Tucker replied with his correct date of birth, his correct social security number, and a military ID number.

Upon arriving home he called his wife, Catherine, explaining his interview with Sgt. Lundblad, and she went totally ballistic. She called her very good friend, the judge, and the judge called the sheriff demanding to know, "Who the hell does that little punk Sgt. Lundblad think he is? What the hell is going on? I want an answer right now—not tomorrow morning, but now, in my office. You tell him to get his ass up here right now."

The sheriff called Lundblad and told him to meet him in Judge Winston's chambers immediately. Lundblad responded as ordered, and when he walked into Winston's office he was met by his boss, Judge Winston, and one other Superior Court judge.

They closed the doors and the sheriff demanded to know, "What is going on? I have never given any orders for my men to record license numbers of people seen loitering around the rest areas."

Lundblad tried to make an excuse saying, "I should have cleared it with you first, but there have been a lot of beatings, muggings, and robberies in the rest areas on Hunter Hill."

The sheriff told Lundblad, "Belay all such orders, and forget about George Tucker completely."

As Lundblad told me, "I have never been so humiliated in my entire life."

When they left the courthouse he told his boss, "I couldn't tell you inside, in their presence, but this George Tucker is a very good Zodiac suspect. I have been wanting to talk to you about it, after I obtained some more background on this guy. He is really weird. Even the FBI said he is a phony s.o.b."

"I don't care who he is," the sheriff barked, "I am telling you to destroy your notes and burn your files. I never want to hear the man's name again, ever."

Lundblad was shocked—he could not believe his ears.

"If this man turns out to be the serial killer Zodiac, you know what you can do with my badge."

When Lundblad told me this story, the first opportunity he had, he said, "I was so furious I could barely drive back to Vallejo. Lyndon, you must promise me you will never breathe a word of this story to anyone, do you understand?"

Lundblad was never so serious, and it was the first time I could remember he had his face in mine, nose-to-nose.

"If you ever tell a soul I will deny it, under oath, and I mean it. You cannot tell a soul."

At the moment he told me this unbelievable story, I truly did not appreciate the gravity of the situation. Then, several days later, it was like someone had turned on a light, and I realized I was in a terrible dilemma.

From that day on, I never received another phone call or message from Sgt. Lundblad. When I made a few calls at his office unannounced, he was no longer happy to see me. It became painfully apparent my presence was putting him in an awkward position. If any of his supervisors were lurking around the office, he would try to ignore me as long as he could.

Before we broke it off, however, he did confide in me two more secrets. He showed me where he was hiding his file on Tucker, telling me he would never destroy it; and pleaded with me to continue my investigation saying,

> "Lyndon, you have a very strong suspect, and you should never quit until he is either exonerated completely without question, or arrested for the

crimes."

He further advised, "We have recently discovered the Lake Herman murders actually occurred on a small piece of property within the Benicia city limits, and this is their investigation to pursue from now on."

Les also told me, "I've been ordered to turn over everything I have to the Benicia police, but due to promises I have made to a bunch of teenagers, I will not reveal or turn over this information to the Benicia authorities."

Years later, I learned from his family members Lundblad continued his own private investigation of Tucker, as he was convinced George Tucker was the Zodiac.

What was Catherine Tucker thinking? What did she know? She was also on a hugging basis with the sheriff, so we wondered just exactly what he told her. Did he say, your husband is a Zodiac suspect? Did he tell her some nut of a CHP officer told Lundblad that Tucker was a Zodiac suspect?

She has a very good legal mind, and she has been around law enforcement all her adult life. While the sheriff might not have told her the real reason her husband was called in, she was much more intelligent than they were giving her credit for. She therefore was left with an enigma, and would not rest until she discovered the truth for herself. She now had to conduct a covert investigation of her own, and the Zodiac web began to weave curious patterns of strange phone calls, platonic relationships, and deceit; a play within a play. And how did Sir Walter Scott say it?

"Oh, what a tangled web we weave,
When first we practice to deceive."

The entire situation was outrageous. Next to the district attorney, the highest-ranking law enforcement officer in the county, the sheriff was ordering his homicide investigator to destroy his files and never mention that man's name again. This was outright criminal and the term malfeasance is insignificant.

One wants to say, “Oh Mr. Zodiac, can we buy you a new .22 or sharpen some knives for you?”

Should there be an internal investigation to uncover the political corruption and the official criminal acts? *They gave him a license to kill!*

Our records of unsolved homicides attributable to Zodiac in the general area of San Francisco, Marin County, Sonoma, Sacramento, and Vallejo, plus one in Stockton, total 22. These 22 homicides were committed after March 1971 and ended in November 1974. There may be more, like the young girl Penny Parker who was stabbed to death in Sacramento on May 7, 1977.

Many of these have been declared possible Zodiac murders by the authorities in their jurisdictions, and we agree with their assessments. As the reader will discover, Zodiac's claim of 37 victims is shockingly real. It is a terrible tragedy that we were so totally ineffective, that our continual pleadings fell on deaf ears.

Once I was told, “No CHP officer will be allowed to solve the Zodiac case,” and they have been absolutely correct.

Jerry and I were shocked years later to discover there were still standing orders in the Vallejo PD that referred to the esteemed Superior Court judge. We were never to learn the exact wording, but the critical essence was so powerful one detective told Jerry, “I would have to get permission from Judge Winston before I could investigate your man.”

Apparently Jerry and I had been sanctioned, as the lieutenant told Jerry, “We are not supposed to give you or Lafferty any more information on the Zodiac case.”

The last half of the fourth paragraph on page 120 of Robert Graysmith's book *Zodiac Unmasked* (The Berkeley Publishing Group, 2002) is the most relevant thing in his entire 585-page book:

> The behavior of the Vallejo Police Department had

> always puzzled Toschi. It was as if a second mystery underlay the watery town of Vallejo, invisibly affecting the investigation at every turn. 'For some reason Lynch and Lundblad didn't want to come to some of our early conferences in Sacramento. And here Bill and I are driving ninety miles up there.'

Just what was the second mystery? This mystery concerned the name of our Zodiac suspect, which Lynch and Lundblad could not even mention. Lundblad was under strict orders to destroy his notes and his files, and never mention the man again. They were withholding evidence, perverting justice, and committing unbelievable acts of unethical and immoral conduct. They were confronted with a terrible dilemma, meeting with members of the DOJ and the Attorney General's office and being asked, "Do you have any other suspects?"

While we will never know the precise details, we can speculate these standing orders were in a bold caption posted on the cover of a file under our suspect's name. Most likely it contained the message, "Contact Superior Court Judge Dennis Winston before any contact with this man."

We are fairly certain this notation is identical to the files maintained by the Vallejo PD and Solano County Sheriff's Dept., as well as the Fairfield, Vacaville, Suisun, Dixon, Rio Vista, and Benicia PDs. Most likely these files have long since been destroyed.

Every investigator was admonished, "You shall not mention this man's name, but if you want to, you must clear it first with your immediate supervisor who will then clear it with Judge Winston. This man has been officially cleared, so leave him alone."

The file would have also contained the names of two investigators, Lafferty and Johnson.

According to the experts, FBI, and other analysts, something happened to Zodiac early in 1971. Bob Ressler, retired profiler for the FBI, and leading authorities on serial killers have a common consensus: Zodiac most likely had a brush with the law, may have been questioned by law enforcement officials, or came very close to being caught in the commission of one of his 37 killings.

After our suspect Tucker was called into the sheriff's office by Detective Lundblad on March 15, 1971, there was a dramatic change in Zodiac's persona and geographic activities. The mind of the Zodiac was clever, one step ahead of the police, like in a sharp game of chess. Consider his preemptive move in anticipation of his scheduled appointment with Detective Lundblad. The latter sent Tucker a short note stating, "I would like to see you in my office on March 15," which fell on a Monday.

On Saturday, March 13 Zodiac mailed another letter from Pleasanton, California, located just south of Walnut Creek in the East Bay. Pleasanton is about one hour away from Tucker's home, a straight drive down Interstate 680 from Fairfield. This letter was addressed to the *Los Angeles Times* and was received on exactly March 15, 1971. The irony is quite fascinating. Zodiac's letter begins:

> THIS IS THE ZODIAC SPEAKING LIKE I'VE SAID I'M CRACKPROOF IF THE BLUE MEANIES ARE EVER GOING TO CATCH ME, THEY HAD BEST GET OFF THEIR FAT ASSES & DO SOMETHING

(letter continues... and ends below:)

SFPD – 0 ⊕ – 17 +

Was he hoping to divert attention away from himself? Was he thinking nobody would be foolish enough to send a Zodiac letter when they had an appointment scheduled with the police?

On December 13, 1970, a lady was living on a remote ranch off Lake Herman Road. Her husband was one of the three witnesses who had reported seeing a 1961 or 1962 white Chevrolet four-door parked at the murder site of Betty Lou Jensen and David Faraday. The witnesses had observed this vehicle, a short time before the two teenagers were shot to death on December 20, 1968. The lady's husband had passed away just three weeks before she received the phone call. A male subject with a childish, high-pitched, and muffled voice told the lady he was the Zodiac. The Solano County Sheriff's report reads as follows:

(L - is for the lady making the report, S - is for the subject making the call)

L: *(Answering the phone.)* "Hello!"
S: "This is the Zodiac."
L: "I can't understand you, would you repeat?"
S: "This is the Zodiac, I'm gonna kill you."
L: "Oh, you are?" *(As though talking to a child.)* "When are you going to do this?"
S: "I'm coming out tonight."
L: "Now honey, tell me who you really are."
S: "I told you, this is Zodiac. I'm coming out to kill you about midnight." *(Hangs up.)*

She received the call about 7:00 PM, and after some consideration became very frightened and reported the incident to the Solano County Sheriff's Dept. at 8:35 PM (case #V-28328).

The lady stated, "I have never received a phone call of this nature in the past, and I am at a loss with regard to suspects." She agreed to take her two sons and stay with relatives that evening.

The report was brought to the attention of Det. Sgt.

Lundblad, who then suggested a plan for a stakeout. At 11:20 PM sheriff's deputies checked the residence inside and out, and everything was perfectly normal.

The officers assumed the phone call was made to force the people from their home, leaving it open and vacant for a burglary attempt. The stakeout was canceled at 6:00 AM.

Did anyone in the sheriff's department suspect the caller might really have been Zodiac?

VI

OTHER AGENCIES

Months before, Sgt. Lundblad had sworn me to another oath of secrecy. He left a message in my CHP office telling me to come to his office right away. When I walked in he said, "Lyndon, you are not going to believe this, but you must promise never to reveal you ever saw it because I am not supposed to have this either."

Lundblad then showed me a "Top Secret" document, eight pages of a federal agency's code decryption. I nearly swallowed my tongue—could not believe my eyes. Our suspect's name appeared as one of three possible names extracted in the last 18 characters of Zodiac's three-part code. The Hardens had deciphered Zodiac's entire message, save for the last 18 letters. Some said these last 18 characters contained the Zodiac's name.

I had been extremely excited about our suspect as we obtained a few pieces of circumstantial evidence here and there, but at this point it was just supposition. Now we had an official agency of the government advising, "We have discovered three possible names, and one of them matches your man." Can you imagine how elated I was?

"My God, the man is truly the Zodiac."

Les himself didn't come right out and say it, as he was trying to remain calm and cool.

"Pretty interesting isn't it? But you can never mention it to anyone."

I wanted to scream at him. "What the hell are you talking about? What do you mean, I can never mention this to anyone?"

"We can get into a hell of a lot of trouble, that's why. I can get in a lot of trouble because this was given to me in confidence, and my hands are tied on this."

I said, "Les, this is bullshit politics and you know it. You have sworn me to *two secrets*, two vital pieces of information, which, whether you know it or not, are absolutely critical to this investigation. I cannot talk about your boss ordering you to destroy your files and never mention the man's name again, and now I cannot discuss this "Top Secret" document, which reveals our suspect's name."

The analysis was most likely requested by the Chief of Police, Jack Stiltz, of the Vallejo PD. However, their principal Zodiac investigator was Detective Jack Mulanax, a very close friend of Les Lundblad, who confided in Les and gave him a copy. Les confided in me and gave me one, and that's the way it goes in law enforcement.

Within a few days, I totally breached security and showed the document to two FBI agents, my friends John Marchi and Floyd Barrus. They examined it carefully and said, "We are not equipped to work on any codes, but the wording strongly suggests it to be the work of the National Security Agency."

"I'm not supposed to have this, so please don't burn me." They laughed and shook their heads, like they understood only too well. They suggested I make contact with Naval Intelligence on Mare Island to confirm the information.

The agent at the Office of Special Investigations (OSI) at Travis Air Force Base in Fairfield, CA was very congenial. He offered to check out the military ID number our suspect gave to Sgt. Lundblad. Thinking this process could take two or three months, I was surprised when the agent left a message for me at the CHP office only two weeks later.

When I called him he advised, "The identification number is invalid and none of the military services—Army, Navy, or Air Force—has ever issued this number to anyone." He also said something to this effect: "The numbers are all wrong and totally bogus."

On January 24, 1972, I called Bill Amick, Mare Island Police Chief, and he gave me the phone number for Naval Intelligence. He suggested I ask for the Senior Agent in charge, Byron Tardiff.

Tardiff, friendly and outgoing told me, "Come right over," which I did. Another agent, Chuck Forrest, was also present.

(In time, Chuck would become an active member of our own Mandamus Seven task force.)

By the time I left their office they had become truly excited, and I was really charged. They joked, "We are going to resign, so we can assist you in your Zodiac investigation."

As weeks rolled by, I became very discouraged. I had not heard one word from Naval Intelligence, and I was not going to bug them by calling. But then on March 31 at 9:15 AM, Chuck Forrest called me at home and told me, "Come to our office immediately, like right now. Lyndon, you are not going to believe your eyes! Get your butt here quick."

With hands sweating and legs shaking, I could barely shave. At 10:15 AM I walked into the small office of Naval Intelligence. After all, these were true professionals, federal agents who had traveled all over the world on their investigative assignments.

Good God! I thought. *They must have something very, very compelling.*

Shocking and startling, the information was an absolute bombshell. Agent Tardiff, more formal than Chuck Forrest, said,

"Officer Lafferty, our sources are the best in the world and extremely confidential."

Tapping the file in front of him he continued, "This information is tightly controlled and highly classified—unlawful dissemination will get you a minimum of five years in prison. We have to show you, but understand one thing—this information does not exist and you never saw it."

I replied, "OK, I read you loud and clear."

Forrest was grinning and shaking his head, "This guy is totally unreal, and if he isn't the Zodiac, I'll eat your hat."

Tardiff told me, "Pull a chair to the front of my desk," and he opened the file of several official documents. Contained there was a highlighted list of four names. Tardiff explained that our suspect was using the four names surreptitiously and unlawfully.

Forrest remarked, "Lyndon, in the thousands of background investigations we have conducted we have never seen anything like this, ever. We had to open a case file number in order to get the information, and we have been asked by the local authorities to assist them in the investigation." Chuck then smiled and asked, "You are an official authority, are you not?"

Then I laid a bombshell on *them*. I opened my briefcase and my file on the National Security Agency code decryptions. The identical names in their classified material matched the names revealed by the NSA code work.

"My God!" They both literally jumped from their chairs. The three of us stared at one another in shocked disbelief, with our mouths agape, in a state of wonder. This was a moment, impossible to describe. It was the most magnificent revelation one could possibly hope for. It was the smoking gun—the concrete evidence, the absolute proof we needed to prove the fact beyond any doubt.

I was shaking and my guts were churning. All three of us were just pacing back and forth, and for several minutes nobody said a word. Chuck Forrest walked out of the building to get some fresh air, and then returned in about one minute, still speechless.

"Jesus! Jesus! Jesus!" Forrest blurted.

Tardiff was shaking his head, and we continued pacing the floor in and out of Tardiff's office. I was so excited I was nearly numb, a feeling I had never experienced.

"Jesus! Jesus!" Forrest blurted again.

Tardiff broke the silence most profoundly when he began,

"Well,"... but then, said nothing.

Finally, Chuck Forrest exclaimed, "Fuck, we are really screwed! We can't even use the information."

And there you have it, good friends, another secret, which can never be revealed. Was this the Pandora's box, an absolute dilemma, or what? I had already been sworn to secrecy on the NSA code analysis, and now I was forced to remain silent on the shocking information provided by Naval Intelligence.

Could I tell my colleague, Det. Lundblad, this highly classified and sensitive information? Absolutely not! A thousand times over I asked myself, *What is wrong with this picture?*

Did I dare trust the police departments? You've got to be kidding! Could I relay this shocking news to the California Attorney General's office? No, I had given my word. Therefore, even at this writing my word is my bond, and I cannot reveal every specific detail of the information revealed to me by Naval Intelligence. As for the FBI, they would never admit they had an open case on the Zodiac, so the best they would do was give advice.

Many years later, they did, in fact, open an official case. Their involvement was predicated on their interpretation of threatening letters sent through the mail.

On that same day I met Naval Intelligence Agent, Jerry Johnson, who walked into the office shortly before I was getting ready to leave. His good buddy, Chuck Forrest, filled Jerry in telling him about our recent discoveries. Jerry also became ecstatic. For some reason I knew instinctively we had a lot in common, and had no doubt these two would become deeply involved with me in this investigation. Chuck, Jerry, and I had lunch at the Officer's Club on Mare Island and we talked for nearly three hours. When I drove home I was "on Cloud Nine" because I had had a great lunch with two of the finest men I would ever hope to meet in my lifetime.

And so it came to be—Jerry, Chuck, and I formed a great alliance and a wonderful friendship over the years.

On April 5 we met for lunch at Denny's. Chuck reminded me, "This is really sensitive material we've obtained, and you must never mention it." But he added, "One of my best friends with Naval Intelligence is a close personal friend of Henry Kissinger, and if we ever need their assistance they could pull some strings."

Jerry advised, "I have contacted a good friend of mine who has just retired from the New York Police Department, and he is checking out one of the names on the list. Also, one of our own agents is checking out another name in Hayward, CA."

I informed them, "I ran all the names through the National Crime Information Center (NCIC) with no hits."

After calling the Department of Motor Vehicles (DMV) and the Department of Drivers' Licensing for an appointment, Jerry and I met our designated DDL assistant on April 8. The assistant had been assigned to me for as long as we needed her. Everything was waiting for us, and we began our long day's work at about 9:00 AM. By hand, the only way to do it, we examined hundreds and hundreds of driver's licenses, among all that were ever issued in the State of California. Our well-defined objective was to try and match the photo of our suspect with any alias on the infamous list obtained through Naval Intelligence.

As I recall, we finished around 4:30 in the afternoon. We had absolutely no luck at all, but it was an important issue, which had to be resolved. Many years later a detective with the Vallejo PD told us that he and his partner discovered something very strange. He said our suspect had applied for a new driver's license in three different DMV offices, disguising his appearance, and on the same day.

On April 19 Chuck, Jerry, and I met with Sheriff Captain Kenneth Narlow at his office in Napa. Narlow was in charge of the Zodiac investigation in the Lake Berryessa case. Bryan Hartnell had barely survived, and Cecelia Ann Shepard had died two days after their brutal and vicious stabbings on September 27, 1969. Capt. Ken Narlow is a fine man, friendly, and all business.

Chuck and Jerry requested Capt. Narlow to write Naval Intelligence a letter requesting their assistance in the investigation. Capt. Narlow was very happy to oblige them with the official letter. Apparently they needed something in writing, and since I personally did not have the authority, they asked Narlow to write it.

This meeting with Narlow would be the first of many over the years. He had his own Zodiac suspect, and he seldom shared any details about him. What little he did tell us did not seem compelling at all. His suspect was 5'8" and weighed 165, and this description did not meet the criteria. Besides, and something we could never understand, Narlow's own sand-compaction tests at Lake Berryessa revealed the suspect weighed about 220 pounds. We would learn later his suspect failed the facts in the profile in most every instance. (Narlow had heard a theory that his suspect was into "snuff" films, and the man was, in fact, a self-styled moviemaker.)

On June 24 Jerry's mother, visiting from Santa Barbara, wanted to see the Zodiac murder sites, so Jerry and I drove her around the area. She was a very charming and gracious lady, and offered to check out all the references she could find, attempting to place our suspect in the Riverside area. Over the next few months she gave us a great deal of research material. During our drive we discovered the property being rented by our suspect now had a "For Sale" sign. Jerry, with unflinching gall, even knocked on the door and talked with the suspect's mother, asking questions about the house, etc.

On November 11 I called the Deputy District Attorney Neal McCaslin at his home. Neal was a man I had already admired and respected for several years, who would soon be elected District Attorney of Solano County. I confided in McCaslin, telling him my story in very brief terms. Neal became one of our strongest advocates, and provided us with a great deal of intimate, inside information. Jerry and I had many luncheons with Neal. Over the years, I regarded him as a prominent and outstanding member of our investigating team, the Mandamus Seven.

Neal told me one day, "Lyndon, as a sworn peace officer, you have the legal authority to pursue this investigation, with or without your department's approval."

Was there a possible Zodiac connection in the murder of Nelda Tally in Stockton, CA on November 20, 1971? The local authorities could not understand the six ritual-like fires, which had been ignited between her legs. There was a theory the Zodiac might be responsible. She'd been found nude, strangled with her own pantyhose, in her employment agency office. She catered to "banking" employees to a large degree.

Jerry and I made an appointment with Sgt. Grudee and a lieutenant in the Stockton PD. Just prior to this meeting, Jerry and I had discovered our suspect may have worked for a Stockton bank sometime in 1971. As the lieutenant knew the bank officials very well, he went over to talk to them. When he returned he advised, "The bank officials feel sorry for your suspect, as they know him very well. They said, 'He had a terrible booze problem, but we did, in fact, hire him to work in our bank.'"

Apparently things did not work out since he only worked nine business days between January 11 and January 23, 1971.

Simply another coincidence? We do not think so. The person setting the fires had used recent employment applications and resumés.

The friends at the bank said, "We think your suspect has gone into professional gambling."

We believe there is a probable cause, based on the strange circumstances. Our suspect had filed an application or resumé with Nelda Tally sometime between the time he left his bank on January 23 and the date of Tally's murder on November 20. He was most definitely in the banking business; was having trouble finding employment; had an uncontrollable hatred for women; was a binge drinker; and was most definitely in the area.

On November 8, 1971, George Pimental had been set up with a blind date for a homosexual encounter. His date was some high-ranking "Big Shot" according to Pimental's good friends and other boozers in his favorite bar, some admitted alcoholics.

When we examined the crime scene reports and the photographs, I discovered something very bizarre: It appeared the killer had actually carved or scratched his name on Pimental's abdomen.

We were told this had never been brought to the detectives' attention. The Vallejo police were unaware of these carved initials or letters. Then, perhaps as an afterthought, the killer commenced to slash over the name repeatedly to obliterate it. The still readable name is the same as our suspect's.

Pimental had made comments to a couple of his friends that he knew who the "Big Shot" was, and was afraid to have sex with him. As one of Pimental's index fingers had been cut off and jammed into his left eye socket, we believe there may be a "left eye" connection between this and two other shootings that occurred on the evening of September 25, 1973. They were both shot in the left eye; one victim in Oakland, and the other in adjoining Berkeley. Both were killed instantly, and ballistics show the bullets were fired from the same gun.

Back to 1971—considering Nelda Tally on November 20 and George Pimental on November 8, we have yet another example of binge-drinking killings.

It is imperative for you, the reader, to exercise a great deal of patience as you try to connect the dots. We are not dealing with a slam-dunk killer or a who-done-it murder. This is not an episode of *CSI: Crime Scene Investigation* where a speck of dust or a strand of hair solves the case in two or three weeks. My advice is to be conscious of how easy it is to become lost in all the dynamics of this complicated story.

"Why," we ask, "was he looking for employment in Stockton when he lived in Fairfield?" Was he going to drive 36 miles across the dangerous two-lane Highway 12, and another 20 miles down Interstate 5, five days a week? Or, like Riverside, was he actually living there temporarily with a friend?

It should be noted that this geographic area is where the abduction of Kathleen Johns took place on a Sunday, March 22, 1970. A man flashing his headlights behind her got her to stop. She had noticed a car starting to follow her from the Modesto/Stockton area on Interstate 5.

Late at night on March 15, 1970, a Vallejo woman was followed by a white 1962 or 1964 white Chevrolet as she was driving to Travis Air Force Base. The man was blinking his lights and blowing his horn, trying to get her to stop. She never did.

VII

BACKGROUND ON SUSPECT

After World War II, in 1945, George Russell Tucker received his discharge from the US Air Force. At the time he enlisted, this branch of service was the Army Air Force, but was renamed during the war. After his radio and code schooling he had also received an MOS (Military Occupation Specialty) in weaponry, the servicing and maintenance of .50-caliber machine guns. In time, he was sent to the Philippine Islands.

Over the years information surfaced that Sgt. Tucker had a few problems, medically speaking, and had spent several months in the hospital while in the Philippines. Apparently, he had developed reasons to despise and hate the female gender. This information, while coming from credible sources, could never be verified. It was during this period of time Tucker also taught code for two years, when reassigned back to the States.

In 1962, Tucker's wife of 16 years charged him with physical and mental cruelty and divorced him. At the same time, he was fired from his job at Wells Fargo Bank in Marin County, after 16 years of employment. He had previously worked at Wells Fargo in Napa and Petaluma, working his way up to the position of loan officer in Marin County. He was fired when the officials of the bank discovered a fraudulent loan Tucker made to a female co-worker, and other questionable loans to known gamblers.

It was also reported Tucker had an uncontrollable and violent temper with his female co-workers, and had, in fact, been cautioned by his supervisors on several occasions. The alleged benefactor of the fraudulent $20,000 loan had moved to Southern California, possibly the Riverside area.

When Tucker promised to repay the money, the bank did not press charges against him. There were rumors Tucker had married the woman he had taken the loan for. We were advised Tucker was also ambidextrous and a professional gambler who played cards for high stakes.

In 1963, a title company closed in Vallejo, and one or more officials were indicted for criminal activities in connection with the business, and sent to prison. Early in the same year, Tucker bought a principal partnership in this same enterprise, but due to the low volume of business, they folded and shut their doors in August 1965. It was reported the two partners lost a great deal of money in their investment. Another reliable source revealed Tucker was an avid gambler, and either very good at it, or very lucky.

On many occasions, Tucker would have to lie down at work; suffering from terrible migraine headaches, so severe, they would literally disable him.

There is one other interesting point that should be mentioned. This title company was located just one-half block from a very popular deli-restaurant, Herb's Troc. Great food with a great atmosphere, their buffet was the finest in town. Judges, attorneys, businessmen of all types would have lunch at Herb's Troc. One of the well-known waitresses was Mrs. Suennen, and she had worked there for several years. Before her daughter went to work for IHOP (International House of Pancakes) on Tennessee Street, her mother trained her at Herb's Troc for six months.

Mrs. Suennen's daughter was Darlene Ferrin, the young girl shot to death on July 4, 1969, by the Zodiac. We ask the obvious: "Is this about the time Tucker first met Darlene at Herb's Troc?"

His office was only one-half block away. We think so. He is "the older man" at the house-painting party, and neatly dressed with a suit and tie—the man driving the white 1961 four-door Chevrolet.

Darlene Ferrin had just purchased a small home at 1300 Virginia Street, Vallejo, in her own name. Her husband, Dean Ferrin, was not recorded on the title to the house. We had heard Darlene bought this house for $10,000 cash. Pamela (Suennen) Huckaby, sister of Darlene, has stated, "I recall vividly the night of the house-painting party because 'the older man' kept harassing Darlene by following her around and asking where she got the money to buy the things in the home."

With varying degrees of certainty, three witnesses have identified Tucker as "the older man" at the house-painting party. The most reliable is retired Vallejo Police Officer, Steve Baldino. There is no question at all in his mind, Tucker was there.

The second witness is Pamela Huckaby who actually picked Tucker out from a six-photo lineup. However, she was not certain.

The least reliable witness is another sister, Linda (Suennen) DelBuono. When shown a single photo of Tucker she replied, "Yes, this is the man."

(We acknowledge our failure by not using a prescribed procedure with Linda, and her statement would be virtually useless in a court of law.)

Pamela Huckaby has also stated, "I am certain it was Tucker who was always sitting at Terry's Restaurant when Darlene was working the night shift."

In this regard, there is yet another witness who has identified Tucker in person advising, "He is the man in the horn-rimmed glasses pretending to read the newspaper while he watched Darlene."

Back in August 1965 when his business failed, it caused a huge monetary loss and George Tucker became despondent. Like many other alcoholics, Tucker resumed his old lifestyle and began to binge again. He had never confided in his wife that he was alcoholic, nor did he tell her this was the main reason his first wife had filed for divorce.

When Lia received a phone call from a good friend in Napa, telling her to come and get her drunken husband out of a bar, she was furious. Rumor or not, we learned Mr. Tucker received Holy Hell—was tongue-lashed and threatened by his new wife. Now engaged in guilt and remorse, feeling more depressed than he had for many years, Tucker began attending AA meetings all over the Bay Area, including Napa, Petaluma, and Marin County.

In May 1966, Tucker received a speeding citation on Highway 101 in Marin County while visiting a good friend in Petaluma. He became a kite without a tail, flitting here and there, trying to land a decent job. In desperation, he packed a few clothes and left to visit his aging mother on the East Coast whom he had not seen for two years. In September 1966 he got another speeding citation in Pennsylvania. It was on this trip we suspect he made the loop to see his ex-girlfriend in the Riverside area of Southern California.

Over the years we have learned that Cheri Jo Bates was a part-time employee with one of the banks in Riverside. While in the area of his old girlfriend and cooling his heels, with his wife in Vallejo not really caring if he returned or not, he began to look for a new job. As banking was his expertise, his path may have crossed with that of Cheri Jo Bates. Purely speculation, but there is one thing we know for certain.

A Riverside detective confided to Capt. Ken Narlow, "An older man with the exact same name as their [our] suspect was sitting in the Riverside College Library on October 30, 1966, the same night Cheri Jo Bates was there." She was murdered later that same evening, just after midnight.

A typewritten letter of confession mailed on November 29, 1966, and a handwritten letter mailed on April 30, 1967, were both sent from Riverside. On the face of it, it would appear the killer did, in fact, live in the area for at least six months. We also find it interesting, in the psychological terms of fixating blame on others, we discover the initials "RH" left as the signature on the desk "death poem" at the Riverside College Library. We find it interesting because the attorneys representing Tucker's first wife were "Robinson and Healy."

This could be another taunting clue left by the Zodiac. Is Zodiac placing the blame on the attorneys saying, "It's your fault I had to kill that girl"? This is nearly identical to the sentiment expressed in his Riverside letter when he states:

> "PUBLISH MY LETTER SO YOU CAN SAVE YOUR GIRLS etc IT WILL BE ON YOUR CONSCIENCE, NOT MINE."
>
> (The Riverside letter)

In this story you will find a common theme of Zodiac's:

> "SOME OF THEM FOUGHT, IT WAS HORRIBLE" and "DON'T MAKE IT SO EASY FOR ME."

Zodiac perceives himself as a moral crusader, killing those people who are found where they should not be, and doing things they should not be doing.

Tucker received another speeding citation on January 11, 1967, in Richmond, and yet another on February 10. When the Department of Motor Vehicles computed his violation points, they placed him on probation from June 1967 to June 1968, as a negligent operator. Most unusual for a man 47 years of age.

Six months later, on December 20, 1968, the young couple (Jensen and Faraday) were shot to death on Lake Herman Road in Benicia. A person by the name of "Zodiac" wrote letters, taking credit for their tragic deaths.

Just prior to their bodies being discovered, two different witnesses, at two different times, reported seeing a dark vehicle parked on the opposite side of their Rambler station wagon. The dark vehicle is further described as having no chrome. However, shortly before this, three witnesses had reported seeing a 1961 or '62 white Chevrolet four-door parked in the area. This matched Tucker's vehicle precisely.

Assuming Tucker was in the Riverside area in October 1966 and April 1967, we tried to discover the events in his life between April 1967 and the acceleration of the Zodiac murders on December 20, 1968. Was he laying low and not driving during his probation period of June 1967 to June 1968, knowing if he picked up another moving citation the Department would revoke his driver's license? Was it simply the booze, or did something else happen to him, something truly traumatic? What triggered his extended spree? Did his wife have something she had to tell him?

VIII

THREE SECRETS AND THREE OATHS

Born during the latter stages of a great depression, I was raised with what we call today traditional American values. My dad always told us, "A man is only as good as his word."

And from legendary role models on the silver screen like Gary Cooper, Robert Mitchum, Humphrey Bogart, Gene Autry, and the Lone Ranger, my brother and I learned that a man's word was a sacred oath. We learned when a friend entrusted you with a secret, they were telling you—you were their best friend in the whole world, and they trusted you with their life. Short of cutting your arms to become blood brothers, these bonds were unbreakable.

So it was with Sgt. Lundblad and me. I never understood what I had ever done to gain his trust. Had I not remained silent, had I ever betrayed his trust, he would have been fired from his job in disgrace, with the possible loss of his pension, medical benefits, etc. He had a great deal to lose. But there were many other considerations. At this time, I did not know his wife was in advanced stages of terminal cancer.

Sworn to secrecy, and faced with the possibility of civil lawsuits for defamation of character, there was one other very critical issue.

As I had been given permission to work with the authorities by my superiors on the California Highway Patrol, Lundblad and I had acquired a considerable amount of detailed information on our suspect. We had already met with members of the California DOJ, CII, the FBI, and the Vallejo

PD. But Les Lundblad, generally a very quiet and reserved individual, told me there was something else he had to tell me, something very important.

He swore me to yet another oath of secrecy, telling me emphatically I could never tell another soul:

> "The suspect's wife is the judge's lover, and they were caught screwing on top of his desk in the judge's chambers."

"Les, I already know. Lew Richey and one of the court bailiffs told me last week."

"My God, don't you ever tell anyone about this."

I truly do not believe Lundblad appreciated the gravity of what he just told me. Suffice it to say, at that moment he was giving me a powerful motive for Zodiac's killing spree, fueled by revenge and unmitigated hatred.

He did not care who he killed; he just needed victims so he could prove to his wife, the judge, and every cop that ever wore a badge that he was better, more clever, and smarter than all of them put together.

> Note: Of those few credible Zodiac suspects over the years, George Tucker is the only person with a *motive.*

While we could never confirm a date or a time period when this act of adultery was discovered, a close friend of Tucker's wife suggested it was a couple of years after they were married. They were married in January of 1964.

When Lundblad showed me his secret hiding place he told me, "I will never destroy my notes."

From that time forward, I inherited the Zodiac case.

It is incredible! All these years, the only person I have shared this with is my own confidant and partner, Jerry. But now I am going to share it with the world.

This one "Top Secret" document became a critical pillar of strength and has been a continual source of inspiration throughout the years. It helped reassure me and give me the confidence to continue. This is a valuable piece of evidence; but we are reminded we are sworn to secrecy and must never tell another living soul. In fact, the document does not exist, and I have never seen it before. And the police departments work together to solve such cases?

There remains one critical question—how many kids have been killed when it might have been entirely possible to prevent their untimely deaths by focusing on a suspect who was given immunity? If this case had been treated with any sanity at all—if they had only listened. But the sheriff, the detectives, and the police felt they had to get permission from the judge before they could investigate our suspect—with the terrible irony that it was—permission from the same judge who was committing adultery with the suspect's wife.

Years later, Jerry showed the NSA work to Det. Jack Mulanax, Vallejo PD. Mulanax told the author Robert Graysmith, "The first time I ever saw that code work was when that guy from Naval Intelligence showed it to me." (He was referring to Jerry.)

Over the next few years Sgt. Lundblad and my friends on the FBI encouraged me to continue with the investigation, even though I had absolutely no jurisdiction or authority, whatsoever.

I did, and I also watched Det. Lundblad turn sullen and withdrawn, living the last few years of his life in quiet rage.

When I confirmed this story with three of his family members, I learned he had continued his own off-duty investigations. He often told me, "Lyndon, don't you ever quit, you are right."

In time, I surrounded myself with professionals and other criminalists, and sought counsel, advice, and assistance.

My partner, Jerry Johnson, and I have been working

together for 39 years, and I have been directly involved for *over* 40 years. From the very beginning, other than political corruption and obstruction of justice, we have encountered a considerable amount of police hostility on a local level, even though for the most part we have received an open-door policy with most departments and agencies.

However, when the author Robert Graysmith, working on a book for St. Martin's Press, interviewed Jerry and me, we were shocked to see in his possession some of our original reports and other material. When we asked him, "Where did you obtain our material?" He told us, "I received it from the COYOTE group of San Francisco." This was one of those moments when, considering San Francisco, we never asked the obvious.

This was a learning experience for us, as it was very clear we did not know who we could trust with our reports of the investigation. Many indiscretions of this type have occurred over the years—some detectives discussing our suspect by name over the telephone with total strangers. I tried to ignore the blatant lies about me by San Francisco PD Inspector Dave Toschi, the infamous Zodiac investigator and distinguished authority, who started writing letters to himself signed "Zodiac."

There were elements in our investigation, which in themselves are fascinating incidents, of an unknown male stalking young females and many murders never suspected of or connected to the Zodiac. There are several murders where we can place our suspect within those geographic locales. Zodiac boasts of 37 victims, and our count is very close to this number, almost precisely so.

We can make 156 matches between our suspect and known facts in the Zodiac case. However, I would like to stress that motive is the fuel in the fire, the primal cause, the driving force behind every criminal act. Our suspect had the most powerful motive known to man, his wife's adultery; the most volatile of all.

The three oaths were a sacred trust, and I could not

violate this trust:

1. The judge had seduced the suspect's wife.

2. Sgt. Lundblad was ordered to destroy his files.

3. The "Top Secret" document revealed the suspect's name.

One more critical factor exists, which must be addressed. Falling also into the realm of supersecrecy is the criminal activity revealed by Naval Intelligence. This information cannot be revealed to lower public authorities, and falls into a category of federal jurisprudence.

IX

ZODIAC CREATED

In order to protect the innocent, directly and indirectly, and for other legal considerations, this chapter will contain a certain amount of fiction. While the dots will be connected in a circuitous manner, the truth will hopefully be the end result. Many points of evidence, including the powerful motive responsible for the insane and vengeful killings, are directly related to this series of events.

The Superior Court judge had a reputation for skirt-chasing, but he also enjoyed an outstanding judicial record and was highly respected. In law enforcement circles, he was considered the "final arbiter." He was not only Solano County's representative of the law, he *was* the law. Judge Dennis L. Winston was a close friend of many influential members of high society, including California Governor George Deukmejian. They had gone to law school together. Judge Winston had another close friend in Catherine Maldonado, who became Catherine Tucker, and they had known one another for many years. Their close friendship began in Sonoma County, when Winston was a deputy district attorney and Catherine a legal secretary.

When her second husband, George Tucker, failed to return from a trip back East to see his mother, and after discovering he was a violent alcoholic, Lia was considering either annulment or divorce.

It was a late Friday afternoon and the courthouse was virtually empty when she visited her intimate friend, the judge.

On this occasion, and they say there were many others, he and Lia were caught in the act. The poor janitor thought the judge's chamber was empty, just like all the others.

Lia's relationship with Winston was no secret to a few senior employees in the courthouse. When she would leave early on Friday afternoons, her co-workers knew exactly where she was going, a routine in place for many years. This day of infamy became Lia's coup de grâce. She knew within a few days the scandal would be known by everyone in the courthouse. She was so humiliated, she wanted to die. When her husband came home around the middle of May, she became frantic. Ashamed and feeling terribly guilty, she had to confess; she had to tell him before somebody else did.

Tucker, who was about the same age as the judge, was known to a few as some "weirdo" who liked to wander in and out of the courtrooms. One of his best friends in the courthouse was a well-known homosexual.

Some said of Tucker, "He is homosexual," while others said, "He is AC/DC."

However, all agreed this man also had a strange and insulting attitude toward women. District Attorney Neal McCaslin referred to him as "El Psycho Grande."

Nobody knew what the "weirdo" did to earn a living, even though he was always neatly dressed, intelligent, and very well-spoken.

The judge learned from Lia, "My husband is a high-ranking official in Alcoholics Anonymous (AA). He travels all over the country opening up new AA chapters, including Canada, and he is always a guest speaker at their conventions and other meetings. He has been with AA for many, many years."

Day after day, Lia struggled with her emotions, trying to work up enough courage to confess her terrible sins. The first thing Tucker did when he walked in the door was take a shower, then put on his white Palm Beach suit on top of a royal-blue shirt, and go to his AA meeting at the church. There was not a hair out of place, and with his matching white shoes he was a sight to behold, totally unreal. Except for being twice as old, he could have doubled for John Travolta in *Saturday Night Fever*—a real dandy!

Now, Lia was faced with the biggest decision in her life. At the time she married George Tucker, she truly believed she loved him. He was the first man who had ever told her he needed her in his life. For many years she blamed herself for the failure of her first marriage; the first time her husband left her, he just vanished into thin air, and she never saw him again.

After long discussions with the judge, the two of them developed a strategy. In spite of the judge's strong admonition to remain silent about the incident, Lia refused. She told him, "Things in the past were totally different because I was single and unattached; now I'm a married woman."

Winston asked Lia, "Do you know what people in the courthouse are saying about your husband?"

"No, I don't know and really don't care." But then she asked, "Just what are they saying?"

Now Winston replied, "Never mind." He was feeling too kind to tell her.

As Winston had planned another trip to the Himalayas with the Sierra Club and would be away for six weeks, Lia agreed to wait until he left. Winston advised the six weeks could act as a cooling-off period.

Lia was fully aware of her husband's good friend in the courthouse, the flaming homosexual. He had refused to attend their wedding because he was insanely jealous. She knew when he heard the rumor he would not wait to tell her husband. Lia knew he hated her; yet, Tucker had said, "He is just a poor lost soul I met at AA."

The judge left on a Sunday evening, and Lia prepared her little speech for the following Friday. She would attempt to rationalize and justify her actions in terms he would understand as an alcoholic.

"I'll blame the booze." True, she was not a drinker at all, but she would explain, "I truly believed you'd left me, like my first husband. The judge just lost a very close family member and was sad and depressed. One thing led to another, and—it just happened." Lia had attended dozens of AA meetings with her new husband, and most of the stories she had heard had a similar theme.

He of all people will realize how powerful booze can be. Indeed, the spirit is willing, but the flesh is weak. He himself has relapsed many times, and God only knows, nobody is perfect! If anyone can understand, he can.

When Tucker came home early, like he did every Friday evening, giving himself time to get ready for his meeting, Lia had prepared his favorite meal of broiled salmon, scalloped potatoes, and garlic bread. Now, the moment of truth had arrived. She began by telling her husband, "You know, you left here the first part of September, and the next time I see you is in May. I would not blame you if you wanted a divorce. I betrayed your trust, and broke every vow in the book."

Then she recited her prepared statement about having a few drinks, something she never did, and how she thought he had left her for good, just like her first husband, and Dennis was so depressed and—"Well, it just happened, and I had to tell you."

George Tucker went into a frenzied rage, throwing one of her Hummel figurines against the wall. He was violent, screeching and hollering, "The judge raped you; he drug-raped you by plying you with booze. I will file charges against him. That pompous, no-good, son-of-a-bitch!" He was so furious. He threatened to kill the lowlife hypocrite.

"All you no-good fucking whores.... The judges and cops all think they are so high-and-mighty... always better and smarter than everyone else. You should all just fucking die—you dog-fucking sluts—I hate your guts."

During the next few weeks George talked with several attorneys about suing the popular judge. Tucker was getting very angry because the first question they asked was, "Have you made a report to the police—and if not, why not?" Tucker tried to explain his reasons for not going to the police.

"The judge is so powerful, the police would find an excuse, some pretense, to frame me. It would be me landing in jail, not the judge."

One considerate attorney told Tucker, "If you want to sue the judge you would have to demonstrate some type of physical or emotional loss—like medical bills, loss of wages, psychiatric counseling, and so forth."

Another attorney told him, "You are wasting your time because there is not one attorney in Solano County who would handle a case against Judge Winston. I would advise you to look for an attorney out of the area."

Another one suggested, "You should go to San Francisco because the city is filled with bleeding-heart liberals."

Following this advice, he made an appointment with the famous Melvin Belli. Tucker was very familiar with San Francisco. When he worked in Marin County he would attend some AA meetings there, as well as the bars and dance clubs. Tucker was certain this affable Melvin Belli would take his case. When they finally met, Tucker became incensed at him, also.

"Look," Belli told him, "you people come in here wasting my time. You don't have any case. You refuse to go to the police, and you will not ask your wife to testify. They will argue she was a willing, if not eager, participant. Besides, the only witness is the janitor, and he probably has a long arrest record, and is a totally unreliable and impeachable witness. And Mr. Tucker, I would like to tell you something else. I know Judge Dennis Winston, and have for years. He is one of the finest men I have ever known in my life. If you had any class at all, you would not be sitting here telling me all these lies."

Tucker squirmed in his seat, grinding his teeth. He was

thinking, *If I had my 9-MM automatic, I would not hesitate to put a bullet right between your eyes.* He finally smiled at Belli and said, "You will never know how lucky you are at this moment."

Belli replied smugly, "Oh, and why is that, Mr. Tucker?" Tucker never said another word, and left the silver-haired fox sitting at his large desk.

Driving across the Golden Gate Bridge to Petaluma and the home of his friend, his AA sponsor, Tucker was developing an intricate plan of revenge, murder, and blackmail.

> *I will show them all. They deserve to die; and for every person I kill, the blame will be placed at their feet. I will taunt the police; I will write letters and codes to prove it is I and I alone, who is better and smarter than all of them put together. I will call myself the Zodiac, like the killer in that Charlie Chan movie.*

By the time he reached his friend's home he was in orgasmic ecstasy....

> *The friend of the governor,*
> *The most highly-respected judge in Solano County,*
> *The most powerful man in Solano County,*
> *A man with high expectations and political ambition,*
> *I NOW OWN YOU—YOU ARE MINE!*

X

SIERRA CLUB INFAMY

At times it is difficult to distinguish between fantasy, speculation, and opinion. In the matter of Zodiac's Sierra Club postcard, with a mailing date of March 22, 1971, the timing of other events is unusual and very interesting. While skeptics may simply call it another coincidence, we should not be so willing to concede that it is. The date of 9-70 on the bottom left corner of the card may refer to the disappearance of Donna Lass, last seen at a casino in Lake Tahoe on September 26, 1970. We have established, from a number of sources, that our suspect is an avid gambler. As Zodiac was claiming victim number 12, many authorities believe he was referring to Donna Lass.

Zodiac is cunning and devious, and he enjoys playing his little games.

Consider the following scenario: Relatives, colleagues, and friends are all talking about the judge's pending appointment as national president of the Sierra Club. He was undoubtedly asked if he would accept the title and position of president, well in advance of his election. Talk and gossip fills the courthouse, everybody commenting, "Oh, did you hear Judge Winston is being elected president of the Sierra Club?"

So, the jealous and raving husband, who is already in a festering, smoldering rage, gets a deranged and fanciful notion. He decides he will start his own Sierra Club.

As the web continues to weave, on May 3, 1971, the local newspapers announce, "Judge Winston named President of the

Sierra Club."

Over five-and-a-half months later, on October 22, they print a story stating the judge has just been released from the hospital because on the previous Tuesday night, at 11:30 PM, some unknown assailant beat him to a pulp. The paper reported Winston saying, "I caught a young man burglarizing my car, rifling through the glove compartment."

He described his attacker as "husky, six-feet tall, weighing 190 to 200 pounds, with blond hair."

This, of course, matches our suspect, except for the age and hair. A private investigator, very close to the source, told me,

"The man who attacked the judge was your suspect—Tucker! *I know, for a fact, because his wife told me.*"

A very similar story was told by the Vallejo Police officer who took the initial report from the judge as he lay in his hospital bed. Years later, the same policeman told me in person, "The judge confided to me the man had accused him of having sex with his wife." The judge also told the cop, "Exclude this piece of information from your report."

The newspaper reported that the beating was brutal, knocking the judge unconscious. Blood was smeared on the side of his car, and there were pools of blood on the ground. Does this sound like some 20-some-year-old punk, rifling through his glove compartment, and being caught in the act? Most punks are simply going to run away in fear, scared to death to be caught. It would appear this was a deliberate stalking and a well-planned assault.

The suspect, being familiar with the judge's haunts and nighttime activities, drives around until he finds his car. He then parks and waits. The suspect needs to teach the judge a very serious lesson, but he must be careful not to hurt him too badly. And the suspect knows the judge will not even fight back.

In this sordid affair of crime and justice, *the suspect needs the judge, and the judge needs the continued acquiescence and silence of the suspect.*

"There is a way, which seemeth right unto a man,
But the end thereof are the ways of death."
Proverbs

The suspect will laugh, all the way to his next killing and brag, "You will never catch me; I am too clever for you."

No, an eye for an eye will not satisfy his raging revenge. He will make them pay, and pay, and pay, as he gloats over every new killing.

The FBI and other institutions, which study criminal behavior, instruct their students to search for a few basic keys, critical factors to aid their investigative efforts. Perhaps the most important, and one, which most juries insist on knowing, is the motive. After answering questions like ability and opportunity, motive is the most significant factor in the entire investigative process. Therefore, the most difficult thing to establish in the large host of Zodiac suspects is motive. Harvey Hines, a homicide detective with the Escalon PD, had developed a suspect by the name of Kane, but with Kane there was absolutely no motive. Was Zodiac just a drive-by killer? The evidence suggests *no.*

There is but one suspect with a huge motive, a very powerful one; and the trail of evidence in the Zodiac case is overwhelming, leading directly and positively to our suspect.

The witchcraft and red homosexual drawings that later appeared around our suspect's home were not put there by a bunch of kids with nothing else to do. No, these red drawings reflect the taunting of "The Red Phantom," designed by evil intent, sinister and threatening, to embarrass and intimidate his wife. The Zodiac is not only getting even, he is proving to the world he is more clever and smarter than the police, and especially the judge who can give them orders.

The Count Marco letter of July 8, 1974, the one, which

made reference to the "shrink," was for the benefit of his wife who had been receiving psychiatric counseling. The Zodiac wanted his wife to see the red homosexual drawings, and this was his intent from the beginning. In his perverted dementia he wanted her to ask him, "Did you see those filthy drawings? There is one right across the road from our driveway, and another just like it on that huge water pipe sticking up in the field."

He would most likely reply, "Oh, maybe the Zodiac put those there. Did you see his Count Marco letter in the *San Francisco Chronicle* signed 'The Red Phantom'?"

It is difficult to explain how conspicuous these drawings appeared, looming up from a barren field in the middle of nowhere. When Zodiac's wife, Lia, would pull from the driveway, she would see one drawing immediately to the left and the other to her right in the open field. The drawings mysteriously appeared about two weeks before the Count Marco letter was printed in the newspaper. The paint was fresh and bright red.

> *The Zodiac went on his killing rampage to prove to his wife he was better than her boss and smarter than all the cops put together.*

This is why it was imperative for him to relate specific details of his crimes that only he would know, and use evidence taken from his victims.

The Zodiac wanted to start his own "Sierra Club," and this is why he sent his Sierra Club card taking credit for his 12th victim, Donna Lass. (It was not commonly known that Donna Lass had worked as a nurse at the Presidio for the Department of Veterans Affairs. As a frequent patient, Tucker may have met Donna at this facility.)

In October 1969, Zodiac drove to the Presidio in San Francisco and parked his car in a strategic area. He went there for one purpose only—with the deadly intent of killing a taxicab driver, and he didn't care which one. The Zodiac wanted a piece of clothing in order to taunt the police. Whenever he needed to verify the authenticity of his letters and the credibility of his threats, he would include a small piece of the shirt of Paul Stine, the taxi driver. This is in keeping with his many letters where he includes details of evidence relevant to his victims.

I have so often reminded myself over the past years that this is the same psychotic individual who pulled beside me as I sat in my black-and-white patrol car in full uniform. Be mindful of the fact the suspect was called in for questioning on March 15, 1971. Seven days later, March 22, 1971, Zodiac mailed his "Peek through the pines... Sierra Club card." Inverted, the date 9-70 appears on the lower left corner. Just another coincidence? If he was taking credit for killing Donna Lass at Lake Tahoe in September 1970, why would the Zodiac wait six months to make reference to the murder? Perhaps, in his twisted insane logic, he was going to play hardball, and was mad as hell because he got called in by Sgt. Lundblad on March 15.

"I'll show you who's boss—I killed a girl at Lake Tahoe last September."

In his book *Zodiac* (New York: St. Martin's Press, 1986), Robert Graysmith stated that our suspect received a traffic citation at Lake Tahoe during the exact time period Donna Lass disappeared. We have never been able to confirm this piece of evidence with the authorities in California or Nevada, and Graysmith tells us he cannot recall how he acquired it.

One month after Donna Lass disappeared on September 26, 1970, (remember the Lake Berryessa killing took place September 27, 1969), Nancy Bennalack, age 28, was murdered in her home, on October 26, in Sacramento. Strange as it seems, Nancy Bennalack was a court reporter, and the attack later on Isabel Watson, another legal secretary like Tucker's wife, may have absolutely nothing in common with the others.

However, as our suspect Tucker has many connections in

these areas—Tamalpais Valley, Sonoma, and Marin Counties—and as Capt. Ken Narlow was convinced the attacker of Mrs. Watson was Zodiac, the possibility does exist. The attacker stabbed and slashed Mrs. Watson when she refused to ride with him. He had deliberately knocked her down with his light-colored vehicle when she stepped from a bus at 9:00 PM on April 7, 1972. The incident is worthy of note because it occurred in the middle of another series of suspected Zodiac murders in Sonoma County.

Capt. Narlow stated, "Mrs. Watson described the Zodiac to a T."

We discovered that during the sudden string of murders in Sonoma County there was a national convention of AA taking place in Santa Rosa. Most likely an official of the affair, but at least in attendance was our suspect, George Tucker.

These homicides included the following:

NAME	GENERAL AGE	DATE	FOUND	GENERAL LOCATION
Yvonne Weber	13	2-2-72	Ravine	Sonoma County
Maureen Sterling	12	2-2-72	Ravine	Sonoma County
Kim W. Allen	19	3-4-72	Ravine	Sonoma County
Jeannette Kamahele	20	4-25-72	Ravine	Sonoma County
Lori Kursa	14	11-20-72	Ravine	Sonoma County

(Three victims were found at the same site.)

In his November 9, 1969 letter, he said he would no longer announce to anyone when he committed his murders.

A staff writer for the *Santa Rosa Press-Democrat*, Randi Rossman, mentioned the Zodiac in her 12-30-99 article stating, "In the early '70s a serial killer was stalking young women in Sonoma County. He killed at least seven and maybe several more."

Was the same person responsible for the vicious knife attack on Mrs. Watson? These sudden episodes of several murders tend to fit a definite pattern found also in Sacramento and San Francisco.

Sierra Club
around in the snow
Sought victim 12
"Peek through the pines,"
pass LAKE TAHOE areas
(9-70)
SAN FRANCISCO POLICE
ELLISON
3-23-71
3-23-71
ORDER RECEIVED BY

XI

SLEEPY HOLLOW

His lonely and mysterious house is nestled in a quiet location from the rest of the world, and surrounded by an unusual grove of whispering pines. The Suisun winds never stop. No stranger's eye can pierce this foreboding veil, behind which a monster dwells, composing his tales of murder and woe, and clandestine secret codes. He is a man possessed by the darkest evil, who feels no remorse. His insanity gives him a type of inner power and satisfaction. His failure as a human being has turned him into a sick, tormented animal, a killer, who calls himself "Zodiac." A perfect lair for nefarious deeds, even for calling up the devil—the terrible remoteness blends well with his psychotic mind.

On those crystal nights with a full moon, he looks upon the shadowy silhouette of Mt. Diablo. Nor does he have any house or hill obstructing a marvelous view of this prominent Bay Area landmark. How fitting then is the Mt. Diablo bomb letter with his code, telling us where it is buried. In a heavy rain, the road in front of the house is always flooded. This was considered another major clue by the DOJ, in the early stages of the investigation, as Zodiac had sent a card advising he would have written sooner, but was flooded out.

Zodiac's Mt. Diablo drawing, with his circle and cross-hair logo is also compelling. The compass reading of zero, if offset to magnetic north as he said—*would point directly to his house.* This was his intention, in our opinion, but he never expected anyone would ever find his house or make the connection.

Perhaps then it would not be unusual, considering his state of dementia, to assume he painted hex and "black magic" symbols truly believing they would help keep him safe and protect him from the authorities. It seems to follow the logic of an insane person, in addition to the dabbling in witchcraft suggested by the DOJ profile. He was spinning a web around his house like a force field, telling all trespassers to beware or die.

While on duty, I would drive by this spooky house at least two or three times a week. This road was used by truck drivers who were trying to evade the CHP scales, so we had reason to patrol the area, which made it very convenient. Then one day, I noticed something very strange. Someone had taken white paint, and painted an inverted cross with arrows on the telephone pole on the right side of his house. With the dribbles running down, it was quite obvious it was fresh, and was approximately thirty inches long.

Then lo and behold, on a concrete water cistern to the left of the house was painted a large hatchet. The freshness of the paint appeared to match that of the inverted cross on the telephone pole. Recalling the *inverted cross on one of Zodiac's cards with the inverted writing*, the paintings appeared to be a significant clue.

Neither Jerry nor I made an issue of these symbols, but we did mention them in our reports. The police naturally regarded them as pranks, drawn by kids with nothing better to do. Can't you just imagine a carload of kids drinking beer, driving around dark and lonely roads, armed with a can of spray paint saying, "Hey, let's go paint an inverted cross on a telephone pole!" (My God, they never had so much fun.)

In addition, covering all the bases, there was another fresh white spray-painting of a voodoo-like face, at a major crossing of Interstate 680 with the road leading directly to the suspect's house. The letters beneath the face were slightly blurred, but A, R, A, C were legible. We found an empty can of white spray paint in the weeds on the other side of the road. Judging by the lack of rust and the condition of the paper, the can appeared fresh and new, also. No latent prints were found on the can, and this itself is quite odd.

If one is inclined to be superstitious, these magic symbols could be intimidating. In our opinion, it is most improbable that kids painted these demonic or occult-type symbols. The hatchet is a detailed, nearly perfect drawing. The bands on the handle show the precise detail not to be expected of some kids just goofing off, and it is very neat.

The inverted cross with the arrow is not a juvenile creation, either. In various forms, the inverted cross has been used in black magic and is still used today. I had actually noticed them around the spring of 1974.

Another amazing coincidence happened about the same time. Painted in bright red spray paint, two more drawings appeared within a few hundred feet of the house. These drawings were nearly identical. One was on a farm labor shack directly across from the house, and the second was on another concrete water cistern in a freshly plowed field. They depicted two nude males engaged in explicit homosexual activity. The drawings were not small, standing about four feet tall. I refer to these drawings as "the Red Phantom" drawings because their appearance occurred near the same time of Zodiac's "the Red Phantom" letter, postmarked July 8, 1974.

We should note at this juncture that another spray-painting occurred on the back road to Travis Air Force Base and bordering Highway 12, in Suisun. Also written with a can of white spray paint, the message read:

"ZODIAC SUCKS AND KILLS"

All of these drawings were subtle hints, clues, and psychological taunting designed specifically, in my opinion, to tease and torment his wife. He wanted, he needed his wife to suspect *he might actually be the Zodiac.* His ego was filled with ecstatic pride, and this gave him a great sense of power. Their daily conversations must have been quite remarkable as he made innuendo and references to his true and mysterious identity. The homosexual drawings were designed to shock her sensibilities, and this gave him the ideal opportunity to play with her emotions, and perhaps drive her to a nervous breakdown. For reasons to be discussed later, I have strong feelings this man had already confessed everything to his wife.

The personal aspect of this bizarre and perplexing case is compatible with the Zodiac profile, to a marked degree. The principal motive of revenge has been satisfied, fulfilled, with creative genius. He not only proved he was better and smarter than the judge, he also took his wife along for the ride. She was, after all, a willing participant by her marital act of treason. Besides, the suspect had all the power over the judge who ordered this investigation to end immediately, an enviable position for a serial killer. It was a big game and he enjoyed every minute.

Dr. Donald T. Lunde, Associate Professor of Psychology at Stanford, interviewed a sudden serial killer, Herb Mullins, of Santa Cruz infamy. In his book, *The Die Song*, Dr. Lunde said,

> Mullins thought he was committing moral acts. This being the case, he may not have known the difference between right and wrong.

He talked to Mullins in jail, and told him a sleep researcher at Stanford had a theory that the hallucinations of schizophrenics might be a dreamlike phenomenon occurring in a waking state. This most certainly matches our suspect. Dr. Lunde also states,

> Another symptom of paranoia is projection—blaming one's failures or antisocial acts on others.

Thus, our suspect could blame the attorneys Robinson and Healy for Cheri Jo Bates's death, and sign his death poem on the Riverside campus desk with their initials, "R.H." They represented the suspect's first wife in his divorce.

When Jerry and I met with Dr. Lunde, he advised us the Zodiac might find the stability he needed and never kill again. He also cautioned, "The trigger mechanism is unpredictable; any one thing could cause another series of killings."

We found two bona-fide witches who owned a business in downtown Vallejo. My diary entry of May 4, 1974, reads:

> About two weeks ago, Jerry and I went downtown to Jim's Gifts, a store owned and run by two witches. They sell all kinds of magic books, spells, charms, herbs, etc. They were very friendly and freely admitted they were practicing witches, but emphasized they were white witches who never tampered with the black arts.

We showed them our photos of the symbols around the suspect's house, and they recognized them immediately as charms to protect the area, or to keep people out.

They said, "The one voodoo face with the letters A, R, A, C is part of the theme, as it fits the other symbols." They also told us, "Before you set foot on that property, you should wear something red touching your skin."

At a later date, we were, in fact, on the property and Jerry was wearing some red cloth, but I was not. The only red I was wearing was the red fire in my .38 snub-nose Smith and Wesson, loaded with 158-grain hollow points. Our car was parked nearly a mile from his house, and it was so quiet on the way. As we veered from the railroad tracks, we found ourselves almost in our suspect's backyard. The ground had recently been plowed, and the moist dirt crushed in silence beneath our feet. We saw what we wanted to see, but also something else, which made our hair stand on end. Crouching in his garden was our suspect, with his back slightly turned in our direction. This could have developed into an interesting, if not awkward, parley of words, or worse. Jerry and I looked at one another, and I raised my eyebrows. We dared not speak because there was not a lame reason in the world to explain our presence on this man's property.

We reached the road and glanced back. Apparently, he never knew we were there, and we were not twenty feet away. Jerry said, "See, I told you—red really works." (Years later, at his birthday roast, Jerry denied that he pulled up his shirt to show me the red cloth.)

So, we continued to ask, "Who the hell is this guy? All we knew for certain was he was an alcoholic with migraine headaches, a high-ranking official in AA, and a man who could destroy a Superior Court judge.

Two Vallejo detectives, Jack Mulanax and James Husted, both stated at different times, "We would have to get permission from Judge Winston before we proceeded with any investigation."

Many years later, this story was confirmed by Detective James Dean, who was Lt. Husted's partner.

It was too outrageous for words. Even as I am writing this years later, I find it almost impossible to believe. *This man had been given a license to kill.* And these guys are sworn, dedicated police officers?

The man on Interstate 80 was always in his white 1961 Chevrolet sedan, and the man on the frontage road beside Interstate 680, at the Cordelia junction (where the voodoo hex symbol was located), was always in an ice-blue/silverish-blue vehicle appearing to be a two-door hardtop. The DMV records showed the suspect owned a 1961 Chevrolet and a 1965 Dodge.

However, it was not until the summer of 1971 that I began to observe the man on the frontage road at Cordelia, several months after the Interstate 80 sightings. As occurred with those, whenever I returned to check out the man on the frontage road, he was gone. He, of course, saw the patrol car, as there was a clear and unobstructed view of the passing traffic on both sides of the freeway. The frontage road is quite narrow, and he was always parked in the same place, a gravel shoulder pull-out directly under a scraggly willow tree.

From the viewing distance, I could not swear it was the same man, but his height, the erect manner in which he was sitting, and the dark clothing he always wore matched the man on Interstate 80. A full head of hair was also identical. And in retrospect, it was the behavioral characteristics and the coincident time periods, which made it so unusual. In my own mind, I was fairly certain it was the same man.

I would guess I saw this individual on the frontage road five or six times, and he appeared to be watching traffic, never reading anything. Of the thousands of trips I made up and down this freeway, year after year, I have never observed another person duplicating this behavior.

As Zodiac prided himself on being the perfectionist, the daytime sightings were most likely practice sessions. If a vehicle is traveling at 60 MPH, let's call this Vehicle A; a pursuit vehicle, Vehicle B, traveling 90 MPH will overtake Vehicle A in one minute, assuming the initial distance at the start is one-half mile. If Vehicle B travels 75 MPH it will catch Vehicle A in two minutes. The hunter in pursuit of his next victim has 8.7 miles to overtake and assess his prey. Assuming he travels the moderate speed of 75 MPH, he can view his target, male or female, and make his judgment call two or three miles in advance of Lake Herman Road-Vista Point exit. It is within this area that he will start flashing his lights. (This was the method used to kidnap Kathleen Johns and her baby in Modesto on March 22, 1970.)

Regardless of his success or failure, he knows it will take the victim at least ten to fifteen minutes to drive to the Benicia police to report the assault. If they broadcast an APB or a BOL (All-Points Bulletin; Be on the Lookout) for the suspect vehicle, the psycho could be drinking a cup of coffee at Terry's in Vallejo, or walk into his front door, which is only 11.3 miles away. In fact, he could be home before the victim ever found the police station.

We learned that a few reports were given at the Concord and Walnut Creek PDs. To disappear with impunity time and again, it was logical to assume the person was a real phantom or perhaps lived in the neighborhood.

The sites of the killings on Lake Herman Road and at Blue Rock Springs Park strongly suggest that convenience, and ease of vanishing without a trace might well have been a factor—an inducement, if not an invitation. They were caught in his web of death.

The diagram (last insert at end of chapter) illustrates the Zodiac's local "web" of operation for capturing his prey and shows a direct route to and from Lake Berryessa and Lake Herman Road. Additionally, it should be noted that the tire casts made by the Napa Sheriff's Department, after the attack on Cecelia Ann Shepard and Bryan Hartnell, fit the wheelbase measurements of a 1965 Dodge. A few witnesses at Lake Berryessa reported a suspicious man driving an ice-blue hardtop. After a few years of investigation and profiling, the DOJ concluded the Zodiac most likely resided in the Fairfield area.

The majority of these sexual assault victims offered the same or a similar description of their assailant: an older white man in his forties or early fifties, slight potbelly, weighing 180 to 200 pounds, 5'8" to 6' tall, a full head of hair with a tint of grey. Most said he had pulled right up on their rear bumpers, flashing his lights up and down, just before they reached the Lake Herman Road exit. If he got them to stop, he would tell his victims, "Yeah, your wheel is really loose. Pull off up here at Lake Herman Road, and I'll check it for you." These incidents always occurred at midnight and later. He would then exhibit himself and tell his victims, "Suck it or die."

One detective told me, "A lot of these women are so

embarrassed and so afraid their husbands will find out, they never make a report." Do these incidents match the general Zodiac profile?

We know, for a fact, our suspect's AA meetings, at least two a week, adjourned at around 10:00 PM or later. With a few cups of coffee, some conversation, or counseling, the witching hour of midnight was very close indeed.

The DOJ profile is absolutely certain about one of their observations:

> *Zodiac hated women—and this precisely matches our suspect.*

A nurse at County Hospital, whom I interviewed around the latter part of 1971 stated, "I am almost positive I was followed from work," which just happens to share a common driveway with a 24-hour detox facility. "I was followed several times, and on each occasion the person behind me would start flashing his lights when I was approaching the Lake Herman Road exit."

She never stopped as she was scared to death. Her shift ended at midnight.

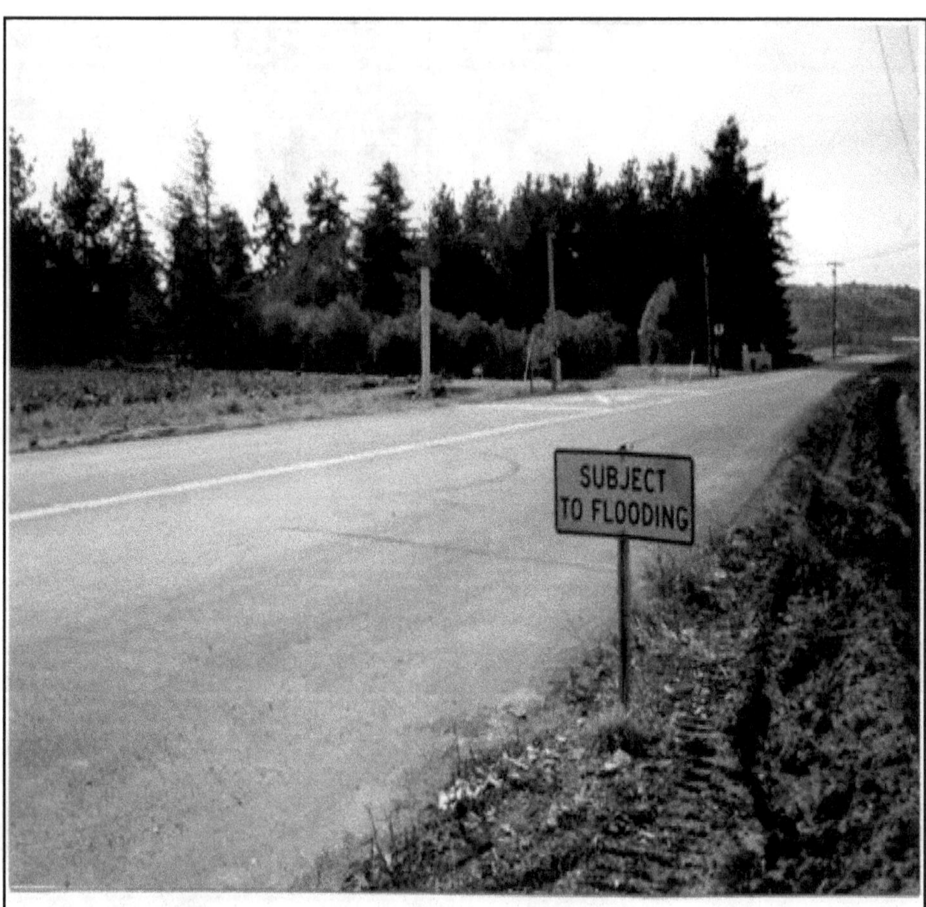

A Department of Justice profile advised the local authorities to look for a suspect who lived in a flood area or a basement subject to flooding. Zodiac's letter of April 20, 1970 stated: "I was swamped out by the rain we had a while back."

Suspect's home in center of and completely hidden by the grove of whispering pine trees.

Zodiac's "Sierra Club" card, received by Paul Avery on March 22, 1971 stated: "PEEK THROUGH THE PINES." (Zodiac would not write again for nearly three years.)

In *This Is The Zodiac Speaking* the authors Michael D. Kelleher and David Van Nuys comment on page 169, "In many ways, Zodiac's last communication of 1971 marked the end of his strange and frustrating relationship with the press."

The "Sierra Club" card was most likely mailed on March 19th or 20th, just five or six days after our suspect was called in for questioning on March 15, 1971. It is our supposition our suspect mailed this card for the same reasons he mailed the other letter on March 13, 1971. It is the mind of the Zodiac!

Mt. Diablo: Looking south from the rear of suspect's rural residence.

Unobstructed view of Mt. Diablo from the rear of suspect's residence. Did this provide the inspiration for Zodiac's Mt. Diablo "Bus Bomb" letter? "Turn the magnetic indicator on Mt. Diablo to North." View is looking directly south. With the compass adjustment the reading from the top of Mt. Diablo would point directly to suspect's residence (Sleepy Hollow). Date of Zodiac's letter—June 29, 1970.

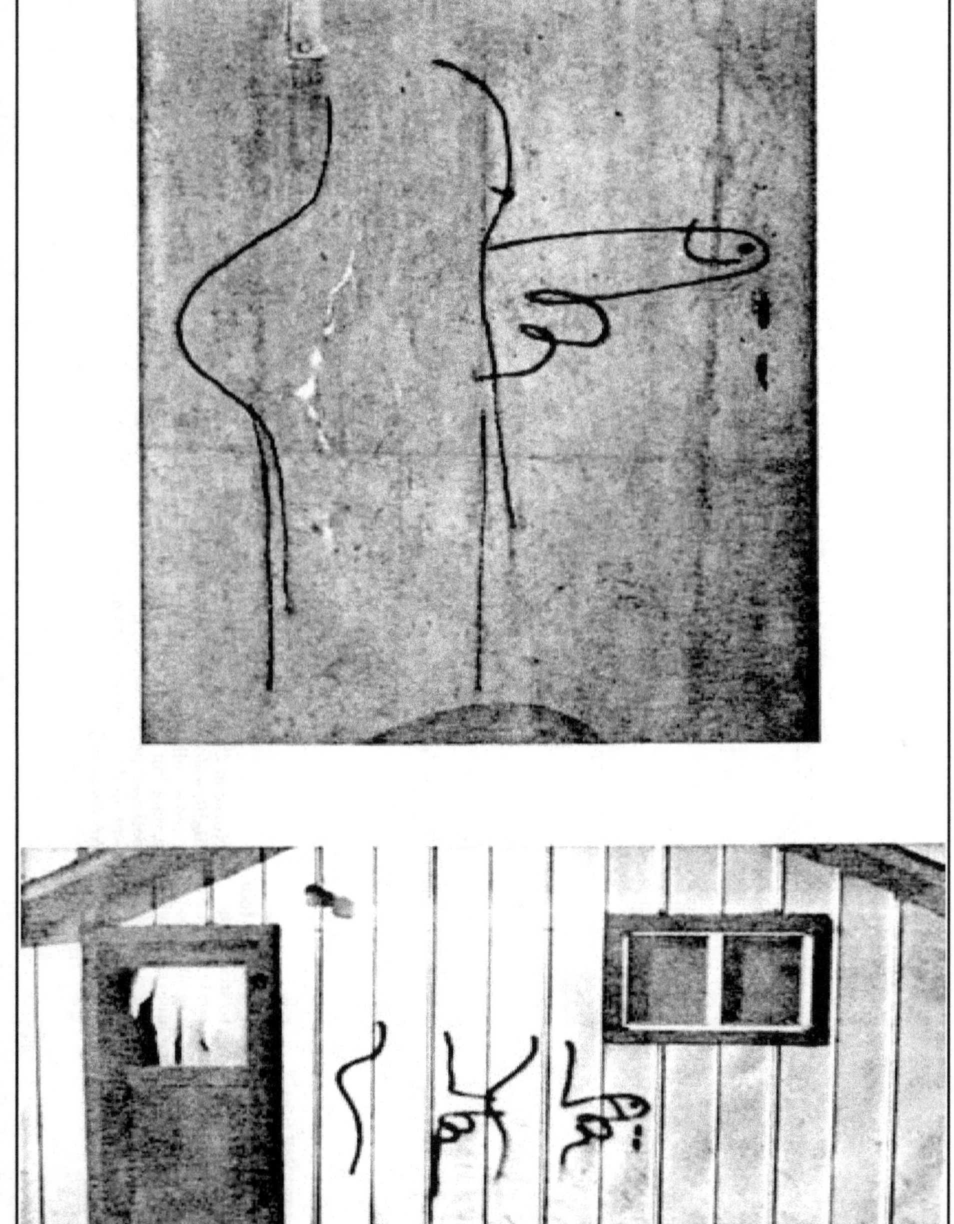

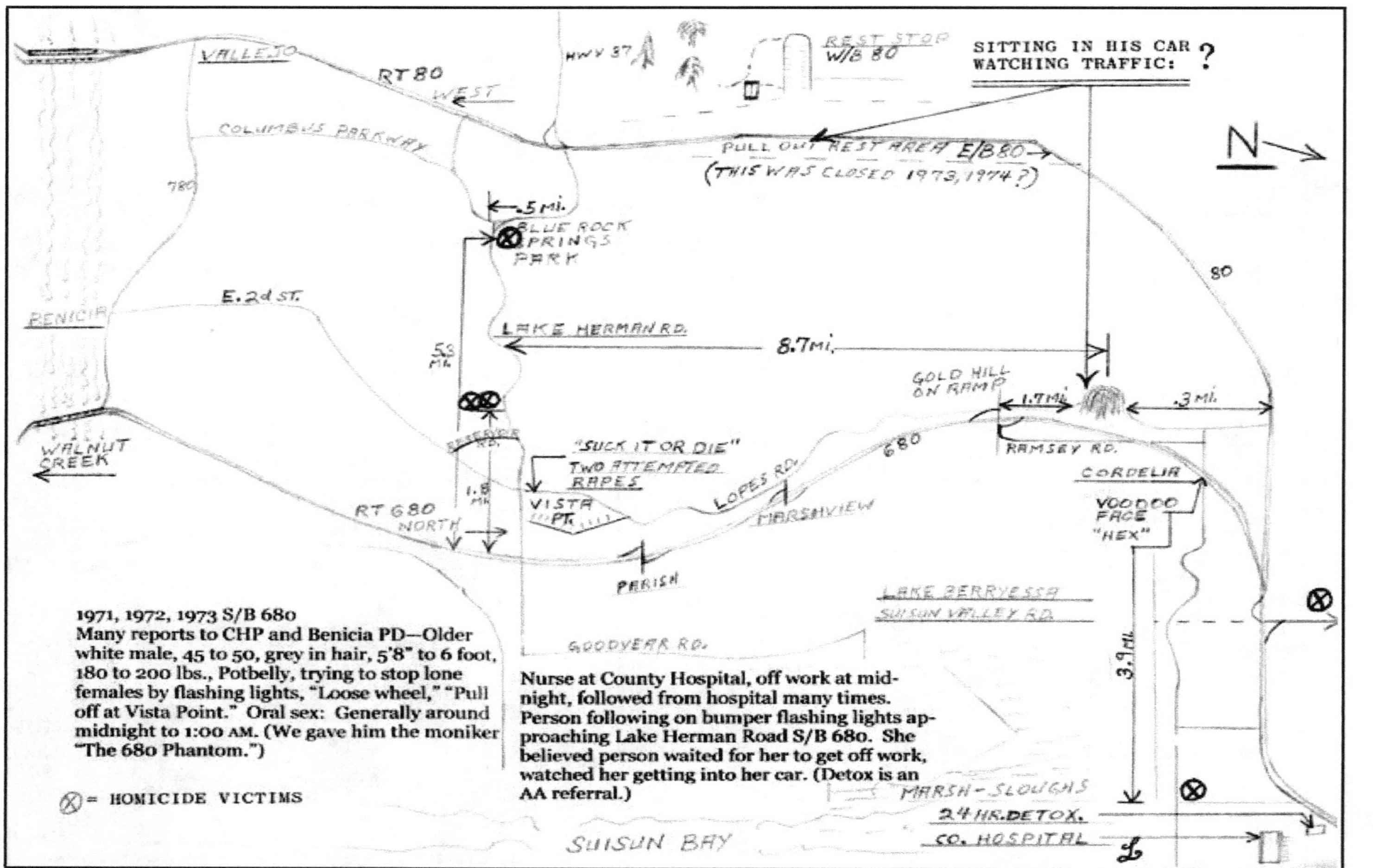

1971, 1972, 1973 S/B 680
Many reports to CHP and Benicia PD—Older white male, 45 to 50, grey in hair, 5'8" to 6 foot, 180 to 200 lbs., Potbelly, trying to stop lone females by flashing lights, "Loose wheel," "Pull off at Vista Point." Oral sex: Generally around midnight to 1:00 AM. (We gave him the moniker "The 680 Phantom.")

⊗ = HOMICIDE VICTIMS

Nurse at County Hospital, off work at midnight, followed from hospital many times. Person following on bumper flashing lights approaching Lake Herman Road S/B 680. She believed person waited for her to get off work, watched her getting into her car. (Detox is an AA referral.)

XII

SLIPPERY FOX

It was March 5, 1973, and our suspect was allegedly working in an office in West Sacramento, just off Mace Boulevard. We had planned for this evening three weeks in advance. He would be attending his AA meeting Friday, and we had developed a plan to place him under surveillance the entire evening. If he took off for Lake Tahoe or wherever, after the meeting, so be it—we were going for a ride. But that didn't happen.

That night, we staked out Tucker's house—Chuck Forrest in his black Dodge, Jerry in his blue Ambassador, and my wife and I in our black-and-white Coupe de Ville. Tucker is very clever and was acting very spooked, like scared. Chuck and Jerry went up about 5:00 PM and saw him come home around 5:20, driving his 1970 green Ford sedan. As planned, my wife and I were in position at 6:30.

Then, at 7:25, a car whipped out of the driveway, and Chuck pulled out behind it at some distance away. I was to continue the surveillance when Chuck got made. When his taillights began to fade, I could not believe the speed I was traveling just trying to catch up. At about 90 MPH I had to back off, and we watched Chuck disappear into a very dark night. Jerry had remained in a fixed position, to keep the house and driveway in view at all times. In about fifteen or twenty minutes, we had returned to Jerry sitting concealed in the orchard. The straight road gave him an excellent view of the suspect's house, which was about 600 feet from his location.

Chuck was really pumped up, telling all of us, "Did you see that guy? I was up to 100 miles an hour, and he just disappeared! I went up to Main Street thinking I would find him, but he was gone."

I told Chuck, "I had to slow down as I was approaching the big curve at 90, and your taillights faded away."

Chuck said, "I have never seen anything like it—that guy is totally whacked!"

Jerry said, "I saw you and Chuck take off, but I never observed our man pulling out of the driveway."

We talked for a while more, went for coffee, and then drove by the AA meeting to see if his car was there. We had to pass Tucker's house again. There was no moon, and it was extremely dark in this remote rural setting.

Jerry was in the lead, Chuck following, and my wife and I bringing up the rear. Jerry and Chuck cleared his pine-shrouded driveway, but just as I drove by, headlights came on, and Mr. "El Psycho Grande" pulled behind me and got right on my bumper. Jerry and Chuck turned off onto another road. To cover the charade I continued to go straight.

I sped up to a modest speed, and soon his headlights vanished behind the rear of our car, as he pulled within a foot or two of my bumper. I increased my speed to about 65 when he tried to pass us over double-yellow lines. He jerked back quickly at the point of a sharp curve. I pulled my Colt Python .357-Magnum from beneath my jacket, laid it on the seat, and then placed it between my legs.

When the passing lane permitted, he pulled broadside, giving us a look from hell.

My wife said, "Oh, my God!"

I hit the brakes and he flew by. Within a few seconds, his brake lights came on and he began to slow down. The situation was becoming nasty, and now I realized how foolish it was to bring my wife along. But she was very willing to play the part of an innocent passenger, to make it look good.

I guessed he was trying to see if I would follow when he sped up and turned left toward town. I also turned, but continued at a moderate speed, letting him get further and further away. He stopped for a red light, and when it turned green he crossed the intersection and pulled to the curb, his foot on the brakes.

When the light turned red again, I stopped, and he waited for the light to turn green. But instead of going straight, I turned left and watched my mirror to see if he would continue to follow us. He did not.

When we walked into the restaurant, Jerry and Chuck said, "Where the hell did you go?" They had not observed Tucker pulling behind my wife and me, and they were totally shocked.

Yes, he was in his green Ford sedan, the same one he was in when he left earlier. There was only one answer to this strange set of circumstances. As Jerry had never left his observation post, *Tucker obviously returned home with his lights off*. Damn clever, all right! He wanted to check us out, and he did just that.

Next morning I called my office at the CHP and asked the dispatcher, "Call DMV and have my license plate number removed immediately from the computers. This is an emergency request." The dispatcher called me about 30 minutes later and said, "They pulled it. I tried running your number again, and it's been removed." (There is a law permitting peace officers to place their personal plates in an "undercover" status.)

But surrounding the lair of Sleepy Hollow, the night was still young. Two days after our frenzied encounter the newspapers had a front-page story of a young black man, who had been shot to death on the same road we were traveling back and forth. He had been murdered either the very same evening or in the early morning hours, not too far from Tucker's house. The man was wearing a back brace, and in a flicker of headlights the brace might well have been mistaken for a shoulder holster.

However, the poor guy had just bought a half-pint of

booze from a nearby Short Stop Market, and was walking down this remote and isolated road. At the location his body was found, there was a dirt pullout between the orchard groves. It is conceivable someone was sitting in his car waiting for this young man to walk by. The victim was shot six times in the chest by a .38 caliber, and at least three times in the back of his skull with a 12-gauge shotgun. The body was still warm when it was discovered around 4:00 o'clock that morning.

While there is no such thing as a friendly or congenial shooting, this was an especially brutal and vicious act. It was very natural for the police to assume at least two people did the shooting because two different weapons were used. In the mind of Zodiac, this would be another ploy. The conclusion of the police department was: "Another drug-related homicide."

Jerry and I immediately made contact with our District Attorney, Neal McCaslin. After explaining the entire story, McCaslin agreed to call the police department and ask them to place an "Information Wanted" notice in the local newspapers. It read:

> Attention—Police asking anyone observing anything strange, out of the ordinary, suspicious persons, or suspicious vehicles, on this road or in the area of a murder victim on the night of March 5 or the early morning of March 6, please contact the police department at (phone number).

This appeared on the front page of the *Fairfield Daily Republic*.

McCaslin told the chief to contact him, if and when somebody called. About one week passed, and Neal told us, "I called the chief and was told, 'Not one soul called in response to your notice.'"

So over the years we've asked, "What does this tell us about our suspect?"

XIII

GENERAL INVESTIGATIONS

In February 1975, the Department of Justice (DOJ) issued a special confidential report on unsolved female homicides. The areas included Northern California and Western America, and covered a time span from December 10, 1969 to September 29, 1974. This report DID NOT include any of the known Zodiac murders, though the first murder listed on the DOJ report, Leona Roberts from Rodeo, is, in fact, one murder we lay on him.

In the annals of criminal history and statistical data, it would be difficult to match the large number of female homicides in a small geographic area in such a short period of time. Ted Bundy, Richard Ramirez (The Night Stalker), and even Jack The Ripper did not even come close to matching these numbers in a five-year period. John Gacy, the contractor clown, did murder 33 young men in six years. Of course, Zodiac claims 37 victims in eight years (1966 to 1974).

The Juan Corona murder case might well be an exception to the above statistics. On May 19, 1971, the first of his 25 victims was discovered, and these murders did occur over a very short period, perhaps no longer than two years. All but three were Anglo-Saxon, not one was Mexican, and they were all adult males, which makes him unlike most serial killers. To this day, there remain serious questions about the validity of Juan Corona's guilty verdict.

The DOJ special report stated that during the five-year period, fourteen young women murdered in Northern California appeared to have been killed by the same person. In 1974, eight other women mysteriously disappeared in the states of Oregon and Washington, and there was the distinct possibility those incidents might be related to the fourteen.

Consider what the Zodiac said on November 9, 1969, that he would no longer announce his murders. Thirty-one days later, Leona Roberts disappeared from her Rodeo apartment. About two weeks later, they found her body in Marin County by Bolinas Lagoon.

These are the fourteen murders the DOJ believes were committed by the same person:

Name	Date
Leona Roberts	12-10-69
Antoinette Anstey	3-13-70
Linda Dudley	8-27-71
Yvonne Weber	2-02-72
Maureen Sterling	2-02-72
Kim Allen	3-04-72
Lori Kursa	11-20-72
Rosa Vasquez	5-29-73
Yvonne Quiltang	6-09-73
Angela Thomas	7-01-73
Nancy Gidley	7-12-73
Caroline Davis	7-15-73
Therese Walsh	9-22-73
Donna Braun	9-29-74

The eight missing females from Oregon and Washington disappeared between January and July 1974, and there was no reported activity in the California murder series during that time. Quoting from the report:

> The unknown suspect in the missing-persons series, apparently, travels about freely, as the unknown

suspect in the California cases is believed to be doing.

Four of these girls were last seen on a campus, two at the University of Washington. We must recall the murder of Cheri Jo Bates late on 10-30-66 on the Riverside campus. The "unknown" killer must have had an affinity for, or some reason to be on, the campus. Possibly a scheduled guest speaker for AA or somehow involved in drug prevention programs at the universities. In the San Francisco murder series, some of the girls were found on school grounds. Of one thing we were absolutely certain:

Our suspect traveled about freely.

If we give Zodiac credit for the fourteen known murders and the eight disappearances, which we might assume are also homicides, we have a total of 22 murders. However, there were several more unsolved murders during this time frame, which were not mentioned in the DOJ report.

For perspective, here are the dates and locations:

3-03-69	Moraga	
3-05-69	Pleasant Hill	
12-01-69	Walnut Creek	
3-07-70	Sacramento	
9-26-70	Lake Tahoe	(Donna Lass)
10-26-70	Sacramento	(Nancy Bennalack)
11-20-71	Stockton	(Nelda Tally)

NOTE:

10-19-71	Judge Winston brutally attacked, knocked unconscious, and in the hospital with a severe concussion for two-and-a-half days.

Adding these seven killings to the previous 22, we have a

total of 29 victims. We include these seven because we can place our suspect in the general area during the respective time periods. And Zodiac even makes a direct inference he killed Donna Lass in Lake Tahoe. Adding the five known Zodiac murders in the Bay Area, including Lake Berryessa, brings the total to 34. If we added Cheri Jo Bates in Riverside we would have 35. If we were to add a young couple in Santa Barbara in June 1963, we would have the exact total Zodiac claims—37. There are, however, four more, which are worthy of review, but have received very little press and notoriety.

It would appear there are a multitude of victims we could blame Zodiac for killing, and I will be the first to say he most likely did not kill them all. It is just like many typical investigations by police departments, when the victim is involved in buying or selling drugs. In the majority of cases, no witnesses can be found or very few come forward. Absent the evidence, the vast majority of these cases cannot be solved. Routinely, the police departments put the matter to rest by making a public statement like, "Another drug-related homicide."

Yet, it is most unlikely that Zodiac could have picked the number 37 out of a hat. Unless he had police access to confidential reports, it is totally unreasonable he could invent or create 37 victims, unless, he is keeping his own personal scorecard. It is my guess the serial-killer profilers and other professionals would agree that Zodiac tells the truth.

Without question, there exist other compelling considerations. After Zodiac's letter of July 1974 and Zodiac's last suspected activity in September 1974, unsolved murders and the murders themselves, virtually stopped.

Dr. Lunde of Stanford University told Jerry and I there were many stabilizing factors, which could cause a serial killer to stop his killings: a job, marriage, health, age, etc. Something in their troubled and sociopathic lives has changed, and in most instances they lose their lust for killing. Impotence and the inability to achieve sexual gratification are powerful qualifiers, affecting their emotional and physical drives.

When Zodiac sent in his last-known letter in April 1978, he said,

"I AM NOW IN CONTROL OF ALL THINGS."

This was another turning point in the Zodiac murders. Literally and figuratively, it would appear he is, in fact, in control of himself. This, of course, corresponds to our suspect, who for the first time in his psychotic and pathetic life, opens his own business on the first of April 1978. One not familiar with the scenario or details in this case would even wonder if the two were not one and the same—they are now in control of all things.

That Penny Parker (murdered on May 7, 1977, in Sacramento), Carol Hilburn (murdered on November 14, 1970, in Santa Rosa), and Susan Lynch (apparently abducted and murdered while hitchhiking from San Diego on July 31, 1971) were all three dumped like sacks of garbage in the same remote field in West Sacramento cannot be a mere random occurrence. This is why the authorities believed the three girls were killed by the same person. It is yet another remarkable coincidence, for our suspect was working in the same area of West Sacramento, many miles from his home.

Dr. Lunde also stressed this: "While many factors could stabilize the psychotic killer, the trigger is always cocked. If anything happens to cause stress, pain, or adversity, the person could resume his killings."

In this regard, we should mention the fact our subject's business failed after a short period of time.

On the face of it, Penny Parker's murder does not fit the "cluster" profile. Yet, the circumstances could have made her a vulnerable and easy target. She had been riding her bicycle, collecting money earned from the customers on her paper route.

She was abducted and killed in broad daylight. Her parents, family members, and friends all said the same thing: "She would *never* enter a stranger's car."

What kind of stranger might she trust? Perhaps a man who was her father's age with gray hair, suit and tie, and driving a nice new car. Pretending to be lost or searching for a street or store, he might say, "If you could show me, I'll bring you right back." She never made it.

Evidence also exists, never made public, that a disguise may have been used by the killer, a black wig.

ZODIAC VICTIMS: KNOWN AND POSSIBLE

** = DOJ PROFILE – SAME KILLER – 14 FEMALES

NAME		AGE	DATE	MO	LOCATION - OTHER
CHERI JO BATES		18	10-30-66	STABBED	RIVERSIDE CAMPUS / BANK / LIBRARY
BETTY LOU JENSEN		16	12-20-68	SHOT	LAKE HERMAN ROAD – VALLEJO
DAVID FARADAY		17	12-20-68	SHOT	LAKE HERMAN ROAD – VALLEJO
DARLENE FERRIN		22	7-5-69	SHOT	BLUE ROCK SPRINGS – VALLEJO (MICHAEL MAGEAU – SURVIVED)
CECELIA ANN SHEPARD		22	9-27-69	STABBED	LAKE BERRYESSA – NAPA COUNTY (BRYAN HARTNELL – SURVIVED)
PAUL STINE		29	10-11-69	SHOT	SAN FRANCISCO – CAB DRIVER
ELAINE DAVIS	N	17	12-1-69		CONCORD
LEONA ROBERTS	N **	16	12-10-69	ASPIRATION – VIRUS	CONCORD/RODEO/MARIN COUNTY
COSETTE ELLISON	N	16	3-3-70		MORAGA
PATRICIA KING	N	21	3-5-70	STRANGLED	CONCORD
JUDITH HAKARI	N	23	3-7-70	BEATEN	SACRAMENTO / SUTTER HOSPITAL NURSE
ANTOINETTE ANSTEY	**	24	3-13-70	BLOW	VALLEJO / BAR / CLEARLAKE
EVA BLAU		17	3-13-70		SONOMA COUNTY
DONNA LASS	NF	25	9-26-70		LAKE TAHOE CASINO – NURSE – SAN FRANCISCO
NANCY BENNALACK	N	28	10-26-70	THROAT CUT	SACRAMENTO – COURT REPORTER
CAROL HILBURN	N	22	11-14-70	BEATEN – CUT	SANTA ROSA – SACRAMENTO
SUSAN LYNCH	N	22	7-31-71	BEATEN	SAN DIEGO – SACRAMENTO
LINDA DUDLEY	**	22	8-27-71	STABBED	SAN FRANCISCO
GEORGE PIMENTAL		67	11-8-71	STABBED	VALLEJO – RESIDENCE: BLIND DATE WITH "BIG SHOT": FINGER EYE – NAME CARVED
NELDA TALLY		46	11-20-71	STRANGLED	STOCKTON – FIRE – EMPLOYMENT AGENCY
MAUREEN STERLING	N **	12	2-2-72	U	SANTA ROSA
YVONNE WEBER	N **	13	2-2-72	U	SANTA ROSA
KIM ALLEN	N **	19	3-4-72	STRANGLED – CUT	SANTA ROSA / MARIN COUNTY
JEANNETTE KAMAHELE	NF	20	4-25-72	[FOUND 7-6-79]	SONOMA COUNTY
LORI KURSA	N **	14	11-20-72	BEATEN	SANTA ROSA / SONOMA
NAOMI SANDERS		57	2-27-73	BLOWS	VALLEJO – APARTMENT MANAGER
SUSAN McLAUGHLIN	N	19	3-8-73	STABBED	UC BERKELEY – PLACERVILLE
ROSA VASQUEZ	N **	20	5-29-73	STRANGLED	SAN FRANCISCO – GOLDEN GATE PARK
YVONNE QUILTANG	N **	15	6-9-73	STRANGLED	SAN FRANCISCO
ANGELA THOMAS	N **	16	7-1-73	SMOTHERED	SAN FRANCISCO – SCHOOL
NANCY GIDLEY	N **	24	7-12-73	STRANGLED	SAN FRANCISCO – MOTEL – SCHOOL
CAROLINE DAVIS	N **	15	7-15-73	POISONING	SANTA ROSA – GARBERVILLE
THERESE WALSH	N **	23	9-22-73	ROPE STRANGLED	GARBERVILLE (HWY 101 SONOMA)
GORDON SWINFORD		54	9-25-73	SHOT – LEFT EYE	OAKLAND – SECURITY GUARD (SAME GUN)
KIRK HUGHES		22	9-25-73	SHOT – LEFT EYE	BERKELEY
DONNA BRAUN	**	14	9-29-74	STRANGLED	MONTEREY COUNTY – IN RIVER
LAURA O'DELL		21	11-4-74	STRANGLED	SAN FRANCISCO
TOTAL 37					
NOTE THE FOLLOWING:					
PENNY PARKER		15	5-7-77	STABBED	SACRAMENTO: FOUND IN SAME REMOTE FIELD AS CAROL HILBURN AND SUSAN LYNCH
SHIRI-DINE BANA		19	5-14-79	STABBED	BLUE ROCK SPRINGS – VALLEJO (FOUND BY LAKE HERMAN ROAD)

LEGEND: N = NUDE U = UNAVAILABLE NF = NOT FOUND

XIV

SCHEMED SEDUCTION

Francois Rochefoucauld, French courtier and moralist:

"It is as easy to deceive one's self without perceiving it, as it is difficult to deceive others without their finding out."

(1630–1680)

~ ♦ ~

George Edward Bulwer, English novelist:

"The surest way of making a dupe is to let your victim suppose you are his."

(1803–1873)

Catherine Aurelia Maldonado, now Catherine Tucker, was a sophisticated socialite, born and raised on a large ranch in Sonoma County, CA. Her grandfather, Joaquin Maldonado, was heir to a large Spanish grant, and they boasted of their friendship with General Vallejo's family. Cathy, or Lia as most everyone called her, was the youngest of four children. Against the advice of her family and friends, Lia married at a very young age. The man turned into a vulgar and abusive alcoholic. One of Lia's uncles, an attorney in Napa, threatened her husband, telling him to end their marriage by just disappearing. The uncle gave the man a choice: either leave on his own terms, or other options would be enforced. The family never knew what happened to Mr. Stuckey Finch; he just vanished suddenly, and Cathy never saw any more of him. Bruised by her disaster, she vowed never to marry again.

As the years went by, she tried to pass the bar examination three times, with no success. She mastered the difficult stenotype machine and began a career in court reporting, making more money than her uncle. Soon Lia was in big demand for her recording skills. She began working in several law offices in the Napa and Sonoma area taking dictation while she still worked for the courts. She was offered a very nice salary to take a job as office administrator in one of the finest law offices, which she accepted. She would be making more money with half the work.

She had vowed she would never marry again, but at a rather older age, she married a man she did not truly know. She didn't know if the man had touched her heart, or if she just felt sorry for this poor lost soul, or if she really loved him. However, with assurances and a little pressure from her family and friends, she married this comical and mysterious man.

She thought, *A woman nearly fifty years old can't be too choosy*. She had no idea who he was, except that he needed her, nor did she know how the rest of her life would be changed irreversibly.

Lia was still a very beautiful woman, and it was no surprise that many of the attorneys and judges in Napa and Solano Counties adored her wiling charms.

Lia maintained their extensive Law Library, kept the books, ordered all the supplies, and set the dates for the attorneys' court appearances. Additionally, Lia did the hiring of the other legal secretaries. She told the attorneys when she would be taking her vacations and how long she would be gone. On certain afternoons, she would simply leave for the rest of the day, and nobody ever said a word to her. When the other secretaries needed a day off, they asked "Catherine." (Calling her

"Lia" was reserved for friends only.)

If the girls' skirts were too short, or they were wearing too much makeup, Cathy would tell them to shape up or go peddle their bodies in some other office. Here was one sharp lady, aggressive, educated, refined, and some said snotty. But she was very attractive, even to much younger men. There were two attorneys, one in Vallejo and one in Fairfield, who pursued her constantly, and they were both married men. The other girls loved nothing more than to talk behind her back. As popular as she was, they could not stand her, and one in particular hated her with a passion.

My wife had been employed as a legal secretary for several years, but was not associated with the same law firm as Catherine Maldonado Tucker, and as yet, hadn't had any occasion to meet her. It was not until the summer of 1976 that Lia approached my wife, at a legal secretary luncheon at the Elks Club in Vallejo, and introduced herself with her ingratiating manner and her words flowing like honey. She asked my wife, "Would you ever consider working part-time? I've heard through the grapevine you've quit working."

As a result, this strange relationship developed into a lot of work for my wife over the next few years. Catherine, however, was a very inquisitive person—always asking questions about me, the kind of car we drove, if we ever went out for dinner, dancing, shows, etc.

When I told Jerry, in detail, the first words out of his mouth were, "It's a set-up."

As things turned out, he was absolutely correct. The situation struck me the same way, but my wife insisted we were all "loony tunes." After a short while, it became impossible to ignore her continual advances and her invitations for dinner and lunch.

As subtle as she was, she always seemed to have a hidden agenda. With the strange phone calls I began receiving at my office and at home, I became very suspicious.

At this time we did not know Catherine Tucker had taken a temporary state-compensated leave of absence, on a disability, a couple years earlier. She had mentioned to my wife, “My office is all messed-up, and some of the girls have just quit.” She was trying to fix things there. This is why she recruited my wife for part-time work, allegedly, but Jerry was not buying any of it.

I could not think of any practical way to cancel this dinner. His wife, Catherine, had orchestrated the entire evening, planning everything, even the reservations. There was no doubt in my mind they wanted to see our car. They wanted to know if we were still driving the same one we were driving the night of our fouled-up surveillance.

If I tried to feign a sickness, it would be too obvious. Then they would know, that we knew, they knew, who we were, and what the hell we were doing.

My God, I thought, *talk about a rock and a hard spot*. It was Murphy’s Law in spades.

“No,” I told my wife, “we have to play this silly game; we will have to go through with the evening as planned.”

Even though I could not share other thoughts with my wife, I had my strategy well thought-out—*I won’t hesitate. If he tries anything at all, I will blow him away, period, end of story.* I was definitely prepared.

The evening before this “arranged” dinner, I retrieved my .38 five-shot Centennial Smith & Wesson hammerless, cleaned and lubricated it, and loaded it with high velocity light-grain hollow points. These bullets explode on impact and are twice as deadly as the conventional loads normally used by the CHP. I adjusted my shoulder holster so it fit snug and comfortable. The five-shot hammerless had a small cylinder, which made it a superb piece to carry in situations like these. I could hit a man at 75 feet, but not predict if I would hit him in the head or foot. It was not very accurate at those distances, but at close range, it was a great little gun.

Next, I checked my small, palm-sized .22 Magnum

Derringer, the "dynamite stick," which holds two bullets. I called my wife into the kitchen and asked her, "Do you still remember how to load and shoot the derringer?"

She asked, "Do you really think all this is necessary? Don't you think you are overreacting? What makes you think they know who we are anyhow?"

"Look," I said, "I have been over this with you a dozen times. Jerry is positive they made us a long time ago, and that is exactly why she singled you out. She wants to find out what the hell we know. With those strange phone calls I have been getting from 'astrological woman,' pumping me for information about the Zodiac case, I think Jerry might be right."

That gal, the "mystery woman," was most likely a friend of Lia's, and her phone calls were designed well in advance. She asked all the right questions obliquely. She was very clever, and one day I would find out who she was, too.

"Now listen up real good," I told my wife. "We cannot anticipate what might happen, but if I get spooked about anything at all, I am going to say something about the kids, like—well, we should get home and check on the kids, something like that. This is my code to you, to put you on alert."

"You are really nuts, you know that?"

"Yeah," I said, "you just know how to get your damn gun. Tell me again—why do they want us to go to their house, and why do they insist on driving? We're only going to Winters."

"Well, because she wants us to see their new house, and because he wants to drive."

"We should just meet them at the restaurant and save all the hassle."

My wife has been shooting my weapons for a long time and she is extremely competent. She has never been shy about carrying a gun when needed.

As we were ringing their front doorbell, I asked myself, *What the hell am I doing? Why in the world did I ever consent to this insane meeting?*

Here I was, getting ready to meet this psycho face-to-face again, a man I felt most likely to be the crazed killer "Zodiac." It was all especially insane when I suspected he actually knew I was the guy who had him called in by Sgt. Lundblad. I never knew what the sheriff had told Catherine, but as they were very close, dear friends, I truly feared the worst-case scenario.

My God! He answered the door. I also thought I detected half-a-smile (like the spider who swallowed the fly), but I was not certain.

"Come in, come in, and have a seat. My wife is in back. I'll tell her you are here." He disappeared down the hall.

The house was ultra-neat and clean, almost sterile. The furniture was classic old, plain and colorless, just like the entire room. Everything was very nice but very cold, with no atmosphere whatsoever. It made me think of an old musty library with dark wooden floors but no books. They showed us through the entire house, and I was looking for the Zodiac books and typewriters, but I saw nothing.

In fact, what was so surprising, except for the bland furniture, was that there was nothing to speak of in any of the rooms. It was rather like a model home. The furniture was there, but you could tell nobody lived there.

I watched him walk back and forth across the room and guessed his height to be about six feet, maybe a little taller. While I could not say he had a limp, there was something unusual about the way he walked—a strange gait, hard to describe.

There was the normal light conversation about nothing in particular, and they asked if we would like to have a drink. My wife took a glass of water, but I told them, "No thanks, I'm fine."

Perhaps it was just my imagination, but I sensed a very subtle tension in those moments of uncomfortable silence. There were those brief interludes when we were all trying to find something to say. (We all know how terribly awkward we feel when that happens.)

So far things were progressing nicely; he was pretending I was not me, and I was pretending he was not him. We had only been there ten minutes when they suggested we leave. It had been raining all day and at that moment a torrential downpour swept over the area. We entered the garage from the kitchen and climbed into his dark-green Ford sedan. For some reason, the idle chitchat turned into somber quiet.

The Tuckers had made reservations for eight o'clock at the Buckhorn Restaurant in Winters. That place was packed like a sardine can, and the bar was elbow-to-elbow. We were early, so I excused myself saying, "I have to use the bathroom."

I crunched my way to the bar for a bourbon and water, twice. I saw our little group walk through the bar into another room in the rear, and in a few minutes I joined them.

For whatever reason, I had a position at the end of the table, and Mr. Tucker was sitting 90 degrees to my right. I guess everyone figured Mr. Tucker and I had a lot to talk about. My wife was sitting directly across from him, and Lia was to his right.

The next hour was one of the most bizarre in my entire life. Staring straight out, at about a 30-degree angle, Tucker appeared to be in another dimension, some kind of "twilight zone." He did not want anything to drink, and Catherine assured us he had not touched a drop of alcohol in several years.

Throughout the entire evening Lia carried the burden of the conversation, but on occasion, she would ask her husband a question saying things like, "Isn't that right, George, do you remember that?"

Whenever she said anything to him, she would grab his arm or poke him, like she was trying to get him to pay attention. At times, he would begin to answer one of her questions while he was still staring into his dream world and then suddenly turn towards her or me while he completed his response.

On two or three occasions, he grabbed my arm forcefully while talking, just to emphasize a point. Once his manner became quite hostile over an innocent remark made by my wife. We were talking about schools, in some context, I cannot recall, and my wife mentioned we had graduated from high school in 1950. George Tucker became serious and said, "Oh, is that right? 1950, huh! So, what do you want me to do now, tell you when I graduated? You think you are so much younger than me? Are you telling me I am old, or just what are you saying?"

We could not believe our ears. The other couple with us, a retired man and his wife, turned away trying to ignore his remarks. He seemed not to be joking at all, but if he was, he did not even grin. He was bitter and vindictive, and Lia tried to laugh, interrupting and changing the conversation immediately. Her actions told us a great deal, that he was very serious.

Then, suddenly, talking about his favorite night clubs and bars in San Francisco, including the dance halls, George Tucker began talking about the attorney Melvin Belli. By the inflection and tone of his voice, it was apparent Mr. Tucker was becoming excited as he talked. He said, "Do you know where Melvin Belli's office is, over there in San Francisco?"

I replied, "I have absolutely no idea where his office is located."

He continued, "Well, it's right on the sidewalk, and you can stand there, right there on the sidewalk, and look into his office. You can stand there—right there on the sidewalk—right there, just stand there and look right into his office—you know what I mean?" As he said the last words he grabbed my right arm again, squeezing very hard, and stared into my face, nose-to-nose.

My wife nudged me under the table, and I knew exactly what she was thinking, *This guy is a whack job, borderline insane, a kite without a tail, and three bottles short of a six-pack.* It was an incredible experience.

When we walked outside, it was still pouring. The other couple had already left in their own car. The parking lot was packed, and there was very little room for navigation, especially if we went straight, as we should have. For a few seconds I thought, *I am back on our CHP EVOC* (Emergency Vehicle Operations Course) *at the Academy.*

Tucker was listing to one side, with his face directly in front of his rear-view mirror. He sped backwards at a high rate of speed, turning the rear of his car into a narrow opening between two parked cars. He then accelerated forward at a reckless speed and exited the parking lot. On reaching Highway 505, I realized why this man had been put on probation by the Department of Motor Vehicles.

The wipers could not move fast enough to clear the heavy torrents of rain, and the visibility was no more than fifty feet. Under these conditions, a safe speed would be approximately 40 to 45 MPH, but this idiot was flying down the road at 60 to 65.

As we passed the Nut Tree and then the Brigadoon Restaurant, he missed his turnoff at Peabody Road. This, I did not like—I did not like it at all. Then, muttering something about not being able to see, Tucker slowed down and turned off onto Cherry Glen Road. It was about 10:30, and it was pitch-black.

He drove across the freeway (Interstate 80), and instead of turning onto the ramp to head back to Vacaville, he continued straight. His wife asked him, "Where the hell are you going?"

"This is a shortcut."

Lia became a little upset and demanded harshly, "I'm telling you right now, turn around and go back to the freeway. You're going to get us lost."

I had been down this road many times, and it is a very remote and lonely road, which leads into the dark foothills behind the California Medical Facility State Prison. It most assuredly is not a shortcut, and it sure as hell did not go into Vacaville.

He is walking a very fine line, I thought.

His silence just added to the sheer panic I was beginning to feel. In fact, I knew something was wrong when he passed the Nut Tree, which was brightly lit. I knew if I saw it, he did, too. I knew his wipers were OK, even though he had been playing with them, or so it seemed to me. I slipped out my .38 snub-nose and told my wife, "I hope the kids are staying dry, not getting soaked in all this rain." I noticed she already had her hand in her purse.

"There!" Lia said, "there is a driveway. Now you get us turned around right now!" Without any hesitation he stopped and carefully pulled into the driveway.

This is it, I thought, *he has stopped the car, and he will most likely try to get me out under some pretext, like helping him get turned around or whatever.*

My adrenalin was pumping a mile a minute, and my palms were wet with sweat.

He turned the car around, and within a few more minutes we arrived back at their new home on Marshall Road. I cannot remember another time in my life when I was so mad. My body was still shaking, and I could not believe how stupid I really was. In fact, I knew better, and this is why I was so angry. I wanted to take that s.o.b. and literally tear him apart.

I said to myself, *Dumb, dumb, dumb!* To put my wife in imminent danger with a person I truly believed was the sick psychopath Zodiac. I could feel the veins in my head were tight and throbbing.

My God! I thought, *did this really happen? Was it all entirely innocent? Is my wife right, am I simply overreacting?*

Well, we will never know.

One thing I know for certain, I did not believe one word he said about not being able to see. I can tell you something else. At that very moment I knew, one day, I would be writing this fascinating story.

When we arrived at their home, he promptly disappeared while the ladies were saying goodnight.

"We should do this again real soon."

"You bet your sweet ass," I mumbled to myself.

In the weeks that followed, something else struck me as most unusual. Normally, when people discover a CHP officer in their midst, they want to know things like drunk-driving policies and enforcement, blood alcohol, sobriety field tests, how fast you can drive without getting a ticket, felony high-risk arrests, and so on. With the suspect and his wife, not one word, nada—nothing whatsoever said about law enforcement. Naturally I have asked myself a thousand times if his eccentric behavior matched the Zodiac profile. There never was any doubt.

Yes, there were other dinners and lunches, and in each meeting I discovered many abnormal characteristics of Mr. George Tucker.

Our investigative team—I called them the Mandamus Seven—continued to meet for lunch, but now, not so often. For some unknown reason, the Zodiac activity had stopped, and the last serious episode we had with Tucker was the Kimberly Lawrence case. She was the young schoolteacher being stalked by a mysterious man, an older man, driving a new dark-green Ford sedan. This was in May of 1974. Tucker was positively identified as the man sitting in his green Ford at Lawrence's apartment in Vacaville. This matter is discussed in another chapter.

On January 3, 1976, Jerry met with Lt. Jim Husted of the Vallejo PD. Husted was extremely interested in the Zodiac case, and at our suggestion, hypnotized Darlene Ferrin's babysitter. However, on this particular date of January 3, 1976, Husted told Jerry that he had been very busy and that there were restraining orders about releasing information to both of us. He added that Det. Jack Mulanax hated Jerry's guts and that he (Husted) did not want to upset Judge Winston by asking for his permission to work on our case.

A few months later we discovered the confessions at AA, and a month or so after that we went ahead with the famous "fish bowl" event. Yes, we were still busy doing what we could, but the years were passing quickly. I continued to wait patiently for the authorities to respond to my pleadings for an examination of my code decryptions. And we believe the psychiatrist played a major role in Zodiac's life. His ad in the *San Francisco Chronicle* appeared on August 26, 1976. Is it not all too amazing how the timelines weave a credible pattern?

Five years after that traumatic dinner in Winters, we received an invitation to celebrate George Tucker's 60th birthday. A small party had been planned at their newly renovated cabin in the Lake Tahoe area (actually, Weimar, CA). During these past five years, my wife and Lia had become very good friends, in spite of it all.

> *This was the principal reason my name could never be mentioned in connection with the Zodiac case.*

My wife actually thought the world of Lia, and truly enjoyed her company. She would never miss an opportunity to have lunch with her whenever she could.

Perhaps the relationship was born out of a "Schemed Seduction," but they remained good friends until she passed away in May 2007.

Possessed with obtaining the critical palm prints, I saw an opportunity presenting itself in this birthday party. We would have to try something we had never done before, and we had made several attempts. The sinister side of my nature, the one who sees deceit behind everything, made me extremely suspicious again. Was he trying to get us into the mountains for some other reason?

I had reason to be concerned because of something that happened to our undercover informant in AA. Ernie (HB) recovered a note one night after everyone had left the meeting. The note was about him, and he became very worried. In essence, Ernie had been made.

We were now asking these major questions: "Has our suspect made the connection between Ernie and us? Has he hired a private investigator?" It was possible.

As usual, we were still not in a position to discover just how much he knew about us and our investigation. With the "fish bowl" caper revealed in Robert Graysmith's book *Zodiac*, and the note saying our informant was a phony, Ernie moved out of the state. His safety had been seriously compromised by Graysmith, and perhaps ours, as well.

XV

PERSONAL PROFILE

In his book, *The Psychopathic Mind*, J. Reid Meloy discusses an unusual but common trait among serial killers: the "Reptilian, Predatory Stare," the central focus being the limbic system, the cortex surrounding the stem. On page 70 Meloy states,

> Clinical observations support the hypothesis of a reptilian stare among certain primitive psychopathic characters [which] is the absence of perceived emotion in their eyes. It is common to hear descriptions of a certain patient or inmate's eyes as cold, staring, harsh, empty, vacant, and absent of feeling. The psychopath's eyes have incited comments like, *I was frightened... he's very eerie: I felt as if he was staring right through me; when he looked at me, the hair stood up on my neck.*

Meloy mentions how adept our movies are in depicting this strange phenomenon with killers such as Richard Ramirez, Ted Bundy, and Charles Manson. We can recall most vividly the unbelievable eyes of Anthony Hopkins as he played the role of Hannibal Lecter in *The Silence of the Lambs*. Meloy states,

> Scoptophilia, the sexualization of the sensation of looking, may be a predominant component of the reptilian stare. The Sicilian fear of the 'evil eye' is based on the visual act of predation.

Personally, I can attest to all the above in my eye-to-eye contact with Mr. George Tucker, a most frightening experience.

Consider the following events, as three more witnesses describe their true-life encounters with Mr. Tucker. An informant, conducting a variety of surveillances for us said, "On one occasion, as I was driving by the church slowly, your suspect suddenly appeared on the sidewalk directly in front of me. My God, it was so weird. I have never seen such a stare—his eyes—I can't describe it. He scared the hell out of me. He is one spooky son-of-a-bitch."

This man, Jones, was a true undercover specialist with Naval Intelligence, and had twenty years experience in the field. He spoke five languages, was cool, and sharp. After two months, we had a camera rolling in his van with its one-way glass. We didn't know what to expect, but we were prepared for just about anything. Jerry and I always kept the van in view from another car while Chuck was manning the camera.

Jones walked into our suspect's office with his briefcase and a long map neatly rolled under his arm. He was a walk-in customer with some questions about the real estate market. He was portraying himself as an investment developer, and he certainly had the appearance of a very successful businessman in a double-breasted suit. Jones was sharp.

He walked right up to our suspect's desk and laid his briefcase down in the empty chair alongside. Jones said, "Hello, how are you? It's so hot!" He took off his coat and loosened his tie. Not saying a word, our suspect literally jumped up from behind his desk and ran out the door. Jerry and I watched as he bolted to his car and drove off.

To present a credible story, Jones then asked if he might speak with the broker in charge, which he did. We watched Tucker drive rapidly toward the freeway. Shortly after, Jones walked from the office and drove off in his van with Chuck. Thirty minutes later, as planned, we met for coffee at the Texaco Truck Stop in Cordelia, where Interstate 80 and 680 join and flow northeast toward Sacramento.

Jones reported the following: "In my entire life, I have never had an experience like this. The person smelled a cop as soon as I walked in the office. He's incredible! He never said one word to me, just jumped up and ran out the door, and I can't believe it... his eyes—he stared a hole right through me. I'm going to tell you one thing for sure, he is your man. That guy is Zodiac. It's amazing, he knew exactly who I was—knew what I was doing—the guy is brilliant. One of the spookiest encounters I've ever had."

Our principal confidant, our top-secret agent, Ernie Bringas, is a highly educated professional, with more than one college degree. A minister and counselor, people are Ernie's business.

Here are some of his comments after going undercover for us: "I noticed a few things as he chaired the one AA meeting [on December 14, 1976, shortly after the Grand Wizard ads in the *San Francisco Chronicle*]. 'I have done things so bad,' he said, 'I could never tell, nor *would* I. *If you only knew.*' And he was very ambiguous about what he said, 'Let's not concentrate on the past.'"

"He always makes fun of the women, makes jokes about them constantly. A woman at the meeting said, 'When I was drunk, I was mean and nasty to my husband,' to which he replied, 'Well, you don't have to be drunk to do that, that fits all women.' He is always cutting down the women, and he seems to be saying things to absolve himself of past misdeeds. He speaks with authority, a low voice, very articulate—an intelligent person."

"On the other hand, I have an impression he has two lives, *that he is not real*. I have noticed when he is not in the leadership position, he never laughs and never gets involved. I have also noticed he doesn't know the people's names, like they don't matter. I also get the impression he's always holding something in reserve, like he's not really there."

"He seems to make negative remarks about women all the time. We were in the kitchen the other day and a woman—I don't exactly remember the remark she made, but he made a negative comment about her personality."

"My summary impressions: I felt like he was trying to say—'*I am a rotten s.o.b.*, but I can't tell you what I have done. I've done things I'm not proud of, and I would never tell you—*terrible things*, if you only knew, but you will never know, and I don't care anymore, it's in the past now.' I get the impression it was far more than just what troubles the normal alcoholic. I not only heard it in his voice, I caught it in his eyes—it impressed me like I was looking at two different people."

"And I sensed a feeling of superiority about him."

We tape-recorded Ernie's comments right after every meeting. On January 12, 1977, he said,

"Last night I went to another AA meeting, and I thought it was very strange, and I want you to record this before I forget. When I went in, he was already there, and I sat down at the end of the table. I had a feeling he was looking at me, so I looked over, and he was—staring at me with such a—penetrating look—like he knew who I was. He was staring right through me. I have never, ever, in my entire life seen anything like it. I didn't know if I should just stare him down or what, but he kept staring. My heart began to race. He really frightened me, but I never let him know it. It was so weird. I just pretended to ignore him, and I turned away."

"I noticed when he is not the chairperson he will just stare off into space and never pay attention. He will say, 'Hi' back to all the speakers if they are men, but he will never respond to a woman, ever."

"And I noticed something else. I have paid close attention to the fact he will never laugh. Even when the jokes are going around, and everyone is laughing, HE will never laugh!"

"But, that look—it really got me, paralyzed me. I've never seen anything like it before. I very definitely get the impression, a distinct feeling, he is two different people."

"He told me, 'I enjoy traveling because I get to stop at all the AA meetings. I have visited AA offices in every state in the country.'"

Raised as a Catholic, our suspect was undoubtedly haunted from time to time, as he contemplated his foul deeds.

Whatever remorse he may have had, it was likely to have been superficial at best. On those certain occasions when he suffered his anxiety attacks and could seize the opportunity to gloat and brag to a large audience, he actually confessed his crimes.

To those of you who are not familiar with the traditions of AA, the nature and atmosphere of their meetings, it may be difficult to comprehend. Alcoholics Anonymous encourages their members to talk.

"Hi, my name is (first name only), and I am an alcoholic." The group, in unison responds, "Hi," or "Hello, (first name only)." Then the war and horror stories begin. Each one more graphic and more disgusting than the one before. "I had no control, I hit my kids, I kicked my wife and shot the dog, wrapped my car around a telephone pole, was in a coma for three weeks; three days later I found myself in South Dakota, etc."

These self-incriminations are part of the curative therapy, and the sharing of these tales helps the other members as well. Some egomaniacs actually feel proud if they can portray themselves as the meanest junkyard dog in town, consuming more booze in a day than any three of the others combined. The message contained herein is, "I was so bad—if I can do it, you can, too."

Tom M. Smith, M.D. has written extensively about the subject. In *Emotional-Behavioral Problems Associated with Brain Damage* he states:

> Studies of brain-damaged individuals reveal many emotional and behavioral problems, which greatly affect the afflicted person, their families and associates. Since alcoholism can cause temporary or long-term brain dysfunction, and even damage, we can notice the same problems in alcoholics as in people with brain tumors, strokes, brain degeneration, and brain injury. Chronic alcohol abuse (as brief as five years of heavy drinking) can definitely cause brain damage.
>
> During sobriety, recovering alcoholics may also experience 'dry drunks,' where the alcoholic thinks and feels in much the same way as if they were intoxicated with alcohol. 'Dry drunks' are a part of delayed withdrawal, where alcoholic thinking, unrealistic behavior (overestimating one's importance, overestimating one's abilities, intelligence, and judgment, living beyond one's means), childish and unrealistic behavior, overreacting, and being self-destructive. Sobering alcoholics share many of the same problems as people with brain damage.

As a layperson, I would have to interpret Dr. Smith's comments in my own language. It appears he is saying there are many people running around as recovering alcoholics who are still very sick, and possibly extremely dangerous. Mr. Tucker fits into such a category very well.

There seems to exist very little research on alcoholics and their predisposition for criminal activity. We know statistically nearly 50 percent of traffic fatalities can be associated with alcohol, and we know the use of alcohol is related to approximately 90 percent of our prison population.

What demons control the type of recovering alcoholic who either lapses into binging stupors from time to time, or the deranged psychotic who has suffered irreparable brain damage?

The AA literature is bloated with redundant tales of the alcoholic's struggle to maintain control, and the factors involved when one loses control. A truck driver who never had a drink in seven-and-a-half years attended three AA meetings in one day. The same evening he drank himself into oblivion, waking up three days later.

This theme is common. For most, the cycle of behavior is well-known. A high-ranking oil executive whom I knew, had a terrible problem. Placed in rehab for the second time in a year, he was determined to beat it. But his wife divorced him, and his three children would have nothing to do with him, isolating him from his grandchildren, also. Then he was told if he didn't stop drinking, he would lose his job. About a year later, he was admitted to the same clinic in an alcoholic coma, and died there the same day.

Drunk—sober—sick—tremors—shame—guilt—resolve to quit—recovering—in control—feeling great—then drinking until drunk—sober—sick—etc. And for many the cycle only ends in premature death. What are the coping techniques of the alcoholic? What patterns of behavior can substitute for a pending, imminent relapse?

In the histories of a few serial killers, we learn they had no motives, no intentions, and no plans to kill. But suddenly something came over them, and they just had to do it. Most studies reveal that lust is the primary force behind these killings. The ferocity and exultation displayed in the stabbing of Cecelia Ann Shepard at Lake Berryessa is a tragically perfect example. Even the spasmodic cycles of several killings in a single geographic locale—Sacramento, Sonoma, San Francisco—tend to fit this demonic pattern. And in George Tucker's case, he had a reason to be there.

HIS VICTIMS WERE CONVENIENTLY LOCATED.

Are the sudden clusters of killings directly related to the bingeing and withdrawal cycles of the alcoholic?

In *Serial Killers* (Anchor, 1989), a book by Joel Norris, intimate profiles of serial killers are combined with a discussion of psychobiology.

> Addicted to the act of murder as if it were a drug, serial killers compulsively and silently troll for their victims amid shopping malls at twilight, darkened city streets, or country roads in isolated rural communities. They are motivated by a force that even they do not understand.

I would also add lovers' lanes.

> Once they have spotted a potential victim, they begin to stalk with dogged relentlessness that does not cease until the victim is cornered, and the trap is sprung. Like tormented beasts of prey, serial murderers do not commit simple homicides. They often torture their victims, taking delight in the victim's agonies, expressions of terror, cries of despair, and reactions to pain. Then, in a period of marked depression that follows the high of the murder, the killers plead for help from the police or newspapers. (page 15)

Does this fit the Zodiac? Every young girl killed by the Zodiac, and 99 percent of his possible victims, were *not* sexually molested physically, but the vast majority were found nude, with no clothing at the scene. It would appear Zodiac was humiliating his young victims by forcing them to take their clothes off. This was in keeping with his self-righteous moral crusade. He would punish them like an outraged father, then kill them to save their sinful souls. Most likely impotent and unable to perform normally, he was nonetheless sexually stimulated here to the point of orgasm. Norris states,

> Between crimes, the serial killer slips quietly back into the fabric of society. He lives and exists in plain sight from day-to-day, but on the sly, he is observing the police who are busily trying to assemble clues but never seeing the larger picture. (page 19)

The Zodiac is not a slam-dunk murder case.

> He may loathe what he does and despise his own weakness, but he can do nothing on his own to control it. Perversely, he wishes for death, and the threat of the gas chamber, the electric chair, or the lethal injection is only an inducement to keep committing murders until he is caught and put to death. (page 20)
>
> He attempts to medicate himself with large quantities of alcohol or drugs, but, like pouring gasoline on a fire, these create an opposite reaction and only feed his lust. (page 25)
>
> He only has to troll like a fisherman spreading his net, plying back and forth across likely seas for abduction. (pages 20, 25)

Zodiac's stalking of the schoolteacher Kimberly Lawrence is a classic example of the serial killer's trolling.

> Most homicide cops report it is the killer's stalking phase that most unnerves a police department once a pattern of serial murders has been established in an area. The problem is compounded by the sensational nature of the news of each murder that appears on television that very evening. This sometimes inspires the serial killer, who is tracking both the police investigation and the media reporting, to change the pattern of his crimes to throw both the police and the

media off the trail. (page 27)

This is exactly what Zodiac did.

> For days or weeks after the most recent murder, the killer will inhabit a shadowy world of gloom in which he feeds on his own sorrow.

(In AA, it is called the pity pot.)

> All the while, he is going about the business of life, as if he were normal. Then, sick of the crimes he has committed, he may send a confessional note to the police or he may even call the local newspaper to ask for help. But driven by the lust of murder, he starts up the car again and drives off into the night to seek out the trolling grounds where his next victims will unwittingly congregate. (page 35)

The phone calls and the letters mailed to attorney Melvin Belli were Zodiac's cries for help.

Dressed in his white suit, white shoes, and royal-blue shirt, Mr. Tucker is not always as effeminate as he appears.

One evening, JJ and I were on a stakeout at the church AA meeting. Shortly before the meeting was to begin, I witnessed a strange incident. While most of the members had gone into the church, a few stragglers were still standing in front. Tucker became involved in a very heated argument with a shorter, but very husky man. From my position, hiding in the bushes, I could not hear what they were saying. Tucker was very hostile and raising his voice every few words. To my surprise, Tucker began to punch the husky man squarely on his chest with his right index finger, which was extended like a spear, his forearm still and locked into a perfect striking position. Tucker, with a great deal of force, punched the man repeatedly, time after time, without stopping, with such a series of blows he literally pushed the man backwards down the sidewalk fifty or sixty feet. Soon the fray was over, but the other man never raised a hand to protect himself. They both turned and walked back into the church.

I told Jerry later, "Most men I know would have punched his lights out, me included."

One of our trusted contacts, a businessman, related the following: "One day, one of my female employees received a phone call from Mr. Tucker, and she reported this conversation to me. She was very upset because this person, a man she did not know and had never met, said some strange things to her. She said, 'His remarks were lewd and suggestive... He told me he would like to do things with me, or to me, etc.... He said something else, which really frightened me—that he knew who I was, he knew all about me.'"

Our friend was very concerned, also, but said nothing. He was perplexed because if he told her to be careful, to watch her mirrors to see if she was being followed, it would scare her half-to-death.

At a surprise meeting one day, my wife and I met Tucker and Lia by chance at a local restaurant. During the course of the conversation, my wife asked Lia, "What do you think about the OJ Simpson trial?"

But before she could speak, Mr. Tucker, in an almost belligerent tone said, "Oh yeah, sure, you women think he is guilty, but us men know he is not. The police set him up with the glove, *and besides, she went way over the line and got exactly what she deserved.*"

We were dumbfounded. Beyond his outrageous remarks, consider that he knows I'm in law enforcement, and he further knows I'm a man. After having made the statement, "men see it differently," wouldn't he have looked at me and said, "Isn't that right, Lyndon?"

No, this did not happen at all, like I was not even there.

Would he have also taken my argument for granted that young girls hitchhiking and girls in lovers' lanes have all crossed the line and deserve to die? Is this guy for real?

The following list contains 26 known facts about our suspect, a small fraction of our accumulated data. While they are more directly circumstantial evidence, they also apply to his personal profile.

Brief summary of most important factors, A to Z:

A. *Motive*: *Revenge—To prove he is smarter and better than the judge and cops*

B. *Confessions at two different AA meetings*

C. *Mobility*: *Travels extensively as AA official*

D. *White Chevrolet sedan*
   1. Three witnesses at Lake Herman Road murder site
   2. Several witnesses re: Darlene Ferrin (murdered July 4, 1969)

E. *Older man*
   1. Wording of Zodiac letters
   2. Witnesses re: Darlene Ferrin
   3. Age update in the SF composite, from age 25-35 to 35-45

F. *220 pounds—Lake Berryessa*

G. *Physical description by San Francisco PD*

H. *Photo lineup re*: *Wilbur Thompson, Pam Huckaby, Steve Baldino, and others*

I. *Kimberly Lawrence incident—positively identified*

J. *Face-to-face display of hate and frenzy*: *CHP officer in uniform and patrol car*

K. *Theft—$45,000 total*
   1. Bank—$25,000
   2. Real estate employer—$20,000

L. *Code training—code instruction*
   1. Matches DOJ and FBI profiles

M. *History of outward display of hatred toward females*

N. *Handwriting analysis—DOJ cannot eliminate*

O. *Never eliminated by DOJ—still a prime suspect*

P. *Bizarre, anti-social behavior observed by many associates and other witnesses*

Q. *Confessed he carries gun in his car—saying, "I am being followed."*

R. *His name found in codes*:
   1. Analysis by author: Probably
   2. Analysis by NSA: Probably
   3. Analysis by Edward Steinke and work of Henry Ephron (past presidents of the American Cryptogram Association)

S. *Geographic locale of residence—matches profile*

T. *Can be placed in the killing areas*

U. *Effort to smudge and destroy palm prints on fish bowls*

V. *Most likely homosexual/bisexual*: *Matches profile*

W. *Voice identified over phone*

X. *Witchcraft symbols and homosexual drawings around suspect's house—matches profile*

Y. *Prominent judge brutally beaten, in hospital with serious concussion—committed adultery with suspect's wife*

Z. *Brutal act against female employee*

NOTE: These *26 factors* are less than one-fourth of the total associated factors and comparisons we have made with our suspect, and the Zodiac.

We now have a total of 156.

XVI

"ALL THE WORLD'S A STAGE"

"All the world's a stage, and all the men
and women in it merely players...
"They have their exits and their entrances;
and one man in his time plays many parts."

William Shakespeare

Fortunately, it was his own idea, and I therefore exonerate myself from any malpractice and undue influence. I'll just be on stage for Acting Workshop 101, and watch the master at work.

Initially, Capt. Kenneth Narlow of the Napa Sheriff's Dept. had a 110-percent belief the sweaty palm print they found on the Napa phone booth on September 27, 1969, belonged to the Zodiac. The phone, identical to the incident in Vallejo, was left hanging loose, and Narlow told us the response time to the phone booth was only twelve minutes. The dusting of prints was methodical and exhaustive, and many latent prints were discovered. Aside from the handwriting, the possible typewriter from Riverside, a wristwatch, a broken penknife, a tire casting, a few shoe prints, controversial fingerprints, bullet casings and a composite sketch, there is absolutely no other hard evidence in the case. However, as discovered, Zodiac's codes and ciphers might be his final undoing.

Unfortunately, the latent prints from Paul Stine's cab

were routinely used to eliminate any and all suspects, a terribly flawed supposition. It was a process of elimination, a convenient tool, but perhaps not so wise. Considering the time element and still-moist palm print, Capt. Narlow placed a great deal of faith in the latter. In fact, there was no doubt in his mind at all, the print had to be the killer's. Some of the many fingerprints were highly regarded as well.

We became obsessed with finding a plan, a method, a ploy, a strategy; anything we could do to obtain a solid and perfect palm print. In addition, we had to do this without him knowing it. Remember, we are dealing with the Zodiac. Holding a cup or a glass wouldn't do it. Leaning on a desk wouldn't work either. Handing him something to hold was an option, if we could figure out what, and where, and under what circumstances, and then have him return it.

The months and years passed until finally we had an opportunity to try one of our ploys. It took us over a year to find the perfect chair, with large rounded armrests, and then several months more conjuring up a legitimate business meeting with one of our sources. It was a perfect plan.

The chair had been thoroughly cleaned and the arms highly polished. As planned, our suspect sat in the chair and placed both hands on the large rounded arms of the chair. My God! It actually worked. You cannot believe the excitement in our little group. The chair was locked up and protected until we picked it up later that same evening. At 9:00 AM the following morning, we carried the chair into the Berkeley PD, as arranged. The detective, a print expert, dusted the chair for the prints, and we were holding our breath. We knew we had just solved the Zodiac case. Neither Jerry nor I could even sit down. After about twenty minutes of dusting, the detective shook his head in dismay. We knew by the frown on his face that things were not going very well. Finally he said, "There is nothing here at all."

The only explanation he could offer was, "The person

sitting in the chair smeared the prints into an obscure mess." He dusted the entire chair with no result.

Several months later, we had another brainstorm. We had to first determine the night of the week he attended his AA meetings, and then the regularity of his attendance. After driving hundreds of miles back and forth to the church in West Sacramento, we learned he never missed a meeting. He always arrived early, and was the last to leave as he had the keys. Next we had to find a young man and a young woman, people we knew we could trust completely. We had to be carefully selective. My soon-to-be son-in-law, Neil, was eager to assist, and I had known this fine young man for many years. Then a friend living in an apartment not too far from the church volunteered to play the part of the young female. My friend "Sher" had actually given us information about our suspect, telling us, "I saw him try to solicit a young man sitting in the restaurant late one night."

Sher advised, "I will be wearing a wig and sunglasses, and even though your man has seen me before, I am certain he will never recognize me in my wig." Her normal hair was bright red, a very charming girl.

The timing would have to be perfect. The stalled car would be parked in the suspect's normal parking space in front of the church, but protruding slightly into the street. The hood would be up and Neil would be working on the "loose wires." Our suspect would drive up, and Neil would close his hood, grab the steering wheel, and try to push the car from the outside.

Sher would then get behind the clean trunk and begin pushing. As Tucker got out of his car, Sher would ask, "Could you lend a hand and help push our car out of the street?"

We felt certain he would assist, and we would obtain two perfect palm prints on the trunk of the car. It would appear very innocent, but there was always a risk involved. One of my CHP partners was with me, and we were parked up a side street with a view of everything. Jerry and Chuck were parked about 200 feet in front of the normal parking area, and on the same side of the street as Neil's disabled car. If anything strange occurred, ominous or threatening, Jerry and Chuck would pull in front of the suspect, while my buddy and I pulled in directly behind. It was a good plan. We were all packing weapons except Jerry. Everything was in place, the stage was set. It was nearly 8:00 PM but still very light.

The meeting was to begin at 8:00. Soon, several members were standing on the sidewalk, still waiting for the doors to open. Things were getting very tense and my palms were sweating. People began to drift into the church, but our suspect never appeared. Six people, three cars, sixty miles from home in the terrible Sacramento heat, and the man does not show. Our months of planning down the tubes—our night was a total bust. We ask, "Did he see us? Did he smell cops?"

Ernie's Plan

It was nearly a year later when we developed another plan of attack. This time it was foolproof, we could not miss. Ernie, who had become a valuable member of the Mandamus Seven, created the idea himself, one in which he was volunteering to perform. It was a pure stroke of genius, but it would require a huge sacrifice of time, extensive traveling, and a strong commitment. Ernie was not only willing to do it, he wanted to. This was serious business because there was a very real element of danger, which we discussed thoroughly.

Ernie said, "Instead of playing these cat-and-mouse games, let's go directly to the source, up close and in person. I will not only get him to confess, but I will also get the palm prints. Lyndon, I've been thinking—I don't believe it, I even surprised myself!" Ernie was laughing, but he was very serious.

"So what already?" I asked.

We listened to Ernie's plan with great interest—and agreed it was brilliant, but possibly dangerous. Ernie would become an educated and informed alcoholic. He began attending some of the AA meetings in another town; he read all the AA literature, and in a couple of months he thought he was ready. I told Ernie and Jerry, "Our suspect will see right through you and I am getting very apprehensive."

I was ready to squelch the entire thing, but Ernie was convinced he could pull it off with no problem. Ernie did not drink, ever; he had never been intoxicated one day in his entire life. Jerry, of course, wanted to proceed with this dangerous and risky plan.

I tried to explain, "It's just like an undercover cop or one off-duty—a con can spot them immediately, and it's the same way with alcoholics."

Jerry told Ernie, "You will be playing the most major role in your life."

There were even minor adjustments made on Ernie's license plates. I admired his confidence.

"This is me you're talkin' to. It'll be a piece of cake—no problem, just trust me. I know what I'm doing. You think I haven't dealt with these people before?"

Ernie was a United Methodist Minister and had several degrees in psychology and family counseling. He was brilliant.

~ Act One ~

And so it began. One night a week for several months, Ernie was driving nearly 60 miles one way. Immediately after each meeting, we tape-recorded everything he had to report. The ice had been broken, and the two diverse individuals were now on a first-name basis (first names only in AA). Ernie made many friends at the meetings, and he always took notes on our suspect's strange and abnormal behavior.

As March 1, 1977, approached our plan was right on schedule. Jerry and I bought the two fish bowls required, one much larger than the other. These bowls would have a major role in Ernie's strategy. Weeks before, Jerry and I had met with a latent-print specialist with the Walnut Creek PD. He was very responsive to our request, and was eager to assist us in our examination.

~ *Act Two* ~

Andy and Peggy, from Orinda, were good friends of Jerry's. They had agreed to the taping and bandaging of Ernie's arm, including a cast. As Peggy was a registered nurse, she could handle the procedure like a true professional. Furthermore, she instructed Ernie on the precise terminology he should use to describe his injury and the progress of his disabled arm. Ernie would continue to attend the AA meetings with his bandaged arm for several more weeks, setting the stage for what was to come.

~ *Final Act* ~

The fish bowls were cleaned with soap and water, dried, and cleaned again with glass cleaner. We were all wearing gloves. We met at Sher's, as she lived in the area, and filled the bowls with water and a couple of live goldfish. Arriving at the church a little early, Ernie asked Tucker, "Would you come outside for a second? I need some help."

On the way he explained, "I'm going to be making a special presentation before the group, and I think they will really enjoy it."

Ernie opened his trunk and asked Tucker, "Could you carry in the two bowls for me?"

Six months of preparation was now dependent on a few seconds. Tucker carried the bowls into the church, one at a time. The large one was heavy and Tucker's palms were pressed tightly against the glass. The plan was working with precision. Ernie gave his presentation, using the fish as principals in his fairy tale, and said, "The group was inspired by my talk."

After the meeting, Ernie again asked for help in carrying the bowls, and Tucker again carried the bowls back to Ernie's car. But then, for some strange reason, our suspect did something totally bizarre. After the bowls were set securely in the trunk of Ernie's car, Tucker slapped the bowls with his palms, several times, and then rubbed the bowls several times, as well.

Ernie said, "I could not believe my eyes—Lyndon, it was like he knew."

I could only think of what Zodiac had once said:

"YOU WILL NEVER CATCH ME,
I AM TOO CLEVER FOR YOU."

The very next day, Jerry and I took the bowls to the detective at the Walnut Creek PD. He was expecting us. After just a few minutes of dusting the bowls, he said, "I'm shocked! I can't believe the bowls are not covered with prints. There's nothing here at all. I don't understand what's going on."

How many ways can you say defeated and disgusted? Jerry and I were feeling them all. We'd previously discussed our plan with the detective and he had said, "It sounds great." He was now truly perplexed.

In a couple of days I called another highly respected print expert with the Contra Costa County Sheriff's Department, a Mr. Cowger, who said, "Bring the bowls over to my office."

Ernie went with me. He was not merely disgusted, he was very angry because he thought someone had initially given us bum information. Cowger also dusted the bowls, and he, too, said the same thing, "The bowls should be covered with prints."

Cowger did, however, find a pinkie print of Ernie's on the extreme bottom of the smaller bowl.

What happened? We had no idea unless the rubbing of the bowls had actually destroyed everything.

A few days passed, and I set up a work area in the garage. I had obtained one of our own CHP fingerprint kits, and while we have received some limited training in dusting for and lifting prints, we generally had no occasion to use the kits unless we were recovering a stolen vehicle. Much to my surprise and amazement, I soon discovered some smeared palm prints on the large bowl, in fact, several. Later, another print specialist told us, "The reason you found them is the glass had a chance to dry out. Prints won't surface on moist glass."

For several days I inspected the one smeared palm print I had found, the best one. With bright lights and a magnifying glass, I thought I could see 17 or 18 points of comparison to one of the lifts from the Napa phone booth—Capt. Narlow had given us copies of his original photos—but I knew absolutely nothing about print examinations. Another print expert at the Fairfield PD examined my findings and said, "It is nothing, *but it could get you a court order for a palm print.*"

It should be mentioned that Mr. Cowger spent a great deal of time comparing one of our suspect's fingerprints to a print found on Paul Stine's taxicab. A couple of times he went—"Hmm... hmm... hmm."

I had to ask, "Do you see something interesting?"

"Yes, there are similarities, but I can't quite make it."

Along with the smudged palm prints on the bowl, I raised something else very curious. In an arc was a pattern like the outline of four fingers. The outer ridge was visible, but the center of the outline was completely blank, no lines at all. Zodiac had said,

"I USE AIRPLANE GLUE ON MY FINGERTIPS,
AND THAT'S WHY MY PRINTS
WILL NEVER BE FOUND."

Lyndon E. Lafferty

January 22, 1993

Re:Latent prints - Fish Bowls
ZODIAC CASE
Napa County - Case #105907

Initially, after 6 months of planning and preparation, the two fish bowls were cleansed thoroughly with soap and water and windex. They were handled with extreme care and caution, being transported in styrofoam containers. Therefore, the bowls were totally and absolutely uncontaminated.

The bowls were handled by the SUSPECT only.

As prearranged, a print expert with the Walnut Creek P.D. dusted the bowls the very first day after being handled. The officer dusting the bowls found no prints at all on the glass. The officer was amazed, stating the glass should be covered with prints.

Approximately 5 to 7 days later I called another highly respected print expert, Cowger of the Contra Costa County S.O and he agreed to examine the bowls. H.B. went with me. Cowger dusted the bowls which were still in the trunk of my car. He handled them with great care using gloves, turning the bowls by inserting his fingers on the inside of the rim. Cowger found nothing, stating the bowls should be covered with prints.

Over the years J.J. and I have talked with various print experts and one individual, cannot now recall, made a comment that the glass was likely still wet or moist, that it might take a couple of weeks to dry out.

Then, after Cowger's attempts, and approximately two to four days later, I dusted the bowls again in my garage. Behold, I found some partial but smudged prints.

Note striking similarity between the top left of #24 and "G's" left index finger. This is not a good copy but it does appear!

Sketch

Napa case # 105907

24

"G. left index

1. Both shaped as the letter A.
2. Both appear to be same size.
3. Both appear to be crossed. (A)
4. Both have an extended left leg.
5. Both have a "dog leg" on lower left.
6. Both have same alignment to adjoining lands.
7. Both have a squared effect on upper left and upper right.
8. Both approximately located in respective positions to left & right & top to bottom.
9. Other adjoining land similarities.

This is a repeat of the writing obscured by the margin.
Striking similarity between the top lift of #24 and suspect's left index finger. NAPA case #105907.
Both shaped as the letter A.
Both appear to be the same size.
Both appear to be crossed.
Both have an extended left let.
Both have a "dog leg" on lower left.
Both have same alignment—lands.
Both—squared effect–upper left and upper right.
Both approximately located in respective positions.
Other land similarities.

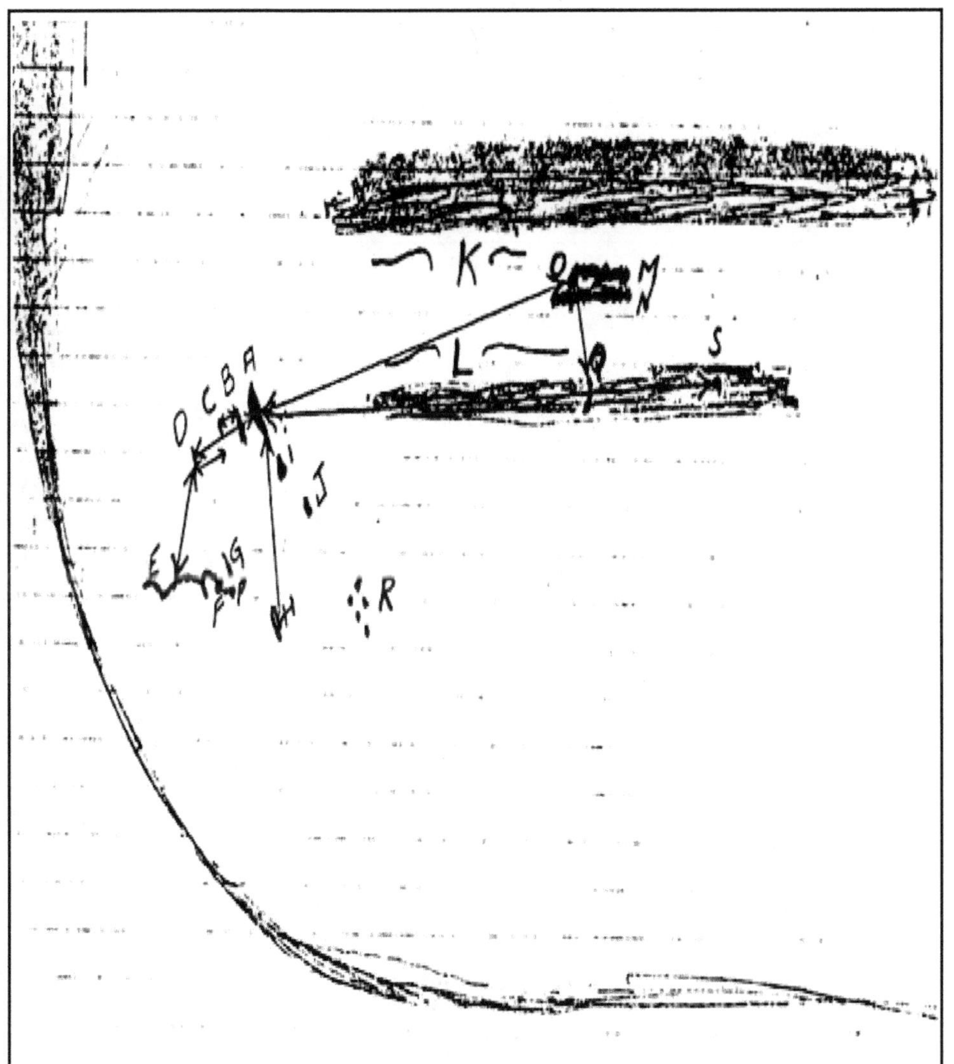

THIS IS A HAND DRAWING OF A PARTIAL PALM PRINT TAKEN FROM OUR SUSPECT. I CAN MAKE THIS POSSIBLE MATCH WITH NAPA SHERIFF'S CASE, #105907. While the Napa authorities have never seen this I have had this reviewed by two experts who have stated it "MAY OR MAY NOT BE, BUT IT WOULD GET YOU A COURT ORDER FOR A FULL SET OF PALM PRINTS".

XVII

THE CONFESSIONS

As suggested in other areas of this story, the Zodiac perceives himself as a moral crusader. In his own demented rationale, he has a valid reason to kill, but he chooses only those that actually deserve to die. These are the young people who are doing things they should not be doing, in places where they should not be. He said things like:

"SOME OF THEM FOUGHT, IT WAS HORRIBLE,"

similar to a sentiment he expressed about the killing of Cheri Jo Bates. He wrote letters to her father and the police saying,

"SHE HAD TO DIE."

Zodiac's needs for revenge and to prove his superiority over the judge and several police departments had been satiated. His lust for killing was always tempered by the set of circumstances. He had to discuss philosophy, religion, concepts of good and evil, and the liberal lifestyles of the young. He talked with Cecelia Ann Shepard and Bryan Hartnell for a very long time before they failed his test. These kinds of debate are in constant play at AA meetings, and they can become very heated at times, even violent.

On November 5, 1973, I was advised Mrs. Tucker (Lia) had recently had a nervous breakdown, for she and her husband were having serious marital problems. She was seeing a local doctor with a sordid reputation—a doctor who had been charged with having sexual intercourse with his patients. However, most people in the community thought highly of this doctor, who had been in practice for many years. As discussed many times by the Mandamus Seven, we believe we know why Mrs. Tucker had her nervous breakdown.

The moment of truth had arrived, perhaps the finest moment in George Tucker's life. The drawings of the axe and the inverted cross, the bright-red male figures having sex, and the tauntings and innuendo of his daily banter had come to their glorious climax. He confessed to her just as she had confessed to him—displaying a type of "sick pride" normal people would never experience or understand.

He most likely told her to sit down, for he had something to tell her. He knew her nature and personality. He did not have to tell her that every killing and every act of revenge was laid at her feet. He did not have to tell her she caused it all when she committed adultery, but he told her anyway. She could never report him to the police because she knew he could destroy the judge, her lover. And now she thought, *He might kill me, too.*

(Two different sources relayed this information, both credible, and one very close to the situation.)

On November 4, 1974, Laura O'Dell was murdered in San Francisco. She was the last victim in the San Francisco-Santa Rosa cluster killings. A newspaper article stated a person passing by on foot witnessed a man removing an object from his car. The girl's body had been discovered there the same morning. The killer probably saw this man and knew he could describe his vehicle, and might even have jotted down his license plate number. In a panic, Mr. Tucker drove his white Chevrolet down to a car dealer in Vallejo and gave his car to a salesman, a good friend. The salesman then took the car to another used-car lot and sold it for $100. This transaction took place on November 6.

On November 8, Mr. Tucker bought a new Ford sedan

and handed his buddy $4,450 in cash for his new car. (Typically, 99 out of a hundred people would have used their old car as a trade-in.)

On November 17, a sailor named Hood, stationed at the Concord Naval Weapons Station, bought the '61 four-door Biscayne for $299. My partner, JJ, actually bought the car from Hood a short time later.

We suspect Mrs. Tucker was becoming extremely paranoid during the next few months, unable to cope with the terrible secret that her husband was the Zodiac. Yet, she did believe him because this explained why he had been called in on March 15, 1971. She became very ill, losing a great deal of weight. Finally, her doctor referred her to a specialist at Gladman Memorial Hospital in Oakland, a well-known and highly respected psychiatrist.

At some point during her treatment, perhaps the first few months of 1974, Lia was convinced her road to recovery was to tell the truth about everything. Besides, everything she would tell the psychiatrist would be totally confidential. He could never tell a living soul. Lia felt trapped and helpless. She lived in fear day and night. If she ever left him, or filed for a divorce, there was no doubt in her mind at all that he would kill her. She had begged him to go talk to a priest. He was raised a Catholic, yet she had never known him to go to mass or any other church service. She said, "His AA is his religion, his higher power."

Yet, in an act of redemption, perhaps feeling some remorse, the Zodiac had sent a card (mailed in Alameda County) to the *San Francisco Chronicle* on May 8, 1974.

> "SIRS, I WOULD LIKE TO EXPRESS MY CONSTERNATION CONCERNING YOUR POOR TASTE & LACK OF SYMPATHY FOR THE PUBLIC... IN LIGHT OF RECENT EVENTS, THIS KIND OF MURDER-GLORIFICATION CAN ONLY BE DEPLORABLE AT BEST... CUT THE AD."

Two months later, on July 8, Zodiac sent another letter of tremendous significance. (This letter came from a mailbox in San Rafael.) It is noteworthy because it makes a direct reference to the psychiatrist.

EDITOR–

PUT MARCO BACK IN THE HELL-HOLE FROM WHENCE IT CAME–HE HAS A SERIOUS PSYCHOLOGICAL DISORDER–ALWAYS NEEDS TO FEEL SUPERIOR. I SUGGEST YOU REFER HIM TO A SHRINK. MEANWHILE, CANCEL THE COUNT MARCO COLUMN. SINCE THE COUNT CAN WRITE ANONYMOUSLY, SO CAN I–

(signed) THE RED PHANTOM

(red with rage)

Borrowing a line from Graysmith's book *Zodiac Unmasked*, page 196:

> Antifeminist columnist Count Marco Spinelli, a former hairdresser, quit the *Chronicle* because of this threat.

(Graysmith has used every bit of my information he could get his hands on, so I guess I can quote him from time to time.)

It is all theoretical, but a reasonable progression would suggest Lia was truly placing her health and safety in the hands of her psychiatrist. Her story was so shocking, so traumatizing, she could not even tell her best friend. And she had nowhere else to turn. As the lights were dimmed and the curtain raised, the stage was set for two events, which are especially intriguing.

The psychiatrist had pleaded with his newly acquired patient, Catherine Aurelia Tucker, to convince her husband to come in for counseling. God only knows she tried. Crying and begging, she told her husband, "He could help us through this crisis! You were not truly responsible for your actions because the chemical imbalance and your genetic predisposition, had a tremendous power over your mind and body, which you were powerless to control."

Tucker simply laughed and mocked his wife, "You're as ignorant as all the other women I've ever known. So what do you want me to do? Walk into the VA (Veteran's Administration) and tell them to pay for my therapy—tell them I'm the Zodiac? They would lock me up in 'Tune Town' and *you'd* never see me again." Lia said, "He is sworn to secrecy, and he can never mention any of this to the police or anyone else. All you have to do is talk to him."

The psychiatrist had a major dilemma himself. Never in his entire career had he been confronted with such a dangerous and deadly potential, inherent in this person, whom he now suspected of being the Zodiac killer. He had the tremendous burden of preventing any other murders—if this woman's husband was, in fact, the Zodiac, and he had some doubts. While he was still evaluating her background and mental proclivities, from all indications she appeared healthy and normal, but suffering extreme anxiety. He made a determination that the only way he could help to resolve the problem was to have a face-to-face conversation with Mr. George Tucker. Whenever Lia tried to hand her husband a note from the doctor, he would go into a raging fit and tear it to shreds.

In the interim, the doctor began a little investigation of his own. He called his good friend on the police department, and asked him to put out a feeler with the DOJ in Sacramento. He told the officer he would like to be notified if any suspicious murders had occurred in the general area, which might have been committed by the Zodiac.

Between March 22, 1971 and January 29, 1974, *Zodiac did not send letters to anyone.*

Our suspect worked in an office in West Sacramento for

almost three years, but obtained a new job in Fairfield, in January 1974. Please make note of the identical dates.

George Tucker was now attending several AA meetings a week. When he was announced as a guest speaker, the attendance was very high. There are over 600 regular AA meetings in San Francisco alone. A man and wife in San Ramon AA referred to Tucker not by name, but as the "Big Shot" in Vallejo AA. The friends of murder victim George Pimental referred to Pimental's blind date the same way. It is our guess Tucker was attending AA meetings in San Francisco, San Rafael, Santa Rosa, Napa, Fairfield, Vacaville, Vallejo, and possibly Jenner by the Sea.

In addition to Tucker's confession to his wife in November 1973, there was the fact of his mother passing away on December 13, 1974. She had been living with her son and Lia. These life-changing events surely had a significant impact on the psyche and behavior of both Tucker, and Zodiac.

In spite of the psychiatrist's urgent requests, George Tucker refused to listen. The doctor developed a strategy, hoping to provoke a meeting with Mr. Tucker. He had not heard one word from his police friend. So, in desperation, the psychiatrist took a bold leap of faith. He realized if Tucker was truly the Zodiac, he could be placing himself in very real danger. Following his conscience, he placed a large ad in bold type in the *San Francisco Chronicle*. Tucker read this paper everyday. On August 26, 1976, the ad appeared for the first time, and he ran it for a full week:

> "ZODIAC," YOUR PARTNER IS IN DEEP REAL ESTATE. YOU'RE NEXT. THE IMPERIAL WIZARD CAN SAVE YOU. SURRENDER TO HIM OR I'LL TERMINATE YOUR CASE.
>
> R.A.

We located a Richard H. Adler, Psychiatrist, at Gladman Hospital in Oakland. Even though we did not make contact with him, we believe he is the doctor in question. By law, he could not talk to us, ethically or legally. The wording of the ad is a true work of art, as it is *specifically perfect*. Since obtaining his real estate license in 1971, this had been Tucker's profession.

Zodiac is being told, "Come in or else."

We never discovered whether or not the Zodiac ever met with the psychiatrist, but we sincerely believe he did. Remember that the DOJ said that the unsolved female homicides ended abruptly in September 1974. The drying-out process for the alcoholic is like being born again. The withdrawal symptoms continue for well over a year because the body does not know how to react without the supply of blood alcohol sugars. There is a dramatic transformation in the mind, body, and soul. The next drink is always waiting for the devoted and helpless alcoholic. This is why their motto, "One day at a time," is so cherished because it actually works. AA is a magnificent organization. The recovering alcoholic is always exorcising the demons within. At the end of 1974, the Zodiac was perhaps for the first time in his life going through a long period of sobriety, the longest he had ever known.

Now, two more confessions: On December 13, 1976, three months and eighteen days after the psychiatrist's ad appeared in the *Chronicle*, our suspect stood before his AA group and, totally out of character, said:

"We must forget the past...
I have done things so bad, so terrible,
I could never tell you because if I did,
You would all go out and get stoned right now."

On March 26, 1977, our suspect stood before yet another group with a large number of members and said:

"If I were to tell you all the horrible things
I have done which I cannot tell you,
You would all go out and get stoned right now."

Additionally, our suspect did something else he had never done before: He apologized to the members for not knowing their names, even though he had been associating with them for several years.

Our informants, who had been attending for a few months, knew most of the regulars by name. Our principal colleague had remarked that our suspect reminded him of two different people.

Over the years, we have interviewed many alcoholics devoted to AA, and they all say the same thing: "While it is routine to listen to some hardcore stories everyone shares at the meetings—hit my wife, kicked the dog, spit on the cop, fell down the stairs, etc.—nobody ever said things like he did. You never tell a recovering alcoholic they might get stoned."

Is it just another coincidence or is the anniversary date of his mother's death, December 13, 1974, significant? That he chose December 13, 1976, to make his first confession, and only three months and eighteen days after the psychiatrist's ad in the *San Francisco Chronicle*, is rather remarkable. Was this an act of contrition? His mother had been living with them for several years. The emotional and psychological life-changing events in Tucker's life most assuredly played a role in his behavior. This extraordinary chain of events cannot be denied and are paramount in our comprehension of Zodiac's redemption.

In the 12-step tradition of Alcoholics Anonymous the 5th step states:

> That we admitted to God, to ourselves, and to another human being the exact nature of our wrongs.

Who else is he going to tell? The confessions were the cleansing of his soul, giving him total absolution. Zodiac's killings had climaxed but this does not mean he would never kill again—if the right opportunity presented itself.

Editor—
Put Marco back in the hell-hole
from whence it came—he has
a serious psychological disorder—
always needs to feel superior. I
suggest you refer him to a shrink.
Meanwhile, cancel the Count Marco
column. Since the Count can
write anonymously, so can I—

the Red Phantom
(red with rage)

Count Marco was born in Pittsburgh, PA and was a satirical, controversial columnist for the *San Francisco Chronicle*. Regarded as anti-feminist, he was a great humorist. He died on October 28, 1996, from pancreatic cancer, at age 77. His real name was Marc Henry Spinelli (Letter sent from the Zodiac— July 8, 1974.)

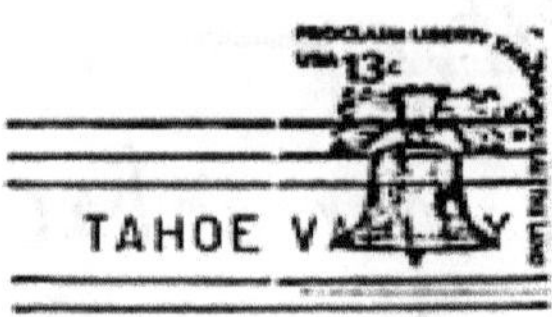

TO Mr & Mrs. D. Peterson
(Name of Correspondent)

COMPLETE OTHER SIDE
CHANGE OF ADDRESS
NOTICE TO
CORRESPONDENTS

PO Form 3573

68 Yosemite Rd.
No. and Street, Apt., Suite, P.O. Box or R.D. No. (In care of)

San Rafael, Ca 94903
(Post Office, State, and ZIP Code)

NAME
Print or Type—Last Name, First Name, Middle Initial
Area Code and Telephone No.

No. and Street, Apt., Suite, P.O. Box or R.D. No. (In care of)

OLD ADDRESS
Post Office, State and ZIP Code

No. and Street, Apt., Suite, P.O. Box or R.D. No. (In care of)

NEW ADDRESS
Post Office, State and ZIP Code

SIGN HERE
Effective Date

COMPLETE OTHER SIDE

The change of address form mailed to Dave Peterson was postmarked on September 13, 1976, a Monday, which means it was likely placed in the mail the day before, Sunday. Peterson was alarmed because he thought some of the writing resembled the Zodiac's. He requested CII in Sacramento to examine the writing and their conclusions were negative.

What is interesting, after 12 years in the same home, our suspect moved to another home in August, 1976. Another taunting—another joke of the Zodiac? Did he just happen to have an extra form in his pocket? The form was mailed from South Lake Tahoe.

Dave Peterson, Journalist for the *Vallejo Times-Herald* newspaper, worked with us on the Zodiac investigation and wrote several articles about the case. Dave thought Jerry and I were playing a joke on him.

We noticed several letters matching Zodiac's writing. Zodiac played games with the *San Francisco Chronicle* writer, Paul Avery, just like this.

As Dave demonstrated "too much interest" in the case, the police considered him a good suspect also.

XVIII

THE LADY BLEW HER COVER!

Like a faint shadow or a phantom in the night, this strange lady would haunt me for nearly four years. In September 1984, I received the first of many phone calls. However, before I tell you about this spy, this double agent, let me lay out the events leading to the "mystery lady's" phone calls.

During this time period, Robert Graysmith was conducting interviews and other research for his book *Zodiac*, and he undoubtedly contacted the Solano County Sheriff's Dept. Graysmith was talking to anyone who knew anything about the case. It was during this same period that he interviewed my partner and me.

He was really stirring the waters, and when Sheriff Renderos got wind of Graysmith's poking around for information, he became alarmed. While we will never know for certain, it is possible he said something to his good friend Catherine Maldonado Tucker. This is pure speculation. It is entirely possible Catherine Tucker heard about Graysmith from other friends, as well. If Sheriff Renderos never mentioned the fact her husband had been called in for questioning, she was nonetheless fully aware he had been. It is not reasonable to assume that in over a dozen years she'd never asked her close friend what was going on, and why he had been called in.

Sheriff Renderos would never tell her the real story. Yet, as we are fairly certain Mrs. Tucker already knew the entire story about her husband, she became fearful of how much we knew. Of course, she could never talk about it to her good friend

Sheriff Renderos. Catherine Maldonado Tucker, a very bright lady, developed a strategy, a covert plan, to pick my brain to pieces. She solicited the assistance of a dear friend she had known for about twenty-five years, and the strange phone calls began.

In September 1984, I was sitting at my desk writing reports when a woman, a total stranger, called me. All the investigators had their own phone, but it was unusual to receive a call from the general public. The lady began telling me, "I have a burning interest in the Zodiac case and know most of the reporters at the *Vallejo Times-Herald.* I was referred to you by Jack Mosely because you and your partner are the Zodiac experts."

She was very polite and seemed to have a sincere interest in the case. I told her immediately, "You've been misinformed. I was involved briefly but it was many years ago. I have no idea what is going on in the Zodiac case since then, none at all."

"Do you know the guy in San Francisco who is writing a book?" Continuing, she asked if I knew several people in Vallejo, mentioning them by first and last name. She asked, "Do you think Zodiac is a Gemini? Have you ever read the first book written on the Zodiac? It is out of print, and I can't find a copy anywhere." (The book is entitled *The Zodiac Killer*, written by Jerry Weissman, published 1979 by Pinnacle Books. I thought it best not to tell this stranger I had a copy.)

She inquired, "Do you know how I might obtain a copy?"

I told Ms. Inquisitor, "I really can't talk to you any longer. I know nothing, and I have nothing further to say."

It was about two or three weeks later when I received another phone call from the strange lady, but this time I was barbecuing in the backyard. I explained, "I'm very busy and you've caught me at a really bad time."

She apologized and said, "I will call back later in the day." And she did just that.

She began by telling me about putting an ad in the paper

in her effort to find a copy of that first Zodiac book. She asked, "Do you know Dave Peterson? Do you know he is one of the Zodiac suspects?"

I told her, "No, I have not heard that, and no, I don't know Dave Peterson."

This had been extremely confidential—there were very few who knew Peterson was considered a suspect. I was thinking, *Who the hell is this gal?* This was strictly inside information.

The lady said, "I have completed several horoscope charts as a favor to the Fairfield courts and some of the judges. I have even done Charles Manson. Do you believe in astrology?"

"I find the people who believe in astrology... interesting."

"What is your sign?"

"I don't know."

She then asked for my birthdate.

"That's too personal."

Then, as if I truly cared, she began telling me about some of her own suspects, explaining how weird they were. She kept me on the phone for about one hour. I still didn't know her name.

Perhaps it was my imagination, but it seemed like my wife was receiving more phone calls from Catherine than ever before. Typically, one would call the other every two or three months, but now my wife was getting at least one phone call a month. Lia was always asking, "When can we all get together for dinner again?"

After the first few calls from the "mystery lady," I became very suspicious. It was becoming too obvious that a conspiracy was afoot. Her questions, cleverly disguised, were specifically designed to test my knowledge of Zodiac suspects.

Several months passed before she called again, but this time she identified herself, just as if she had told me a long time ago.

"Hi, Mr. Lafferty, this is Doris Beckner again, and I

haven't talked with you for awhile."

I always had the feeling she was HBD (had been drinking) before or during her phone calls; she was so glib and silver-tongued, and she barely took a breath. (In about three years this would be her undoing.)

"There is a CHP officer who knows all about the Zodiac case, but he has retired and gone to work in Mare Island Naval Shipyard as a machinist. Do you know him?"

She continued, "I can tell you this, as far as I've heard they've run out of Zodiac suspects. What do you think?"

She rattled on about some man she met in a lounge on Redwood and Tuolumne Streets at the Redwood Inn (Judge Winston's favorite hangout), explaining he was totally weird. When he told her his date of birth, she freaked out because his house was in the rising quarter of whatever, and he resembled the Zodiac composite sketch perfectly.

She said, "He asked me if I would like to take a ride, and he spooked me half-to-death."

Then later she and her girlfriend followed the man to his car and wrote down his license plate number. She asked me, "Do you want the number?"

I told her, "There is no reason in the world I would want his license plate number."

These eccentric phone calls continued sporadically for the next two years. In one she tried to bait the conversation with a most bizarre comment. I had the feeling she and her co-conspirator were getting desperate and very frustrated, and I also had the feeling I was being tape-recorded.

This "mystery lady," Doris Beckner, said, "A really strange thing happened to me." She had finally discovered the publisher's name of the first book on the Zodiac and the author's name and had requested a copy.

"It was the strangest thing. They told me they would send it to me, but when the book came it was not delivered to me. For some reason I cannot begin to understand, the package had my name on it, but the address was totally different. It was addressed to the Law Library at the Fairfield courthouse. Mr. Lafferty, why would they send the book to me, in my name with an entirely different address, and why the Law Library at the courthouse?"

"I have absolutely no idea at all. It makes no sense whatsoever."

Hello, there? Anybody home? The address was correct—the Law Library where Catherine was employed.

In 1986, Robert Graysmith's first book, *Zodiac*, appeared in the bookstores. Doris Beckner soon called again with her mundane and frivolous prattle. She wanted to know, "Have you read the book yet?"

"I didn't even know it had been published."

She mentioned the CHP officer referred to in the book and asked, "Do you know him?"

I told Beckner, "I worked with a CHP officer who had an interest in the Zodiac case, back in 1970. He might be the one mentioned by Graysmith."

Doris Beckner may have called another two or three times in 1986, but in 1987 she became another Titanic as she sunk herself in booze.

Was Doris Beckner a good friend of Catherine Maldonado? Were they engaged in a covert enterprise of espionage, a conspiracy to investigate the investigator? Well, I suspected this was the case, by my third or fourth conversation with the mystery lady. It was a futile attempt.

The very last conversation between Beckner and myself began with the typical routine of astrological humbuggery and reasons why the Zodiac was either dead, in prison, or in a mental institution. The stars were never wrong. The incessant chatter went on and on about nothing, and then it happened—her coup de grâce.

Suddenly, in the middle of one of her comments she said, "And *Aurelia* told me that what I should do is to take the such-

and-such, and then do such-and-such. Then I could find out who such-and-such."

She finally paused, and I asked her, "Who did you say told you to do such-and-such?"

There was a very long moment of silence before she spoke another word.

"I never mentioned any names."

"Well, it doesn't matter."

She said, "Goodbye," and hung up immediately.

I never heard from her again.

XIX

THE RAID

As an orange glow crept over the horizon on that day in May 1978, I knew the light of morning would soon be here. To make the caper look real, Ernie and I had stuffed plastic bags with wadded newspapers, and piled them in the back of my pickup truck. Using heavy string, we also tied some newspapers into a few bundles. These were our stage props.

After he opened his new office we took a long shot, like a "Hail Mary" with two seconds on the clock. Hopefully, Mr. Tucker would clean house—out with the old, and in with the new. Whether it was fate or just plain luck, we hit pay dirt, a true bonanza.

Dressed in old Levis and a tattered army jacket, I walked to the garbage can, pulled off the metal lid, and dropped it. Ernie, holding the empty bag, cringed. We were trying to be very quiet so we would not wake the neighbors. We filled Ernie's plastic garbage bag, tied the top, and threw it in the truck with the rest of the bags. The entire operation took about a minute. I knew the police officers on the day shift would be in briefing, and the graveyard shift gone to the office to turn in their paperwork. It was about 5:30 AM, and I truly did not want any dialogue with the police.

The timing was everything and we were very lucky. Our primary objective was to find more handwriting, but we found a great deal more. If one did not know better, one might say it was meant to happen, and perhaps it was.

Incidentally, the Supreme Court has ruled that any

garbage, disposed of by the owner, is fair game.

Poor Ernie was really out of his element, and scared to death we were going to get caught. Actually, this was not a routine part-time job for a minister, but he was convinced we were doing the right thing. On the way home Ernie laughed out loud and said, "Lyndon, we did it."

After I bought Ernie's breakfast at the Texaco Truck Stop in Cordelia, he was feeling much better about his mission. Of course, my ace in the hole was another of the Mandamus Seven, the district attorney, and he was the highest-ranking police officer in the county.

Many gun enthusiasts, sportsmen, and hunters belong to the NRA (National Rifle Association). They have a huge membership of many millions. Whether or not the Second Amendment Foundation is regarded as a radical fringe group or not, I cannot say. Though I have been a member of NRA since the Korean War, and consider myself fairly aware of various organizations and their agendas, I was surprised to learn that this group, the Second Amendment Foundation, even existed. It would be my guess that the members have passionate and obsessive attitudes on gun-ownership. It is likely these individuals own a variety of guns, some of them, quite possibly, unregistered.

As Mr. Tucker was qualified to operate and repair .50-caliber machine-guns in World War II, he undoubtedly had an avid interest in weapons.

We might mention Zodiac's terminology in some of his letters, phrases like "WIPE THEM OUT" and "SPRAY THEM WITH BULLETS," all direct references to military machine-gun slang and tactics. Consider the description Zodiac employed when he discussed the school bus bomb. He referred to some of the problems he was having in "ADJUSTING THE TRIGGER MECHANISM," etc.

Was the Zodiac smart enough and cautious enough to consider the possibility the FBI might check membership rolls of the Second Amendment Foundation? Was he concerned his name would appear there? That unregistered guns might somehow be traced?

Perhaps, Zodiac thought, *this is a good time to cancel my membership*, and threw away his membership card. Was this brilliant strategy or just paranoia?

Indeed, the Zodiac did exactly the same thing, and for the same reasons, when he literally changed the name on his library card.

He might have thought, *If they ever trace the codebook to me, I could be in trouble.* (It was checked out many times in a matching time frame.) *They will never check, but if they do, they won't find me.*

This is the same thought-process, the same rationale, he was using when he smeared and ruined his palm prints on the fish bowl. If he is not a genius, he is at least a great deal smarter than the cops. He is still free, and still laughing.

Second Amendment Foundation 1977 Annual Report

1978 ACTIVE MEMBER
SECOND AMENDMENT FOUNDATION

Membership No.

Alan M. Gottlieb
Chairman

Jeffrey L. Kane
Executive Vice President

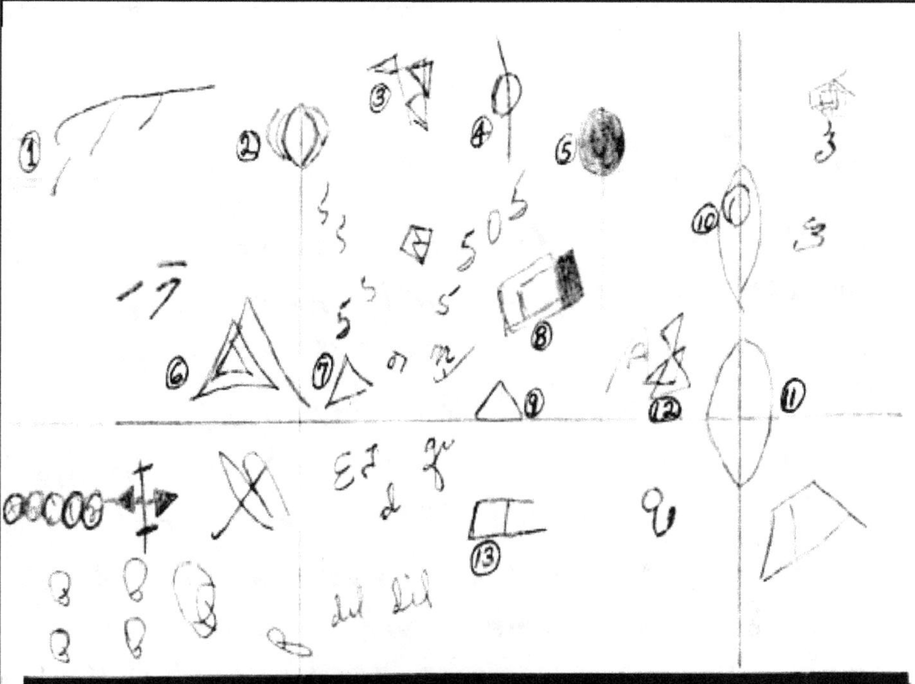

JUNE 1978

"PAPER DRIVE"

This is not the calendar:
This is a 2003 calendar:
Used for illustration only.
The actual calendar was
17 by 22 inches.

SUSPECT'S DESK CALENDAR, MAY 1978:

Random "doodlings"—13 Zodiac cipher symbols. First letter from Zodiac in four years: "I AM HERE, I HAVE ALWAYS BEEN HERE"—etc. "I AM NOW IN CONTROL OF ALL THINGS." This was Zodiac's last letter, and it was mailed in April 1978.

The above drawings were traced from the calendar itself. Note the strange glyph, upper right-hand corner, re: Bates letter. Note the oriental-type glyph above number 6, re: Red Phantom - Exorcist.

The reader may dismiss the symbols as just another coincidence, but we have another 155 to go with this one. What would a clinical psychologist say about these subconscious doodlings?

Dear Editor
This is the Zodiac speaking I am back with you. Tell herb caen I am here, I have always been here. That city pig toschi is good · but I am ~~bu~~ smarter and better he will get tired then leave me alone. I am waiting for a good movie about me. who will play me. I am now in control of all things.

Yours truly :

⊕ - guess

SFPD - 0

Zodiac returns with his letter of April 24, 1978, to the *Chronicle.*

(Yet another remarkable coincidence? Suspect opens his own office April 1, 1978)

XX

HANDWRITING AND OTHER EVIDENCE

Sitting on the shore at Lake Berryessa—alone, depressed, and contemplating the miseries of life—the young man looked up and saw an older man walking directly toward him. The cove was serene, isolated from the world.

"I am the Zodiac," the older man said standing over the young one.

"Oh really," the young man replied. "Well, my parents just died and I just lost my job, so, now you're telling me you are the Zodiac? Really, that's just great."

After the short exchange, the older man turned and walked up the path to the parking area. The tragic date was September 27, 1969, the same day Bryan Hartnell and Cecelia Ann Shepard were attacked.

Many years after the fact, Bill White, an investigator for the Napa County District Attorney, conducted an interview with this young man. White asked him, "Did you ever contact the police or the sheriff's department and tell them this amazing story?" "No," the man said, "you are the first official I've ever told."

Bill White's father was the ranger mentioned in all the Zodiac books, and he was the first person to arrive at the scene of the murder. Bill was only sixteen years of age at the time of the attack. His father showed him the murder site, and they visited "Zodiac Island" together several times, over the years.

Ranger White died in 1993.

If there is any evidentiary value in this strange conversation, it would lie within the confines of Zodiac's attitude. Assuming it is all true, we can only guess at the reasons Zodiac would try to shock the young man by making such a startling statement. Was this a rehearsal? Was Zodiac testing his mettle and resolve, knowing he was going to kill someone before the day was done?

It is very important to make note of one critical factor—that the young man did not have a girl with him. He was doing nothing wrong, and he did not need killing. One thing seems clear: If the older man *were* Zodiac, he did not find a mild-mannered pussy cringing in his shoes. In fact, the older man found just the opposite. He was confronting a young man who had just lost everything precious in his life—who was moody, highly temperamental, and liable in a second or two to stand up and kick the living crap out of this intruder. The older man became alarmed; in his fleeing moment he gave his admonition—*"Don't you ever tell a soul this conversation took place"*—and got the hell out of Dodge real quick.

Bill White was born and raised in the little town of Monticello, and sadly witnessed his home disappearing under the rising waters of Lake Berryessa. There is nothing about the area that Bill White does not know.

He told me, "One of the twin oak trees had fallen down years ago," and gave precise directions to the murder site. Yes, Bill White believed the man's story was true, and I believe Bill White.

On four separate occasions, I had submitted our suspect's handwriting and hand printing to the DOJ in Sacramento. Responding on a timely basis, usually within a month, the specialist advised, "We could not make a positive identification with the limited material we had to work with." When contacted by phone, as they are very cautious about putting anything in writing, they admitted, "The suspect's writing is such we could not eliminate him either." Therefore, they always requested more material.

This was our primary objective when we raided his garbage can in May 1978. After that, we had a great deal of material we did not have before. Figuring the third time would be the charm, I prepared another batch for them, but it was returned with the same conclusion. They asked for "more printing," and it was very difficult to obtain.

David Moore was a certified handwriting expert with the DOJ, and when I met him in 1985 he agreed to take a fresh look at our suspect's writing. He told me, "Send it to me personally."

So, this being the fourth attempt, I included some of the best material we had, plus some new writing, which had never been examined. A couple of weeks after I mailed the package, Moore called me and advised, "I am so upset and angry because due to the pecking order in my unit, I am not allowed to examine the material you sent me. Anything and everything labeled 'Zodiac' goes to one examiner only, a senior member of our staff."

In a couple of months the material was returned, and the cover letter said it had already been examined with inconclusive results. I know, for a fact, some of the writing had been examined previously, but there was other writing that had never been submitted. Apparently, the new material was unexamined.

Inserted among the papers, however, I found what appeared to be a silent message, as though the examiner was trying to tell me something, without saying anything. This was the first time an examiner had left their "working samples of writing," their work pages, in the returned material. Included were a wide variety of letters, loops, connecting letters, etc., attached to the suspect's writing. After four submissions of material, this was the first time I had ever seen anything like this. Was it like the examiner was saying, "Hey, this looks pretty good to me, send us some more"? Or perhaps the examiner was trying to tell me something else like, "Show this work to another agency, our hands are tied."

Wild speculation, no doubt. We have been told that if the DOJ cannot positively make a match, their policy is to state the suspect had been cleared on handwriting. While appearing to be unreasonable and irrational, there is most likely a reason for this unusual and controversial policy.

In December 1976, with the consent and blessing of our district attorney, arrangements were made to tape-record a phone conversation with George Tucker. We were primarily motivated by a newspaper article describing the amazing talents of one of our local psychics. This lady had achieved notoriety by assisting a police department in one of their homicide investigations, and over the years she had been consulted on other criminal cases as well. She had also received a few phone calls from a man claiming to be Zodiac, asking for help.

Our psychic lady was very cooperative, and a meeting was scheduled to make this recording in a private office at the *Vallejo Times-Herald.* While she listened on another phone, a lengthy conversation was recorded; and everything went even better than we had hoped. The psychic said, "He has the same gravelly voice, he cuts off his words, and the accent is the same. I would say this is the same man who called me, claiming to be the Zodiac."

Perhaps it was just an oversight, but it would appear the Vallejo PD did not share the critical information concerning Arthur Leigh Allen's handwriting. Sherwood Morrill was considered the ultimate handwriting expert in California. Please note the date on the DOJ letter, July 29, 1971.

From that moment on, the Zodiac authorities knew, without any doubt, *Arthur Leigh Allen was not the Zodiac.*

There was no equivocation whatsoever in Mr. Morrill's statement. He did not say there was a possibility the writing matched, and he did not say he needed to see more. He said, *"It does not match,"* period.

A truly sad note for law enforcement; they had only one

other strong suspect besides Allen, but following orders, they could not investigate him.

A fellow CHP officer and good friend, Royce Brooks, had started his own private business, Brooks Security Service, in Benicia. Royce approached me one day and said, "I've learned you're working on the Zodiac case with Sgt. Lundblad. Would you like to interview a man who claims he may have seen Zodiac at Lake Berryessa, the day that Shepard and Hartnell were attacked? Wilbur Thompson is a very credible person, a longtime Benicia resident."

Royce offered the use of his office, and we set up a meeting with Mr. Thompson. Jerry and I prepared a photo lineup and composed a list of questions I would ask. Jerry and his wife had planned an extensive trip to another country, and he would not be able to attend this meeting.

It was May 6, 1973. After nearly four years, I had little hope that Mr. Thompson would recall many details, and least of all, identify our suspect.

The first question I asked Mr. Thompson was: "Have you ever notified or talked with the authorities in Napa, or any other police official?" He said, "No."

A Benicia police officer told Jerry and I, "Tucker is a frequent customer and regular gambler at the various poker clubs in Benicia."

The officer positively identified Tucker from our photos, and even told us the man smoked Pall Mall cigarettes. He also said, "Tucker is a buddy of our city manager."

We were wondering if this might influence Wilbur Thompson's identification.

Thompson described the man in question as 5'10" to 6' tall, maybe 185 pounds, white, about 35 or older, stocky, thick-necked, well dressed, very neat, wearing slacks and a tan long-sleeve pullover sweater. The man was wearing heavy horn-rimmed glasses.

Thompson and several other customers were sitting in

the small café, Moskowite Corners, having lunch when this strange man came in acting all weird, asking questions like, "Which road is the quickest out of the area and the fastest way to the town of Napa?" (Moskowite Corners is a prominent landmark and a major intersection at Lake Berryessa.)

Thompson said, "All the customers were making eye contact with one another, raising their eyebrows, like, *Here is one real whack job!* The man asked for a map, and the proprietor of the little country store gave him one."

When the man left, Thompson and a couple other diners actually left their seats to watch him as he walked to his sky-blue, two-door hardtop. Thompson said, "I saw a California plate on the car. No, the man had nothing to eat, nor did he buy anything in the store."

The next phase of this interview was extraordinary, one moment in time, I shall never forget.

I said, "Wilbur, I know it has been a long time since that day at Berryessa, but when you look at these photos I am going to lay out on the table, try to focus on the face and the man you saw in the café. And the photo of the man you saw might not be in this lineup—do you understand?"

Wilbur replied, "Yes I do, certainly."

I laid out the six photos, all black-and-white 5x7s, and told Thompson, "So I won't disturb you, I am going in the next room. You take your time, and try to concentrate on the man you saw."

Before I took one step, Wilbur Thompson said, "You don't have to go anywhere, this is definitely the man right here."

I was shocked. Mr. Thompson did not equivocate in the slightest. When I asked, "Pick a number from one to ten—ten being absolutely positive, five being possible, and one not at all."

Thompson said, "Number ten."

I had identified the photos by numbers on their reverse, and Thompson had picked number three, George Tucker.

"In your own words, would you simply write a short

statement saying you identified number three?" Which he did. (See first insert at end of chapter.)

Nearly one year later, on May 3, 1974, after Mr. Thompson had returned from a trip to Missouri, Jerry took him to an AA meeting to view our suspect in person.

Thompson identified our man again in person, and this is what he had to say: "Well, there is this one guy who caught my eye, but he had grey hair. Otherwise, his face and his voice match perfectly. I think he is nervous—kept fidgeting in his chair, straightening his glasses; and he gave me the impression of being well spoken—rather quick, and well educated."

Jerry, of course, was waiting in his car. Thompson left the meeting quickly when it was over. Waiting for everyone to leave, about forty people, Thompson pointed out our man to Jerry as he walked from the building.

Unfortunately and tragically, Wilbur Thompson was killed in an explosion, which occurred on May 11, 1974, just eight days after his in-person identification of Tucker. Wilbur was painting the interior of a commercial building in Sonoma. (See second insert at end of chapter.) The fire department stated, "The paint fumes were ignited from the flame of a water heater."

This was a terrible shock and tragedy for the Thompson family, and Jerry and I were devastated, too. Of all the witnesses we had interviewed, Mr. Thompson was one of the most credible and reliable. Even though several years had passed, his statement and demeanor were extremely positive. In addition, he recognized the suspect's voice as well, not a slight matter at all. On cross-examination, an attorney could present plausible reasons why his memory could be flawed, but most jurors would be persuaded by his self-assurance and calm manner. He would not be the only witness to identify our suspect.

(I would like to add that our suspect was frequently changing the color and shape of his hair. At one time he was wearing his hair in a black Afro-style just like Judge Winston, only the hair on each head was pure white.)

Whether you call it skimming or outright theft, Tucker committed yet another underhanded scheme when he stole approximately $20,000 from his own broker. The affected firm, for fear of creating a nasty scandal and terrible public relations, did not press charges against Tucker. The only positive thing the owner of the business could do was fire him, and this is exactly what he did. One could say our suspect was not conducting himself with ethical, businesslike professionalism. Unusual behavior for a man in his fifties. Yet, we should not forget his "legal immunity." His blackmail had no boundaries.

The reader is asked to tap into the mind of the Zodiac. Is he bold, brazen, and insanely brilliant? The man had a habit of getting fired: the bank of Marin County; the bank in Pleasant Hill; the bank in Stockton; and now this termination in his hometown.

In January 1973, I met Linda DelBuono (née Linda Suennen) when she was working at Denny's Restaurant in downtown Vallejo. Linda is an older sister of Darlene Ferrin, who was murdered July 4, 1969, at Blue Rock Springs Park.

Linda said, "I have never been interviewed by the police or anyone else. I have a lot to talk about and would be glad to meet with you both."

I lost track of her for a short while but then on February 7, 1973, she called giving me her new address in San Jose. Jerry and I met with her on February 12 and she told us several things we had never heard before, and confirmed several other bits of information accumulated over the years.

Linda said, "Darlene bought the pink house on the corner [1300 Virginia Street in Vallejo] with her own money. I do not know who she bought it from. Darlene did, in fact, work at Herb's Troc on Tennessee Street, where our mother was training her to be a waitress. I believe this was just for two weeks, in 1968, working in the late afternoons."

"Darlene knew Cecelia Ann Shepard from singing

together in choir at Hogan High School, and a Napa school. My younger sister, Christine, also knew Betty Lou Jensen, but Darlene didn't know her. Some twin brothers [Mageaus] knew Darlene, and were jealous of one another over Darlene. And there was a Jim something who had an AKA or alias name, but I can't recall that either. He changed his name because he had killed two other girls. He was from San Francisco, and then came back to Vallejo."

"Our mother worked at Herb's Troc from 1963 to 1966, and Darlene also worked there, about 1967. Darlene also worked at the International House of Pancakes (IHOP) on Tennessee Street in 1967, for eight months. Darlene started working at Terry's Restaurant in late 1968. My dad and I went to see Darlene at 2:00 AM, and Mr. McKee was sitting there in Terry's all the time. As soon as we walked in, he would walk out. He was always reading the newspaper, in his black horn-rimmed glasses. I don't recall how he was dressed, but he was always neat. He, Mr. McKee, was also asking Darlene where she got the money for the new tables she bought. He was always very nervous. He was nice to everybody else, but he was mean to Darlene. Darlene told me, 'He is one of my customers.'"

"It's spooky. I would swear it is the same man. It looks just like him. His chin is just a little bit more pointed; hair the same; glasses are the same. I would say he is about 44 years old—in his 40s anyhow. Yes, I would say this is the same man."

"Darlene had just joined some group or society, and she introduced me to Cecelia. They sang in musical dramas. There was a play at Hogan, *The Mouse* and something. Cecelia came to see Darlene in this play, and Darlene did a solo. (Cecelia also did solos.) Darlene graduated in June 1966 from Hogan. She told me, 'I may have met this guy McKee at Herb's Troc, as many customers from there have followed me to Terry's.' This guy was always dressed neat—never in a suit, but dressed in sport coat and slacks." (Even though Linda made reference to the man as "McKee," she was not actually certain this was the man's name.)

Without any prompting whatsoever, she would frequently refer to the person as "the older man," and would not mention any name at all.

My diary notes of January 15, 1974, refer to the cook at IHOP on Tennessee Street, Vallejo. In 1967 Darlene Ferrin worked there, also. Jerry drove the cook to another AA meeting and the cook said, "Yeah, that's the guy who used to come in and sit and stare for a long time. He would stare at Darlene and pretend to read the newspaper."

Jerry said, "The cook is a boozer and therefore unreliable."

For some reason, Jerry never told me about taking the cook to see our suspect until months after the fact, and I thought this peculiar and totally out of character.

Steve Baldino, retired Vallejo Police Officer, identified our suspect as the neatly dressed "older man" at Darlene's house-painting party.

Pamela Huckaby (née Suennen) also identified our suspect as the neatly dressed "older man" at Darlene's house-painting party, and as the same man sitting in Terry's Restaurant, who was bugging Darlene.

Christine Suennen, Darlene's youngest sister, was with Darlene the night of July 4, 1969. Christine said, "Darlene came out of Terry's Restaurant around 10:00 PM, walked over and began talking with 'the older man.'"

Christine described "the older man's" car as "bigger than Darlene's Corvair, an all-white four-door, maybe a 1961 or '62, maybe a Chevrolet."

The caretaker's daughter at Blue Rock Springs Park told her father, "An older man in a white car was arguing with a young girl, sitting behind the steering wheel of a smaller car, and there was a young man with the girl."

The time was 12:00 midnight. Within a few minutes, the caretaker and his daughter heard popping noises like firecrackers, but said, "They could have been shots fired from a gun."

Jerry and I were informed the caretaker and his daughter had never been interviewed or questioned by any officer or detective from the Vallejo PD, and we were the first to hear their story.

Officer Steve Baldino had related another remarkable story over the years. He has told Jerry and me the same story at least two different times, and as I recall he has told me three times:

"On a stakeout one night with a female partner near Blue Rock Springs Park, I observed brake lights on a car, which had just passed us. I did not get a good look at the car when it passed by us the first time, but I became suspicious when I saw the brake lights come on, as I watched the car in my rearview mirror. The time was around midnight, and there was absolutely no traffic on this remote road except for that car, which had just passed us. I was ready. Within four to five minutes, the car returned with its high beam lights on, blinding me and my partner. I jumped from the car with my .357-Magnum revolver, placing myself in a protected position across the hood of the car. The other car flipped around in a U-turn and raced off. I could not see anyone in the vehicle, and the only thing I could say is it was a white four-door Chevrolet of 1961 or '62 vintage."

Steve said, "I don't know if this was Zodiac or not, but I probably scared the hell out of him." Steve said this incident occurred sometime in 1970 or '71, he could not recall exactly.

Freedom of Information and Privacy Acts: Subject: ZODIAC KILLER. File Number 9-HQ-49911.

Even though I offered to pay half the fee, Jerry paid for the entire FBI Zodiac file. It was huge and cost $81. Names, dates of birth, social security numbers, and other personal data were deleted by blacking out sensitive information. However, I was thrilled and very excited to discover four Zodiac letters, which had never been made public. But, the most amazing thing, two of the four letters were postmarked Fairfield, CA. And there is a great deal more. The handwriting analyst stated, "It appears these questioned documents quite possibly were written by the writer of the other Zodiac letters."

Ironically, one of the letters mailed in Fairfield was postmarked on Pearl Harbor Day, (December 7) 1969. The letter begins:

"THIS IS THE ZODIAC SPEAKING
I JUST NEED HELP
I WILL KILL AGAIN."

It ended with:

"I WILL TURN MYSELF IN OK."

The other Fairfield letter was postmarked December 16, and addressed to the *San Francisco Examiner*. It began:

"THIS STATE IS IN TROUBLE."

The second page contained a drawing of a knife with a message:

"THE BLEEDING KNIFE OF ZODIAC."

One of the four letters was postmarked Sacramento, CA, December 10, 1969, and addressed to the *Sacramento Bee*. Enclosed was a page from an astrology book with a forecast for Cancer on page 59.

(On this same date, Leona Roberts was followed from Pleasant Hill, abducted, and murdered. Her death was the first in the DOJ profile.)

The fourth letter was postmarked San Francisco, CA,

December 11, 1969. It was addressed to the San Francisco Newspaper Printing Company. Enclosed was another page from likely the same astrology book with a forecast for Leo, on page 61.

Another Zodiac letter, not one of these four, was mailed on December 20, 1969, and had already been printed in the newspapers. The Zodiac had a very emotional and frenetic December in 1969, much like a binge. His insanity was consuming him, and his guilt was forcing him to plead for help. Page 43 of the FBI analyst's report states:

> The writings contain some distortions and are not written as freely as the others.

It would seem obvious the Zodiac might try to alter or disguise his writing knowing he was going to mail two of them from his hometown.

Does anyone know whether or not these envelopes and letters have been processed for prints or DNA? Apparently, these four "questioned documents" are still in the possession of the FBI. In my opinion, the letters mailed in Fairfield are critical pieces of evidence and match the earlier profile of the DOJ, which stated, "Zodiac most likely lives in the Fairfield area."

Much of our evening television is glutted with crime themes: *CSI*, *NCIS*, *Law and Order: Special Victims Unit*, *Criminal Minds*, *The Shield*, *America's Most Wanted,* etc. We tend to dismiss or diminish the value of evidence if something cannot prove the fact positively by itself. Forensic science is now playing a dominant role in our current investigations, and DNA is a key factor in many situations. Many clever and brilliant attorneys can totally destroy arguments involving circumstantial evidence. Therefore, it is quite common for scriptwriters to infuse a tone of mockery, or otherwise portray points of circumstantial evidence in a pejorative manner. The negative attitudes spill over when the cops say, "Forget this, it's all circumstantial anyhow."

This was not always the case, and many cases have been brought to successful convictions based on circumstantial evidence alone, even first-degree murder. When two or three witnesses all swear under oath that Robert Blake asked them to kill his wife, this "circumstantial evidence" is very strong. It is not in itself conclusive, nor should it be. But if his wife turns up shot to death, and Mr. Blake had the opportunity, the circumstantial factors are developing into a powerful case to prove his guilt. (This, in fact, turned out to be the case.) There is a pervasive lack of understanding about the nature of evidence.

As required by law, a judge must read verbatim the exact specifics of evidence to the jurors in a first-degree murder trial. Principal excerpts are as follows:

> Evidence consists of testimony of witnesses, writings, material objects, or anything presented to the senses, and offered to prove the existence or nonexistence of a fact. Evidence is either direct or circumstantial. Direct evidence is evidence that directly proves a fact without necessity of an inference. It is evidence, which by itself, if found to be true, establishes the fact. Circumstantial evidence is evidence that, if found to be true, proves a fact from, which an inference of the existence of another fact may be drawn. An inference is a deduction of fact that may logically and reasonably be drawn from another fact or group of facts, established by the evidence. It is not necessary that facts be proved by direct evidence. They may be proved also by circumstantial evidence or by a combination of direct and circumstantial evidence. *Both direct evidence and circumstantial evidence are acceptable as a means of proof.* (Emphasis added.)
>
> Neither is entitled to any greater weight than the other. However, a finding of guilt as to any crime, may not be

> based on circumstantial evidence unless the proved circumstances are not only (1) consistent with the theory that the defendant is guilty of the crime, but (2) cannot be reconciled with any other rational conclusion.

The admonition continues, dealing with matters of reasonable doubt, etc. Probably no one on the jury would fully comprehend these judicial instructions upon hearing them for the first time.

> Motive is an element of the crime charged, and need not be shown. *However, you may consider motive or lack of motive as a circumstance of the case. Presence of motive may tend to establish guilt. Absence of motive may tend to establish innocence. You will therefore give its presence or absence, as the case may be, the weight to which you find it to be entitled.*

Selling and changing cars became nearly routine. The only two Zodiac killings where his vehicle might have been compromised were at Lake Berryessa on September 27, 1969, and in San Francisco in May 1974. In both instances our suspect sold the two "suspect" vehicles immediately. In the Lake Berryessa episode, Wilbur Thompson observed the strange man drive off in a sky-blue or light-blue two-door hardtop, possibly a 1965 or a '66 Ford, possibly a Chevrolet.

Later in the day, two girls reported there was a strange man "ogling" them, or stalking them, as he appeared suddenly on two different occasions, separated by a couple of hours. The two girls described the car as a sky-blue or powder-blue two-door hardtop, maybe a 1965 or a '66, but of an unknown make. They did say it was an American car.

The man I observed on numerous occasions sitting broadside to southbound Interstate 680 (old Highway 21) on Lopez Road, just south of Cordelia Road, was always in a sky-blue, powder-blue 1965 or 1966 two-door hardtop. I would guess the vehicle was either a Chevrolet, Plymouth, or Dodge. Our suspect owned a 1966 two-door hardtop, a Dodge, and he sold this vehicle approximately two weeks after the Lake Berryessa killing. A 1966 Dodge was one of the very few vehicles matching the wheelbase tire prints at Lake Berryessa.

In October 1977, our suspect told his AA group the following: "Before I joined AA I was in real bad shape. I was afraid I would either be killed or go to jail, so I carried a gun in the trunk of my car all the time."

We had previously checked with the CII (Criminal Identification & Investigation) division of the DOJ for gun ownership, and they had no registrations for weapons in the suspect's name. (However, in hindsight, we never checked the other names being used by the suspect revealed by Naval Intelligence.) As suggested in another chapter, his membership in the Second Amendment Foundation reveals his fascination with and knowledge of guns.

Please pause and deliberate on the suspect's unusual statement. It is difficult to imagine what he was doing to cause such terrible fear. What criminal activities was he engaged in? What is a person doing that if caught at it, could cause his death? If he was in such bad shape, and arrested for drunken driving, why would he need a gun? Did he think he needed a gun because he might be involved in a shootout with police? This man, our suspect, is a weapons expert, certified to maintain and operate .50-caliber machine-guns. It is most unlikely he would tell the cops, "Oh, just wait a minute while I get my gun out of my trunk."

But, of principal concern, why would he own a gun or guns not registered in his name, and how would he obtain them in the first place? Yes, it is easy to buy guns from a variety of sources: private sales, gun shows, friends, etc., but by law, they should be registered.

Does this explain why Michael Mageau said, "The guy

drove off and then came back in about five minutes. It was the same car."

It would make sense because the Zodiac had decided to shoot them. He drove down to the golf club driveway, stopped, removed his gun from the trunk, and then returned with his bright lantern-type flashlight. This would require about five minutes. In 1969, the golf club entrance was about 300 feet south of the Blue Rock Springs parking area, around a curve and out of sight.

The set of circumstances on this devastating evening of July 4, 1969, needs to be told in its entirety: While members of the family were waiting with fireworks for Darlene to return to her new home, at 1300 Virginia Street, Darlene and Christine made a last-minute stop at Terry's, around 10:00 PM. Christine, the youngest sister, was waiting in Darlene's Corvair. Darlene came out of the restaurant and halfway to her car, she turned around and literally ran back into the restaurant. She had most likely seen "the older man" in his white Chevrolet, who had been driving around trying to find her, and had just pulled into the parking lot. Darlene told one of her friends to watch her when she went back out because *her friend* was madder than *hell*, and she had her younger sister in the car.

Darlene went back out and began talking to "the older man," and Christine was watching everything. Darlene then drove Christine to her parent's house on Jordan Street, just across the freeway from Terry's about two minutes away. (The back of the Suennen's home looks down on Terry's Restaurant.) As Darlene was walking out of her parents' home she made a strange comment to her mother, something like, "Something is going to happen, and you will read about it in the newspaper."

In a mild panic, fearing she was being followed, she made a quick phone call to her good friend Michael Mageau. She may have told him to dress warm because it could be a long night. This would explain Mageau's attire of two pairs of pants, two shirts, and a sweater. She may have told him it was an emergency and to be ready, as she was coming right over to pick him up.

Mageau was living in the East Vallejo area, off Springs Road, about a ten-minute drive from Jordan Street. When Darlene pulled up in front of Mageau's house, she honked the horn rapidly and Michael flew out of the house on the run, leaving his stereo blaring and his front door swinging wide open. The time was then 11:00 PM or slightly later.

In the hospital the next few days Mageau told a close friend of his, who just happened to be a patient at the same time, "After Darlene picked me up, she drove around East Vallejo, back and forth on Springs Road because she thought she was being followed."

She had just received her driver's license and was still uncomfortable behind the wheel. Then, feeling safe and not spotting the car following her, she drove out to Blue Rock Springs Park only two miles away.

In a few minutes a man pulled up by their car. Mageau was now very frightened, and he asked her, "Who is this guy?"

Darlene replied, "Never mind, it's only him."

Mageau said that Darlene definitely knew the man. The time element would correspond to the caretaker's statement that about midnight a man in a white car was arguing with a girl sitting in her car.

Michael Mageau never told the police this story. This would explain Mageau's vanishing act when he was released from the hospital, because Mageau knows a great deal more than he ever revealed, and quite possibly the true identity of the Zodiac. Mageau became a missing person for years. As he had been positively identified in the police reports and the newspapers he most likely was in great fear for his life.

When Warner Brothers and Paramount Studios caught up with him some 36 years later, he told a different story. In the Editor's Cut version of their movie *Zodiac* Mageau states: "Boy, were we ever chased." He said, "The car the killer was driving was a light-colored four-door, possibly a Chevrolet," and described their assailant as, "a white male, maybe in his late 40s, about six feet tall with jet-black curly hair, and horn-rimmed glasses."

Con-wise and streetwise, Mageau also will never put his life on the line again. He nearly lost it once, and he sure as hell is not going to give the killer a second chance. In the Editor's Cut, he stated that Darlene also made the following remarks when the man pulled up to their car: "I saw him kill someone in Mexico, and if he knew I was talking to you about this he would kill us, too."

Our witness, whom Jerry and I have interviewed on two occasions, was a close personal friend of the Mageau family, and by coincidence, a patient in the hospital at the same time Michael was brought in. She talked to Michael several times while they were both recuperating.

When Jerry interviewed Dean Ferrin, Darlene's husband, he was struck by the man's quiet and reclusive manner. He gave Jerry the impression he did not know a great deal about Darlene's friends or activities. Jerry was given a few items of Darlene's: personal phone book, a couple of letters, and a Kodak photo envelope, which appeared to be fairly new. (No photos in the envelope.)

We have read all the letters, gone through the material and discovered nothing of value. However, the Kodak envelope was curious. Written on the envelope were some words: *cut*, *hacked*, *stabbed*, *testify*, and one partial word, *Acqu--?* It appeared the writer was trying to write "Acquit." We think it might be related to the strange comment she made to her mother: "You will read about it in the newspaper."

Additionally, this could also be related to a spontaneous remark Darlene made to her babysitter a few weeks earlier. The babysitter had told Darlene, "A man has been calling you, but will never leave his name. An older man has been sitting in front of the house in a white car." Darlene then said to her babysitter,

"Oh, I heard he was back in town—I saw him kill somebody once."

This is the same babysitter who had told Jerry, "Yes, Darlene did tell me his name; it is a short, one-syllable name."

She could never recall the name, not even under hypnosis. Lt. Jim Husted, Vallejo PD, acting on our suggestion, had her hypnotized by a professional with negative results. Her husband did not want her to repeat the procedure.

Was Darlene living in fear, anticipating she might have to "testify" about something? Was it true—did she actually see the person kill someone? Over the years, the Mandamus Seven located other friends and acquaintances of Darlene Ferrin, and they could shed no new light on her case.

However, at least two other witnesses who had never been interviewed, confirmed the fact of "the older man." They knew nothing about this man, and certainly did not know his name. They stated, "The man would transport Darlene here and there, taking her shopping and to the bank. He was always driving a white four-door Chevrolet, either a 1961 or '62 model."

When I met David Moore, the handwriting analyst with DOJ, I mentioned the fact we had a tape-recording of our suspect, Tucker. Subsequently, I received an unexpected phone call from a Fred Shirasago of the DOJ in Sacramento. Shirasago, at this point in time, was the person in charge of the Zodiac case for the State of California. In this capacity, he was generally regarded as either a principal profiler or the DOJ's Zodiac expert. Any and all information regarding the case was referred to him.

He began his phone call by asking me, "Did I hear correctly—you have a tape-recording of your suspect?" "Yes, we do have a recording." He continued by asking a series of questions—why this, why that, how did you do this, do that—and on and on.

As there were several of my co-workers sitting nearby, I could not answer any of his barking questions. He got very demanding, using a tone of voice, which irritated the hell out of me. Years ago Jerry and I had developed a very strict policy about talking to strangers over the phone. Unless we saw some kind of official identification, we never discussed our case, ever, and there were no exceptions. We had already been there and done that.

In my calm and polite manner I tried to explain to Fred Shirasago, "I am in a small office with several people and I would be happy to schedule an appointment with you, at your convenience." Shirasago did not respond to my offer and continued his questions.

I did tell him, "I submitted a report to the Chief Deputy Assistant to the Attorney General, Mr. Michael Franchetti, in 1982, when I met with him personally in his office in San Francisco. This meeting was at his request. And I suggest you read this brief summary." Shirasago said, "I know you did; he and I read it together."

"There is a great deal more, but I cannot discuss it here and now." He continued, "Just tell me what the strong points are in your case?" I said again, "Mr. Shirasago, we can make an appointment. I have told you now, two or three times, I cannot talk to you at this time."

Then he mellowed out, but again refused to acknowledge my offer for an appointment. He continued, "If you can, will you send me your tape as soon as possible? Sure appreciate it."

I told Double J later, "If I could have pulled that arrogant idiot through the phone line, I would have punched his lights out." Jerry and I were shocked, stunned, and unbelieving. This was the most important phone call I had received in nearly fifteen years. Why was it important? This was absolutely the first time the authorities had revealed that our man was still a viable suspect.

Over the years, time after time, we heard from one agency or another that our man had been cleared. We, of course, knew why the false information was being given, and we knew everything on file was a terrible lie. It is important to note this information was not coming from a podunk police department, it was coming from the ivory towers of the DOJ of the State of California. This is the department, which has examined every piece of evidence, every witness, every letter, and every detail known in the entire Zodiac case, from every police agency in the state.

So, just as Shirasago requested, I mailed him a copy of our recording. I never heard another word from him.

Shortly after, we learned through our grapevine that a police department had received a collect call from someone claiming to be Zodiac. The caller was quite persistent, apparently, calling more than once. The calls were coming from Canada.

The Benicia note, found at the front door of the Benicia High School, appears to be the ruminations of a lunatic. The note reads:

> "(IM SORRY) BUT BY SON SOULD HAVE SAID ANYTHING ABOUT TIME BLOW UP THE SCHOOL SO I WILL DO IT BETWEEN NOW AND THE 22 OF DEC. SO I KILL BY SON AND YOU WILL FIND HIM UP BY LAKE HERMAN ROAD. IF YOU GET UP THEIR IN TIME YOU WILL FIND HIM BEFORE THE DOG EAT HIM UP I HOPE THEY DO."

GUESS WHO

OFF

YOU DIE

ZODIAC

THIS HIS BLOOD

IM GONA DO MY THING AT AIR SCHOOL

(this was inverted)

Neither the Vallejo PD nor the Sheriff's Dept. had ever seen this note. A copy was given to me by a sergeant on the Benicia PD. When I showed Capt. Wade Bird and Sgt. Lundblad they both laughed and never regarded it as an authentic message from Zodiac. It is much easier to dismiss it as a hoax, and it may well be just that; yet there are several clues in the note, which should have been considered. Zodiac's comment about bombing the school had never been made public when this note was discovered. The only thing published at that time was the reference to the "school bus bomb." The letters "f" and "A" are identical to Zodiac's. The abbreviation SON for Sunday is like Zodiac's FRY for Friday. Zodiac had also said "IM GONNA DO MY THING" in another letter. Zodiac uses the open dot when he dots his I's and at times he will reverse his letters. In Naomi Sanders's murder, the police were looking for a pilot, an instructor who taught flying at some "air school."

However, the most important clue is in the usage of two words: "ABOUT TIME." It is most unusual that Zodiac used the exact comment on the Cheri Jo Bates murder in Riverside in his letter of confession:

> "I SAID IT WAS ABOUT TIME. SHE ASKED ME 'ABOUT TIME FOR WHAT.' I SAID IT WAS ABOUT TIME FOR HER TO DIE."

Almost legendary in the Zodiac case, the white 1961 Chevrolet four-door had achieved a kind of mythic status. Observed by three witnesses on Lake Herman Road, shortly before Faraday and Jensen were shot to death; described by Darlene Ferrin's younger sister on the night Darlene was shot to death; described by several other witnesses as the car being driven by "the older man"; described by the CHP officer (your author) as being parked on the freeway on numerous occasions; and pulling alongside in a threatening manner–the car, like its owner, was a mystery. Was it Zodiac's primary machine of death?

On December 1, 1973, at 5:00 PM, I met Jerry and a sailor, Mr. Hood, at the main gate of the Concord Naval Weapons Station. Mr. Hood said the white 1961 Chevrolet sedan had slightly over 82,000 miles on the odometer when he bought it. By this time, Hood had added another 3,000 miles on our phantom car. I looked under the front seat and found and old U-Save receipt and a toothpick. I ran my hand between the seat cushions, and then noticed a white button on the rear floor. Apparently, the button was dislodged by my hand, as it had not been seen on the floor before. I removed the rear seat and scraped up a variety of leaves, pine tree needles, a couple of burnt paper matches, cigarette butts, a couple of dead bugs, weed stickers, etc.

Mr. Hood advised he had cleaned the trunk and had thrown away an old blanket. However, when I checked under the trunk mat I found several other pine needles. Two of the leaves found under the rear seat were somewhat fresh, not brittle-dry, and one was green and still pliable.

I asked my wife and Jerry, "How many buttons have you lost in your car?" I have never lost a button in my car. Have you ever known anyone who had ever lost one in their car? This is a single, lonely white button, nearly translucent, about three-fourths of an inch in diameter. It appears to belong to the female gender, perhaps from a blouse or sweater. I have never checked out the button with the authorities. There is a remote possibility the button could have significant evidentiary value, and it is still in safekeeping.

Was the button ripped off in a struggle? The prospects are very haunting. In fact, under what circumstances does a person accumulate a variety of vegetation under the rear seat of their car? Very strange indeed! Even if the leafy material was spilled or dropped from a torn plastic bag on top of the seat, it is difficult to imagine how it would get under the enclosed seat. One possible scenario would be the lifting or pulling of a heavy object from the rear seat, which then might dislodge the entire cushion. The vegetation would then simply fall onto the floor under the seat.

Jerry actually bought the 1961 Chevrolet from Mr. Hood, and the last he had heard, the car had broken down somewhere in Oregon and was abandoned. Jerry had loaned the car to Mr. Hood.

~~This is~~

THIS PICTURE CLOSELY MATCH'S THE PERSON I SAW AT MOSKOWIT CORNERS ON DATE TO YOUNG PEPOL WAS SLAIN AT LAKE

Wilbur Thompson

5-6-73 at Brooks Security Service Office, Benicia 10:00 A.M.

by Lyndon Lafferty

4 — Times-Herald, Vallejo, Tuesday, May 14, 1974

Man Dies Of Burns

BENICIA — Wilbur L. Thompson, 41, of 345 West K St., died Monday in a San Francisco hospital of burns received in a fire and explosion in Sonoma Saturday.

Mr. Thompson was spray-painting the interior of a commercial building for the Redwood Homes firm when the paint fumes were ignited from the flame of a nearby water heater, Sonoma authorities said.

A native of Missouri, he was a Benicia resident for 23 years.

Mr. Thompson was a member of Painters Local No. 376.

Mr. Thompson is survived by his widow, Patricia; a son, Michael; two daughters, Catherine and Wanda, and his parents, Mr. and Mrs. Melvin Thompson, all of Benicia, and a brother, Lloyd of Missouri.

A funeral service will be held at 10 a.m. Wednesday in the Passalacqua Funeral Chapel with Rev. Marshall Luckey of the First Baptist Church officiating.

Burial will be in Skyview Memorial Lawn.

Friends may call after 3 p.m. today at the mortuary.

The family prefers contributions to the St. Francis Hospital Burn Center in San Francisco.

[Diplomatic Reproduction]

Wilbur Thompson had lunch at Moskowite Corners - café/store on September 27, 1969.

I met with Wilbur Thompson in Royce Brooks Security Office in Benicia but many years after the killing at Lake Berryessa.

I laid out the photo lineup and told Wilbur to take his time, there was no rush. I told him I would wait in the next room so I would not disturb his concentration.

Before I took one step he said, "Don't bother, this is the man right here."

I asked him if he thought it was a strong possibility or perhaps—maybe. He said, "No absolutely, there is no doubt in my mind at all. We were all looking at this guy, he acted so strange. He was very nervous and asked the owner of the store which was the fastest way out of the area, and did he have any maps or a map. I got up and kind of walked out behind him just to watch him drive off—real weird. He got in kind-of a light blue car like a 2-door sedan."

This interview took place just a short time before his accident, around April, 1974.

ACKNOWLEDGMENT OF RECEIPT

I, MICHAEL FRANCHETTI, of the Attorney General's office, State Building, 350 McAllister, San Francisco, California, do hereby acknowledge receipt of Lyndon Lafferty's ZODIAC SUSPECT file consisting of 60 pages, plus attachments.

DATED this 14 day of April 1982.

ATTORNEY GENERAL

By: Michael Franchetti
MICHAEL FRANCHETTI, Chief Deputy

I submitted my Zodiac suspect report to the Chief Deputy Assistant to the Attorney General, Mr. Michael Franchetti, in 1982, when I met with him personally in his office in San Francisco. This meeting was at his request.

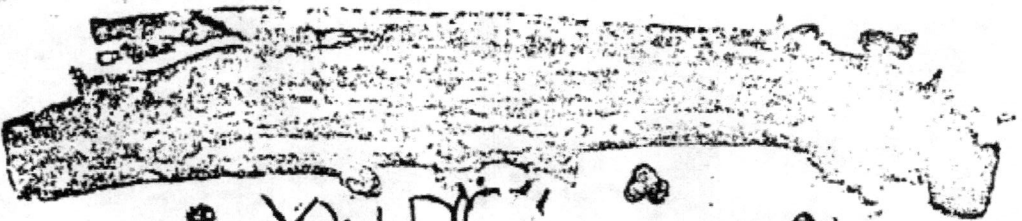

(IM SORRY) BUT BYSON SOUID OF SAID ANYTHING
ABOUT ME BLOW UP THE SCHOOl SO I WILL DO
IT BEWEEN NOW AND THE 22 Of DEC.
SO I KILL BYSON AND YOU WILL FIND
HIM UP BY LAKE HERMAN ROAD.
IF YOU GET UP THEIR IN TIME YOU WILL FIND
HIM BEPORE THE DOG EAT HIM UP I HOPE THEY
DO

GUESS Wha it This Hiz Blood

YOU DIE

ZODIAC

I'm GONA DO MY THING AT OUR SCHOOL

NOTE FOUND AT THE FRONT DOOR OF THE BENICIA HIGH SCHOOL. 1972 - 1973 ?

XXI

LES LUNDBLAD JR. AND MISCELLANEOUS

While I was checking a disabled motorist on Interstate 680 by Lake Herman Road, a truck driver stopped to report some unusual writing on the roadway. He said, "I make deliveries to Travis Air Force Base once a week. I always use the south-gate entrance to Travis, and the writing wasn't there last week."

When I drove to the site on Scandia Road, I saw white spray-painting, bold, fresh, and very conspicuous. Covering half the road, the writing designed to shock, said,

"ZODIAC SUCKS & KILLS."

The letters were huge. I took a few photographs and then called my dispatcher to notify the Vallejo PD suggesting, "They might want to take some photos."

A few days after I picked up my photos, I took them to the Vallejo PD. A senior captain advised, "We have taken our own photographs." He laughed and said, "A bunch of kids did the spray-painting." He also informed me, "We have already made comparisons, and this painting does not match Zodiac's handwriting." Yes, he was totally serious. This spray-painting occurred approximately one-and-a-half years before "The Red Phantom" homosexual drawings appeared by our suspect's residence. The grove of eucalyptus trees, at this spot, was also used as a lovers' lane by the local teenagers. It was a favorite hangout because this remote road was the only one leading to the south gate of Travis Air Force Base. While heavily used in the day, the south gate was always closed during the evening. There was absolutely no nighttime traffic on this lonely road except the beer-guzzling kids and a vicious killer who was stalking them.

As the evidence supports the opinion that our suspect and the Zodiac are homosexuals or latent homosexuals; as we know our suspect is driving around late at night; and as we know the site of this spray-painting is approximately a two- or three-minute drive from his AA meetings, we have reason to believe this is a message from the Zodiac. Additionally, the language of the message itself, so vulgar and threatening, seemed beyond the norm for a bunch of kids.

Let us recall the homosexual murder of George Pimental on November 8, 1971. Very typical of Zodiac to want the publicity of a newspaper article, which he received. In addition, one must admit the spray-painting and the letters themselves are very neat. (Pimental's murder in Vallejo closely matched the time of this writing.)

The captain on the Vallejo PD was not entirely correct when he mentioned the spray-painting did not match Zodiac's handwriting. As handwriting analysis is a very sophisticated science, most experts will tell you it is not possible to compare spray-painting with a person's normal handwriting, and this is what they have told us. In fact, there are a few similarities with the upper and lowercase letter usage.

I received a three-page letter from Leslie Lundblad Jr., Sgt. Lundblad's son (see inserts 3, 4, and 5 at end of chapter—edited version). In an earlier letter I asked if he would send me a short note or letter pertaining to his father's involvement in the Zodiac case. I had met Sgt. Lundblad's widow, Emma, as well as Leslie, Jr. and his wife, Nancy, several years after Sgt. Lundblad's death in 1977.

Sgt. Lundblad had been ordered to destroy his notes and

his files, and terminate his investigation of George Tucker immediately. He was ordered never to mention the man's name again. Sworn to secrecy, I, too, became a "silenced badge." Les always told me, "Lyndon, don't you ever stop, you have a strong case here." Whenever Lundblad saw Jerry he would say, "Tell Lafferty to keep goin', don't stop, he's got a strong suspect."

I was sworn to secrecy, and the continued investigation became a carefully orchestrated covert operation. From time to time, the sheriff and I would lock our eyes together, but never say a word. He never knew that Lundblad had confided in me, but his soul betrayed his guilt and remorse, and I could read him like an open book. Today the retired sheriff is stooped and withered, a broken man with nothing but shame hanging around his neck. Dismayed, rejected, and totally neutralized, Sgt. Lundblad spent the last five years of his life in sullen withdrawal.

Detective Sgt. Leslie Lundblad, Sr. was buried on October 11, 1977, only 61 years old.

Zodiac's "The Exorcist" letter was dated January 30, 1974:

I SAW & THINK "THE EXORCIST" WAS THE BEST SATERICAL COMIDY THAT I HAVE EVER SEEN. SIGNED, YOURS TRULEY:
HE PLUNGED HIM SELF INTO THE BILLOWY WAVE AND AN ECHO AROSE FROM THE SUICIDES GRAVE
TITWILLO TITWILLO TITWILLO

PS. IF I DO NOT SEE THIS NOTE IN YOUR PAPER, I WILL DO SOMETHING NASTY, WHICH YOU KNOW I'M CAPABLE OF DOING.

Me – 37
SFPD – 0

Zodiac's signature was a strange symbol, the characters resembling a type of oriental writing. His "Titwillo" was a reference to *The Mikado*, the Gilbert & Sullivan opera set in Japan. There has been speculation the symbol-signature might also be of Japanese origin. A few Japanese friends have examined the symbol, and they cannot identify it as being Japanese. The 7th insert at the end of the chapter shows the four Japanese alphabets, and there is nothing similar to Zodiac's strange symbol.

However, as mentioned in another chapter, the homosexual spray-paintings and other drawings strongly suggest an obsession with some type of penile disorder. Does Zodiac suffer from some glandular problems? Is he impotent? Has he had any surgical procedures or operations? The strange symbol also tends to portray the separation of one of the testes and, in fact, matches the red homosexual drawings around his house. Did this happen to Zodiac? Would this abnormal condition have any relationship to Zodiac's extreme hatred of females? Did he incur any STDs (sexually transmitted diseases) while in the military service in World War II, perhaps in the Philippines, where he was hospitalized for eight months?

On October 17, 2007, the *Vallejo Times-Herald* printed an interesting letter by attorney Robert Tarbox submitted as an advertisement. He had remained silent for some thirty-five years, not sharing his information with the police for legal and personal reasons. Additionally, in the interest of his own safety and that of his partner Joseph Jit Jue and his wife Rita Mok Jue, he too was caught in a traumatic "catch-22," and dared not betray his oath of confidentiality.

A few Zodiac experts and other cops have questioned why Tarbox did not come forward earlier with his shocking information, but I can assure you that not one of them has ever been placed in jeopardy by a personal association with the Zodiac. Could the police actually handle this matter with complete integrity? No, they could not.

Is Robert Tarbox's story true? Consider the fact that his letter is in essence a most noble act of conscience and justice. He was willing to break his silence and testify that the man who confessed to him was not Arthur Leigh Allen, if Allen was ever charged for the Zodiac killings. Consider also that Mr. Tarbox paid the *Vallejo Times-Herald* $650 to print his letter on a half-page of their newspaper. Instead, they gave him a full page, which his letter deserved; a nice gesture by the editor. (They never mailed Tarbox a copy of his published letter, but I did at his request.)

Personally, I believe Mr. Tarbox totally, and I also believe his confessor was, in fact, the terribly flawed and deranged Zodiac. To Zodiac, an interview with an attorney would be tantamount to a heart-to-heart with his priest. (This also supports the information related by the author that the Zodiac did, in fact, have a serious dialogue with the attorney Melvin Belli.) Remember, that in his letter to the Riverside authorities he stated,

"I AM NOT CRAZY, I AM INSANE."

Was he exploring the possibility of a plea of insanity, with all the legal and psychological parameters? Recall also, in a few of Zodiac's letters he expressed feelings of contrition, afraid he might lose control and kill again.

Why would the confessor offer any identification? He was certainly under no rule of law or any other obligation to identify himself and attorney Tarbox never asked for any. It seems obvious! The person knew he must use false identification because he was, in fact, the Zodiac. Knowing he could not trust the attorney to remain silent, in spite of the attorney-client privilege of confidentiality, he very astutely offered a fake document. He could not assume the attorney would not immediately call the police. Additionally, Zodiac was an avid reader of the newspapers and he would have known there had been a persistent and popular theory that the Zodiac might be in the military service or the merchant marines. Zodiac is a master of deceit, always thinking ahead. The merchant marine ploy was an excellent choice for the person to use, and attorney Tarbox had no reason to question or doubt the man's identification.

When I asked Mr. Tarbox the color of the person's eyes he replied, "Once I found out what was going on, I tried not to make eye contact with a serial killer."

Tarbox described the man as being lighter than himself, when he weighed 225 pounds, white, 5'11½" to 6'1", not blond, with some gray in his hair, casually dressed but upscale, well-spoken and highly educated. He agreed that the revised age reported by the San Francisco PD, 35 to 45, would be correct. Tarbox stated the man was very sincere.

When I asked Mr. Tarbox if he believed in his heart he was truly talking to the Zodiac killer, he replied, "Absolutely! There was no doubt in my mind, and he chilled me to the bone."

"Did he express any remorse about his killings?"

"No, none at all. He paid me $50 cash, and I gave him a receipt."

"My office was between Melvin Belli's home and his office, and I would see him frequently, almost daily, as he walked to work. Maybe the guy wanted to talk to Belli, but most of the offices were already closed. I'll tell you one thing, I got so stoned that night my friends put me up in one of their rooms over the bar. The guy literally scared the hell out of me. I could not look into his eyes. I had shut and locked my office door, and he was sitting there between me and the door, and yes, I was really frightened."

Mr. Tarbox has deep roots in Vallejo. He graduated from Vallejo High School and would be attending his 66th reunion in 2010. He had family members who were high-ranking officials on the Vallejo PD.

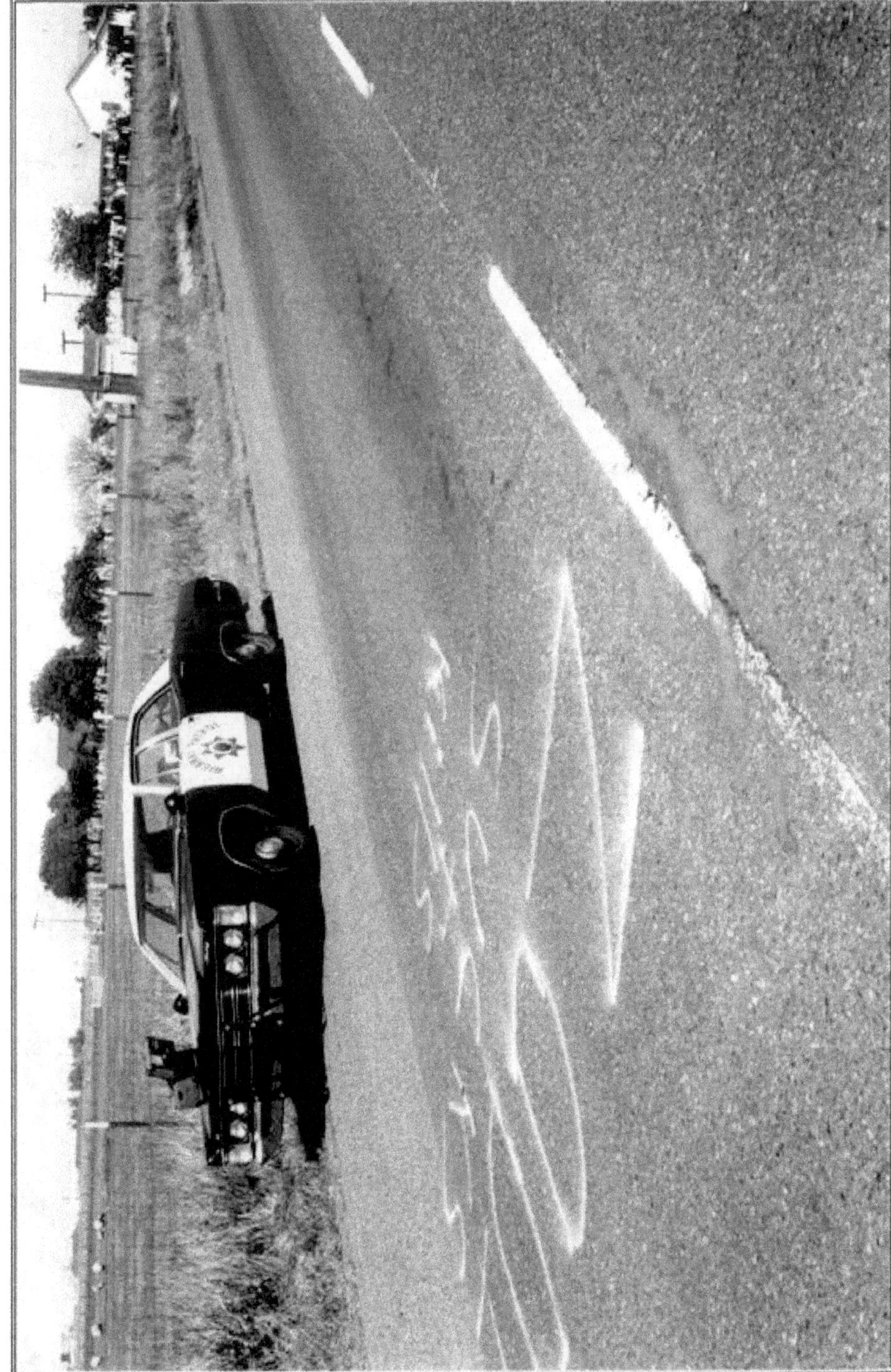

23 APRIL 95
SUNDAY

DEAR LYNDON

IM SORRY, IT HAS TAKEN ME SO LONG TO RESPOND TO YOUR LETTER. I

I WOULD BE HAPPY TO COOPERATE WITH YOU REGARDING THE ZODIAC CASE.

MY DAD AND I DISCUSSED THE CASE, ONCE A WEEK - SUNDAYS - WE ALWAYS HAD A FAMILY DINNER, AT MY PARENTS HOME AT 1016 OHIO ST. IN VALLEJO. DAD WOULD TELL ME ABOUT HIS CASES AND CERTAINLY THE ZODIAC CASE WAS THE MOST IMPORTANT CASE HE EVER HAD.

-5-

23 APRIL 95.

only TO WALK IN ON THE JUDGE AND [redacted] IN THE ACT OF LOVE.

SHORTLY AFTER THE INCIDENT OF WALKING IN ON THE JUDGE - SHERIFF [redacted] TOLD DAD - TO DROP [redacted] AS A SUSPECT.

DAD WAS DISGUSTED - IT WASN'T LONG AND HE RETIRED. }

ARRESTING ZODIAC SINCE HE KILLED OUR NEXT DOOR NEIGHBORS WIFE.

WHEN I MET YOU – I TOLD YOU BEFORE YOU TOLD ME – WHO DAD THOUGHT WAS THE ZODIAC.

I could PIN DOWN SOME DATES SLIGHTLY BETTER – IF I HAD A CHRONICLE OF THE EVENTS,

DO YOU WANT ANYTHING ELSE

Lee Lundblad Jr.

IS THE AUTHOR OF THIS LETTER A MORON OR A GENIUS?
WHO IS HE, AND WHY DID HE WRITE IT?

I saw + think "The Exorcist" was the best saterical comidy that I have ever seen.

Signed, yours truley :

He plunged him self into
the billowy wave
and an echo arose from
the sucides grave
titwillo titwillo
titwillo

Ps. if I do not see this note in your paper, I will do something nasty, which you know I'm capable of doing

Me - 37
SFPD - 0

Letter written January 30, 1974

katakana

アイウエオ
カキクケコ
サシスセソ
タチツテト
ナニヌネノ
ハヒフヘホ
マミムメモ
ヤ丰ユヘヨ
ラリルレロ
ワ井ウエヲ
ン a i u e o

イロハニホヘト
チリヌルヲワカ
ヨタレソツネ
ナラムウイノ
オクヤマケフ
コヘテアサキ
ユメミシエヒモ
セス ン
IROHA

hirakana

あいうえお
かきくけこ
さしすせそ
たちつてと
なにぬねの
はひふへほ
まみむめも
やいゆゑよ
らりるれろ
わいうえを
ん

いろはにほへと
ちりぬるをわか
よたれそつね
ならむういの
おくやまけふ
こへてあさき
ゆめみしえひも
せす ん.
光 順 . 伊藤
mitutaka. Ito.

ZODIAC's SIGNATURE

Mc - 37

SFPD - 0

EXORCIST LETTER
1-30-74

There exists an abundance of evidence and other commonalities to satisfy even the most skeptical that Zodiac is responsible in many if not most all of these brutal killings. That Maureen Sterling, Yvonne Weber, and Caroline Davis were found at the exact same spot in the Santa Rosa hills. Jeanette Kamahele and Lori Lee Kursa were found within 100 yards of one another. Penny Parker, Carol Hilburn, and Susan Lynch were found in a remote field in West Sacramento, CA. Considering the fact that Carol Hilburn was abducted in Santa Rosa, that Susan Lynch was last seen in San Diego and hitchhiking to Sacramento, and Penny Parker was the only girl from Sacramento, the odds are staggering that their killer is one and the same psychopath.

Identical to the white plastic clothesline used at Lake Berryessa, many of the other victims in Sonoma County were found still bound with the same type of clothesline, and others had evidence on their wrists, neck, and ankles that they had also been hogtied.

On page 253 of Robert Graysmith's book, *Zodiac*, there appears a Chinese symbol that Graysmith states matches the symbol on an empty two and-a-half foot wooden barrel which was being carried by Kim Wendy Allen on March 4, 1972. She too had been strangled with a white clothesline and marks indicating she had been spread-eagled with the same line. She also had superficial cuts on her chest. It is reasonable to assume that the strange signature Zodiac used on his *The Exorcist* letter was inspired by this Chinese symbol.

Wednesday
October 17, 2007

This letter is to the family, relatives, and friends of
MR. ARTHUR LEIGH ALLEN:

My name is BOB TARBOX. I practiced law in San Francisco with an office on upper Montgomery St. My law partner was Joseph Git Jue. One night in Early 1970's, I was sitting at my secretary's desk around 5:30 p.m. A male approached the office door which was open and I motioned him to come into the office. He indicated he wanted to have a legal consultation so I locked the front door and went into my office. In the office, the individual produced as identification a MMD (Merchant Marine Document). Since I did Jones Act cases (personal injury at sea), I assumed he had a Jones Act case. He indicated to me that it was not a Jones Act case but a criminal case, and wanted to pay for an hour of legal consultation. We agreed upon the amount of $50.00 for the hour consultation.

The individual proceeded to inform me that he was the Zodiac Killer and we proceeded to talk about this legal jeopardy based on the facts provided. Having been pre-med at UC, I took some courses in psychology and I perceived this confession to be of a cathartic nature wherein the individual is changing his life's path.

For many years, I have been under both legal and personal constraints with regard to this matter. The legal constraints still remain, but the personal constraints were severed by the death of my law partner and recent death of his wife RITA MOK JUE.

To the family of Mr. Allen: I have for years monitored Mr. Allen's trails and tribulations in the investigation of the Zodiac Killer until his death in the early 1990's. If he had been placed in actual legal jeopardy for these crimes, I would proffer my limited testimony to his defense attorney and I would have testified at any trial as to the prior confession of another individual. Since I have seen photos of Mr. Allen, I can express unequivocally that he was not the individual that confessed to me!

The big question I ask of myself is "why me". I think it was my connections to Vallejo and the fact that I practiced both ADMIRALTY and CRIMINAL law.

My conclusion as to why he was so elusive to law enforcement departments was his occupation as merchant seaman. He had the ability if the trail became too hot to make a pier jump to exit the Bay Area without people becoming suspicious by his absence.

BOB TARBOX
Las Vegas, NV

[Diplomatic reproduction: an original version, no corrections made]

'WHEN HE WAS DOING THIS STUFF (DIVING) HE WAS SORT OF A LOCAL HERO. THE KIDS WOULD FOLLOW HIM AROUND.'

— Frank Wetmore
former coach

'Local hero' or serial killer?

Arthur Leigh Allen: *Vallejo Times Herald* February 23, 2007 (photo circa 1949)

Mild, courteous, and obliging, Leigh was also a "straight A" student, without even trying. His natural diving skills placed him as the second best diver in Northern California and he later placed eleventh best in national events. His friends, that knew him well, were outraged at the conduct of the police, saying he was totally incapable of committing the Zodiac killings. Leigh always had a smile on his face.

OUNGER
NERAL

STATE OF CALIFORNIA

BUREAU OF CRIMINAL IDENTIFICATION AND INVESTIGATION

MAILING ADDRESS:
P. O. BOX 1859
SACRAMENTO 95809

Department of Justice

3301 C STREET

July 29, 1971

Refer: INV-Nicolai
Case INV 1-15-311-F9-5861

William R. Garlington
Chief of Police
P.O. Box 1031
Vallejo, California 94590

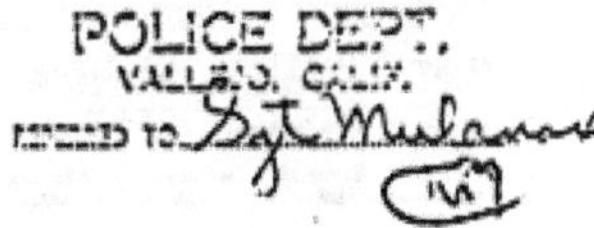

JUL 30 1971

POLICE DEPT.
VALLEJO, CALIF.
REFERRED TO Sgt Mulanax

Attn: Sergeant Jack Mulanax
Investigation Division

Dear Chief:

Enclosed are the exemplars of Arthur Leigh Allen, CII 1 311 511.

Mr. Sherwood Morrill, Questioned Document Examiner, has compared the printing on the submitted documents with the printing contained in the Zodiac letters and advised they were not prepared by the same person.

Thank you for your cooperation and assistance in this investigation.

Very truly yours,

A. L. Coffey

A. L. COFFEY
Chief of Bureau

MHN:jj
Enclosure

CERTIFICATION OF VITAL RECORD

STATE OF CALIFORNIA

DEPARTMENT OF HEALTH SERVICES

92-135325 (STATE FILE NUMBER)

CERTIFICATE OF DEATH
STATE OF CALIFORNIA
USE BLACK INK ONLY

39248 001355 (LOCAL REGISTRATION DISTRICT AND CERTIFICATE NUMBER)

DECEDENT PERSONAL DATA

1A. Name of decedent—First (Given)	Arthur
1B. Middle	Leigh
1C. Last (Family)	Allen
2A. Date of death—Mo, Day, Yr	Found August 26, 1992
2B. Hour	Fnd 1510
3. Sex	M
4. Race	White
5. Hispanic—Specify	☐ Yes ☒ No
6. Date of birth—Mo, Day, Yr	December 18, 1933
7. Age in years	58
8. State of birth	HI
9. Citizen of what country	U.S.A.
10A. Full name of father	Ethan W. Allen
10B. State of birth	KS
11A. Full maiden name of mother	Bernice Hanson
11B. State of birth	CA
12. Military service	19 56 to 19 58 ☐ None
13. Social Security No.	572-44-8882
14. Marital status	Nvr. Mrd.
15. Name of surviving spouse (if wife, enter maiden name)	–
16A. Usual occupation	Teacher
16B. Usual kind of business or industry	Education
16C. Usual employer	San Luis Obispo School District
16D. Years in occupation	10
17. Education—Years completed	17

USUAL RESIDENCE

18A. Residence—Street and number or location	32 Fresno Street
18B. City	Vallejo
18C. Zip code	94590
18D. County	Solano
18E. Number of years in this county	18
18F. State or foreign country	California

PLACE OF DEATH

19A. Place of death	Residence
19B. If hospital, specify one: IP, ER/OP, DOA	–
19C. County	Solano
19D. Street address—Street and number or location	32 Fresno Street
19E. City	Vallejo

CAUSE OF DEATH

21. Death was caused by: (Enter only one cause per line for A, B, and C)

	Cause	Time interval between onset and death
Immediate cause (A)	Arteriosclerotic Heart Disease	Years
Due to (B)		
Due to (C)		

22. Was death reported to coroner? ☒ Yes Referral number CCI-256 ☐ No
23. Was biopsy performed? ☐ Yes ☒ No
24A. Was autopsy performed? ☒ Yes ☐ No
24B. Was it used in determining cause of death? ☒ Yes ☐ No
25. Other significant conditions contributing to death but not related to cause given in 21: Diabetes Mellitus, Cardiomegaly
26. Was operation performed for any condition in item 21 or 25? If yes, list type of operation and date: No

PHYSICIAN'S CERTIFICATION

I certify that to the best of my knowledge death occurred at the hour, date and place stated from the causes stated.
27A. Decedent attended since / Decedent last seen alive (Month, Day, Year)
27B. Signature and degree or title of certifier
27C. Certifier's license number
27D. Date signed
27E. Type attending physician's name and address

CORONER'S USE ONLY

I certify that in my opinion death occurred at the hour, date and place stated from the causes stated.
28A. Signature and title of coroner or deputy coroner: By: [signature] Deputy Cor. James E. O'Brien, Coroner
28B. Date signed: 8-27-1992
29. Manner of death: Natural
30A. Place of injury
30B. Injury at work ☐ Yes ☐ No
30C. Date of injury—Month, Day, Year
31. Hour
32. Location (street and number or location and city)
33. Describe how injury occurred (events which resulted in injury)

FUNERAL DIRECTOR AND LOCAL REGISTRAR

34A. Disposition(s)	CR/SCT
34B. Place of final disposition—Name and address	Off coast near San Rafael, CA.
34C. Date Mo, Day, Year	8-28-1992
35A. Signature of embalmer	Not embalmed
35B. License number	–
36A. Name of funeral director (or person acting as such)	Wiggins-Knipp Funeral Home, Inc.
36B. License no.	FD-353
37. Signature of local registrar	[signature]
38. Registration date	AUG 27 1992

STATE REGISTRAR

A	B	C	D	E	F	Census tract
8	X	1				

(REV. 3-81)

MAKE NO ERASURES, WHITEOUTS, OR OTHER ALTERATIONS

This is to certify that this document is a true copy of the official record filed with the Office of State Registrar.

Molly Joel Coye, MD, MPH, Director and State Registrar of Vital Statistics

by: Michael Davis
MICHAEL DAVIS CHIEF
OFFICE OF STATE REGISTRAR

890054

DATE ISSUED

2

274

dhs

LETTERS

Our Zodiac Complex

You did a most interesting story on the Zodiac [Dec. 21, 1986], this being about the 18th anniversary of his bursting upon the scene.

I remember well getting a telephone call about 4 in the morning when it was still pitch dark outside. It was the Zodiac. He wanted to meet me at KGO-TV and go on the air. He would only talk to me by telephone, not appear in person.

I called the police to pick me up to take me to the TV station for an 8 o'clock telecast. They met me in a police car with guns drawn and searched my basement to see if Zodiac was around!

It was a very dramatic thing when I arrived at the station. There were cops on the surrounding roofs with rifles, and when we went into the studio, sure enough, Zodiac phoned. We got about an hour's conversation with him. He was smart enough not to stay on the phone too long, so his calls could not be traced.

He made an appointment to meet me out in the Mission at a church rummage sale, provided I wouldn't bring any cops. I agreed and went out to the rummage sale, but when I got there the place was swarming with police. One of them was even in the toilet — with drawn gun.

Zodiac didn't show. But he apparently drove by, because he phoned me later at my office saying, "Mel, you broke your promise — you had police." They had come to protect me, even though I asked them not to. Thinking back, I couldn't blame them.

For the next month or so Zodiac would call me at my office or my home, and once during the day he appeared at the front door of the penthouse where I was living on Telegraph Hill. My German housekeeper invited him in, and later on she told me she had given him a "good home-cooked meal — the poor fellow looked hungry and that's want he wanted." I almost fainted.

I got some letters and telephone calls sporadically after that, but suddenly they ceased.

Since everybody else has a theory, I have one too: He's back in jail, where he doesn't have to make any decisions, and thus his mania isn't disturbing to him. When he gets out and suffers the ordinary vicissitudes of our strenuous life, when he has to make even simple decisions, I think we'll hear from Zodiac again!

Melvin M. Belli
San Francisco

[Diplomatic Reproduction]

Freedom of Information and Privacy Acts

Subject: ZODIAC KILLER

File Number: 9-HQ-49911

SECTION 4

Federal Bureau of Investigation

FEDERAL BUREAU OF INVESTIGATION

FREEDOM OF INFORMATION - PRIVACY ACTS

ZODIAC KILLER

OPTIONAL FORM NO. 10
MAY 1962 EDITION
GSA FPMR (41 CFR) 101-11.6

UNITED STATES GOVERNMENT

Memorandum

TO : DIRECTOR, FBI (9-49911)
ATTENTION: IDENTIFICATION DIVISION,
LATENT FINGERPRINT SECTION, LATENT CASE #A-10042

DATE: 4/1/71

FROM : SAC, SACRAMENTO (9-68)

SUBJECT: ZODIAC
EXTORTION

On 3/24/71, Sgt. [redacted] Solano County Sheriff's Office, Fairfield, California, requested that the unidentified latent fingerprints previously developed in this case be compared with the fingerprints of [redacted] SSAN [redacted] He was born [redacted]

b7C

b7C

REC-115 9-49911-157

APR 3 1971

EXP. PROC.

36

2 - Bureau
1 - San Francisco (9-2296) (Info)
1 - Sacramento
FBB:jam
(4)

L.F.P.

9-49911

Report

The h.p. on the Q85- Qc100 letters show a wide range of variation and various writing speeds. Additionally, portions of the material, particularly the three Riverside letters, may have been disguised or deliberately distorted.

For the above reasons, the handprinting examination of these letters was inconclusive. However, consistent hand printing char. were noted in ~~the~~ the Q85- Qc100 letters which indicate that one person may have prepared all of the letters including the Riverside letter and the message found on the desk top in the Riverside case.

The submitted evidence was photo. & is enclosed herewith.

For legal and other reasons, pages 43 thru 48 are proprietary rights of the FBI examiner and are hereby excluded. However, they shall be referenced to support the premise that Zodiac does, in fact, live in Fairfield, California. These are prefixed with "Qc" (Questioned documents.)

1) Qc 34 Envelope: *SF Chronicle*, postmarked Fairfield, CA, December 7, 1969.

Qc 35 Letter: "This is the Zodiac speaking—I just need help—I will kill again ... I will turn myself in O.K."

2) Qc 36 Envelope: *SF Examiner*, postmarked Fairfield, CA, December 16, 1969.

Qc 37 Letter: "This is the Zodiac speaking—I just want to tell you this state is in trouble."

Qc 38 On second page was a drawing of a knife with a message—"The Bleeding Knife of Zodiac."

3) Qc 39 Envelope: *The Sacramento Bee*, postmarked Sacramento, CA, December 10, 1969. **(Note: Leona Roberts)**

Qc 40 Enclosed was a page from an astrology book captioned *Day-By-Day Forecast For Cancer*.

4) Qc 41 Envelope: "San Francisco Newspaper Printing Co.," postmarked San Francisco, CA, December 11, 1969.

Qc 42 Enclosed, page from as astrology book captioned *Day-By-Day Forecast For Leo*.

These four letters were never made public. This cluster of letters is synonymous with Zodiac's binge-like acts of murder. The synchronic stalking and homicide of Leona Roberts is not a coincidence. When she left work at the Pleasant Hill shopping mall in Concord, CA, she was followed to her duplex apartment in Rodeo, CA, abducted, and killed. Her body was found in a remote area of Bolinas Bay, in Marin County, where George Tucker spent several years of his life. After he mailed his letter in Sacramento his blood lust was too much to control.

XXII

MATHEMATICAL ANALYSIS

In the very beginning, every investigator we spoke to viewed our information with mild curiosity. However, without exception they stated, "Your suspect and information are very interesting."

In our opinion, the term *interesting* is now better defined as *relevant*. As stated previously, we have not been able to present the entirety of our information to any agency, as of yet, due to the complex web of intricate details in this case.

The following facts and information are also relevant, but they lend themselves more to the circumstantial indicators, which seem to have a very definite association with the Zodiac case and our suspect. Many of these factors, 156 and still counting, would be classified as problematic or speculative, while many others are totally factual. Therefore, the sliding scale of probability is based on a numerical value, which comes from a subjective process of evaluation.

Mr. Leo Hertoghe, in charge of the Administration of Justice program at the California State University at Sacramento, had given me his approval to establish a special course in order to work on a special project involving a computerized analysis of our accumulated data. It was a generous offer and would additionally give me four units toward my degree. I elected not to pursue this academic opportunity primarily because of reasons of confidentiality. Even though the results of such a study would never convict any suspect, I nonetheless considered such a study as a tool for a unique approach to the investigative function. Additionally, I was hopeful that if the results of such a project could prove on a mathematical basis that our man was the Zodiac, the authorities would be prompted and motivated to begin an in-depth investigation of him. And, Mr. Hertoghe seemed to have a genuine interest in the concept.

In an attempt to make a chart of comparisons between two characters or persons and ascribe to these comparisons a numerical value, we shall hope to achieve a "probability factor" of equating the two as one person.

We shall ascribe the known traits of one as "Z" for Zodiac, and the others as "A" for suspect. A numerical scale of 1 to 10 shall be used, and this shall be supposition, guess, or judgment, not related to any actual mathematical statistics.

We hope to show our two are one and the same, as far as a mathematical analysis will indicate.

Obviously, an expert is needed for this project. I shall, however, record those known traits and facts, and using my own judgment, indicate a corresponding number value.

Let us say there are a certain number of clues and evidence we know about the Zodiac and then compare the correlations of number values to the suspect. A pattern should develop, and a "probability factor" would be determined.

Values: 0 = unknown
1 = very weak
2 = weak
3 = fair
4 = good
5 = very good
6 = excellent
7 = outstanding
8 to 10 = perfect match

While we have always attempted to relay and share our

information with police agencies, I have always considered disclosure to any other source totally out of the question. I felt there would be no way I could maintain the integrity, or control, if I involved the assistance of university faculty or others who might become privy to the information.

In an attempt to clarify this mathematical analysis, while I am certain to repeat myself, I will cite a few examples.

If we regard the Zodiac as being closer to the age of 50 than say 30, we shall give that a value of 6. Number 6 is excellent. We say 6 because of the revised statements and other evidence. We could use 7, but a number 7 is too positive. 6 is a fairly reasonable number to use. Now, inasmuch as our suspect is or was very close to being exactly 50 years of age at the time of the taxi driver killing, which we know for certain, we shall ascribe a number 10 to the suspect. Therefore, we will attempt to prove that the corresponding related values, 6 to 10 are greater than, let's say, 4 to 10.

While 156 associations have been discovered over these past 40 years, there are bound to be many more, which I am certain have been overlooked.

I suppose we are dealing with the laws of statistical probability. A coin flipped in the air 100 times should turn 50 times heads and 50 times tails. The odds against the coin landing consecutively 50 times, on either heads or tails, are undoubtedly astronomical. It would probably be considered impossible.

This is the entire purpose and objective of this study. Odds are very good that thousands of persons might fit one or two clues in the Zodiac profile. Yet, conversely, the odds that so many clues could be associated with only one person, is also unbelievable. What are the odds of a person matching the description, which can be associated with ten clues? or thirty? or *156? Our suspect does.*

The Vallejo PD could make 30 matches with their suspect Arthur Leigh Allen, and they believed they had a very strong case.

The nationally acclaimed and very popular Vincent Bugliosi, prosecutor from Los Angeles, has stated, “Give me a suspect with 48 points of circumstantial evidence, and I will show you a guilty person.”

SITUATION ANALYSIS
CIRCUMSTANTIAL INDICATORS

		"Z" is	"A" is
1	Strange erratic behavior	10	10
2	Murder—in Benicia	10	7
3	Murder—in Vallejo	10	7
4	Murder—in Napa	10	7
5	Murder—in San Francisco	10	5
6	Murder—in Stockton	4	5
7	Murder—in Pleasant Hill	4	5
8	Familiar with code	10	10
9	Intelligent	10	10
10	Handwriting	10	7
11	Composite drawings—physical identification	10	7
12	Gambler	10	10
13	Astrological dates of incidents	5	4
14	Mobility	10	10
15	Motive	10	10
16	Cunning	10	10
17	Wit	7	3
18	Homosexual	7	7
19	Witchcraft	7	8
20	Headaches	5	10
21	Sonoma Murders (AA)	7	5
22	Temper	10	10
23	Hates females more than males	10	10
24	Strange behavior (girl—real estate)	0	10
25	Strange behavior (surveillance)	0	10
26	Silent time period	10	10
27	Letter clue (Sierra)	10	7
28	Letter clue (swamped)	10	7
29	Letter clue (trees)	10	10
30	Assault of Judge	0	5
31	Eyewitness (Lake Berryessa)	5	5
32	Eyewitness (Darlene Ferrin)	5	4
33	Dr. Hoey's analysis	10	10

SITUATION ANALYSIS CIRCUMSTANTIAL INDICATORS

		"Z" is	"A" is
34	Graphologist	10	10
35	Chemicals (bomb)	10	10
36	Symbols	10	7
37	Criminal background	10	6
38	No record of criminal background	7	10
39	Silent period—re: police interview	10	10
40	Extraction of name in code (NSA)	7	7
41	Extraction of name—second code (LL)	7	10
42	Similar car seen at murder scene	10	10
43	Pennsylvania (9-66)	0	10
44	Appearance change past few years	5	10
45	Loss of money, job, stress time factor	5	10
46	Unemployment—opportunity	7	10
47	Has pity on people he meets (code, AA)	10	7
48	Re: Authorities—geographic residence	10	10
49	Kimberly Lawrence note—letter A	6	8
50	Zodiac's question mark— ?	10	10
51	Attorney Melvin Belli—(letters—behavior)	10	8
52	Another witness—white four-door— older WMA	10	10
53	Another witness—ID photo	6	10
54	Zodiac—collect phone call (Vancouver, Canada)	9	9
55	Request of tape—Fred Shirasago, DOJ	6	6
56	Medical/health problems	7	7
57	Slaves in afterlife, Mindanao, Philippines re: authority profile	10	10
58	Opportunity—mobility—AA and unsolved female homicides: surrounding Bay Area	6	10
59	Strange—threatening behavior (Darlene Ferrin)	8	8
60	Shooting—Suisun cop—(green four-door Ford)	7	7
61	Zodiac—220 pounds—1969—Napa	10	10
62	Failure to notify police—3 suspect vehicles, black male shot to death,		

SITUATION ANALYSIS CIRCUMSTANTIAL INDICATORS

		"Z" **is**	"A" **is**
	1 mile from residence	6	10
63	Cordelia—Lake Herman Road—Hwy 21 incidents, females followed—stopped with flashing lights, attempted rape ("Suck it or die)—(nurse)	8	8
64	Physical description given by at least two female victims—re: incidents above	8	9
65	Travis—back road, writing in white paint, covering entire width "Zodiac Sucks and Kills"	10	10
66	Red-paint drawings (sodomy) near residence, Red Phantom (two sets: shed and water pipe)	8	10
67	Time relationship of drawings above	9	10
68	Suspect's stalking—parked on and beside hwys	10	10
69	Statement—"He is a phony s.o.b." (FBI)	10	10
70	Opinion—many professionals, subject is a very strong Zodiac suspect	10	10
71	Sgt. Snook, Napa—(testifies as expert on handwriting)—("Looks good to me.")	10	10
72	Zodiac may be ambidextrous	6	10
73	Detective's opinion, actions—(Lundblad)	10	10
74	Letter—Benicia High School—re: body along Lake Herman Road—"FIND HIM BEFORE THE DOG EAT HIM UP." (school bus bomb)	7	7
75	Suspect observed near murder site immediately after departure of police—(Dewey—Lundblad)	9	10
76	Evading confrontation, high speed (CHP—me)	9	10
77	Strange, unexplained phone calls—("Court asked me to do a chart on Charles Manson.")—("The Zodiac book I ordered was mailed to Law Library.")—(mentioned name and then denied)—(The Lady Blew Her Cover!)	5	10
78	Seeking—social relationship	5	10

SITUATION ANALYSIS
CIRCUMSTANTIAL INDICATORS

		"Z" is	"A" is
79	Reason to be in LA area (Riverside)—phony loan (Wells Fargo Bank)—girlfriend/wife?	10	10
80	Fired from bank—cautioned many times, hostility toward female employees—(16 years)	5	10
81	Troubled—problems in military service	5	10
82	Mikado clue—(have a little list)	10	7
83	AA religious aspects, overtones	5	5
84	Murder—in Vallejo—(Naomi Sanders, booze)	4	5
85	Strange behavior—(one source)	0	10
86	Driving record—probation, time element	5	5
87	18 undeciphered letters and suspect	10	10
88	Loner—dislike for people	10	10
89	Appraisal—professional as to character	10	7
90	Verbal confession before large group–1st time	6	10
91	Verbal confession before large group–2nd time	6	10
92	Palm prints	10	7
93	Abnormal behavior (trunk of car)	0	10
94	Owns a gun	10	10
95	No record of gun (official—DOJ)	7	10
96	Familiar with gun laws, purchasing, etc.	10	7
97	Mount Diablo	10	7
98	Hates kids (never had children)	7	7
99	Note on desk in college library, Riverside (RH—Robinson and Healy—Attorneys)	5	5
100	Open hostility, hatred toward police	10	10
101	Lied to police	0	10
102	Knowledge—compass	7	10
103	Military background	7	10
104	Murder—in Riverside	10	10
105	Use of typewriter	10	10
106	Access to Teletype paper	7	7
107	Access to legal information	5	10

SITUATION ANALYSIS CIRCUMSTANTIAL INDICATORS

		"Z" is	"A" is
108	Unusual interest in handwriting (Corona trial)	5	10
109	Light-blue vehicle (Lake Berryessa)	7	10
110	Is an alcoholic—(reformed—active AA)	5	10
111	Lake Tahoe—(Donna Lass)—(gambling)	10	5
112	"Paradice"—(Pair of Dice)—(key-ring clue)	3	7
113	"Gone two or three days at a time"	7	10
114	"I am now in control of all things"—(clue)	10	10
115	Psychiatric counseling—(connection)	9	9
116	Count Marco—("shrink" letters)	4	4
117	Voice identification—(Jeanne Borgen)	3	7
118	"New England"—"Boston" background due to terminology used	7	10
119	Terminology used—Lake Herman Road	7	7
120	Plays golf—("golf clue"—Lake Tahoe)	5	7
121	Relationship of time between first Zodiac murder (Oct. 66) and (possibly 1963)—and divorce of first wife	7	7
122	Sophisticated, older, businessman	6	6
123	Holds a "lever" over prominent judge	5	10
124	Statement—"Police framed OJ Simpson."	5	10
125	Statement—"Nicole Brown Simpson stepped over the line—got exactly what she deserved."	7	10
126	Machine-gun expert: Maintenance; operation—"Adjust the trigger mechanism."	10	10
127	Road rage—uncontrollable anger	6	10
128	Raised—Catholic faith	4	10
129	Attack—Isabel Watson, Marin County, Court Reporter—WHITE CAR	10	5
130	Residence—DOJ Profile—Fairfield area	10	10
131	Letter #1—postmarked Fairfield, CA—FBI	10	10
132	Letter #2—postmarked Fairfield, CA—FBI	10	10
133	Letter #3—postmarked Sacramento, CA—FBI	10	10
134	Letter #4—postmarked San Francisco, CA—FBI	10	10

SITUATION ANALYSIS
CIRCUMSTANTIAL INDICATORS

		"Z" is	"A" is
135	Age—Inspector Dave Toschi (older man, 50)	10	10
136	Age—Language of Zodiac (several)	10	10
137	Age—Language of Zodiac ("Fiddle & Fart")	10	10
138	Age—Language of Zodiac ("Rub Noses in it")	10	10
139	Riverside—College Library: (man, same name)	5	5
140	White Chevrolet four-door, 1961-1962, many witnesses	10	10
141	Murders—in Sacramento and Davis—and time period	10	10
142	Several "road rage" attacks—green Ford sedan	7	10
143	Suspect owned two identical green Ford sedans at the same time—relevant time periods	5	10
144	Murder—George Pimental meeting "Big Shot"	7	8
145	Name (first name) carved on abdomen—tried to cover—obliterated by slashing	7	8
146	Homosexual acts—Fairfield Motel (1st instance)	6	10
147	Homosexual acts—Fairfield Motel (2nd instance)	6	10
148	Met Darlene Ferrin—Herb's Troc	10	10
149	Writing—scratch marks, Terry's Restaurant ("Bates Had to Die.")	10	7
150	Zodiac symbol—penile drawing, Blue Rock Springs Park	10	7
151	Celebrity Cypher—(*Vallejo Times-Herald*) (1990)	10	7
152	Systemic pattern discovered	10	10
153	Prominent view of Mt. Diablo; influencing the Mt. Diablo bus bomb and code radians, etc.	8	8
154	Table kick—Terry's Restaurant	8	10
155	Shootings—sniper attacks, Interstate 80, Fairfield areas	6	6
156	Brutal act against female employee	8	10

There are a *total of 156 circumstantial indicators*, factors, or relationships between known facts in the Zodiac case and our suspect. An expert in mathematical statistical science would be required to analyze the odds involved in these comparisons.

ZODIAC MAKES A UNIQUE QUESTION MARK

LIKE THIS (writing)

ZODIAC ***SUSPECT*** ALWAYS MAKES A UNIQUE QUESTION MARK

LIKE THIS (writing)

XXIII

LAKE BERRYESSA

The residents in the area, very few in number, call it Zodiac Island. In the middle of winter, when the water level is high, this roundish mound is surrounded by water. In late summer, early fall, the water is found on three sides. A gravel-and-sand pathway leads from the parking area, angling downward and onto the barren island. Even after so many years, the scene is desolate and foreboding. The lone pitiful oak tree stands like a saddened sentry—leaning, waiting; maybe even hoping to die. The only living witness—and she is not talking. The other oak fell several years ago, but the two together gave the picnic cove its original name, Twin Oaks.

As stated by Cecelia Ann Shepard before her death, and by Bryan Hartnell, who barely survived, this island is bounded by groves of oak trees. The groves, one to the north and one to the south, are both situated about 150 to 200 yards away. This is where Cecelia first saw their attacker as he was watching them from the grove to the south. As the terrain slopes down to the water's edge, at a modest-to-steep angle, a couple in a prone position would never see anyone walking either behind or in front of them. The nearly flat area directly under the oak tree is quite small, perhaps no larger than eight by eight feet.

This small area is the only area suitable to stretch out a blanket. In the late afternoon, this small patch of land would be in the shade, as the sun would be behind them to the west. Most likely, the terrain and surrounding topography is very much like it was then. In general, there are no shrubs, no Manzanita, or other types of vegetation in the area, save for the small patches of weeds. Ninety-nine percent of the growth consists of the few scraggly oak trees. Although the trees may be slightly larger than they were, passing cars on the highway above are still visible from the parking lot.

The Zodiac stalking his prey was (using a crude and insensitive vernacular) "road hunting." From the highway, just one-quarter mile away, the Zodiac could easily observe the victim's car in the parking lot. Even if we assume the parking lot had not yet been built, any car parked in the area would have been visible from the highway. As there were no other cars in sight, only the single Karmann Ghia parked by itself, the young couple became prime targets.

The footprints, described by Capt. Kenneth Narlow of the Napa County Sheriff's Dept., became a critical clue to the killer's identity. Without any hesitation or reservation, Capt. Narlow still defends his assessment, still maintains the killer weighed at least 220 pounds, and he may be totally correct.

However, there are a few major considerations, which have never been mentioned. Capt. Narlow had one of his large deputies, weighing 210 pounds, walk in line with, and directly to the side of, the Wing Walker boot prints. The killer's prints were much deeper than the deputy's so Narlow concluded the killer weighed at least 220 pounds. Now, it is essential to know the deputy's shoe-size, in order to factor in the many variables in this calculation. While we can assume the depth of the sand was exactly the same for the killer and the deputy, we do not know for certain. Weight distribution, the surface absorbing the weight, and corresponding depressions are crucial elements in the equation. Additionally, it is unknown if damp sand will compact or depress equally with completely dry sand. Walking on an ocean beach is something we have all experienced. There is a small area of sand that is neither too dry nor too wet, which is best for walking. In this narrow strip of sand, we find we sink very little.

The entire cove was surely closed and protected as a crime scene late that night. Early the next morning, Capt. Narlow returned with his team to conduct a thorough search and investigation. In late September there would be a great deal of moisture in the night air. Therefore, not knowing the difference in compaction variables, wet or moist vs. dry (6:30 PM vs. 7:00 AM), the depth of footprints could be very misleading. If Capt. Narlow conducted other sand compaction tests at the scene, it was never mentioned. I know he never discussed it with us.

A rectangular bar of steel will depress sand much deeper when placed on its end, than it does when placed on its side. The weight of the bar is the same, but the pressure is distributed over a larger surface area when it is placed on its side. There are other factors, which were never mentioned. We have never known the length of the gait, which could be a clue to the killer's height. Posture is yet another factor. A person walking in an entirely straight position will exert more pressure on their heels, while a slightly forward-leaning position will place more pressure on the ball of the foot.

The results of many dozens of sand compaction tests are interesting and perplexing. Walking in a variety of sands, both controlled studies and in the field, including Lake Berryessa, we discovered the depressions made by the 220-pound man were identical to the same man when he carried an additional 25 pounds of iron weights. Repeatedly, time after time, in sand from one-half inch deep to four inches, the measurements were identical. The physics involved must be very complex, and above my ability to understand or explain.

We also discovered that there is a minimum of sand around Lake Berryessa and the Twin Oaks cove. The small area of fine, loose sand seems to be concentrated near or at the high-water mark of the lake. Below and above the sandy area are gradients of rock and gravel. Therefore, the measurable prints would be very few, perhaps no more than two or three. Granted, this area was investigated many years after the fact. There may have existed more sand then, than today, but I would guess there is a great deal more now.

It is our conclusion and opinion the killer at Lake Berryessa *could* have weighed 220 pounds. However, considering the many variables involved, especially the foot-size difference, it is impossible to know. The killer Zodiac could have weighed much less and possibly more, but to say Zodiac weighed around 220 pounds is very inaccurate and terribly misleading.

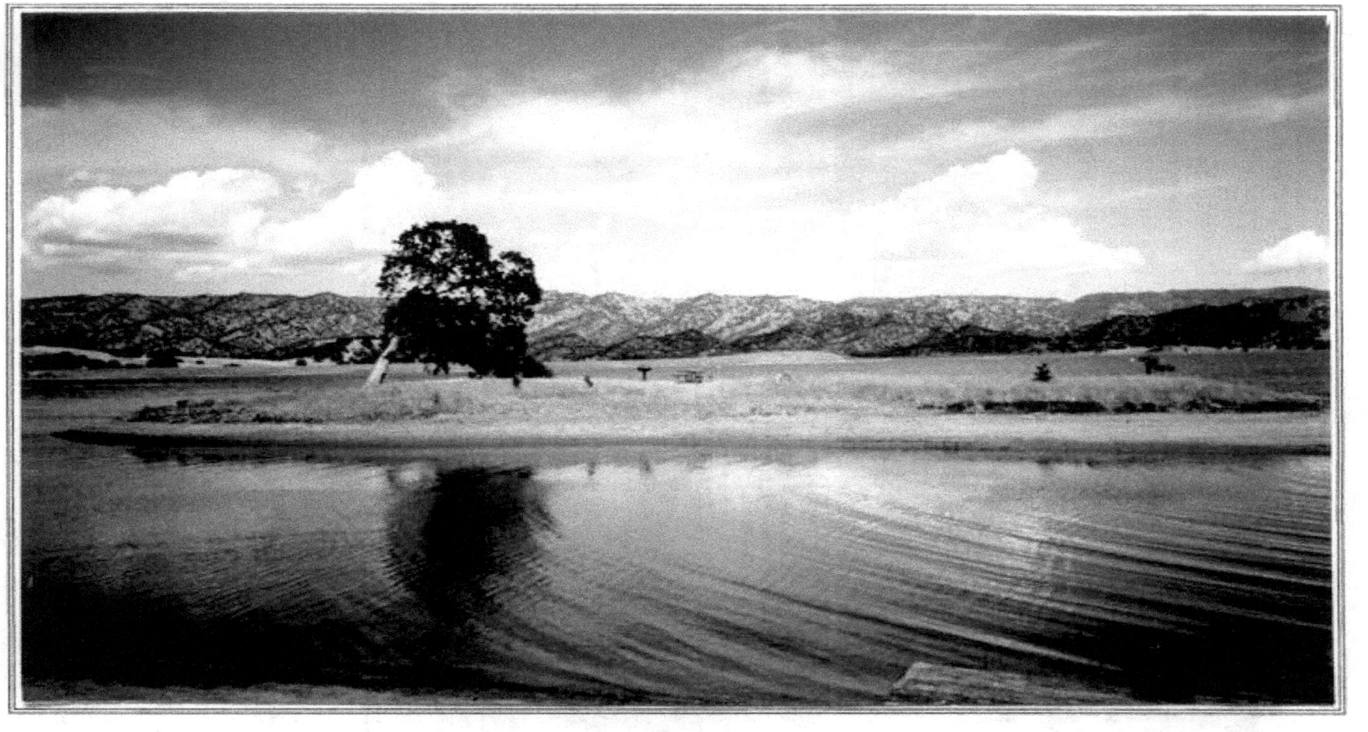

The local residents have named it "Zodiac Island":
AKA – Twin Oaks Cove, Lake Berryessa, CA.

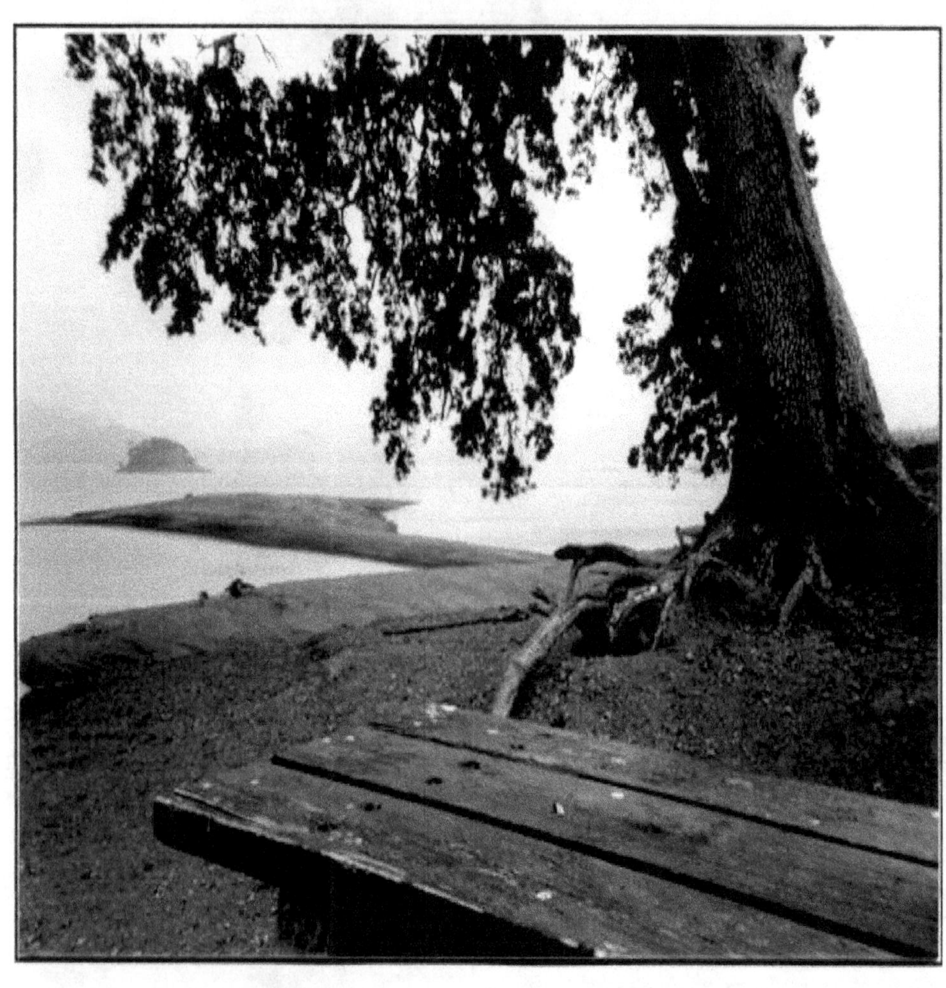

Lake Berryessa, Twin Oaks Cove. Cecelia Ann Shepard and Bryan Hartnell under this tree on September 27, 1969 when attacked by the Zodiac. Shepard died of multiple stab wounds—Hartnell survived.

Hill and cluster of trees to the right is where Shepard saw a man watching them a short time before they were attacked.

Moskowite Corners, Lake Berryessa, CA:

This is the small café where Wilbur Thompson was having lunch on September 29, 1969. Mr. Thompson said that several customers were making eye contact with one another, reacting to the strange behavior of a middle-aged man, maybe 45 years of age, who walked into the store asking unusual questions like—"Which is the fastest road out of here?", etc. He was acting so strange and bought nothing. Everyone left their seats to watch the man as he got into his light, powder-blue car—a two-door hard-top.

XXIV

I WATCH YOU A LOT

The Kimberly Lawrence incident in the spring of 1974 provides incontrovertible evidence our suspect was stalking this young schoolteacher. It is entirely possible our intervention may have saved her life. This situation was documented by both the Vacaville and El Sobrante Police Departments.

Neva Tracy, who knows Kimberly Lawrence, was a close friend of my mother-in-law, and the family had known Neva for many years. An older lady, who helped support herself by giving "readings" and making astrological charts, Neva was a very charming and gracious person. In conversation, she would never mention her craft unless someone else brought up the subject first. No, neither Jerry nor I have ever believed in these pseudo-sciences, fortunetellers, or anything remotely similar. However, we were always conscious of the fact the Zodiac might dabble in witchcraft, according to the profile experts, and on one occasion, we did interview two "white witches."

(Years later, interviews with a most charming and beautiful lady, Darinka Luke, gave me a new perspective on telepathy and the science of the mind. A former employee of Solano County Social Services, Darinka is still actively engaged in her amazing profession. Her abilities are truly remarkable.)

So Neva, never knowing why I asked, made up an astrological chart based on our suspect's birthdate.

Then, on May 15, 1974, Neva called me and asked, "Please come to my home in El Sobrante right away. I have something very important to tell you and I do not want to discuss this over the phone."

When I got there, Neva proceeded to tell me about a beautiful young girl, a schoolteacher in the Fairfield area. The school was in a country setting a few miles out of town.

"The girl lives in an apartment complex in Vacaville, but because of some terrifying things going on, she has returned home to her parents. The people live right next door to me."

Neva, who always took methodical notes, began reading what Kimberly had told her.

"On May 7, 1974, just a few days ago, Kimberly told me, 'I have just started to receive some strange phone calls and letters. I am being stalked by some psycho. The phone calls come late at night, and I can only hear rushing wind and heavy breathing.' The calls have continued, and Kimberly said to me, 'I told some of my friends and my apartment manager, and I am really frightened.'"

Kimberly could not understand how the stalker discovered her parent's address or phone number, which was unlisted, but after she received two more calls late at night, she was terrified. It appeared the psycho stalker had followed her to her parents' home. They changed their phone number, but she received two more cryptic letters through the mail.

Kimberly said, "I made out police reports with both the Vacaville and El Sobrante Police Departments."

Returning home I called Double J and told him the entire story. The very next day Jerry was sitting in Neva's home, and in a short time he was next door talking with Kimberly and her parents. Within a day or two he obtained copies of the police reports and the cryptic notes Kimberly had received in the mail.

Jerry then interviewed the apartment manager at the Alamo Garden Apartments, who said, "One of the other tenants reported seeing an older man sitting in his new Ford, a dark-green four-door. The man was parked in the private parking area near Kimberly's apartment."

She said, "I also observed the same man on several

occasions *just sitting in his car.*"

This was the exact time period when Kimberly received her silent phone calls. Our suspect had just purchased a new dark-green Ford sedan.

Strangely enough, the manager even reported another odd conversation she had with a man who told her he was with the Chamber of Commerce, or something like that, or some real estate firm doing surveys on rental factors, vacancies, and such things. It was about the same time as the other tenant reported seeing the man in the dark-green Ford.

The man was in a suit and tie, fairly neat and very well-spoken, and she invited him into her apartment. Jerry asked her, "Do you think you could identify him if you saw him in person?"

She said, "Absolutely!"

Within a couple of days, Jerry and the apartment manager went to an AA meeting.

Jerry said, "I'll wait for you in the car. You don't have to stay for the meeting, just go in and see if you can spot him."

This was a meeting, which was always heavily attended, maybe thirty or forty people. The manager returned after a few minutes and told Jerry, "The man is most definitely in there."

She told Jerry exactly where he was sitting, and described his attire perfectly. In order to confirm her identification, it was necessary for them to wait until the meeting was over. When our suspect walked out, the manager said, "There he is, that's him right there."

Jerry observed his clothing, and it matched precisely with her previous remarks. Jerry then said, "Now we are talking about the man that just such-and-such?" (Describing his movements.)

She said, "Yes."

"The man with the such-and-such?"

She said, "Yes, that's him. There is no doubt in my mind at all—that's the man I was talking to in my apartment."

Then Jerry, in a near panic, called me a couple days later and asked, “Can you take off work tomorrow? I have just learned Kimberly has gone on a long trip to see her grandmother in the mountains.” Jerry was sincerely concerned for Kimberly’s safety.

I told Double J, “There is absolutely no way I can take off work.” (And frankly, I was not nearly as concerned as Jerry.)

As things turned out, he was absolutely right.

Jerry called Kimberly’s mother explaining his concerns, and the next day he picked up Mrs. Lawrence and they went to the mountains above Fresno, a very beautiful area in the Sierras. Three days later, Jerry called and we met for lunch, and he told me this fascinating story:

“After a four-hour trip to Bass Lake above Fresno, we found the small resort, and there was Kimberly alive and well. Her mother was greatly relieved. I’m sure I scared the hell out of Kimberly’s mother. The family didn’t tell the grandmother the spooky story because they didn’t want her to worry.”

“In private, Kimberly told me, ‘It’s absurd for you to follow me. Your fears are totally unfounded. I haven’t been followed by anyone. There is nobody else staying at my grandmother’s small resort, just me.’ She was quite irate over the entire matter.”

“Later, when I was alone, I walked into the little grocery store and began talking with the grandmother. I was curious to know if anyone else had shown up after Kimberly arrived. The grandmother was somewhat surprised by my question, and she replied, ‘Why, yes! There was a nice-looking man, an older man, with grayish hair here. He was so neat, and he came into the store. I asked if I could help him find something, but he never said a word. In fact, I tried to start several conversations with him, but he didn’t talk at all. He just kind of stared at me and left. I saw his car. It was a big American car, and it was dark-green, but I couldn’t tell you what kind. He just turned around and drove off.’”

“I showed the grandmother a photo of our suspect, and

she said, 'Well, if he now has long bushy hair down to his collar, I would say this is the same man.'" (At this time, our suspect was wearing his hair long and bushy, down to his collar.)

"Later that evening, Kimberly made a passing comment: 'I thought I heard creaking noises from the stairs, which lead to my little room, but I didn't think anything about it.' I said, it occurs to me the man could still be in the area. I suggest we leave at once. We immediately drove back to El Sobrante."

I asked Double J in a mocking tone, "Did you carry a gun?" He shrugged and replied, "You know I hate guns."

"Great job, Double J! You make me proud!"

There was little doubt in my mind; Jerry had just saved this girl's life. Yet, she didn't have a clue.

The handwriting experts had stated the notes Kimberly Lawrence received were in a forced and contrived writing, and it would be impossible to make a comparison with Zodiac's writing. However, there are a few similarities between the Zodiac's contrived writing and our suspect's fancy-style writing, with the notes in question.

I would be remiss not to mention one other witness of a related incident. Another apartment manager Jerry and I knew, here in Vallejo, also identified our suspect. While looking at a photo she stated, "Oh yes, this is the man who was here asking questions about some survey or something about rental vacancies—he was with some real estate firm."

This lady had absolutely no knowledge of the incident in Vacaville.

Jerry and I are still convinced this episode with the young schoolteacher, Kimberly Lawrence, matches the Zodiac stalking profile one-hundred percent. She was fortunate to survive his insane drive and lust for killing.

June of 1974 was a dramatic turning point in the Zodiac murders. In our suspect's personal life, many things were taking place at this exact period.

One other important factor in the Kimberly Lawrence

matter: the country-school setting was rather remote. The primary road Kimberly would have been traveling to and from her school was the road on which our suspect lived. Therefore, it is no stretch of the imagination to assume our suspect first observed his young beautiful prey as she drove by his house, twice a day. He followed her to her apartment in Vacaville; and then when he did not see her for a day or two, he went to the school instead of waiting for her to drive by his house, and followed her to her parents' home in El Sobrante. Then, from her apartment in Vacaville, he would follow her to Davis to her boyfriend's home on Silveyville Road. Was she going to be Zodiac's next victim? We think so, without any doubt!

I seen you on Silvyville at that house. I like you I followed you. You live in Vacaville. I watch you there and Dixon and Davis. I watch you alot. I call you alot. I like to watch you and call you alot. I get mad cause your telephone doesnt ring at night now. You better let it ring or I get to mad and bad things will happen. I tell you once. let it ring or else.

Look at the letter "a." Remember, this writing has already been declared to be "definitely contrived." Remember also that Mr. ________ has been identified, in person, as the same man who came to the apartment manager asking "rental" questions. Also, the large, 4- door green Ford seen about the apartments on several occasions. Also, even the terminology and the threatening statements fit perfectly the Zodiac M.O.

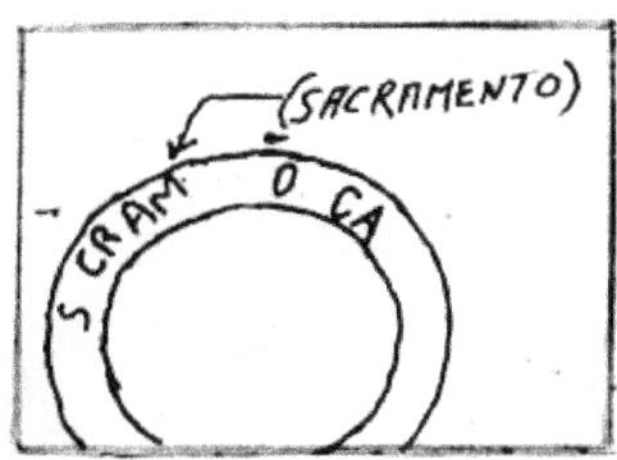

1567 Alamo Drive No 15

Vacaville, California

NOTE: As the above note was fading to an unreadable condition it was traced over with a fountain pen on 3-1-2000.

XXV

RELATED INCIDENTS

When the Riverside Police Department reconstructed the group of people, who were assembled in the campus library the night Cheri Jo Bates was murdered late on October 30, 1966, an older man with our suspect's name was officially reported as being present. This was confided to us by Capt. Narlow, who was in charge of the murder case at Lake Berryessa. In thirty years of requests, we have never had a reply from the Riverside authorities, and have not been able to confirm this information. Narlow promised he would confirm this bizarre story, but never did. If it is true, if our man was, in fact, there, he knew he had to respond to the request of the Riverside police to attend the reconstruction, as someone else knew he was there. Had he not attended, he knew he could be held under suspicion. Capt. Narlow told us, "This information was reported to me verbally by one of the Riverside detectives."

Did our suspect check out a book, using his real name? Did he borrow a friend's student library card? Was he, in fact, a student? Narlow mentioned that "the older man" was not a student, but we have had absolutely no cooperation from the Riverside authorities.

Another observation is the fact that the person etching the "death ode" on the library desk, found some two months after Cheri Jo's death, had to do it at some later date. This would indicate the killer had a reason to return, like returning a book.

Was he a part-time student, perhaps taking just one class? Our Mr. Tucker *was* a part-time student at Solano

Community College on Suisun Valley Road in Cordelia, in 1971, when he was 51 years old.

On November 8, 1971, George Pimental, 67 years old, was stabbed to death in his home at 471 Woodrow Avenue, Vallejo. The knife was still in his lower chest: multiple knife cuts on his chest; severe slashing of his abdomen; penis cut; nose cut; and throat slashed. His left eye was gouged from its socket. Mr. Pimental was not wearing any pants or shorts, but he was still clad in a shirt, socks, and shoes.

The crime was more than an act of murder, but rather vicious and brutal, the act of a rabid beast, savagely insane. When we obtained the report, along with the color photos, I observed something very odd within and under the multiple slash marks. Turning the photo one way and then another, trying to focus my eyes, a very clear letter became apparent. It was not one of the straight-line slash marks, but faintly carved in a circle. Then behold, another letter, and a third became most evident. Now they were obvious. With much deeper slash marks, angled up and down, across, sideways, and at other angles, the killer was trying to erase, or obliterate the letters he had just made.

With a great deal of examination and computerized enhancements, we all agreed. The letters visible were the letters of our suspect's name, and in proper sequence. As an afterthought, the killer decided he should not leave his name carved into the man he had just slaughtered. (The Vallejo police never noticed the carved letters.)

Typically, Pimental spent his evenings in a local bar, and one of his friends had set up a blind date with a man referred to as the "Big Shot," well known in the gay community. We should mention a man and his wife in the Danville/San Ramon area, who were former residents of Vallejo and devoted AA members.

They asked me, "Do you know the 'Big Shot' in Vallejo AA?" They could not think of his name. They said, "Everyone calls him the 'Big Shot.'" (I could note a mocking and derisive tone when they said "Big Shot.")

We believe some of these nightly bar patrons, mostly alcoholics, have attended AA meetings. It is entirely possible this is how the blind date was set up.

We know Judge Winston was beaten to a bloody pulp in October 1971, outside a popular Vallejo bar, and rushed to the hospital. We know that on November 18, 1971, Nelda Tally was murdered in Stockton in her office. Also, just ten days earlier, on November 8, 1971, Pimental was slashed to death.

Pimental had made a comment to one of his friends, "I'm scared of this guy."

Did he mean he had seen the "Big Shot" at some of the AA meetings? Perhaps had even met him at one?

One of Pimental's fingers had been severed and sadistically stuck in his left eye socket. Is this some type of ritualistic message? Is it related to the Gordon Swinford and Kirk Hughes murders, when they were both shot in their left eye? They were killed on the same night in 1973, Swinford in Oakland and Hughes in Berkeley. Ballistics proved they were killed by the same gun. Swinford was a security guard at an Oakland car dealership. He was found sitting in his locked car with the driver's window lowered just a couple of inches. Perhaps this was the "cop" the Zodiac referred to when he said, "I killed a cop sitting in his car."

Hughes was a very young man just walking down a sidewalk in Berkeley in the early morning hours. Both victims were killed around midnight or slightly later.

And there was one other clue we find interesting. Within a few days of Pimental's murder, Det. Jack Mulanax, Vallejo PD, received a strange note (see 11th insert at end of chapter). The "CON" for the word "constantly" is identical to words and abbreviations used by Zodiac (e.g. "FRY" for Friday), as is the almost template-perfect printing, similar to letters addressed to Attorney Melvin Belli, and the lowercase "thanks." The most chilling and compelling part of the note is, "LEND AN EYE."

The note itself is in keeping with the Zodiac's taunting and teasing, and is also like the short note received by Kimberly Lawrence. And, for the record, nobody by the name of White lived at 401 Idora, and the residents did not know anyone by that name. Is George Pimental a Zodiac killing? If we could show you the carved letters on poor Pimental, you, too, would begin to wonder. There are two other clues in the short note, which definitely match our suspect Tucker—the "mirror" and the "speedo retard."

While the note asked the police to keep watch over his wife's home, we could never locate her. We also tried to trace the signed note from an "H. White" in Lake County, with no luck. After an extensive and thorough investigation, the Vallejo detectives developed no leads in this brutal killing.

Consider the most unusual connection between a fifteen-year-old girl, Cosette Ellison, who disappeared from the Walnut Creek/Moraga area, and the unsolved murder of Ms. Naomi Sanders in Vallejo. On a good day with moderate traffic, a motorist can drive from Vallejo to Walnut Creek in about 22 to 25 minutes, and from Fairfield/Cordelia in about the same time. Cosette Ellison vanished in March 1970, and Ms. Sanders was murdered on February 26, 1973.

A few mystery telephone calls in the Ellison case were traced to a "Realty Investment Company" in Oakland. On subsequent checks, it was discovered the number was for a phone in the lobby of an Oakland hotel.

In addition to the realty investment firm, the phone was also used by a black male entrepreneur who lived in the hotel as well. This man had an FBI, CII rap sheet about ten feet long. A large majority of his offenses were sexual in nature, and his business card listed his professional services as "Minister, Marriage Counselor, Boxer, Fight Promoter, Masseur, and On-Call Specials." He was no stranger to the CHP night shift in the Vallejo/Fairfield area.

Based on the realty investment aspect and our suspect's

real estate development self-employment, the series of phone calls and their nature, we thought there might be some connection, however slim.

We had one of the local police departments call the man in. We had prepared a photo lineup for the lieutenant, who happened to know the man very well. The man looked at the lineup and said, "Oh yeah, sure, that's the guy I had sex with a couple of times. The last time we met, he was just wearing a blue bathrobe when he opened the door. I forget his name, but I can show you the motel on West Texas Street in Fairfield—the Travis Sands Motel."

As the Vallejo police were searching for a possible suspect by the name of Lonnie Alexander in Naomi Sanders's death, we discovered through our own investigation of Sanders, manager of the Oakwood Garden Apartments in Vallejo, that she was the former manager of the Travis Sands Motel in Fairfield. Royce Brooks, owner of Brooks Security Service in Benicia, told me, "Naomi Sanders worked for me for two years, and she could not stop talking about the Zodiac killer. She really thought she knew who the Zodiac was."

Evidence in her apartment revealed she was making dinner for two, and other factors strongly indicated she knew her killer. From the time frame mentioned by the black male, it is possible Naomi Sanders was the motel manager when he met our suspect for their sexual encounters. Other than our suspect's defense of homosexuality, we have confirmed other information, which strongly suggests he is AC/DC.

Another mysterious and unsolved murder—on February 26, 1973, Naomi Sanders, the apartment manager at the Oakwood Garden Apartments, 1055 Oakwood Street in Vallejo. Poor Naomi! Did she tell the wrong person she knew the identity of Zodiac? She boasted to her close friends she knew it, for a fact. During her part-time job at Brooks Security Service in Benicia, she always drove the lonely Lake Herman Road in an excited state of trepidation reliving the murder of the two teenagers on December 20, 1968.

She maintained an extensive newspaper file on the Zodiac. While the exact time period is not known for certain, it appears she was, in fact, the manager of the Travis Sands Motel in Fairfield around 1969 and 1970, and rented a room to George Tucker for his homosexual encounters.

Naomi was cooking dinner for two as evidenced by two uncooked steaks, still in the pan on top of the stove. Four partially-smoked unfiltered cigarettes (Pall Malls) and two filtered Camels were found in the ashtray in the living room, and more of the same in another ashtray in the bedroom. It would appear they were having a lengthy conversation. (George Tucker smoked Pall Malls, as reported to us by a Benicia police officer who saw him frequently in the gambling parlors there.)

The police report on Naomi said she'd been vaginally and rectally assaulted, and strangled to death with her own pantyhose.

Six days after her murder, on March 4, 1973, a close friend received a phone call at 2:45 AM. The male caller said in a low, calm, and well-educated voice, "I am going to rape and kill you just like I did Naomi." Was this a fortuitous act of fate, or something else?

At 10:30 PM on the very night her killer was smoking a Pall Mall cigarette in her living room, Naomi made a secret phone call to a very close friend she had known for 17 years. In hushed tones there was a brief conversation, very short, and she hung up. Their conversations normally lasted an hour or longer.

As Naomi always left her drapes open, it was strange they were closed; and she did not respond to the tenants' welfare check. Her body was discovered in her bedroom around 3:30 the next afternoon.

Close friends stated that Naomi had had a serious drinking problem in prior years, but had rehabilitated herself to a seldom-to-moderate drinker recently. We suspect this is where she met the "Big Shot" at the AA meetings in Fairfield. One tenant stated that Naomi was "nosey and horny."

She was born March 3, 1915, and was 57 years old. Close friends also recalled that Naomi had a six-foot-tall, grey-haired boyfriend about her age, by the name of Lonnie. He lived at Travis, flew out of Travis Air Force Base, and trained aviators in the Fairfield area. It was reported he had given Naomi a large check ($1,500) to purchase a trailer, so he would have a place to stay when he returned to the area.

Shortly, the police were searching for a suspect named Lonnie Alexander, who taught flying around there. The Office of Special Investigations (OSI) at Travis Air Force Base conducted a search for both military and civilians. Neither they nor other authorities could find any person by that name in the entire Bay Area.

Yes, we were curious about the bizarre note found at the Benicia High School and the notation at the bottom, which said, "*Air School.*"

Royce Brooks told me, "Lyndon, I kid you not, she was obsessed with the Zodiac, and she swore she knew who he was." Royce believes Naomi was killed by him.

So we continue to ask, "Is there is a connection in this confusing mix of obscure coincidence: a missing fifteen-year-old girl, followed by strange and threatening phone calls to her family members; the phone traced to an Oakland hotel and a 'Realty Investment Company'; our suspect's employment; a homosexual black male using the same phone; sex with our suspect; and a murdered apartment manager, who was the manager of the motel where the sex occurred."

The police had developed some information that the Lonnie Alexander in question was either a pilot or gave flying lessons at some air school. After a long search at every air school they could locate in the general area, they could neither identify nor locate anyone by the name of Lonnie Alexander.

The connection was never made to the strange note left at Benicia High School signed "Zodiac." On the bottom right-hand corner of this bizarre note, and only if it were turned upside down, two words are visible, just barely—"Air School." To our knowledge, the Vallejo PD has never seen this note. This is the note making reference to blowing up the school, and to a body by Lake Herman Road. As in the Pimental case, the Vallejo police were baffled, and the case remains unsolved.

The lieutenant assisting us with the hotel resident was initially very outgoing and friendly. As he, too, had developed an interest in our suspect, he tried in vain to make an appointment with the San Francisco police detectives handling the Zodiac case. Eventually he made a special trip there.

A few weeks later, Jerry dropped by the lieutenant's office and was told, "The detectives in San Francisco were so rude, so totally disgusting, I left their office madder than hell. The minute I spoke your suspect's name, they came unglued. They told me they never wanted to hear your suspect's name again."

From that moment on, Jerry was an unwelcome visitor. The lieutenant even told Jerry, "You should not believe one word my informant told you. He is totally unreliable, and I will not call him in again."

Jerry and I shrugged it off, asking, "What else is new?"

Even though the binge-style killings came to a sudden halt in 1974, the Zodiac was still running around the countryside, and up and down the freeways. He travels freely, at will, and extensively, driving first one dark-green four-door, and then the other. Both Fords, and both the same year—identical in every respect, except the license plates. (How many people do you know who own two identical cars?)

Yet, still lingering in his guts was a savage lust for killing. He truly enjoyed the stalking and cornering of his prey, and the final act of murder itself.

Realizing he was no longer invincible, and trying desperately to maintain control over his nightmarish alcoholism, he became very selective. He may not have pursued his victims any longer, but if the opportunity presented itself, if the circumstances were perfect—if "THEY ARE ASKING FOR IT"—then he would kill. We believe this is exactly what happened to Shiri-Dine Bana on May 10, 1979.

Shiri-Dine lived with her mother in a mobile-home park on American Canyon Road, and disappeared on her way to school at Napa Community College. There are several facts in this case, which make Jerry and I believe it to be a Zodiac murder.

Eight days after she vanished, her body was found among the weeds, on the west side of Reservoir Road, less than one-quarter mile south of Lake Herman Road. This is very close to the double-murder site of December 20, 1968 (Faraday and Jensen).

The autopsy revealed she had been struck on the head and strangled. And matching the frenzy of Cecelia Ann Shepard's death, Shiri-Dine was also stabbed "at least" 25 times.

However, another part of the mystery is Shiri-Dine's car. It was first observed by a Solano County sheriff's deputy on May 12, two days after she disappeared. Her car, a 1969 Ford Torino, was parked at a 90-degree angle to the parking stalls, occupying three spaces at Blue Rock Springs Park. This is the same site of the July 4, 1969, attack on Ferrin and Mageau by the Zodiac. According to one Benicia detective, the car was apparently returned to the park and abandoned. ("Returned" is the critical word.) The detectives also assumed the girl was murdered where she was found because her eyeglasses were still on her head.

As there were no indications or traces of blood in Shiri-Dine's car, it would be only natural to find large accumulations of blood at the murder site. However, this was not the case, and the obvious conclusion would be she had been killed elsewhere. The killer may have had possession of her car for a day or two, or at least had the keys to it, and knew where it was parked, moving it to Blue Rock Springs Park a day or two later. The killer's own car would be parked within walking distance, and if not at Blue Rock Springs Park, then perhaps the golf course parking lot just across the road.

A little over a year later, I had a pleading phone call at home from Mrs. Branowski, Shiri-Dine's mother. She explained, "I have heard there were two investigators who were experts on the Zodiac case. I have obtained your name and phone number from an unidentified source. Could I meet with you and your partner? Because I think my daughter has been killed by the Zodiac."

As Jerry and I were always searching for new leads, we met with Mrs. Branowski at Denny's Restaurant on Sonoma Boulevard in Vallejo.

Mrs. Branowski, a lady I guessed to be in her early 50s, olive-complected and attractive, was very anxious and a little nervous when we first met. She soon relaxed, and we talked for nearly two hours.

"I have been fighting with the Benicia PD," she said, "trying to get my daughter's car returned. They have been holding onto the car for evidence, and it is still officially impounded." "You will not believe what we found in the car!"

She continued, "This is why we wanted some other police department to investigate, and they would not do it. Someone told us about two men who were investigating the Zodiac case, and this is how I got your name."

Her eyes were dark, hollow, and intense. We could see the terrible pain she was still suffering; her voice was beginning to crack. Jerry reached out and held her hand as she began to sob.

"We had to have the car towed, and when we got it home, we opened the left door, the driver's door, and we looked down, and could not believe our eyes. Lying on the floorboard, between the seat and the doorframe, was a large butcher knife, with either blood or rust stains on the blade. And, there was a Timex wristwatch hanging on the turn-signal lever."

She told us, "I called the Chief of Police in Benicia, but he told me, 'We have already spent more money on this investigation than we should have, and there is nothing more we can do on the case.'" Jerry and I were stunned.

"We suggest you submit the knife and the watch to the Benicia PD, and make certain to have them issue you a signed receipt with a date stamp."

It was all too incredible. What might possibly be the murder weapon itself, the butcher knife, was still in the car along with the Timex wristwatch. She also stated, "I have never seen the knife before, and the watch is not my daughter's."

One of the detectives reported, "No real clues were found in Shiri-Dine's car."

To remind those of you who may have forgotten, the only evidence in the murder of Cheri Jo Bates in Riverside, in 1966, was a broken knife and a Timex wristwatch. Was Zodiac reverting to his usual persona of taunting and teasing? Is it possible the Zodiac stalked *Shiri-Dine* as he did *Cheri Jo*? (What's in a name?) Did Zodiac watch and wait for Shiri-Dine at the Napa college, just as he did with Cheri Jo at UC Riverside?

We met with Mrs. Branowski at least one other time. While we did not get too involved, we discovered there was a borderline 51/50 (mentally disturbed) young man living in the mobile-home park. Apparently, Mrs. Branowski had previous dealings with the young man, who flirted with her daughter. We also learned, from one of the detectives, this man had made some random and idle threats against Shiri-Dine that were not taken seriously. From what we discovered he was never a suspect, and it appeared this young man could not have possessed the means or the ability to kill her.

Is it possible the Zodiac met Shiri-Dine at an AA meeting or a drug-counseling class or seminar at Napa Community College? We know the colleges and universities offer these special programs for their students having problems with drugs. Was this the key, the door-opener, used by the Zodiac to murder so many coeds on college campuses in California, Oregon, and Washington? AA or NA (Narcotics Anonymous) meetings offer the perfect opportunity for a serial killer to find vulnerable victims. Cloaked in a deceivingly supportive disguise, he is trusted completely. When offered a ride in his car, they do not hesitate for one second, as he reminds them of their own father.

As late as March 9, 1984, the *Vallejo Independent-Press* printed a short article, which read:

> *IDENTIFIED*
>
> Placer County officials have identified the body of a teenage girl, found strangled, as Hope Dierking, 15, of Hayward. Sheriff Donald Nunes said the girl was last seen alive last Friday, hitchhiking near Vacaville. She was reported missing Saturday.

Poor little Hope Dierking! There was no way she could have known she was in the center of Zodiac's web of death.

(Following are 23 pages of graphics, primarily newspaper clippings from 1972-99, describing other incidents with the Zodiac M.O., which lend credence to the likelihood that he didn't really stop killing in 1974.)

Zodiak Killer suspected in murders here

A nine-year-old long beach murder case may have been the work of the infamous Zodiac Killer, according to the sheriff's office.

The bodies of Linda Edwards and Robert Domingos, both of Lompoc, were found near an isolated stretch of beach north of Santa Barbara in June, 1963. They had been shot to death.

Sheriff John Carpenter said that evidence gathered over the past three months points to the murders as being the work of the Zodiac, who gained fame in 1966 by claiming to have murdered six people in San Francisco, Vallejo and Riverside.

However, at a press conference, no facts were disclosed to substantiate the theory.

THE FIRST alleged Zodiac killing was in 1966 in Riverside, according to authorities – three years after the Edwards- Domingos slayings.

"Over a year ago, detectives began a thorough study of the case," Carpenter said. "They examined and re-evaluated all aspects of the crime. Many hundreds of hours have been spent compiling information concerning the possibility that this man could have been responsible for the 1963 killings.

"ALTHOUGH THE anticipated response of this statement would be one of skepticism, let me say that we do not make this assertion frivolously."

Detective William Baker, in charge of the investigation, said that local sheriff's officers have been in contact with other law agencies from areas where the Zodiac had reportedly been responsible for other murders.

"We have found that there appears to be a high degree probability that the Zodiac is responsible for the double murder in our county," he said. "Several significant similarities between our case and others all tend to connect the Zodiac with this crime. WE also have information, to be investigated further, which may place him in the Santa Barbara area in 1963."

BAKER AND Carpenter said they couldn't divulge the exact nature of the similarities.

"I would like to emphasize that we are not using the notoriety of the Zodiac to dispose of a difficult case, nor are we closing our minds to the possibility that he may not be responsible," Baker said.

The alleged "Zodiac" became a suspect in the Vallejo, San Francisco and Riverside murders when he wrote flamboyant letters and made phone calls to newspaper reporters and lawyers telling them of details of the murders.

Sheriff's officers are requesting that any persons with information pertaining to the case notify the sheriff's office.

Date: October 30th, 1966 - Sunday night

Time: Approximately 6:15 PM

Victim: Cheri Jo Bates - Female Caucasian, 18 years
Riverside City College freshman

Location: Riverside City College campus

Victim parked her vehicle in front of Riverside City College library just prior to 6 PM and entered library building. Suspect disabled victim's vehicle by removing coil wire and evidently waited for victim to return. Suspect then either forced or enticed her approximately 300 feet to an unpaved parking area between two vacant houses where he attacked her with a small knife having a blade approximately 3 ½" in length and ½" in width. Victim suffered seven lacerations on her throat and death was due to hemorrhage of the right cartoid artery. There was no evidence of sexual molestation. No witnesses.

Heelprints identical to those worn by Air Force personnel and a Timex wrist watch indicating that the suspect had a 7" wrist circumference were found at the scene of the crime.

Suspect mailed typewritten confession letter from Riverside to the Police Department and Riverside Enterprise newspaper on November 29th, 1966, claiming to be the perpetrator of the crime.

Three additional handprinted letters were mailed in Riverside by the suspect on April 30th, 1967, again claiming the Bates homicide and indicating there would be more.

Evidence:

Handprinting
Latents
Military heelprints
Timex wrist watch
Typewritten confession letter

Riverside Police Department case #352-481

Investigating officer: Captain I.L. Cross

LESLIE B. LUNDBLAD

DETECTIVE SERGEANT

10-31-66
(HALLOWEEN)

Sick of living/unwilling to die

cut.
clean.
if red/
clean.
blood spurting.
dripping.
Spilling;
all over her new
dress.
oh well
it was red
anyway.
life draining into an
uncertain death.
she won't
die.
this time
Someone ll find her.
Just wait till
next time.

rh

Message found on Riverside Library desk!

RIVERSIDE,
APR 30
PM
1957
CA
PRESS Enterprise
3512 14th Street
Riversidc,
California

BATES HAD

TO DIE

THERE WILL

BE MORE

Z

LETTER OF 30 APRIL 1967
Executed in three copies on three-ring binder paper, this letter was mailed to the Riverside newspaper, the local police, and the victim's father. Note the signature: the letter Z has been altered to make it resemble an Arabic numeral 3.

May 1, 1987: Rod's Hickory Pit, formerly Terry's restaurant, Vallejo, CA.

"Double J" standing guard while "Double L" takes photos.

As Darlene Ferrin worked at Terry's when she was murdered, the term Zodiac and Terry's became synonymous. Very typical of Zodiac's taunting and teasing, telling us,

"I AM STILL HERE—I HAVE ALWAYS BEEN HERE."

Compare this with the "Bates Had To Die" letter in Riverside, May 1967. The note was scratched in the glass mirror of the men's bathroom. According to several witnesses, the "older man" was always in the restaurant, watching Darlene.

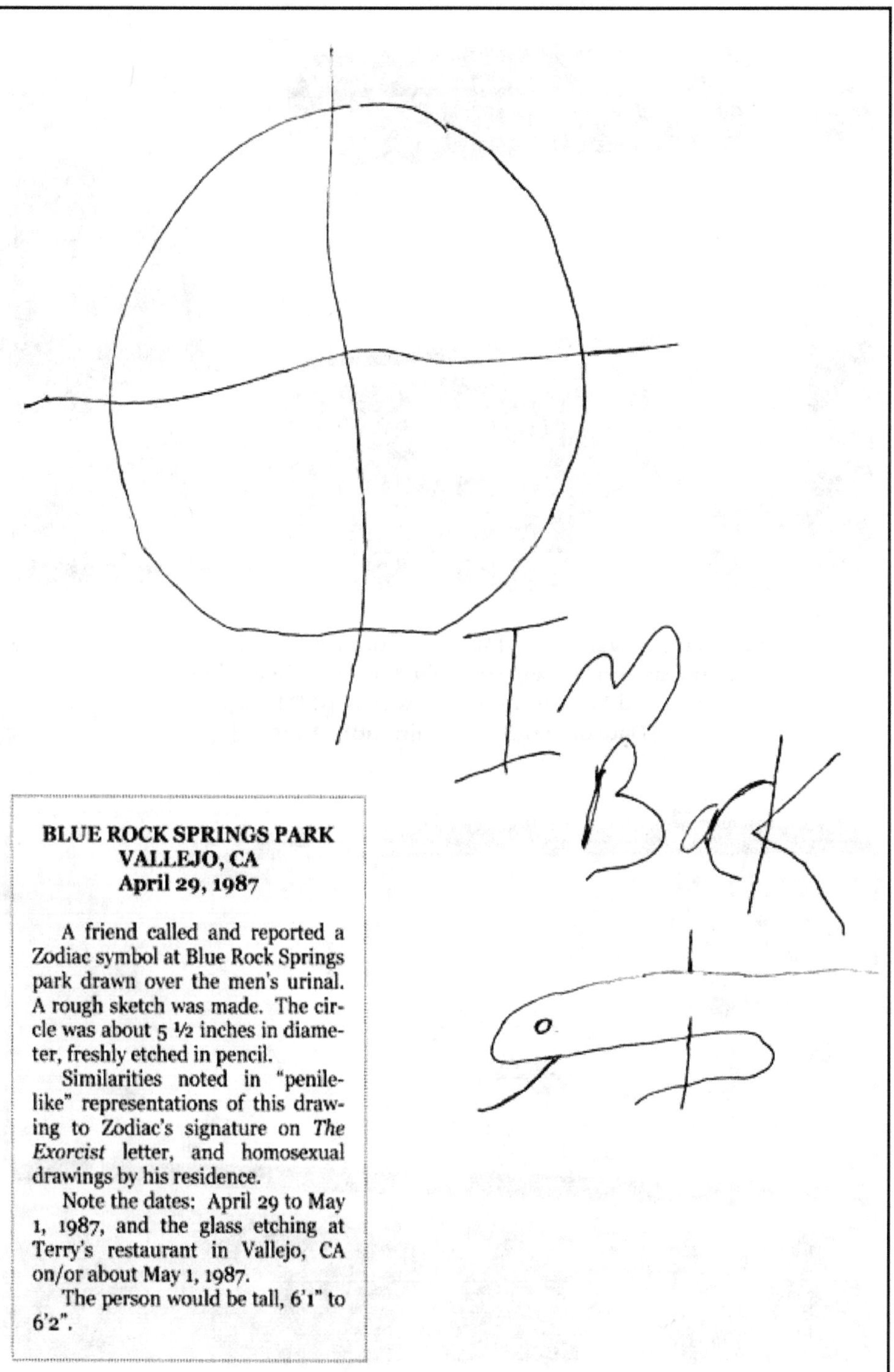

BLUE ROCK SPRINGS PARK
VALLEJO, CA
April 29, 1987

A friend called and reported a Zodiac symbol at Blue Rock Springs park drawn over the men's urinal. A rough sketch was made. The circle was about 5 ½ inches in diameter, freshly etched in pencil.

Similarities noted in "penile-like" representations of this drawing to Zodiac's signature on *The Exorcist* letter, and homosexual drawings by his residence.

Note the dates: April 29 to May 1, 1987, and the glass etching at Terry's restaurant in Vallejo, CA on/or about May 1, 1987.

The person would be tall, 6'1" to 6'2".

13 bullet holes suggest a 9-MM automatic and the diameters match.
(Faraday and Jensen were killed by .22-calibre bullets.)
(Ferrin and Mageau were shot with a 9-MM automatic.)
[Date of photo uncertain—1987 to 1988]

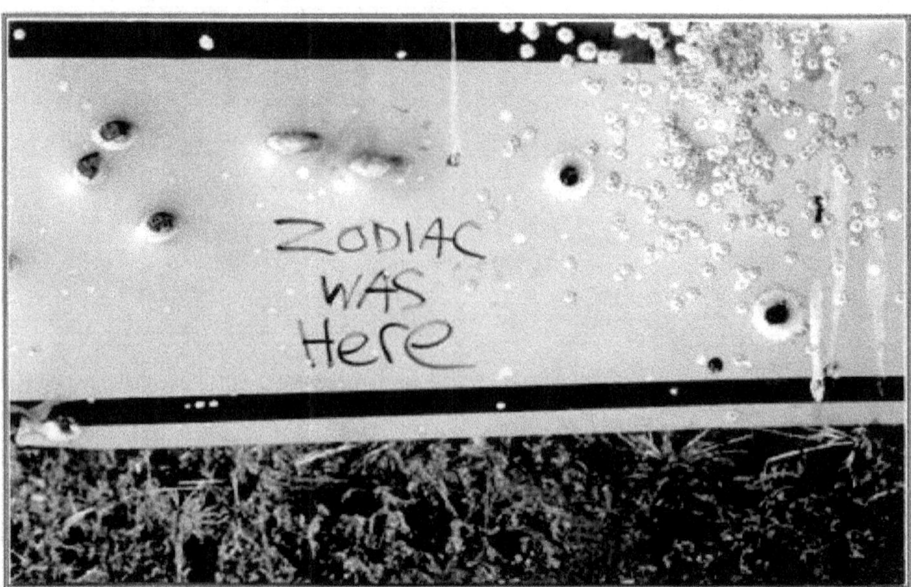

Woman Attacked By 'Insane' Man

WATSONVILLE (UPI) — A "horribly insane looking" gunman fired at least 17 shots at a woman motorist early yesterday, but she escaped uninjured in a frantic chase along a country freeway.

The woman, Mrs. Mary Elizabeth Grant, 36, of Flagstaff, Ariz., told police the man peered into the window of her car before the shooting.

"He had the most horribly insane look on his face I've ever seen," she said. "I stepped on the gas and got out of there."

When she heard the first shot, Mrs. Grant said, she ducked down in the driver's seat but kept going. Officers later counted 17 bullet holes in the rear and side of her car.

Mrs. Grant said she was alone about 3 a.m. driving from Santa Cruz to Watsonville where she was staying with friends. On an isolated section of the freeway she saw a car parked at the edge of the highway.

"It was just like he was waiting for me," she said. "He pulled onto the road as soon as I passed."

She said the car followed her so closely for a time that she decided to let it pass, but the driver would not go past her and continued tailing her auto, only "inches from my bumper."

Mrs. Grant said she decided to stop, thinking the other motorist might be in trouble. A man got out of the car and when she lowered the window he looked at her with the "insane" face. She sped off.

She said she had never seen the man before and described him as being in his 30s, about 5 feet 9 inches tall, with light brown hair. He was driving a light colored Ford sedan about 15 years old.

When Mrs. Grant drove off the freeway at Watsonville, the pursuing gunman abandoned the chase. She went directly to the police station where officers found her car punctured with bullet holes and with a flat tire.

More than a dozen .22 caliber shell cases were found along the freeway at the scene of the reported shooting.

5-23-79

Slain Woman's Car Discovered At Park

By DAN SHRYOCK
Times-Herald Staff Writer

BENICIA — A car driven by a murdered Napa woman was found parked at Vallejo's Blue Rock Springs Park Friday afternoon shortly after the woman's badly decomposed body was discovered along a secluded county road north of here.

The light blue 1969 Ford Torino, styled with a "fastback" rear section, was first noticed as early as May 14 by a park caretaker, Benicia Police Detective Bob Fletcher said Tuesday.

The dead woman, Shiri-dine Bana, 19, of 260 American Canyon Road No. 4 in Napa, was reported missing by her mother May 10 after she disappeared on her way to classes at Napa Community College.

Her body was found at about noon Friday — eight days after her disappearance — among weeds along the east side of Reservoir Road, less than a quarter-mile south of Lake Herman Road. An autopsy showed she had been stabbed at least 25 times in the chest, neck and back areas.

The autopsy, however, could not determine the exact cause of death because the body was so badly decomposed, Fletcher said. Investigators believe the woman had been dead a week when her body was found.

There is also a possibility the woman may have been strangled or killed by a blow on the head. Both neck and head injuries were discovered during the autopsy.

Fletcher said he is seeking public assistance in the murder investigation. "Does anyone remember seeing this car parked at Blue Rock Springs between the evenings of May 11 and May 12?" he asked.

Fletcher noted that the car was found illegally parked across three parking spaces instead of occupying the normal single stall. The detective speculated that persons using the park on a traditionally busy Saturday may recall seeing the vehicle.

He also wants to know if any persons were seen in or around the car. Anyone having any information concerning the parked car or any other aspect of the investigation is encouraged to contact either Fletcher or Sgt. Dave Eger at the Benicia Police Department — 745-3412.

The recovered vehicle was turned over to evidence experts from the state Department of Justice crime lab from Sacramento for examination. There were no traces of blood found in the car, however, and no personal possessions belonging to Bana were found either. Fletcher said no real clues were found through the car.

Fletcher speculates Bana was murdered at the Reservoir Road site where the body was found. He partially based the assumption on the fact the woman's eyeglasses were still on her head when she was found.

Eyeglasses would most likely have been jarred loose in transport had she been killed elsewhere and later dumped along Reservoir Road. "The facts so far show she was murdered where she was found," he said.

The car was apparently returned to the park and abandoned.

The investigation also indicates a large, strong person may have been responsible. Both Fletcher and Solano County deputy coroner Mark Berto said it would take a physically strong person to inflict the stab wounds the woman suffered. One stab went through the woman's sternum.

Berto said it would take a lot of strength to first force a knife through the sternum, and then be able to remove the blade as well.

Benicia Police Chief Pierre Bidou said Tuesday that despite the woman being a Napa resident, the investigation is solely Benicia's responsibility because the body was found here. He said he is optimistic a solution to the crime will be reached soon.

Fletcher said the investigation is being conducted in Napa, Solano and Contra Costa counties. He did not specify what aspects of the case included the Contra Costa County area.

5-24-79

Police Seek Public Help In Murder

By DAN SHRYOCK
Times-Herald Staff Writer

BENICIA — Benicia police are still seeking public assistance in the investigation of the murder of a 19-year-old Napa woman.

SHIRI-DINE BANA
...found dead

Shiri-dine Bana, 260 American Canyon Road, No. 4 in Napa, was last seen May 10 when she reportedly left for classes at Napa Community College. Her badly decomposed body was found Friday along a secluded stretch of Reservoir Road north of Benicia.

Police investigators said the woman had been stabbed at least 25 times in the back, neck and chest.

Bana's automobile was found later Friday abandoned in the Blue Rock Springs Park parking lot on Columbus Parkway in Vallejo. The car, a light blue 1969 Ford Torino, was parked across three parking spaces for several days, Benicia police Detective Bob Fletcher said.

Fletcher is asking persons who may have used park facilities on Thursday, Friday or Saturday, May 10, 11 or 12, if they recall seeing the car or anyone in or near it.

Fletcher said the car was first noticed May 12 by a Solano County Sheriff's deputy and later seen in the same location by a park caretaker May 14.

The first official note on the car came May 17 when a Vallejo Police Department officer tagged the car as abandoned. The car would have been towed from the scene 72 hours — or three days — later.

Both the body and the car, however, were discovered May 18.

Fletcher said Bana's mother reported the woman missing May 15.

The detective asks anyone with any information concerning seeing the car at Blue Rock Springs Park between May 10 and May 12 call him or Sgt. Dave Eger at the Benicia Police Department — 745-3412.

DET. MULINAX
V.P.D. 111 AMADOR

VALLEJO, CALIF.
94590

471 BANDIT MAY BE IN IDORA
TO WOODROW AREA. SPEEDO
RETARD WHO CHECKS REAR
VIEW MIRROR CON. PLEASE
LEND EYE TO MY WIFE'S HSE.
AT 401 IDORA. SHE IS ALONE
THIS AREA MIGHT PAY OFF.

Thanks
H. White

DON STRIEPEKE
SHERIFF

County of Sonoma
Sheriff's Office
2555 MENDOCINO AVENUE
SANTA ROSA, CALIFORNIA 95401
TELEPHONE 707 - 527-2511

ROBERT HAYES
UNDERSHERIFF

FEMALE HOMICIDE VICTIMS

All victims known to hitchhike or were hitch hiking.

Feb. 4, 1972

1. STERLING, Maureen L. WFJ DOB: 2/18/59
2. WEBER, Yvonne Lisa WFJ DOB: 1/29/59

Last seen 2/4/72, Friday night, 9:00 PM.
Location - Steele Lane, Santa Rosa, Redwood Ice Skating Rink.
Last seen by Richard Sanchez, WMJ, 12/30/55
Found - 12/28/72, approximately 4:00 PM.
Found by - Frost, Glen Jack WMJ, DOB: 9/3/55
Brooner, A. Dave WMJ, DOB: 10/29/56
Location - 2.2 miles north of Porter Creek Rd., on Franz Valley Rd.
Bodies approximately 66 feet from roadway, east side
Condition of bodies - bones only.
Cause of death - Unknown
Scene of death - None. No clothing found at scene, presumption, bodies were nude when dumped.
Evidence at scene: One (1) gold chain necklace with cross.
One (1) earring
Suspects - None
Crime Report #2756-00
Sexual assault - Unknown

March 4, 1972

1. ALLEN, Kim Wendy WFA DOB: 9/22/52

Last seen - 3/4/72, Saturday, approximately 5:20 PM.
Location - Bell Ave., Freeway entrance 101 Hwy. northbound, at San Rafael
Last seen by - Tony Ferrari, DOB: 3/31/48
Found: 3/5/72
Found by: John A. Bly WMJ DOB: 7/6/54
Scott J. Bunting WMJ DOB: 2/9/54
Location - Enterprize Road, approximately 3 miles from Bennett Valley Road, body lying in ditch approximately 20 feet from roadway.
Condition of body - Good
Cause of death: Strangulation with rope-wire, or similar type material. Victim had also been bound at wrists and andles as if spread-eagled.
Scene of death - None. No clothing or personal property found - except:

One (1) gold earring, loop type
Suspects: None
Crime Report #2663-96
Sexual assault, semen in vagina

December 14, 1972

1. KURSA, Lori Lee WFJ DOB: 2/26/59

Last seen - November 20, 21, 1972, Monday or Tuesday, 5:30 or 6:00 PM
Location: U-Save Market, was with mother, who reported victim missing 11/11/72
Last seen by Barbara Scerbo
Found by: Moore, Lex Frecrick WMA DOB: 8/11/52
Location: In ravine, Calistoga Rd., approximately 50 feet from roadway.
Condition of body: Fair, body was frozen due to extreme cold. However, victim had been dead for 1 to 2 weeks.
Cause of death - Dislocation of 1st and 2nd cervical vertebra, with compression and hemorrhage of spinal cord - due to trauma.
Scene of death - None. No clothing or personal property found. Victim did have two wire loops in pierced ears. No earrings attached.
Suspects - None
Crime Report #2752-78
Sexual assault - Negative.

July 31, 1973

1. DAVIS, Carolyn N. WFJ DOB: 12/3/58

Last seen: 7/15/73, Sunday, 1:50 PM.
Location - Hwy. 101 on ramp, Garberville, Calif.
Last seen by: Grandmother, Adelia Cook.
Body found: 7/31/73
Found by: Apel, Randal Lee WMA DOB: 11/21/46
Location, 2.2 miles north of Porter Creek Rd., on Franz Valley Road (same as Sterling and Weber)
Condition of body - state of putrification.
Cause of death: Strychnine poisoning.
Scene of death - None. No clothing found at scene or personal belongings.
Suspects - None
Crime Report #2823-94
Sexual assault - Unknown.

Zodiac-Like Knife Attack

On April 7, 1972, another secretary was stabbed savagely in the back and neck. The San Francisco authorities said the attack may have been committed by the psychopath, Zodiac.

It appears she had been followed from the courthouse in San Francisco to her home in Tamalpais Valley in Marin County. As she stepped from the bus and began walking, a light-colored car swerved, hit her, and knocked her down. It was 9:00 PM and dark.

Apparently she was not hurt but the driver got out of his car, apologized, and offered her a ride home. She refused and the man became enraged. "Please let me drive you home," he pleaded again and again—she refused. He became furious, pulled out a knife and began stabbing her. Alerted by her screams the neighbors went to her aid and the man jumped in his car and sped off.

Captain Ken Narlow of the Napa County Sheriff's Department said that Isabel Watson, 33, who had been rushed to the Marin General hospital, described the Zodiac to a "T" (perfectly), and he believed that Zodiac may have been her attacker, "better than a 50–50 chance."

INFORMATION BULLETIN

SAN FRANCISCO POLICE DEPARTMENT

NO. 61-73 HOMICIDES 08 AUGUST 1973

Between May 29, 1973 and July 15, 1973 the nude bodies of four females have been found in various locations in this city. The cause of death in all four cases is either strangulation or suffocation. In two cases the bodies were located in schoolyards and in the other two cases, one was found in Golden Gate Park and the other in an empty lot at the end of Galvez Street. Although the background of the deceased show no prior relationship there are strong similarities in their deaths. They were all relatively young, all were found nude, in two cases sexual activity was apparent and all were found after either a weekend or holiday.

TUESDAY, 29 MAY 1973, the day after Memorial Day, the body of Rosa Vasquez, WFA, 20 years, was found in Golden Gate Park above Arguello Drive. She was nude and dumped in that location. Autopsy revealed subject had sexual relations as seman was located in her vagina, rectum and mouth. Subject last known to be alive on 28 May 1973.

SUNDAY, 10 JUNE 1973 the nude body of Yvonne Quilantang, NFJ, 15 years, was found in an empty lot at the end of Galvez Street. She was last known to be alive on Saturday, 09 June 1973 and had allegedly left her foster home to purchase cigarettes. Just prior to her departure she was heard to be arguing with a male on the telephone.

MONDAY, 2 JULY 1973 the nude body of Angela Thomas, WFJ, 16 years, was found in the schoolyard of Benjamin Franklin Jr. High in the early morning hours. Subject was last known to be alive during the evening hours of 1 July 1973 in the Presidio of San Francisco and several hours later was identified as exiting a vehicle (A 1972-73 Plymouth Duster, dark blue, 2-door with black racing stripe on the rear) in a gas station on Lombard Street. At that time she was nude and asked attendant for key to washroom. The occupants of the automobile were two WMA's, one with dishwater blond hair, longish, early 20's, 5'10" to 6 feet. No further description on the other suspect.

SUNDAY, 15 JULY 1973 the nude body of Nancy Gidley, WFA, 24 years, was located in the parking area of George Washington High on the 30th Avenue side. As in the other three homicides, she had been deposited after the crime. She had arrived in San Francisco on Thursday, 12 July 1973, checked into the Roadway Inn at 895 Geary. She had spent that night in her room, but not Friday or Saturday. She claimed to be here to be Maid of Honor in a wedding; however, this information proved to be incorrect. This victim is missing an unusual type of hammered silver cross, celtic in nature, normally worn around her neck. Autopsy revealed subject recently had sexual intercourse.

All four cases have similar causes of death (manual asphyxiation), all were found nude and the crime scene was elsewhere than where the bodies were dumped. All identification and clothing is missing. All patrol units should pay particular attention to schoolyard areas during night watches and special attention given during weekends and holidays.

ANY INFORMATION:
Homicide Detail Phone: 553-1145
Inspectors McKenna/Podesta/
Coreris/Schneider
Refer Cases: #73042926/73046374/
7352131/73055838

DONALD M. SCOTT
CHIEF OF POLICE

(MISSING PERSON 7-15-74)

VALLEJO GIRL'S SKELETON IDENTIF

Ex-Policeman Has Tip Leading To Girl's Name

A skeleton found Tuesday in an open field at Columbus Parkway and St. John's Mine Road was identified tentatively Wednesday by Vallejo police as the remains of an 18-year-old Chinese girl from Sonoma.

Det. Richard Hoffman said the skeleton is presumed to be that of Deana Hooper who had been reported missing here last July 15 by her sister, Mrs. Tonna Albright, of 901 Georgia St., with whom she had been staying.

Hoffman said Mrs. Albright made the tentative identification after viewing the clothing and sandals found at the scene of the discovery and recognized them as her sister's. Hoffman said Mrs. Albright also identified the ruby-colored birthstone ring on the right hand as that worn by her sister when she disappeared here nine months ago.

Hoffman said the first clue to the skeleton's tentative identification came from Harold Thacker, a retired Vallejo police sergeant and now a criminal investigator at Mare Island.

Hoffman said Thacker supplied the name of the missing Chinese girl after reading yesterday's Times-Herald account of the discovery of the skeleton. Thacker told Hoffman he recalled talking to the missing girl's father at Mare Island when he had made inquiries at the shipyard after his daughter reportedly last had been seen there.

Hoffman said a check of Police Department records uncovered a missing persons report involving Deana Hooper which had been filed by her sister in Vallejo. Police immediately contacted the sister with the result the first lead to the skeleton's identity was developed.

Hoffman said confirmation of the identification rests with an examination of the Sonoma girl's dental charts which have been released by a Napa dentist for checking with the skeleton's teeth.

According to the missing person's report filed last July by Mrs. Albright, Hoffman said, her sister last had been seen on July 11 at the Enlisted Men's Club on Mare Island.

Hoffman said Mrs. Albright gave no reason for delaying the report of her sister's disappearance until July 15.

Hoffman said Deana Hooper and Tonna Albright had been adopted about eight years ago from an orphanage in Hong Kong by their foster father, Dean Hooper, a Caucasian ex-serviceman who now lives at 234 Thomson Ave., Sonoma.

Hoffman said he notified Hooper that the skeleton found here had been tentatively identified as his missing adopted daughter. According to Hoffman, Hooper confided he had suspected all along that Deana was dead after she disappeared without a trace last July and that Mrs. Albright's confirmation of the identification of the skeleton came as no surprise to him.

Hoffman said it is his belief the skeleton found Tuesday by an Oakland chiropractor and his 9-year-old son flying kites on the Azevedo ranch had lain in the field undetected since last June 12.

He indicated the location of the skeleton in high weeds 40 feet east of the nearest roadway would have made it virtually impossible for someone to see the remains unless a passerby stumbled by accident on the site.

Hoffman said the skeleton now is being examined by an anthropologist at the University of California at Davis in the hope of determining the cause of death.

Meanwhile, he said, the police investigation into the girl's disappearance and death is continuing.

DEANA HOOPER, 18
... Skeleton Identified

The Sacramento Union

It's Thursday, May 12, 1977 — 15¢

HOME EDITION

Parker slaying tied to others?

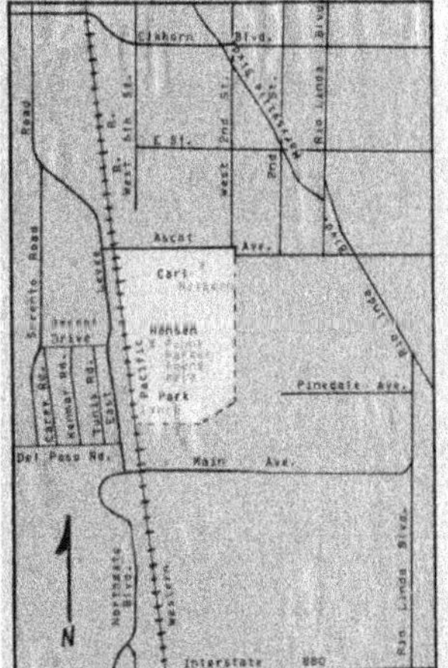

Where body of Penny Parker and two other recent murder victims were found.

Investigators probing the death of 15-year-old Penny Parker said Wednesday they are looking at the possibility her death could be related to the unsolved slayings of two other women whose bodies were found in the same North Sacramento field in the past seven years.

"We're not tying it in per se," said Sgt. Ray Bryers. "We are looking at the possibility (they could be connected) because they were found in the same general vicinity. We're not discounting it."

The Parker girl, a ninth grader at Las Palmas Junior High School, was last seen by her family about noon Saturday when she left her home at 209 Santiago Ave. to collect for her newspaper route. She was seen by an acquaintance about 5 p.m. riding her bicycle in a parking lot around the corner from her home. Her body, stabbed numerous times in the chest, was found about 7 p.m. Tuesday in the field north of Main Avenue and east of East Levee Road.

It was in a small depression adjacent to a water filled drainage canal. The area is in "very close proximity to where the others were found," Bryers said.

The other murder victims found nearby were Carol

—To A2, Col. 1

Penny Parker murder

Other slayings linked?

—From A1

Hilburn, 22, of Santa Rosa, whose nude body was found at the northeast end of the field on Nov. 14, 1970, and Susan Lynch, 22, of San Diego, whose body was found in a sandy grave along East Levee Road on July 31, 1971.

Lynch had been raped and beaten. Hilburn had been beaten and her throat was slashed. Parker was stabbed in the chest and had a superficial slice on her neck, coroner's officers said. It had not been determined if Parker had been sexually molested.

Meanwhile, police combed the fields where Parker's bicycle was found (just south of Main Avenue near railroad tracks on Sunday) and where her body was found north of Main Avenue.

Although he would not say what it was Bryers said additional evidence was found by the searchers Wednesday.

He indicated there is a possibility Parker knew her slayer. "We have found nothing to indicate she was taken in there forcibly. It's very possible it was someone she knew."

Parker's parents, Mr. and Mrs. Robert Parker, said their daughter was not the type to run away and friends of the girl said "she wouldn't even get in my car on a rainy day. That's the kind of girl she was. She wouldn't have taken a ride."

In order to defray funeral expenses a memorial fund has been established in Penny Parker's name at the Wells Fargo Bank, 1501 Del Paso Blvd. In addition funds are being raised at Las Palmas Junior High and Norte Del Rio High School.

2 — Times-Herald, Vallejo, Wednesday, Sept. 7, 1977

NEWS IN BRIEF

No Murder Clues

DAVIS (AP) — Police were without a suspect or a motive Tuesday in the murder of a woman whose body was found among packing crates in an apartment she had rented before starting a new teaching job.

The victim was identified by Yolo County coroner's deputies as Elizabeth Mary Wolf, 27, daughter of a Marin County physician.

She was stabbed about 12 times in the back. Police said there was no evidence of sexual assault or robbery.

The victim, a 1972 graduate of the University of California here, had completed further studies in the San Francisco area. She moved back to Davis over the weekend and was scheduled to start teaching Tuesday at Green Gate Center, a Yolo County school for deaf mutes in Woodland.

The coroner said she had been dead for 12 to 18 hours when her body was discovered Monday night by a former roommate, who had stopped by for a visit.

Like Penny Parker who was stabbed numerous times in the chest, she too may be a victim of the same deranged psychopath who was then working in his new Real Estate office in Davis. Did she find her new apartment at his place of business?

Did Mr. Tucker, living and working in Marin County for several years, know her father?

8 Wednesday, December 10, 1986

Suspect sought in slaying

By MICHAEL MALONE
Times-Herald staff writer

VALLEJO — Police are looking for a suspect in the apparent slaying of a Vallejo woman whose body was found along State Route 37 on Sunday.

Detective Ed McKee of the Solano County Sheriff's Department said the body of Belinda Vandeveer was discovered by local residents on Sunday afternoon at a location four miles west of Mare Island. Deputy Coroner Bill Braker said the woman had been shot, but refused to disclose details of the death.

McKee confirmed the woman had been shot but added, "We don't know for sure if the gunshot wound was the cause of death." He said the death is being investigated as a homicide.

McKee refused to divulge where the woman was shot or how many wounds she suffered, saying the release of such information might compromise the investigation. He also withheld a description of the weapon used in the crime.

Vandeveer's death is the second homicide investigation taken up by the Sheriff's Department in the last two months and is the fifth homicide in the unincorporated areas of the county this year.

Early in November, an immigrant farm worker, Luis Rodriguez Medina, 61, was bludgeoned to death in his home at a farm labor camp on Silveyville Road, near Dixon.

No new leads have turned up in the investigation of his death and no one has been arrested in the case.

Wednesday, December 10, 1986 5

Dec. 10
Another anniversary date!

TWO MURDERS ARE CITED IN THIS SHORT NEWSPAPER ARTICLE.

SILVEYVILLE ROAD IS THE REMOTE COUNTRY ROAD MENTIONED IN THE THREATENING NOTE RECEIVED BY KIMBERLY LAWRENCE. ANOTHER STRANGE COINCIDENCE?

The Zodiac Killer remains a mystery to police almost 20 years after brutally murdering an estimated 40 victims — some of them in Solano County.

But he isn't the only killer on the loose. The Solano County Sheriff's Department has been unable to solve 25 murder cases since 1968.

On Sunday, the Daily Republic chronicles the Zodiac killings and other unsolved murders.

Read about Solano County's oldest murder and the most notorious killings.

And find out why these crimes go unsolved.

Who knows? Perhaps you have some information locked away that can help unravel a secret investigation.

Only in the Daily Republic.

Date of Publication — April 27, 1991

Police warn of man trying to run women off rural roadways

CONTRA COSTA TIMES
JANUARY 1, 1994

An unknown man is apparently trying to run women off rural East County roads, warns the Contra Costa Sheriff's Department.

The department is warning women driving in that area to be careful and not stop for anyone. In three separate incidents, women driving alone have been threatened by another driver.

"We've had about three incidents in three months," said Sheriff's Sgt. Ed Johnson. "He comes up from behind, flashes his light and tries to turn them off the road."

The most recent incident occurred at 7:20 p.m. Wednesday. A Tracy woman driving on Marsh Creek Road saw a car come from behind and blink its lights. When the woman did not stop, the man driving the other car pulled alongside the woman's car and tried to force her off the road.

Similar incidents have occurred on Vasco Road and Route J4, after it splits from Highway 4.

The offending vehicle could be a dark-green sedan. However, night vision may have hampered witness descriptions, Johnson said.

"It's happened to women who have been riding alone at night," he said. "Women should try to avoid the area. If they have to go there, they should try to have someone with them."

Should they collide with another vehicle, don't stop, Johnson warned. Drive to the nearest public area where there are other people.

NOTE THE REFERENCE TO THE DARK-GREEN SEDAN.

MARSH CREEK ROAD IS A WELL-KNOWN SHORTCUT, FROM CONCORD TO BRENTWOOD AND IS USED A GREAT DEAL. CONNECTS TO HIGHWAY 4, AND BRANCHES OFF TO VASCO ROAD LEADING SOUTH TO INTERSTATE 580. MARSH CREEK ROAD TRAVELS ALONG THE BASE OF MT. DIABLO.

COMING UP FROM BEHIND AND FLASHING LIGHTS, THE SAME IDENTICAL TECHNIQUE USED ON ROUTE 680 FROM CORDELIA TO LAKE HERMAN ROAD.

Diplomatic reproduction

A little known fact in the December 20, 1968 killings of Betty Lou Jensen and David Faraday is a mysterious bold-type ad in the *Vallejo Times-Herald.*

The ad, ironically, appeared directly under the "Personals" section for Alcoholics Anonymous. The prophetic ad read in all capital letters:

"BETTY LOU--PLEASE LET ME HELP YOU.
CALL ME COLLECT ANYTIME AFTER
6:00 PM OR ON WEEKENDS.
916 925-7339 JANET WHITE"

Neither the police nor the local newspapers ever mentioned this to the public and it is likely they were never aware of this announcement.

We received this information approximately 11 years after a letter had been mailed to the local police on March 9, 1983, nearly 15 years after this tragic homicide.

Every attempt to track down the "Janet White" by name or phone was fruitless, and the author of this strange missive could not be located.

The ad ran for 3 days beginning on yet another anniversary date, December 10, 1068. (We have the ad.) It was December 10, 1969 that Leona Roberts was abducted and murdered.

THE PRESS DEMOCRAT, THURSDAY, DECEMBER 30, 1999

CRIMES OF THE CENTURY

Notorious acts changed face of county

Gamut of mob hits, lynchings

By RANDI ROSSMANN
Staff Writer

A killer stalked young women in Sonoma County, killing at least seven, but was never caught.

The serial killer, 1972

In the early 1970s, a serial killer was stalking young women in Sonoma County.

He killed at least seven and maybe several more, said sheriff's detectives who tired to solve the puzzling string of murders.

The first found was Kim Wendy Allen, 19, a Santa Rosa Junior College student who had disappeared while hitchhiking the day before her body was found near a creek bed in Bennett Valley. She'd been raped and slowly strangled.

Six other nude and decomposing bodies were found in rural areas northeast of Santa Rosa. The youngest victims were 12 and 13, students at Herbert Slater Junior High who had just finished an evening of ice skating. The oldest was 23, a married woman who was hitchhiking home.

Frustrated sheriff's detectives traveled the country researching whether serial killer Ted Bundy, or the Zodiac killer or the Hillside strangler in Los Angeles or others could have been responsible.

The cases were never solved.

"What keeps nagging at me are the seven little girls killed and nobody knows who did that," said Mullins. "The unsolved ones bother me the most."

[Diplomatic Reproduction]

XXVI

THE LIBRARY! WHO, ME?

Zodiac's "Mikado" letter of July 24, 1970, included a recitation from Gilbert and Sullivan's opera, *The Mikado*. However, because of the variations in the lyrics, Inspectors Armstrong and Toschi were convinced the Zodiac was reciting part of the opera from memory. Based on this frivolous and erroneous assumption, the two detectives spent a great deal of time finding and questioning, onetime Ko-Kos. They had a theory the Zodiac actually played this role in his younger days, perhaps as a student.

Beginning with San Francisco's own Gilbert and Sullivan theatre group, the two detectives tracked down every member of the cast, conducted interviews, obtained handwriting samples, and made physical comparisons to the official composite sketch. Days and weeks were spent on this wild goose chase. Why they limited their investigation to San Francisco was never mentioned or discussed.

Actually, there was a more logical theory they should have considered, but it never occurred to them. Zodiac's "Mikado" letter was filled with misspelled and bogus words, with some words and phrases missing entirely. If he was reciting this opera from memory, he would have known the correct words, and if he was copying the opera from the written word, he would not have made so many mistakes, if any at all. How then did he do it? It is not all that difficult.

It is my opinion the Zodiac was actually using a legal secretary's transcribing machine. The process is really quite simple. By recording the opera onto a small cassette tape, the person can then play it back while typing. The transcribing machine allows the typist to start and stop the tape whenever necessary.

However, the typist would make errors on words and phrases they could not clearly distinguish. A perfect example would be the word "POMPHIT," when the correct words were, "PUFF IT." Another example is "GIRL WHO NEVER KISSED," when the correct phrase was "THE LADY NOVELIST." Another, "IMPLORE YOU WITH IM PLATT," when the correct phrase was, "FLOOR YOU WITH EM FLAT." These are all mistakes based on hearing. Comparing the actual wording of *The Mikado* with the Zodiac's rendition; thirty-four mistakes were counted, and there are likely more.

It should be noted that a transcribing Dictaphone machine would be used extensively in most legal and other professional offices. As Tucker's wife was employed as a legal secretary most of her adult life, it would not be unusual for a busy secretary to have one in her own home.

There was another theory I wanted to explore, even though it was a long shot. This involved the nature of Zodiac's ciphers and codes. Having considerable code experience myself, I always felt Zodiac's work was too sophisticated for and totally foreign to military application. And unless someone is doing some serious research on the subject, they would not have his expertise. Therefore, just like the record, the Zodiac would need an excellent reference source to help him create professional ciphers.

Our suspect, of course, had the military background in code, and certainly had the aptitude, and this may have influenced his behavior. Indeed, the motive behind his killing spree was to gather evidence to prove his superiority, and his code-writing is but another gem in his psychotic crown of ego.

The next stage of testing my theory was to check our local libraries. Again it was a long shot, but a necessary one. I was shocked by what I found.

At the John F. Kennedy Library in Vallejo, there was a badly worn LP (long-playing phonograph record) of *The Mikado*. The due-date card on the album was permanently affixed, and the due dates showed the record had been checked out six times in 1968, three times in 1969; the very last time was March 17, 1970. I found the record in 1975. The John F. Kennedy Library had no books, whatsoever, on code.

In checking the Fairfield Civic Center Library, I found they did not have *The Mikado* record, but they did have an encyclopedic book on code—David Kahn's *The Code Breakers*, a large, detailed, and comprehensive analysis of literally hundreds of codes, ciphers, and symbols.

Like *The Mikado* LP, Kahn's codebook had its due-date card affixed permanently to it. The book had never been checked out before February 1968. It had been checked out seven times in 1968, and five times in 1969.

The person still had possession of the book on August 1, 1969, when Zodiac's three-part cipher-code, his first, was mailed to the newspapers. The book was due on August 20. It was not checked out again until January 1974, and not again until I found it in 1975.

But the best was yet to come. A writer creating pure fiction could not invent such a story as this.

The next logical step in this quest was to find out if our suspect had a library card. What I discovered was hard to believe. In perfect alphabetical order, I found our suspect's library index card. The card was typed by the librarian, which was the routine procedure in those days. Clearly typed was the last name and first name, in that order: Tucker, George.

Wow! I thought. *What a stroke of luck.*

When I looked at the signature on the bottom of the card, I was at first confused, surprised, and then bewildered. The name did not match the cardholder's name at the top of the index card. The signature was Tucker, Floyd. (Our suspect's middle name is Russell.)

I took the card to the librarian and asked her what the story was on the card. She opened her eyes widely, and tilted her head commenting, "I have never seen anything like this before."

I asked her, "Do you have any idea why a person would sign a different name?"

She said, "I cannot imagine why anyone would ever do anything like that."

I made a couple of photocopies of the card and examinations of the one name, Tucker, and it appeared to have been written by our own George Tucker. A positive match, however, could not be made.

Before continuing, pause and reflect on the significance of this discovery. There is only one obvious reason a person would sign a bogus name, a different name, on their library card—to conceal or disguise and hide their true identity. It matches the mystique and the paranoia, the profile of the Zodiac.

As in several other situations, the Zodiac has demonstrated his rationale. In his cleverness, he is always anticipating the worst-case scenario. He is brilliant enough to know there may always be some cop, detective, or FBI agent tracing *The Mikado* record or Kahn's codebook back to him.

While describing his bus bomb, he said, "I would send you pictures but you would be nasty enough to trace me back to the developer," etc.

Therefore, in the strategy and logic of Zodiac, he can say if ever accused, "Hey, that's not me, that is not even my signature, you guys are nuts."

And this is why he decided to cancel his membership in the Second Amendment Foundation, just to be safe—"They might check."

The following is a list of due dates on David Kahn's *The Code Breakers* and Gilbert and Sullivan's *The Mikado*:

The Code Breakers		***The Mikado***
	1968	
		02-05-68
02-13-68		02-17-68
		04-02-68
05-20-68		05-23-68
06-12-68		
07-12-68		
08-13-68		08-17-68
		09-03-68
10-14-68		
10-23-68		
	1969	
02-10-69		
		02-19-69
02-25-69		
03-12-69		
		03-22-69
04-01-69		
08-20-69		
		12-22-69
	1970	
		03-17-70

The book and the record were located in 1975. Neither the book nor the record had been checked out before the above-listed dates, and neither had been checked out after those dates. Both were checked out for the first time in February 1968. The due dates are remarkably similar. It appears the same person had possession of both during the same time periods. Zodiac is both: the code and cipher expert, and Ko-Ko, the Lord High Executioner in *The Mikado* (and Charlie Chan's nemesis in *Charlie Chan at Treasure Island*). With excellent reference sources, he is also a genius.

DATE DUE

May 20'68			
Jun 12'68			
JUL 12 1968			
AUG 13 1968			
OCT 14 1968			
OCT 23 1968			
Feb 10 1969			
Feb 25, 1969			
Mar 12, 1969			
APR 1 1969			
AUG 20 1969			

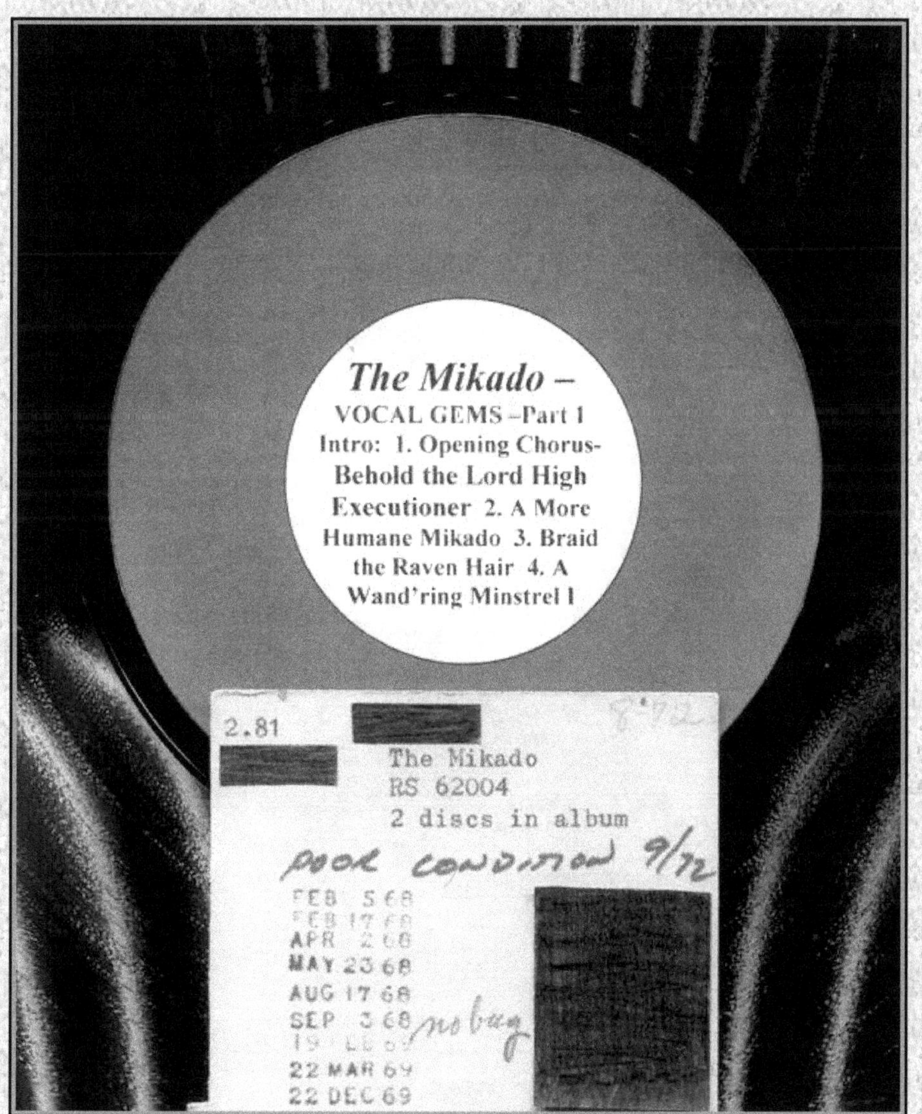
The Mikado –
VOCAL GEMS –Part 1
Intro: 1. Opening Chorus-
Behold the Lord High
Executioner 2. A More
Humane Mikado 3. Braid
the Raven Hair 4. A
Wand'ring Minstrel I
2.81
The Mikado
RS 62004
2 discs in album
poor condition 9/72
FEB 5 68
APR 2 68
MAY 23 68
AUG 17 68
SEP 3 68
no bag
22 MAR 69
22 DEC 69

XXVII

THE MOUNTAIN RETREAT

Only God and the Zodiac know how many victims may be rotting in the area surrounding Lia and Tucker's remote cabin in the mountains, near Weimar. It is so ironic that the local law enforcement, and a few members of the district attorney's staff enjoy free use of this isolated resort for their never-ending parties and drunken brawls. Several attend every year, but only the elite are ever invited. Never suspecting for a minute their good friend Lia had recently married an insane sociopath killer, they would never discover the few bones scattered by the animals in the deep ravines.

These annual gatherings were actually business meetings and "think tank" seminars, but of course, the wives were never invited. Catherine and her brother had inherited the property from their father, but in over twenty years, she had only been there four or five times. She hated the drive, and the dark chill of the night air.

Ever since the late-night surveillance, when the suspect drove home with his lights off, ending up three feet from my rear bumper, my partner was convinced that Tucker knew who I was. Jerry knew the suspect's wife had many connections, and at least one good friend in law enforcement, who could have run my license plate with no problem at all. This was all very true.

The prior incident, on that stormy night after dinner, was enough to make my blood curdle, but this new invitation was keeping me awake every night. I told my wife repeatedly, "Their invitation is totally bizarre. We are not actually friends. In fact, we barely know one another."

My wife countered by saying, "Lia and I are quite close. We have worked together for a long time. Besides, she thinks you are someone really special, and she likes you a lot."

"Bullshit," I said. "She doesn't know me any better than she knows her sick husband, 'El Psycho Grande.' I do know she hugs and kisses me like I am one of her long-lost lovers—a real phony bitch."

"She is a lovely person, you just don't know her."

"No, I don't, but *she* knows *me* well enough to ask me to spend the weekend with her overnight?"

During subsequent phone calls and another lunch, Lia explained, "Only a few people have been invited to the party, and if anybody wants to spend the night, they should bring their own mattress and sleeping bags. But, we are so close to Lake Tahoe, some might choose to stay there."

The party was scheduled for 2:00 PM, so there would be plenty of time to drive to Tahoe before it got dark. This last option made attendance more practical, as I knew from the get-go I would never spend the night in their cabin.

Double J called at least twice a week asking, "Are you going, are you going?"

Chuck Forrest called and told me for the second time, "Do not go to this party."

Another member of our crew, the district attorney, told me, "In my opinion, you should not go. I could give you some strong arguments why you should not go."

God, if I did not go, Jerry would never talk to me again.

Catherine had told my wife about the newly enclosed deck her husband had built onto the cabin, with a beautiful view of the river.

"A portion of the North Fork of the American River runs through the property," she said.

"My husband has been spending a lot of time traveling to and from the cabin. He just loves the mountains."

We were, of course, intrigued with the possible connection to missing females along the I-80 corridor, and the strange disappearance of Donna Lass. The record was clear. Strange murders occurred in areas wherever our suspect happened to go. Anomaly, chance, fate, or pure coincidence?

Dave Peterson, of the *Vallejo Times-Herald*, was the first person to alert us to the murder of a priest in the Weimar area, right around Halloween. The murder occurred on the property of a religious retreat named the Esoteric Society. The priest's collar had been discovered in the ashes of one of the cabin stoves. The police had not developed any leads in the investigation, and Peterson said, "I have reason to believe this might be a Zodiac murder."

Jerry wanted to check it out due to the occult connection, but his real motive was to pay a visit to our suspect's isolated cabin. We planned to conduct a photo lineup, and interview the management personnel at the Esoteric Society, if possible.

Dave Peterson was a truly nice man. He had been a news reporter for many years, and wrote a few articles on the Zodiac. In fact, his own obsession with the case unwittingly turned him into a Zodiac suspect. One of the local detectives advised his superiors, "Peterson is showing way too much interest in the case." He thought since Dave worked as the night reporter, and wore horn-rimmed glasses, and had an interest in the occult and astrology, he could be the killer.

Jerry and I had many discussions with Dave Peterson. In his later years, Dave co-authored a book attempting to make a connection to the Zodiac with a Gerald Davis and Charles Manson. Dave's theories are simply not supported by the facts in the case. Dave was basing a great deal of his suppositions on the San Francisco composite sketch, not a tenable argument. Additionally, Dave began a serious research into astrology, and was convinced that the Zodiac killings were all related to this nebulous field of knowledge. He was convinced the priest's murder at Weimar was a Zodiac killing.

Jerry and I paid a visit to Dave after he and his wife moved to a beautiful community on the coast, several years ago, and he did not look well.

The teachings of the Esoteric Society are based on the prophetic writings of the Bible, especially the book of Revelations, combined with astrology. This fraternity was founded in Boston in 1891. They practice meditation and farming, and publish books, which encourage the suppression of sexual activity. The Applegate Fraternity was established in 1898.

Our visit to the Esoteric Society was interesting, but uneventful. The resort itself, with the huge expansive views over sweeping meadows and the rolling foothills, is absolutely beautiful. Very old and majestic in its style, the main building built of old-growth redwood is truly grand. Two little ladies greeted us, along with an older man. While they were extremely polite and cordial, I had the eerie feeling Double J and I were making a commercial for *The Blair Witch Project*, as the setting was perfect. Both ladies were wearing long black dresses to the floor, and I know we were getting the "sorcerer's eye" from one of them.

After they escorted us into a small cozy room with a small fireplace, I couldn't help noticing they'd left the door cracked open about two inches. From time to time, I observed the older man peeking through the tiny opening. In a few minutes, after Jerry mentioned the word Zodiac, one of the ladies excused herself immediately, and I am certain she placed a call to their local Mounties. It was all very comical. Other than being placed under observation and followed by two plainclothes police detectives, our visit was uneventful. (I had made a note of the only car parked at the Esoteric Society, and it had current Utah license plates.)

We interviewed one witness, the lady with the "eye," and she stated, "The day before Halloween, at about 7:45 PM, I clearly heard six rapid gunshots."

As the victim was shot twice in the chest and once in the

forehead, it appeared the killer was making the sign of the cross. This was mentioned in one of the newspaper articles, which caught the attention of Dave Peterson.

Our trip to the cabin was impeded, in fact, canceled, by our unwanted and disturbing surveillance. Jerry was really upset by the police intrusion, as this *was* the primary reason we had driven such a long distance. The trip consumed a whole day.

The entire area was like a ghost town—deserted, dark, and gloomy. I spotted the undercover police car parked in the shadows on a side road as we drove away. When we reached the highway we stopped at a little café we had noticed earlier, to get something to eat. In about two minutes, the plainclothes cops pulled up in their conspicuous undercover car. They walked in and parked themselves at the extreme end of the counter. They sipped coffee, and our eyes made contact many times, but they never said a word. Such is life in the big city!

A week or so before the party, my wife and I made reservations to stay at our favorite motel at the state-line, The Inn By The Lake. Jerry was obsessed with his strategies and plan of attack. If one thing did not work, he had a backup. With his Virgo nature, he even began writing scripts, things I should say and do, and was driving me nuts.

The twisting road leading to their cabin was terrible. In a very short time, we knew why their family called it a "Confederate conspiracy." Yankee Doodle Dandy Road sounds as bad as it is. The fine powdery dust was so thick, we had to crawl at five miles per hour, close the windows, and turn off the air.

Eventually, after 1.2 miles of pure hell, we spotted the yellow ribbons hanging over the private driveway. Five cars were already parked in the small clearing, and we knew we had found their remote and isolated cabin. My stomach churned, but I had programmed myself into a mild state of dementia, forcing a relaxed and self-composed demeanor. I would be cool, and just play it by ear. Besides, I knew we would not be staying more than a couple of hours.

My wife knew one of our local attorneys and two ladies from the courthouse, one of whom she had worked with for about two years. It was old "home week" for my wife, but I did not know one person, except for Mr. Tucker and Catherine. As usual, Catherine, Lia, hugged me and gave me a peck squarely on the lips. She is most charming, and a very attractive lady. Unfortunately, like many women her age, she keeps her hair dyed in a God-awful mousy red, and it looks ridiculous.

Mr. Tucker was behind a bamboo bar mixing drinks, and he never looked up or acknowledged our presence in any way, even though we were standing not more than ten feet from him. My wife, outgoing butterfly that she is, nudged me to the bar.

"Happy Birthday, George!" we said in greeting. He looked at my wife and said, "Thank you," but never made the slightest eye contact with me. It was very awkward, but I extended my arm for a handshake and felt like a complete idiot.

He shook my hand while staring at my wife, asking her, "Would you like something to drink?" It was totally weird.

My face was flushed and I thought, *If he treats my wife like he is treating me, I will have to remind him what an outrageous asshole he is*. But I said nothing, and my wife was oblivious to it all.

Fortunately, Aurelia introduced me to a fine older gentleman, John Cunningham, a retired police chief of a small community in Yolo County. Although retired for ten years, he was one of the sharpest officers I ever met. We had some great conversation about law enforcement in general, crowded courts, and the necessary evils inherent in plea-bargaining. There was nothing about the Juan Corona trial he did not know. When he mentioned the attorney, Richard Hawks, and how he failed to present his case in defense of Corona, Mr. Tucker himself blurted into the conversation: "The police planted a note at one of the gravesites, and also the bloody knife. The so-called death list—the list of names—is phony bullshit."

While Cunningham and I were having a calm polite talk, Tucker's face became red, and he could not control or mask his anger. He even poked his index finger into the chief's chest (almost like he did that night outside his AA meeting) and said,

"Shoot the fucking cops—put them on trial where they belong, with the judges—you know, you know what I mean."

The chief glanced at me quickly, and I could read his mind like I knew he was reading mine: *This is one sick puppy here.* Even though he was engaged in conversation with another person, he had been listening to every word the chief and I had spoken. The chief walked away briskly, and I jiggled the ice in my glass saying out loud, "Good time for one more," and headed for the bar. Now everyone was mixing their own.

If the reader is familiar with the Juan Corona case, you would know our suspect had just mentioned a few of the most salient points of evidence. We know our suspect attended the trial quite often, and was there everyday during the handwriting testimony. The temptation for me to mention the Zodiac case was overwhelming. As smart as Tucker is, he was most likely amused by the fact I did not mention it. We have all experienced this phenomenon—when it is obvious a person will not or does not say something they should. In short, a normal response. If a person asks, "What time does the shuttle leave for the airport?" One might reply, "Where are you going?"

The cabin was built in 1899 as a hunting lodge and has six huge bedrooms downstairs, all bare of furniture, except one. It had a tremendous loft upstairs, which could sleep twenty or more. The newer additions consisted of an indoor bathroom and the enclosed deck with a fine wire-mesh screening. It was primitive, but actually very comfortable, at least for a short stay. The new Buckwood stove, with a metal flue extending to the loft area, did a great job of heating the entire cabin.

My attention, however, was drawn to a huge stone barbecue grill a short distance away. Catherine said, "This is my husband's pride and joy." (I have had occasion to roast a whole pig over a four-foot barbecue.)

Tucker's grill was huge, at least six feet long by three wide. A couple of us walked outside to inspect it, and on our heels was George. He showed us the chain and its gears, which lowered and raised the grill, and the enclosed propane tank. I looked down at the caked-ash residue, which covered nearly the entire surface of the grill grates. He must have cooked for a hundred guests.

It was nearly five o'clock when the birthday cake was cut and served. The chips and dip were fine, but my wife and I were starved. Tucker and a couple of his good AA buddies were cooking hot dogs and hamburgers on his monstrous grill, and I noticed one of them was getting smashed. I'd already seen him behind the bar at least three times. I walked over to my wife and pointed to my watch, and she understood I was ready to leave right now. I didn't know if any of the others had planned to spend the night or what, and I sure as hell didn't care. Lia pleaded with us to spend the night, "You could use one of the front bedrooms. I don't think anyone else is spending the night, and it would be really nice, just the four of us around a cozy fire. We could play bridge."

"I've never played bridge in my life," I said.

My wife mentioned, "We already have our reservation at Lake Tahoe." She inclined her head toward Lia, "Besides, his back is going into spasms again."

I noticed Tucker was nowhere in sight as I strolled casually over to the grill and picked up a hamburger bun. I opened my penknife, and while pretending to scoop up a piece of cooked meat, I scraped off some of the charred residue from the end of the grill and spread it on one of the buns. Going through all the motions, I wrapped the take-out burger in a couple of napkins. I told Lia, "A snack for the road," and she just smiled.

I never knew what to call Catherine, but before we left, I

was using her preferred name, Lia. She didn't seem to care, one way or the other.

We thanked her for the invitation, telling her, "We truly enjoyed seeing your quaint home here in the mountains. We had a really nice time."

I grabbed my wife's arm and we began walking down the dirt trail to their little parking area. Halfway down, we met George walking up the trail toward their cabin. We exchanged another handshake and told him, "We enjoyed your party." He looked at my wife and said, "You should spend the night."

I told him, "We are going to spend a couple of nights at Tahoe, but thanks for your generous offer."

As we continued, I whispered to my wife, "I sure as hell hope our car starts," which it did.

My wife said it first, "Do you think anyone else was actually invited to spend the night? Come to think of it, it was never mentioned in the invitation." She was reading my mind.

"There is a neat little café right by the road where we turned off to head into the mountains. Jerry and I stopped there when we came up here a few weeks ago."

"When the cops were following you?"

When we walked in, we were surprised to see the chief, John Cunningham, and his wife sitting inside. They began to laugh, and so did we. They had just ordered a hot roast beef sandwich with mashed potatoes, and we did the same.

Cunningham told us, "I have known Lia for a very long time. I first met her when she worked in the district attorney's office in Marysville. Then, when her only son was killed in a car crash, she became very ill, you know, she just lost it. The boy never knew his father, some guy she married in Sonoma. One day he just disappeared. Lia never talks about him or her son. It's a real tragedy because she is such a lovely person, she has a heart of gold."

My wife was shocked. She never knew about Lia's son. After we ate, the ladies visited the bathroom while Cunningham and I waited outside.

I said, "Chief, you're a cop, and you will always be a cop!"

"It's in the blood I guess; my dad was a cop, too."

"And I'm a cop. Let me ask you, strictly confidential. I bet you know a lot of cops who would have jumped all over his ass when he made those comments—right or wrong?" He knew exactly what I meant.

"Quite frankly, I can't remember a time when I wanted to smash somebody's face so badly, I was furious, and I just had to walk away."

"I know, I saw your reaction."

"That guy is—well, he's twisted somehow. We don't know if it's the booze, but we tried to tell Lia this, long before they ever got married. My wife can tell you, something is terribly wrong there."

"You saw him by the car when you left?"

"No, the last I saw of him he was still cooking the burgers, but then he went inside. Why?"

"You and your wife got here about, what, five minutes before we came in?"

"Yeah, it was maybe five minutes."

"It's no big deal. My wife and I met him walking back up the trail, and I just wondered what the hell he was doing down there. Well, you and your wife opted not to spend the night either, huh?"

"Oh, I never knew anything about that, but I wouldn't stay anyhow because we have too much to do tomorrow, and we have to get home. But just between you and me, I wouldn't want to spend the night with that guy—nowhere, no time."

Judith Anne Hakari

The case of the mysterious button (see last insert in Chapter XX of the button).

In Chapter XIII there is one homicide listed with the date of March 7, 1970,—Sacramento. The details of the abduction and murder of a beautiful young nurse, age 23, Judith Anne Hakari, are quite remarkable.

(As a side note, her apartment was only one block away from the court reporter, Nancy Bennalack, and each was in direct view from the other.)

In Tucker's personal profile, a considerable amount of information was not revealed.

However, as several young female homicides were either nurses or worked at hospitals, the following narration should be told:

After Tucker's discharge from the US Air Force in 1945, he persisted in an on-going battle with the Department of Veteran Affairs. Therefore, while there is no hard evidence, it is not unlikely that he had sought medical attention at both the Presidio in San Francisco (Donna Lass 9-26-70), and the Sutter Memorial Hospital in Sacramento, CA.

Hakari left work on March 6 at 11:30 PM, and drove home in a huge storm. The next morning her car was found in her parking space at 1740 Markston Road. Her car door was ajar. Evidence shows she did not go meekly as buttons, ripped off her raincoat, were found on the rear floorboard. She was then placed or forced into another car.

On April 26, 1970, she was found by hikers in a shallow grave near an old cabin, two or three miles West of Weimar, CA. She had been placed in a white laundry bag. She had been strangled, and had her pantyhose still wrapped around her neck, still in her uniform and raincoat, and still wearing a very expensive ring.

Yes, Mr. Tucker was obsessively disturbed by his advancing age, and he was celebrating another birthday—precisely. It was unknown whether or not she had been sexually molested.

Did the button we found in Tucker's car come from her

raincoat, or perhaps her nurse's uniform? We are still checking.

The detectives from Placer County and the Sacramento County Sheriff's Depts. believe there was/is a connection with the murders of both Nancy Bennalack and another nurse, Donna A. Lass of South Lake Tahoe ("Peek Thru the Pines").

Similar to Cecelia Ann Shepard, Bennalack had been stabbed over thirty times, and had not been sexually molested.

XXVIII

SAN FRANCISCO POLICE DEPARTMENT

From the moment Inspector Dave Toschi began telling lies about me in 1971, spreading the rumor I had somehow "invented" a suspect, to the recent confrontation I had with Inspector Michael Maloney, I now realize why we had moved from San Francisco. We did not want our daughter to suffer the stigma of being born in this liberal, deviant community of immoral lifestyles.

In February 2003, the San Francisco PD was under serious investigation with grand jury indictments, and possible intervention by the California Attorney General's Office. These indictments are now purely allegations, but the evidence appears valid and compelling.

On March 1, 2003, the bold headlines of the *San Francisco Chronicle* stated that the San Francisco PD was under indictment, a shocking revelation to the entire state of California. They were being charged with a "Conspiracy to Obstruct Justice," involving the chief of police, his top deputy and five other police officials.

So we ask ourselves, *Can we depend on them to tell us the truth about the Zodiac DNA—or anything else?*

December 7, 1941, was not the only day of infamy in our recent history. In the Zodiac case, there was a day so outrageous and so unbelievably disgusting, every cop in San Francisco should have hung their head in shame.

On November 6, 2001, a special news bulletin was released on San Francisco PD's recent work on the Zodiac DNA examinations. The TV crew was in the lab of San Francisco PD, and they were showing a few of the actual Zodiac letters and envelopes, all neatly protected in sheets of plastic.

Suddenly, the camera panned a Zodiac letter, revealing an excellent palm print. The details looked remarkably clear. Either the lab technician or one of the detectives casually mentioned the palm print did not match Arthur Leigh Allen's palm prints. *This critical piece of evidence had never been revealed.*

For over 30 years the San Francisco PD had never mentioned any palm print. The DOJ has never recorded a San Francisco PD palm print in their Zodiac evidence file.

I called Jerry immediately, and he had seen the same news. Like me, Jerry was shocked. Considering the palm print lifted from the phone booth in Napa on September 27, 1969, was perhaps the most valuable evidence to ever surface in the entire Zodiac case, Capt. Narlow would have jumped out of his socks to make this comparison. It's almost unbelievable that he knew nothing about San Francisco PD's palm print.

When Jerry called him a few days after the news bulletin, he asked, "Do you know whether or not your phone booth palm print had ever been compared to San Francisco PD's palm print?"

Narlow said, "I have no idea."

In Robert Graysmith's farcical fairy tale *Zodiac Unmasked* (2002), he mentions Dave Toschi's chagrin as Toschi wonders why the Vallejo detectives never attended any of the DOJ task force meetings in Sacramento. Now we must wonder if Capt. Narlow ever attended any of these meetings because Graysmith states,

> "The San Francisco Police Department has never heard of any Captain Narlow."

Fearful of severe incriminations by the Attorney General's office and the DOJ, the Solano County authorities concealed our suspect's identity by failing to attend the Zodiac task force meetings. Undoubtedly, this too was a major factor in their desperate, but futile, attempts to prove the case against Arthur Leigh Allen. While Lt. Jim Husted had developed a sincere and dedicated interest in our suspect, it appeared that he, too, was ordered to avoid Jerry and me and terminate his investigation of our suspect. (Many years later, Detective James Dean, Husted's partner, confirmed this as being absolutely true.)

From all indications, the San Francisco PD has no interest at all in the Zodiac case. We know because they have actually told us on more than one occasion.

On March 3, 1971, Inspector Toschi mailed me a short note that said, "The Zodiac could be as old as fifty years of age."

Months later Toschi was telling other investigators I had created the entire story, and went out and found a suspect who matched the description, a man about fifty. I was totally shocked by his ridiculous remarks, and I simply could not imagine anyone actually being that ignorant. Yet, one would think, if he had any brains at all, he could have simply picked up the phone and called me. Before I ever heard his remarks about me, I did have another phone conversation with him telling him a few things about our suspect and asking, "Are you interested in reviewing my notes?"

He said, "I can't step into your case."

Thirty-two years later, Inspector Michael Maloney, San Francisco PD, told me the same thing. They know absolutely nothing about our suspect, *and they do not want to know.*

In 1995, our meetings were continuing at Lyons Restaurant in Fairfield, at least twice a month. Our agenda at this particular time was to try to prove, once and for all, that Arthur Leigh Allen was not the Zodiac.

Jim Lang, Deputy District Attorney for Solano County,

was working with the Vallejo PD in their obsessive determination to file charges against Allen. Jim told them, "You have no evidence, and no case at all against Allen."

Lang told us, "I told the Vallejo PD to focus their attention on *your suspect* because they would have a much stronger case." As time passed, we had convinced Lang the only way to clear Allen's name was through a DNA analysis. Arthur Leigh Allen died in October 1992.

Within a few months, Lang reported, "I have discussed your proposal with Captain Roy Conway (Vallejo PD), and he agrees it is an excellent suggestion." There was no doubt in Conway's mind the Vallejo PD could then take official credit for resolving the Zodiac case, and at the same time redeem their integrity with the public-at-large. They could boast by saying, "See, we told you all the time, he was the Zodiac."

When Jim Lang met with us again a few weeks later he said, "Conway has talked with Lt. Tom Bruton of the San Francisco PD, and they agree to the DNA examinations."

It was the last time we met with Jim Lang. He did not look well, and we couldn't believe how he saturated his food with salt. A couple of years later we heard he had passed away.

It was on February 2, 1996, when a brand-new special series on Channel 5 was announced. Dave McElhatton, their announcer, informed the world he would be having monthly specials on the Zodiac killer, focusing especially on the DNA testing by the San Francisco PD. Now we saw our plans and strategies were successful. Such examinations should have been done years earlier, and we felt especially proud we were instrumental in this investigative process. (DNA examinations had never been discussed previously.) There is no doubt in my mind–Jim Lang never mentioned us to Capt. Conway, but it truly does not matter one way or the other.

Another strange event occurred. Dave McElhatton's special lasted about three months and then–ZAP. Without a word of explanation, his Zodiac special came to a screeching halt. Even though he was on the nightly news, he never said a word about the cancellation of his special program.

Jerry and I had met with the FBI at their offices in San Francisco in 1994. There was speculation San Francisco PD began their DNA examinations at the request of the FBI. Some were saying the Zodiac and the Unabomber could be one and the same. As Jerry and I had maintained extensive files on the Zodiac case, we had compiled a long list of technical information we thought they might like to have. Neither Jerry nor I actually believed there was a connection between the Zodiac and the Unabomber, but there were several circumstantial indicators, which were intriguing.

Early in 1997, perhaps January or February, a female lab technician at San Francisco PD failed in her attempts to find any DNA on the Zodiac envelopes.

In March 1997, another technician, David Allen Keel, did obtain DNA from one of the envelopes.

In this same month of March, Inspector Richard Adkins, San Francisco PD, obtained brain tissue specimens of Arthur Leigh Allen from Jim O'Brien, Coroner of Solano County. These DNA cells would be compared with the DNA found on the Zodiac envelope. Shortly it was announced there was a strong possibility of a match being found, but this had not yet been confirmed.

In April 1997, a forensic expert from Foster City determined that a match did NOT exist. This same expert was successful in further tests, and stated definitively he found DNA cells on the envelope.

On April 23, Jerry had a lengthy conversation with Inspector Richard Adkins, who finally confided to Jerry, *"Arthur Leigh Allen has been eliminated—he is not the Zodiac."*

Double J was ecstatic; he could not believe his ears. Jerry then asked him, "Would you like to have our suspect's DNA to match with Zodiac's?"

"Yes!"

They would start from scratch, and if there was a match with our man, he would call Jerry immediately.

"You'll be the first to know."

Jerry was "on Cloud Nine," and he called me immediately with the good news. Truly, it was not very exciting for me because I always knew Allen was not the Zodiac, plain and simple.

Some call it a tap dance; some call it smoke and mirrors—now you see it, now you don't. More strange things began to happen.

On May 2, a full nine days after Jerry talked with Adkins, Jerry made a phone call and was informed that Inspector Adkins was on vacation. Jerry thought, *That's strange, Adkins never mentioned he was taking a vacation.*

On Monday, May 5, Adkins called Jerry at 10:00 AM and advised, "There is no match with your man and the Zodiac's DNA. The DNA differed on three of five categories."

Jerry asked, "Does that mean our guy does match two of the five?"

Adkins did not reply to that, and said, "We checked out only one Zodiac envelope for DNA."

It seems incredible! The lab technicians themselves, or at least their supervisors, would realize the absolute importance of establishing a positive known sample. This procedure is absolutely necessary to confirm the authenticity of the DNA being compared. They can assume any cells discovered on an envelope or stamp belong to the Zodiac, but unless you verify a positive match between at least two sources, they will never know for certain. It would appear the entire process is seriously flawed. In running a person through the breathalyzer, to determine their BA (blood alcohol) level, the officer must first check and measure a known sample to make certain the machine is calibrated and in perfect working order. Without this critical first step, the officer cannot testify with any degree of credibility, and he will most likely lose his drunk-driving case. In fact, most of the time, a sharp defense attorney will ask the officer to produce the calibration chart, as this confirms the check has been performed.

Jerry called Adkins again on May 7 and provided the telephone number of the retired Capt. Narlow, for Adkins had told Jerry he wanted to check out Narlow's Zodiac suspect also. Jerry also gave him the phone number of the Escalon PD, so Adkins could attempt to locate retired Detective Harvey Hines.

Hines's suspect, Kane, was never a viable one as far as Jerry and I were concerned. We spent many hours with Harvey Hines reviewing his material at his home. Poor Harvey Hines! He was very passionate about his case against Kane. He told us, "Fred Shirasago (DOJ, Sacramento) and I hate one another. He hates my guts immensely."

Harvey showed us his code work on Zodiac's "MY NAME IS," the 13-character cipher, and he explained the three 8's used in the code: "As there are three 8's, you simply multiply three times eight and get twenty-four. My suspect Kane was born in 1924."

What could we say? Well of course, Jerry and I were totally unimpressed. Hines was convinced this was the full message contained in this short code, and in his mind this was a strong factor in his entire investigation.

He told us, "Shirasago has told me repeatedly not to bother him again."

Hines told us how he had gained the confidence of a local TV station, and with cameras rolling stormed into a bar where Kane was sitting. The situation became very explosive as Hines confronted Kane, accusing him of being the Zodiac. It was poor Harvey Hines who checked out the ritualistic site in Lake Tahoe, alleging this was the burial site of Donna Lass. Lass had mysteriously disappeared from one of the Tahoe casinos.

While Jerry and I have been accused by the Vallejo PD of having tunnel vision, devoting all our time to only one suspect, we know how critical it is to stay focused on reality. Many armchair sleuths have simply gone round the bend trying to prove their suspect is the Zodiac.

As the years rolled by, Darlene Ferrin's younger sister, Pamela Huckaby, eventually found Harvey Hines. Jerry and I would learn years later that Pamela obtained our suspect's name from him. Pamela had spent the entire night reviewing Hines's reports and other material, when she discovered the information we had left with him. Jerry and I were furious, as Pamela was totally unpredictable. We were chagrined to think Hines would be so careless.

Inspector Adkins told Jerry, "I called the Escalon PD and was informed Harvey Hines has either moved to the Midwest or down South. They have no idea how to make contact with him."

I told Jerry a couple of weeks later, "Call Narlow and ask if Adkins ever called him." Jerry called and Ken said, "No, I have not received any calls from San Francisco PD."

On June 4, 1997, the *San Francisco Chronicle* printed a disconcerting article revealing the demotion and investigation of two veteran police detectives, Vincent Repetto and Richard Adkins. The article stated, "The two detectives will be removed from street investigations, and will be assigned administrative duties pending results of a bookmaking probe."

Simultaneously, a fraud supervisor, Lt. Tom Bruton, was assigned to the Zodiac case.

Approximately six months passed, and the remaining members of the Mandamus Seven continued to meet as we had done for many years.

On January 26, 1998, Lt. Bruton returned Jerry's phone call and revealed shocking news: "The Zodiac envelope used for testing was not an authentic envelope. Therefore, all known suspects are still viable. We are in the process of testing another envelope, but are having no luck whatsoever."

Bruton advised Jerry, "I have never heard of your suspect, and, in fact, the San Francisco PD has never heard of Capt. Kenneth Narlow, and I know nothing about his suspect, either. Would you send me your suspect's prints and any handwriting you might have?"

Jerry called me immediately, and I told Jerry, "Tell Bruton, we will hand-carry our material to him, and have him sign for the material. This would be a good door-opener for us, to meet him in person."

When Jerry returned Bruton's call suggesting a personal meeting, Bruton became very hesitant, making a comment, "Well, I'm very busy, and I will let you know if my schedule permits."

I told Jerry, "Don't send him a damn thing."

Needless to say, Bruton never called Jerry to schedule an appointment. Bruton's attitude was very strange. He asked for our man's prints and handwriting, but he did not want to meet with us in person. Why would he not want the particulars of our case? Was it possible they were withholding something from us, something very important? Did they actually see some potential for a possible DNA match with our suspect?

During this same time, Jerry and I met again with Dr. Edward T. Blake, a forensic serologist who owned a private business, Forensic Science Associates in Richmond, California. We invited Dr. Blake's assistant, Jennifer, to have lunch with us, as she was the person who actually ran our suspect's DNA. When we related the convoluted story the San Francisco PD was giving us about the DNA, I asked her, "Can you think of any reason whatsoever that the San Francisco PD would lie to us?"

She replied, "Yes, I can. They do not want you to know what they are doing."

Incredible! However, I believe there are many reasons why they would be elusive. The San Francisco PD cannot afford to tell us the truth because they would be charged with criminal malfeasance and be unable to defend their neglect. The media coverage would crucify them, and the family members of 37 murder victims would be enraged. Considering I brought our suspect to Inspector Toschi's attention around March 1971, this is a reasonable conclusion. Additionally, in solving the case, the San Francisco PD would never share the credit with anyone.

We ask again, "Which Zodiac envelope was the bogus envelope they tested?" They're not telling. We assume it is either the envelope from the 1974 letter or the 1978 letter. There is a strong opinion within the San Francisco PD that their esteemed Inspector Dave Toschi is the true author of these two letters. Toschi, of course, denies that, but he does admit previously writing other letters. However, the ones he admits to were never intended or designed to be Zodiac letters, and the San Francisco PD is well aware of this.

Is it true that because of these "alleged Zodiac letters," Toschi was removed from the Zodiac case in humiliation and assigned to the pawnshop detail? He and his partner Armstrong had already become bitter enemies, and we heard from other credible sources that Detective Armstrong would never talk to Toschi again.

Over the next couple of years, Jerry became *persona non grata* with our female lab assistant at Forensic Science Associates in Richmond. We can only guess that she might have received some backlash from San Francisco PD or perhaps her boss. In any event, she became inaccessible and refused to return Jerry's calls.

In this DNA episode, we should mention that neither Richard Adkins nor Lt. Bruton ever made contact with retired Capt. Narlow. Apparently, San Francisco PD has no interest in comparing their DNA results with any other Zodiac suspect—not then, not now.

On October 5, 1999, Jerry and I paid another visit to Forensic Science Associates Lab in Richmond, and Dr. Blake was not exactly enthused to see us, not happy at all. Jerry had sent Dr. Blake a letter, but he hadn't read it yet.

David Allen Keel, the former lab expert at San Francisco PD, was now employed by FSA (Forensic Science Associates), and this was the real reason we were there. Jerry asked if we could speak with him.

Sternly, Dr. Blake replied, "No." It was really embarrassing. "Keel is absolutely swamped and too busy for us to disturb him."

"We just wanted to confirm something, to get clarification on the DNA work Keel performed in San Francisco," said Jerry.

"OK," Dr. Blake relented.

In about five minutes, a pale and mild-looking man, 5'9" to 5'10" tall, thin with black hair, about 35 to 38 years of age, walked into the library. We introduced ourselves, shook hands, and Keel was very cordial, but obviously very tense. I had the feeling he thought, *Are they getting ready to arrest me for something, after they advise me of my rights?* Keel's manner was guarded, his posture very stiff, and it was obvious he was studying Jerry and me intently, wondering, *Who the hell are these guys?*

Jerry gave Keel a quick summary of our backgrounds and involvement in the Zodiac case, making reference to our dealings with Richard Adkins and Lt. Bruton.

I asked Keel, "Were there at least two envelopes that had been matched together in order to authenticate the 'known' sample?"

Jerry asked, "How did you know the envelope you tested was bogus?"

Keel relaxed a little, got a smirky smile on his face, and said, "I did all the work on the envelopes on my own time, and I brought everything with me. I have it all." He continued, "The 1974 and 1978 letters were written by Toschi, but he will not cooperate and give us any body fluids so we can test his DNA. We can't have somebody follow him all day long, waiting to catch him spitting."

"The '74 and '78 envelopes were full of DNA cells; but all the rest, the earlier letters, it's almost like they were sealed with tap water because there were virtually no cells at all." I asked,

"Did the '74 and '78 envelopes match each other?"

Keel said, "Yes, they did match."

He seemed very reluctant, very reserved when he gave the answer. After several more minutes of dialogue, most of it pointless, Jerry asked, "Were the results the same on the '74 and '78 envelopes?"

Keel replied, "No, they did not match."

Hello? What did he just say? During this confusing interview, Jerry showed Keel the George Pimental note and said, "This is why we wanted the Pimental envelope checked against our suspect's DNA."

Then, as he is inclined to do, Jerry became very theatrical and in his typical impression of Jonathan Winters or Andy Devine (it could be Tim Conway), he began to explain the name carved on Pimental's abdomen, and I nearly fell out of my chair. It is certainly no big deal, but as I was the one who ended up with the enlarged color photos, and upon examining them carefully with a magnifying glass, I am the one who discovered the name. Truly, it means absolutely nothing, but when Jerry told Keel, he was shocked when he saw the name. I could not believe it. Jerry continued to talk over me, just like I was not even there. Oh well! That's Jerry.

This meeting was cordial, and I think Keel almost smiled once. Keel did not know us at all, and most likely had never heard our names. It was my distinct feeling he did not want to talk to us at all. I was left with the feeling, *Here is a man I do not trust*. Just before we left, almost like an afterthought, Jerry asked, "Were the results the same on the '74 and '78 envelopes?"

Keel replied, "Yes, they were the same."

It was like a man asking a stranger, "What time is it?" And the stranger says, "How do I know, I don't even live around here."

Perhaps bewildered, or working too hard, possibly confused, Keel reversed his statement again, for the third time. At lunch Jerry asked me, "Are my ears going bad or what?

Didn't Keel say the results were different, and then later say they were the same?"

"That is what I heard, too."

Sometimes I truly worry about my partner Double J. He once confessed, "My memory is not what it was a few years ago."

I told him, "Mine is better than ever."

As we had not yet asked Commander Slaight to listen to our tape, Jerry agreed there was nothing to lose. In 1969 Slaight was working as a dispatcher for the Napa PD. He is the one who actually talked with the Zodiac on the night of September 27, 1969, when Zodiac stabbed Cecelia Ann Shepard to death.

Jerry never knew how angry he made me when he asked, "Do you have the tape in your hot little hands? If not, call me back when you do because I don't want egg on my face."

This was totally out of character for the affable and mellow Jerry Johnson.

I had to remind him, "In the hundreds of times we have met over the past 26 to 27 years, I have never come unprepared or been one minute late."

I had a few other pointed comments, which serve no purpose here and now.

Driving home after our interview with Allen Keel I told Jerry, "I have a letter from Dave Toschi with the envelope seal intact. Keel might want to check this envelope for Toschi's DNA cells."

As Keel indicated, Toschi had refused to cooperate with their request for body fluids. Jerry thought this was a great idea.

When Jerry got home and called him about Toschi's sealed envelope, Allen Keel sounded extremely interested telling Jerry, "Send it to me."

I told Jerry, "Keel will have to maintain a legal chain of custody, and sign for it in person."

Keel told Jerry, "I will get back to you a little later in the day."

Jerry left his home and when he returned found a bizarre message on his phone recorder. We have listened to this tape many dozens of times. This is Mr. Keel, word for word:

> Mr. Johnson, this is Allen Keel at Forensic Science Associates, uh—I just spoke to you in regard to, uh—to a potential reference sample to Inspector Toschi and, uh—I had forgotten we had already eliminated Mr. Toschi by means of an envelope from his uh, uh, from his records in San Francisco that was provided by Lt. Bruton. So, uh, it's not necessary to, uh, drop by the envelope, we already know the answer to that question, and we have in fact, uh—it does?—doesn't? match with the 1978 letter, and he actually admitted writing it. So that's pretty much it, updating and I was just, uh—had not remembered properly what, what we had done in regard to, uh—that issue. So thanks a lot, see you later.

Allen Keel's message was strange indeed. Did he call Lt. Bruton after we left? Did Bruton tell Keel what to say? His comments sounded like he was reading notes he had made. His statement, "We had already eliminated Mr. Toschi," is perplexing. They had eliminated Toschi, meaning he did not write the '78 letter? If that's true, then it would appear Keel did, in fact, say, "It doesn't match with the '78 letter."

Then to add "he actually admitted writing it" does not make any sense at all. And if Keel was actually making reference to the 1974 letter, he never said so.

When *Primetime* aired its Zodiac special in October 2002, it announced the San Francisco PD had recently completed a successful DNA test, and Arthur Leigh Allen had been eliminated as a Zodiac suspect once and for all. Two more suspects had also been cleared: one a prominent San Francisco businessman, and the other from back East. But in a surprise twist, the very next day, the Vallejo PD criticized and debunked San Francisco PD in a major newspaper article stating,

"Their work on DNA was flawed, and Arthur Leigh Allen is the Zodiac."

And the most ridiculous of all, the Zodiac expert Robert Graysmith stated, "The DNA results prove what I have been saying for years, Arthur Leigh Allen, the Zodiac, had a partner who wrote all the letters and sealed all the envelopes."

Rod Serling, move over! These people have just moved here from *The Twilight Zone*.

"Change a man against his will, he's of the same opinion still." Do not confuse us with the facts; Allen was the Zodiac.

A few days after *Primetime* made its blockbuster announcement, I talked with Inspector Michael Maloney, San Francisco PD. In one of his more congenial moments (I must have ruined his whole day) he told me, "The public announcement on the DNA was premature."

I asked him, "Are you actually saying the DNA tests were not valid?"

He paused a few seconds and said, "Yes."

Finding and lifting reliable cells for DNA testing has been an enormous challenge. Methods and procedures vary greatly from one lab to the next, from the FBI to local police departments. Yet, there exists another monumental problem, one we have selectively ignored over the years. It is a sad state of affairs to confess our fragile position, and it is one I have attempted to explain to my partner on a few occasions. If we can assume the San Francisco PD has, in fact, made an accurate and reliable DNA analysis from the Zodiac envelopes and stamps, which they claim sufficient to eliminate a few markers, but not sufficient enough to make a positive match to any suspect, then we still have a major dilemma.

Do you remember when Detective Philip Vannater was walking around with OJ Simpson's blood evidence in his briefcase? Do you recall how the forceful Barry Scheck and the other members of the "Dream Team" challenged this evidence? Well, our situation is much more egregious.

The legal phrase "fruit of the poison tree" refers to any kind of evidence, which was obtained covertly or unlawfully. It is a violation of a person's Fourth Amendment rights, an invasion of privacy, and illegal search and seizure. There are many sound reasons for the law. In our case, we have no proof our specimen is actually from our suspect. We have been assured it is, of course, but we could never prove it in a court of law. Our source can never be revealed. And from the initial change of hands, we do not have a recorded chain of custody. Even if our suspect's DNA matched the Zodiac's perfectly, it would be thrown out as inadmissible anyway—"fruit of the poison tree."

Michael N. Maloney, Homicide Inspector for San Francisco PD, retired after 30 years of service. He died on February 11, 2007, at the young age of 58. With 800 leads to pursue on his assigned 50 homicide cases, he and his partner attempted to work on the Zodiac case in their spare time and weekends. To their dismay, their supervisor intervened, ordered the case closed, and told Inspector Kelly Carroll, "Close the case and never respond to questions about it in the future from anyone, forever."

Based on his personal commentary given to a popular web-site on November 9, 2005, Maloney said, "The Zodiac case will never be solved until my boss is removed from his official status as manager of the homicide unit."

Maloney was depressed and disgusted with the unscrupulous behavior of his ego-infected supervisor. This perhaps explains his curt manner when I talked to him in 2002.

Maloney also stated, "My supervisor knew very little about the complex Zodiac matter," but even Maloney was unaware of critical evidence in the case. He asked, "Did the same person touch or lick all of the envelopes? If not, how many other traces of DNA are we dealing with?"

Obviously, Maloney knew nothing about the analysis of their principal DNA forensic specialist, David Keel, who told us in person, "There were absolutely no cells on the envelopes whatsoever."

Keel still had the envelopes in his possession even though he had left the San Francisco PD and was then working for Dr. Blake at Forensic Science Associates in Richmond, CA. Furthermore, Maloney did not even want to see our case file.

With the recent scandal and investigation of the San Francisco PD's crime laboratory, April 2010, it is quite apparent that any DNA evidence in the future will be regarded with suspicion, most likely tainted, and untrustworthy. Hundreds of cases are now in limbo while other drug offenders, prosecuted and sentenced to prison, are being released.

An agent with Naval Intelligence reported to one of his colleagues and one of our Mandamus Seven group, "I observed an old cardboard box littering a hallway in the San Francisco PD's homicide unit containing Paul Stine's shirt." He further commented, "A janitor could have very easily picked it up and thrown it in the garbage."

It's not just the theft of evidence, but the critical chain of evidence, required by law, which the San Francisco PD was *not* in compliance with.

XXIX

ROBERT GRAYSMITH

Graysmith's second book about the case, *Zodiac Unmasked*, seems worth reading to a lot of people. Every Zodiac expert, especially those armchair website, chat-room, half-witted savants, must buy the book for their collection.

Literary license is one thing, but when important matters are presented falsely, the author has stepped over the line. Whether Graysmith is lost in his quagmire of notes or just confused, he has distorted a few facts. One of the "alleged interviews by other detectives" Graysmith refers to was actually conducted by my partner and me. He related it word for word from some of our official reports over the years. Furthermore, his account of Arthur Leigh Allen's fight with "the Marines on a San Francisco street" is entirely bogus. The fight took place on Marin Street in downtown Vallejo.

One night, shortly after I received my driver's license at age 17, I was driving home from a movie about 10:00 PM. As I passed Frank's It's Rich Café on Marin Street, I saw four or five punks in civilian clothes walk out and surround Lee as he walked up the sidewalk. I pulled over to the edge of the street, and then backed up thinking, *I will get out and help Lee because I know these guys are going to kick the crap out of him.* (Nobody ever needed a reason.)

I was shocked. In less than thirty seconds it was all over. One shoe was flying out in the middle of the street along with its owner; another attacker had been thrown into the wall, and he appeared to be unconscious. Another guy was bleeding and holding his mouth, and the fourth was backing up trying to get away. I did not even have time to get out of the car.

I said, “Lee, you all right? You want a ride home?”

He was walking just as though nothing had happened and said, “No, Lyndy, it’s OK.”

A few days later at school, Lee told me he had been taking judo lessons, which had become very popular during the war. It was truly amazing because during school, much like myself, Lee was rather slightly built, but muscular.

Growing up in Vallejo during the war you knew trouble when you saw it, and well before it happened. Lee was built like a bowling pin with large hips and thighs and powerful legs, which gave him great strength. He was of average height at that time, maybe 5’9” to 5’10” and weighed about 165 to 175 pounds, with jet-black hair always parted on one side. He was definitely a loner—quiet, extremely polite, with excellent grades—yet, I never knew one person who did not like Lee. He had a unique persona, which tended to command respect from the other students. Had he been more outgoing and social, he could have been elected class president with ease. Lee was one of those students who always carried a binder and his books. These were the kids who were headed for college.

When I discovered Lee was the most favored Zodiac suspect of the Vallejo and San Francisco PDs, I couldn’t believe it. They are still trying to prove it, hoping in futile desperation to make a match between the Zodiac stamps or envelopes and Lee’s DNA. I had several dealings with Lee when he worked at Ace Hardware, but he never recognized me; we hadn’t seen one another since school. There was never a time in Lee’s adult life that he matched the composite sketch of Zodiac produced by the San Francisco PD. At 6’2”, 240 pounds, with a very round face, he was not even close.

Two veteran detectives in homicide, Jack Mulanax and Leslie Lundblad, interviewed Lee when he was in prison. They both laughed because they were absolutely certain he was NOT the Zodiac. After having him print sentences from the Zodiac letters, word-for-word, they stressed the fact, over and over, that there were no similarities at all. His writing was cleared by California's chief handwriting analyst in July 1971. In addition, they learned that during the time period of one of the Zodiac killings, Arthur Leigh Allen was in custody.

Lee was always in great pain, in deep anguish over the police treating him worse than a dog, trying to force a confession. A mutual friend confided, "Lee often shared his innermost feelings. Once Lee told us, 'The police are going to put me in my grave.' He talked of a lawsuit, but had no money for an attorney."

He told my friend, "I am not the Zodiac," and she believed him without any reservation. He was being treated for high blood pressure. He lived about one year after this conversation, and died in October 1992.

On page 178 of *Zodiac Unmasked*, Graysmith begins relating a fascinating story. The ex-highway patrolman is me, and for the record, Graysmith has the facts nearly correct. (These two pages alone are worth the price of his book.)

Sgt. Lundblad's son, Leslie Jr., told me in person how his father was ordered to destroy his files and never mention the suspect's name again. These orders did, in fact, follow the chain of command from the judge. Emma, Sgt. Lundblad's wife, told me the identical story.

Sgt. Lundblad laughed at the suggestion Allen was a valid suspect, and, in fact, continued his own secret personal investigation into the bizarre life of his favorite suspect, George Tucker. Until the day he died, Lundblad knew in his mind and heart, the true identity of Zodiac.

Even Narlow, on page 179, told Graysmith:

> I always got the feeling Lundblad knew who the Zodiac was.

Narlow was certainly not referring to Arthur Leigh Allen.

Ann Tompkins, Lundblad's personal secretary, knew from March 1971 that Lundblad became a different person—sad, depressed, and rejected. Lundblad could not tell her the truth, and she never knew the terrible anguish he was suffering.

Personally, I do not find it strange Lee would wear a Zodiac brand wristwatch, a gift from his mother. These are excellent Swiss watches, made especially for water sports and diving. Lee did spend a lot of time in the water.

To think he created a maniacal lifestyle based on the image of a watch is totally absurd. Yet, it is entirely feasible Lee's arrogant flaunting of the watch, and his "Z" ring, were part of a strategy laying the foundation for a huge lawsuit against the Vallejo PD. Had the police been more discerning, they would have discovered the perfect chrome "Zodiac" emblem on both sides of his Buick Skylark. This is perhaps the only reason he bought it in the first place.

It is incredible to think the police recovered so many items tending to match the evidence in the case: the knife, in a case with brass rivets; .22-caliber pistols and rifles; and even an old-style Royal portable typewriter, like the one used in Riverside. Of course it is all speculation, but with his high IQ and his pronounced hatred for the Vallejo police, this is entirely possible. Close mutual friends confided to me, "Lee was planning and hoping to file a lawsuit."

In Graysmith's second book you will discover where the pressure was coming from, the "squeaky wheel" getting the grease, the lady who insisted Arthur Leigh Allen was the Zodiac. What is it they say, "follow the money"? Why would Lee tell a pseudo-friend the police failed to find a "silencer" wrapped up in his socks in a dresser drawer? Do you think Lee told his "friend" knowing full well this person would report it back to the police? Of course! (And she did.)

I learned a few things from *Zodiac Unmasked*. I learned the Vallejo PD's Zodiac expert, retired Officer Bawart, reported they had recorded 30 circumstantial factors, which in his opinion prove Arthur Leigh Allen is the Zodiac. We record *156 factors* to prove *our suspect* is the Zodiac.

Most criminal attorneys would recognize the fallibility of showing a victim a photo lineup after 23 years. Since Allen's photo had been spread all over the country in newspapers, magazines, and live television interviews, it is likely Michael Mageau's identification would be unreliable, at best highly questionable.

Circumstantial factor number 28, on page 498 of Graysmith's book, is also totally false. The "MY NAME IS" code was deciphered by me, of which Graysmith has absolutely no knowledge. Yet, he is actually referring to the anagram, "Robert Emmett the Hippie," which comes from the first cipher with the 18 unsolved letters and symbols, and has no relationship to the "MY NAME IS" code.

Graysmith, if he has his facts straight, states,

> Dave Toschi had never heard of Captain Roy Conway of the Vallejo Police Department, and Captain Narlow was never advised or briefed on Arthur Leigh Allen. All three officials were in charge of their own respective Zodiac murders.

On page 432, Graysmith quotes Det. Bawart saying,

> A Naval Intelligence Agent and two CHP officers pursue the investigation as a hobby, and that's wonderful.

Bawart does not have a clue. By the time he got involved in the Zodiac case in 1989, Jerry and I had already devoted over 17 years of our lives to it. No, this case has never been a hobby. Bawart admits he never knew much about our suspect. Like all the other detectives in the case, if he had wanted to know, all he had to do was pick up the phone and call. Like Graysmith, he never did.

The following exchange between Graysmith and Det. Jack Mulanax is most interesting:

> On page 236 Graysmith said,
>
> "I understand Les Lundblad had a guy he liked a lot."
>
> Mulanax replied, "He was inclined to get real high on a suspect where I wasn't."
>
> Graysmith asked, "Was this Leigh (Allen)?"
>
> Mulanax replied, "That was the only suspect I ever developed that I had any strong feelings about."
>
> Later in the interview...
>
> Graysmith asked, "Did you ever have anyone besides Allen?"
>
> Mulanax replied, "The only one that ever turned me on was Allen."

Note the effort made by Mulanax to avoid answering Graysmith's questions, and the ease of Graysmith connecting Lundblad to Allen. Det. Mulanax would not and could not tell the truth because he himself had betrayed the oath of his badge, and his own personal integrity. He, too, was complicit in his silence and felt a great deal of guilt and shame, knowing full well they were all ordered to leave our man alone, and never mention his name.

Additionally, he and Les Lundblad were very close friends and Mulanax would say nothing to betray their trust. As I said in my chapter about our suspect being called in by Lundblad, the fourth paragraph on page 120 tells it all, the most important thing Graysmith said in his entire book.

Graysmith's journalistic sensationalism not only placed several people in danger, it also compromised and interfered with an official investigation. Decency and moral integrity were issues of no concern to him. Then in 2002, in *Zodiac Unmasked*, he not only disclosed my name, but also mentioned other confidential matters.

In *all* the years of this investigation, *prior to this outrageous exposure*, my name had never been publicized in relation to anything about the Zodiac, a matter I had insisted on from the very beginning. Many members of my extended family had never known of my personal involvement in this case.

Painting images of Arthur Leigh Allen suddenly rising from the murky waters like *The Creature from the Black Lagoon*, staring like a demon at the cars driving by, is an outlandish fabrication. I know every creek, every spring, every pond and quarry in the entire area, and the waters described by Graysmith do not exist. Who in the hell has he been talking to? Are people in San Francisco still relapsing from the experimental virus sprayed over their city in the 1950s by the government?

And now, as the recent DNA analysis has definitely or *allegedly* cleared Arthur Leigh Allen, Graysmith is insisting his original theory was correct. He is telling the world Arthur Leigh Allen had a partner. In his ludicrous speculation, Allen did all the killings, and his partner wrote and mailed all the letters.

I say, "Only in San Francisco!"

One final word about Arthur Leigh Allen: Were it not for an emergency trip to Ohio with my mother and the Korean War, I would have continued my studies at Vallejo Junior College. I would have also remained active in Phi Beta Rho (ΦBP), a select group of guys. Even though we were all expelled from school for two weeks for hazing, I was proud to be a member. Had I the opportunity, I would have nominated Lee Allen for membership in our fraternity.

XXX

PAMELA (SUENNEN) HUCKABY

Pamela Huckaby is still suffering from the pain of losing her older sister, Darlene Ferrin, who was shot to death at Blue Rock Springs Park on July 4, 1969. Most of her tormented anguish springs from the frustration she feels knowing the insane killer Zodiac is still at-large. Pamela is bewildered, baffled by both the cunning genius of the Zodiac and the unforgivable incompetence of the various law enforcement departments working on the case.

My ex-son-in-law, working for a private contractor on Mare Island Naval Shipyard, casually mentioned one day, "A friend of mine is dating a sister of Darlene Ferrin, the girl who was killed by the Zodiac."

The girl had told her boyfriend that another sister, Pamela, had some letters or something from the Zodiac. My son-in-law asked me, "Do you want to meet the sister, Pamela?"

I told him, "I'll think about it."

At this point, I would like to mention that for many years Jerry and I had been getting tips and receiving a great deal of information from people seeking our assistance or advice on the Zodiac case. Generally, we would tell them to contact the police department. Some of these people knew Darlene Ferrin, or David Faraday, or Betty Lou Jensen very well, and most expressed a sense of dismay as they had never been interviewed by the local police. I was curious, but I did not want a personal relationship with strangers. It was extremely important for me to keep a low profile in this investigation. In fact, I was upset because my daughter had been talking out of school. My family members had been cautioned and instructed never to discuss my involvement in the matter with anyone.

About one week later, my son-in-law informed me, "The sister, Pamela, does have a Zodiac letter, and some guy from San Francisco is going to their family home on Jordan Street, and Pam is going to give this guy the letter."

My son-in-law did not know if the man was a San Francisco police detective; he had no idea who he was.

Thinking the letter could actually be real, and not knowing who this Pam was dealing with, I decided I should meet her.

Jerry and I have always maintained the theory that Darlene's murder was not at random. She was killed by someone who knew her. Therefore, it seemed entirely possible the letter in question could be from Darlene's killer, a person known to the family.

Around 7:00 PM, I was being escorted by family members into a small and cramped bedroom. Pam, sitting cross-legged in the middle of the bed, ordered the door shut. Looking at me with a scowling face she asked, "And who the hell are you?"

I identified myself, and tried to explain why I was there. She became excited and told me, "Blaine T. Blaine is coming to our home this evening, and he sent me a long letter, which disclosed the identity of the Zodiac. The guy, the Zodiac suspect identified in the letter, is a genius, he makes movies, is a homosexual, and he and Blaine T. Blaine are... you know?" Pam, barely catching her breath, went on, and on, and on, then asked me, "Do you want to meet this Blaine T. Blaine?"

This explained why the house was full of people, they were all family members waiting to meet this guy. As soon as I heard the name, I knew I never should have come. It just didn't sound like a real person.

Pam said, "Blaine is late, and he should be here any minute. How the hell did the CHP get involved in the Zodiac case, anyhow?"

My God, my guts screamed, *get me the hell out of Dodge, right now!*

Before I left their house, Pam insisted I hear the letter; and as I would not read it, she read it to me. As I suspected, the letter was of no value at all. It sounded like an accusatory letter written by a scorned lover. This was a copy of a letter Blaine T. Blaine had mailed to his boyfriend. *Good God almighty!* I left as fast as I could squeeze through the relatives.

From then on, Pam has been a constant source of information and consternation, and my phone has never stopped ringing. No, I did not want to see the letter, and I did not want to read the letter. I wanted no part of their hysteria.

Pam is a lady who has lived in a state of fear—at times frightful panic at strange and unexplained happenings. Notes and letters and other writing appearing on the front door, with an infamous Zodiac symbol, were the beginning of a series of events that plagued her life. The Pittsburg and Antioch PDs got to know Pamela Huckaby very well. After responding to her frantic phone calls on too many occasions, they became wary and skeptical.

In fact, Pamela was walking on the edge, and before long had a nervous breakdown. Her husband, Ray, was always there for her, but Jerry and I believe he, too, had become tired and perhaps somewhat jaded, resigned to the fact there was nothing he can do. She would say she'd been stalked, followed, forced off the road, shot at, or stabbed; that she had received threatening notes, letters, or numerous phone calls from persons who disguised their voice or simply hung up. Somebody, it appeared, was trying to drive her out of her mind.

Panic attack supreme, Pamela was becoming hysterical. As the weeks progressed, drawing closer and closer to July 4, 1987, the anniversary date of her sister's tragic death, the situation was nearing critical mass. Zodiac was planning to kill Pamela on July 4, 1987, and there was absolutely nothing anyone could say or do that would convince her otherwise. The letters, notes, phone calls, and other bizarre events were all designed to alert Pam to her date with death.

"Lynn, you and Jerry have to help. The police will not do anything, and I don't know what I'm going to do. And that Jerry—huh—Jerry does not believe me, either."

"Pam, the phone calls and letters are not real—none of it. We have tried to tell you. Sure, it appears like someone is, in fact, harassing you, but it is not the Zodiac, Pam."

"Well, who is it? Who is doing all this to me? How do you know it is not the Zodiac?"

"This is not his method or his style, and we have eliminated the handwriting in the letters. Besides, we know, for a fact, it is not the Zodiac."

"Why won't you tell me the truth about your suspect, Lynn? What is his name? Where does he live? What kind of car does he drive? How old is he? Why won't you tell me, Lynn—what are you hiding?"

"Pam, I have told you, Jerry has told you, we both have told you a thousand times, we cannot tell you anything. But I can tell you that our suspect is not the person who has been taunting you."

"Lynn, you have to hide me. He follows me everywhere I go. You are the only person I can trust—the only person, Lynn. I have nobody, and the cops are useless. Ray works graveyards, and I am here every night by myself. They told Ray that if I keep calling him at work, they are going to fire him—I can't even call him."

"Pam, there is nothing I can do. Dial 911 if something happens."

"You've got to be kidding. Lynn, can I stay at your house?"

"Hell no, Pam. Yvonne [my wife] would never tolerate such a thing."

"Where can I go, Lynn? I have to get out of town."

This would be an appropriate place to mention that my partner, Jerry, on those special assignments he delegated to himself, at Pam's insistence, spent two different nights at Pam's apartment for surveillance. On another occasion Jerry spent the night in a separate room at the now-Ramada Inn Motel, 1000 Admiral Callaghan Lane in Vallejo. All were futile attempts to catch the alleged culprit.

A meeting, arranged by a whispering voice over the telephone, the alleged Zodiac, had been scheduled about one week prior. I was on standby alert in the event Jerry needed to call me. This was another sleepless night for both of us. I told Jerry, as I did on several other occasions, to pack a gun. His usual reply was, "Double L, you know how I hate guns."

(Today, in retrospect, neither Jerry nor I can believe we were so gullible and trusting.)

And there was one other occasion when Pam was meeting her sister's killer, about two years before this one. Pam must have liked this particular Ramada Inn in Vallejo, as she would be holed up there, also. On this weird and unbelievable night, I was to apprehend and identify the person who would be meeting Pam "where it all started," at Terry's Restaurant. I told my wife she would be going with me to act as an undercover partner and a witness. We were both carrying weapons, and my wife also had the tape recorder.

Pam failed to show. About 11:00 PM, two hours after the meeting time, we found Pam's car at the motel and knocked on her door. She opened the door immediately and told us we had gone to the wrong place. She said, "When I came out of the Denny's Restaurant downtown, I found a 'golden bullet' under my windshield wiper blade." She showed it to us and said, "It's was a warning from Zodiac."

Another time, Pam started calling early, begging, and pleading in tears for my assistance. I went to see a good friend on the CHP, my graveyard partner, and in the presence of his wife I tried to explain that I needed a safe place for a friend to spend the night. But as I could not reveal the true nature of the circumstances, I felt like a fool. While his wife glared holes through me, he said, "Gee, Lynn, I don't know." That remark was all I needed to hear.

I said, "I don't blame you, I wouldn't either," and left. Then, doing a very dumb thing, I stopped in to see my father, who lived in his big home in the Vista De Vallejo. After hearing a long story he finally agreed to a one-night stay. The entire escapade was straight out of an Alfred Hitchcock thriller or perhaps the animated TV show *Southpark*.

I created a most complicated series of driving maneuvers for Pamela, in order to lose anyone who might be attempting to follow her from Pittsburg to Vallejo. Pam would drive Highway 12 to Fairfield and then take Interstate 80 to Vallejo.

"Pam, you must follow my directions precisely—to the letter."

"OK, Lynn, what do I do?"

"The traffic will be moderate and when you intersect 80 from Highway 12, it will only take you about 10 minutes to reach the rest area on top of Hunter Hill, which overlooks Vallejo."

"Yes, I know where it is, Lynn."

"Make certain you are in the right-hand lane, slow lane, so you can turn off into the rest stop. Be sure to turn right into the actual rest stop for cars and not where the truckers park. You follow?"

"Yes."

"OK, I will be in a car you do not recognize, a friend's car, watching you as you turn into the rest area. And I want you there at exactly 2:00 PM." (My CHP buddy and I were both packing—me with my Colt Python and him with his off-duty Colt .45 semi-auto.)

"You get out, lock your car and walk down to the restroom. We will be watching to see if you are being followed, for anything suspicious. OK?"

"Yes."

"Then, continue down 80 to Redwood Street off-ramp—take the Redwood off-ramp and turn right onto Redwood. You will go just a couple of blocks to Tuolumne Street, which is the first signal-controlled intersection you come to. Turn right on Tuolumne, and you will see a big supermarket and a big parking lot immediately to your right. Turn into the parking lot and park, and we'll be watching for any cars that might have followed you off the freeway. OK?"

"OK, Lynn, I will be there at 2:00, in the rest stop. I wrote it all down."

I had left my car in the supermarket parking lot, and I was going to have Pam follow me to a very safe and secluded parking spot not far from my dad's home. Nobody was following Pam, and she followed the directions precisely. After parking her car, she retrieved a small suitcase from inside. I introduced her to my father, and they struck it off amazingly well. I was surprised, but he was glad to have a little company.

She walked into my sister's bedroom and said, "Wow!"

"Pam, there is not a person alive who could have followed you. Your car is so well-hidden, the cops couldn't even find it. So relax, and I will call you in the morning."

The situation was very hectic and frustrating, as I was having a large 4th of July barbecue party in my backyard and was already preoccupied.

Around midnight Pamela called waking up everyone in the house, and I was still in a state of exhaustion.

"Lynn, you have to come get me right now and take me to my car, and be sure to bring a flashlight. It's an emergency—I need something I left in my car, and don't forget a flashlight."

"What the hell, Pam—what is so damn important? God, it's almost midnight."

"Lynn, I really need it or I would not call this late. Lynn, be sure to bring a flashlight."

I told my wife, "Get up; whatever is going on, I need a witness."

We dressed, I grabbed a flashlight, drove to my dad's house, and picked up Pam. It was cold and with a new moon, it was very dark.

Pam asked, "Did you bring a flashlight?"

We drove a few blocks to Pam's car, which I had had her lock when we parked it. My wife sat in our car as I stood outside across the street watching Pam. She walked around her car and examined the wheels or the tires with the flashlight. I was not sure what the hell she was looking at. This secluded neighborhood was extremely dark, cold, and deadly quiet. Suddenly, there was a shrill, blood-curdling scream, which shattered the silence, and I jumped three feet straight into the air.

My God, I thought, *she found a body or somebody's head in her car.* I ran to her car and asked, "Pam, what the hell is going on?"

Her voice was quivering and her body shaking violently, lurching in spasms. Stuttering almost incoherently she said, "Loo—loo—look, look, Lynn!"

She could barely speak. She had opened her driver's door and tilted the seat forward. There covering the entire back of the seat was a huge Zodiac symbol. It had been drawn with a black felt-tip marking pen.

"Lynn, he's found me—he's found me, oh my God!"

I wrapped my arms around her shaking body and said, "No, Pam—it's impossible. There is no way he could have found your car—trust me. This thing was already there before you left home and you just never saw it."

"Really?—Oh my God!"

"Pam—really. It was already there." (You bet.)

We walked Pam back into my dad's home and asked if she was all right—telling her not to wake my dad and go to bed. She did take another small case out of her car, but she never said what it was she needed, and I never asked.

On our way home my wife said, "You know what?"

"Yes, I'm afraid I do. Forget it." "Is she for real?"

We never saw Pam the next day. She walked to her car and left early in the morning.

Here is a list of perplexing events Pamela submitted to the Pittsburg PD on March 14, 1987:

Pittsburg Police Department
Case # C87-1102 (Re: C87-1013):

February 7, 1987:	Writing found on front door —187 TR O.
March 1, 2, 1987:	Scraping noise at front door —foot steps 12:04 AM.
March 3, 1987:	St. Patrick's Day card found under front door.
March 3, 1987:	Phone call—"Your body is next."
March 5, 1987:	5:30 AM—Dome light found on in car—window pried.
March 5, 1987:	Kaiser Hospital—cartoon under wiper blade.
March 11, 1987:	2:30 AM—Husband hears doorknob turning.
March 11, 1987:	Zodiac symbol drawn on yellow paper—under door.
March 12, 1987:	11:28 PM—Obscene phone call. Pam calls Jerry.
March 12, 1987:	Note found at mailbox— "In desperation, remember."

In one paragraph of this Pittsburg PD report, a Lt. Millicam states:

> On July 6, 1987, at 0936 hours, I received a phone call from Pam Huckaby relative to alleged threats she has received from the Zodiac. Ms. Huckaby informed me she had to go into protective custody in Vallejo over the weekend as the Zodiac had set July 4th as her doomsday.

The voluminous police report is 125 pages long.

When Pamela spent the night at the home of Harvey Hines, the Escalon PD Detective obsessed with his Zodiac suspect, Kane, she read his entire report. Unfortunately, he allowed her to read our report, also. We had shared our report with Det. Hines in the strictest confidence.

Our sensitive information was betrayed and Pamela Huckaby betrayed my confidence as well. Her poor lack of judgment resulted in tragic consequences when she shared our critical information with a despicable low-life leech, a man with absolutely no integrity, moral values, or common sense, a man whose name I shall never grace by writing.

He is the ultimate Zodiac whore, and the one individual who most likely bears the responsibility for alerting the Zodiac to danger and causing the destruction of vital and critical physical evidence. In his depraved need for publicity and notoriety, his gross stupidity and arrogance, he most likely destroyed 32 years of covert investigations, possible grand jury indictments pending on the horizon, and a successful prosecution by the DOJ.

Considering the facts, which surfaced, it is not surprising that Pamela and her family truly believed that Darlene's killer was known by Darlene, or involved with the family in some manner. There were the mysterious phone calls to the parents' home shortly after she was shot to death, the caller remaining silent, only the sound of rushing wind. And the fact that Zodiac was using the phone to call the police. The puzzling comment Darlene made to her mother as she was leaving the house, and shortly after the argument with "the older man" in front of Terry's Restaurant: "Oh, you will read about it in tomorrow's newspaper." And when Darlene said to her friend Michael Mageau—"Oh, it's him, just ignore him," as the car pulled up behind them at Blue Rock Springs Park at midnight.

Years later, Michael Mageau told Pam that the person who attacked them called her sister by her nickname, Dee, during the attack.

"She knew him," said Michael.

> *This information was never revealed to the police. This explains why Michael Mageau virtually disappeared when he was released from Kaiser Hospital. He was convinced the killer thought he knew his identity and would kill him next. Nobody could find Mageau for several years.*

"Lynn, I want to thank you and Jerry for the dozen roses, and I am feeling a lot better."

"What are you talking about, Pam, what do you mean?"

"The roses, they are yellow; how did you know? They're Darlene's favorite color, and she loved yellow roses."

"Pam, where are you?"

"I'm still here."

"Still where?"

"Didn't Ray call you?"

"No, what's going on, Pam, where are you?"

"Well, you must know, you sent the roses."

"Pam, I did not send you any roses."

"Uh—uh—uh," sounding short of breath, stuttering and whispering like someone was listening, she said, "Lynn, I'm still in the hospital and you have to come right now, they are from him—he knows and he signed your names. Quick, Lynn—come over right now, oh my God, Lynn."

"Pam, settle down. Signed whose names?"

"Yours and Jerry's," she said, still whispering.

"The card has your names on it. Oh God, Lynn, he knows I'm here—I've got to get out of here."

"Pam, I will call Jerry and see what he is doing, and if he can't make it, I will come anyhow. You be sure to save the flowers, and we need to see the note. OK, Pam?"

"Oh, Lynn, what am I going to do? He knows."

I called Jerry and we met at the hospital two hours later, about 1:00 PM, and found Pam sitting up in bed. A tray of food was still on her small table, half-eaten.

"Oh thank God, Jerry, you and Lynn are here. I have to get out of here right now—he knows—he knows I'm here. You know, I guess they think I'm nuts or something and they just don't believe me. I've got to have a cigarette."

Pam pulled a cigarette out of a pack in her drawer and lit it. Jerry told her, "Pam, you can't smoke in here."

"I don't care, I'm going to smoke. "

At that moment a nurse walked in and promptly snatched the cigarette from her hand and stuck it in a glass of water.

She told Pam, "We have told you, there is no smoking allowed."

Pam said, "Let's go—come on."

Pam crawled out of bed with her pack of cigarettes saying, "I know where we can go, down to the snack room."

"Pam, where are the roses?" I asked.

"Oh, I guess they threw them away."

Jerry said, "Pam, we want to see the note. You did save the note didn't you—*Pam*?" (In an accusatory tone.)

"Well, I would have if I knew they were going to throw them out—I had no idea. They never asked and they never said anything. I've been out you know—the drugs and all. They keep me heavily sedated."

Pam smoked her cigarette in the snack room and as she shuffled down the hall back to her room she began to swoon and sway, and collapsed on the floor. Just as she began to fall, I grabbed her and gently laid her down.

"Jerry, quick, go get a nurse."

Jerry ran around the corner to the nurse's station and returned in about one minute with a nurse in hand, both running. Scared the hell out of us. Pam regained consciousness, stood on her feet, and leaning on the nurse and me, she was able to walk back to her room.

"Well," she laughed, "I guess you saw everything I have."

"No, not really Pam. I can't speak for Jerry, but I can truthfully say I never looked."

The only thing Pam was wearing was a sheer pink negligée, and a person did not really have to look to see if she had on anything else.

Pam had been ordered into the hospital by her doctor for rest and observation, her blood pressure was extremely high. As I recall she was there for about one week. Before Jerry and I left she was telling the nurse she wanted to go home, she was feeling much better. Jerry and I decided we would never mention the roses, and strangely enough, Pam never mentioned them again either.

Pam has appeared on a few television programs, and is still sought after by the media-at-large. When Pam speaks, everybody listens.

When William Beeman called his press conference at the fairgrounds in Vallejo, Pamela Huckaby stole the show. Beeman, a highly respected criminal attorney in Vallejo, had written a book, actually a two-book set, explaining in detail why his brother, Jack, was the Zodiac. William and Jack Beeman were good friends of old *Ironside*, Raymond Burr. They grew up together here in Vallejo and became good buddies.

Designed to commemorate Zodiac's first murder in Riverside, Cheri Jo Bates on Halloween 1966, Beeman's major news release was for Halloween, also. This was a clever ploy, a publicity stunt we think, so Beeman would have an excellent opportunity to promote his book *Jack the Zodiac.*

Jerry and I got there very early, about the same time as several television crews. We helped Beeman set up the rows of chairs, and after he discovered our interest in the case, he told us everything about his brother Jack.

The district attorney pleaded with Beeman not to go through with this public announcement because his brother, Jack, was certainly not the Zodiac. (This was Neal McCaslin, one of our Mandamus Seven.) But Beeman was convinced, and he would listen to nobody.

The turnout was amazing (with dozens of undercover cops, deputy district attorneys, and other officials from all over the Bay Area), and the large room was beginning to overflow. Of course, Jerry and I had reserved our own seats in the rear so we could count heads, see faces, and take notes. Every car entering the Solano County Fairgrounds was being recorded on film, with the license plate number duly noted. Would Zodiac be dumb enough to attend this book promotion? We didn't think so.

Pam and her entourage arrived when the hall was about nearly filled. As her leg was in a cast and she was walking with crutches, she had no trouble finding a seat. Beeman did an excellent job with his presentation, which was obviously well rehearsed. He was a bright and well-spoken individual, very convincing. However, when he began to take questions, some of them very focused on facts in the Zodiac case, Beeman, it seemed to Jerry and me, started to get nervous.

Very shortly he was questioned and challenged by Pamela, and she would not stop. In a matter of seconds, the television cameras were focused on Pamela, and she was now getting all the press coverage. At the end, William Beeman was still standing inside the hall, while the cameras followed Pamela all the way to her car.

At a later date, Pam identified our suspect from a photo lineup.

"I am certain this is "the older man" at Terry's Restaurant, in the late evenings when Darlene was working." She also said, "He is the same man, well-dressed and older, who was at Darlene's house-painting party. The man was bugging Darlene, following her around the house, asking her where she got the money for this, money for that, etc. Darlene had told me previously to stay away from the man, and not even to talk to him as he was a really bad person."

Of course, Pam's sister, Linda, had also identified our suspect.

In the late 1990s, I received a frantic phone call from Pamela at about 11:00 PM. She said, "This is an emergency! Ray is working, and I dare not call him again or he'll lose his job."

She was pleading with me to come over, it was very important. I grabbed my gun and drove to Pittsburg. I met with Pam in a supermarket parking lot. I had absolutely no idea what the hell was going on, and with Pam, one never did.

She got in my car, her right hand in her purse. I will not go into the teary eyes or her emotional state, but she was very upset. She demanded to know, "Why, after all these years, have you never told me you knew and dated my murdered sister Darlene?"

I told her, "I have absolutely no idea what you are talking about. I don't know where you're getting your information."

"A detective from the Pittsburg or Antioch Police Department told me." I could not believe my ears.

"If I had known your sister, Darlene, I certainly wouldn't have had any reason not to tell you. Plain and simple, I never met Darlene."

Pam asked, "Well, didn't all you guys on the CHP go into Terry's?"

It was an absurd notion. Even though a lot of the day-shift guys did go to Terry's, very few on the graveyard shift ever went there, and 99 percent of the time I worked the day shift. Whenever I had to pull a night shift, we always had our dinner at the Red Top Restaurant by Cordelia. I was beginning to fume.

"Tell me the absolute truth because I am furious."

"I would swear on the Bible one of the detectives [she told me his name] told me you knew and dated Darlene."

I asked Pam, "Have I ever lied to you about anything, anything at all?"

"No."

Pam had her right hand wrapped around her husband's .357-Magnum revolver.

Good God, I thought, *that asshole could have gotten me killed*.

I could understand why this would have shocked Pam. So lucky to be alive, I drove home in a mild state of rage.

Yet, what Jerry and I could never quite resolve was why Pam had a tendency to create issues not always supported by the facts.

The next day, I was getting ready to call the chief of police, or the detective, or perhaps go over and confront the asshole detective in person. But as usual, trying to maintain my anonymity in the case, and certainly not wanting any conflict, I decided to cool off and deliberate while I reflected. As discretion is the better part of valor, I let it slide, just as I had with Inspector Dave Toschi in the early 1970s. I was fairly convinced Pam was making up the entire story anyhow. After all, this was an outrageous lie, and I truly did not believe there was a cop alive who would ever say anything so vicious. We had heard talk of Darlene dating a CHP officer, but the officer turned out to be a Vallejo policeman, who was interviewed extensively.

Several years passed and Pam and her husband, Ray, moved to Oregon. Pam, always working on the case, continued her frequent phone calls. She was always frustrated because she accused Jerry and me of "never doing anything with your case."

One day Pam asked me, "Do you want a copy of the police report from Pittsburg/ Antioch Police Department?"

I told Pam, "I do not need or want the report, but you could send it, if you want."

"I found a thick report bundled up and placed at my front door. I have no idea who might have put it there."

Pam sent me the report, and it was, in fact, an official copy of a police report. It meant absolutely nothing to me, but I did review it one night. On one page the Pittsburg PD detective referred to Jerry and me in a meeting with Capt. Ken Narlow in his Napa office. The report stated we were making a movie about the Zodiac case, and our investigation should not be taken seriously because we were motivated by monetary considerations. The innuendo implied that our entire case was fabricated, all fiction, and could not be trusted. Then, near the bottom of the page, I discovered the source of the vicious and outrageous lies about me. The detective wrote: "Fred Shirasago, DOJ, told me Officer Lafferty knew and dated Darlene Ferrin."

Would you care to guess which person or which department started these false and unbelievable rumors? Who gave the orders to Lundblad to destroy his files, his notes, and never mention the man's name again? Does a lie not become more believable when it is supported by other lies?

In the Pittsburg PD detective's official narrative concerning the movie Jerry and I were making, he even mentioned a couple of movie stars by name—Meryl Streep was one. It was all a bunch of egregious lies stacked on one another, and made a person wonder: Did this detective call Capt. Narlow? Was Narlow the original source? It boggles my mind.

The issues of trust and integrity have been a perplexing challenge for all these years. To what lengths would an official go to discredit a fellow police officer's story? How low would a person stoop to defame the CHP officer? Actually, in retrospect, the perfect story and a great strategy would be just what they did. Dirty politics by a dirty cop. Fred Shirasago did not invent this outrageous story, somebody told him, and at this writing he is still alive.

If, in fact, I had known Darlene Ferrin as even a slight acquaintance, I would be remiss not to mention it in this telling. However, since we had never met, I cannot embellish or personalize this story in that way. In fact, of all the CHP officers the rumors said she met, I have never known of even one.

XXXI

AMERICA'S MOST WANTED

On November 13, 1998, the celebrity John Walsh was being interviewed on a radio station in San Francisco. Mr. Walsh was promoting his popular television program, *America's Most Wanted,* to be aired the next day.

During his interview he stated, "The Zodiac has been writing to me for nine years and has sent me several letters, all signed in blood. The FBI has verified the letters as being written by the Zodiac."

"My television program will disclose the names of four Zodiac suspects, which have never been mentioned or revealed by any other source."

Mr. Walsh also gave the telephone number to order their special edition of *America's Most Wanted* magazine featuring the Zodiac killer.

While we cannot challenge the veracity of such a notable and distinguished public figure as John Walsh, it is unrealistic to believe it is possible to conceal such critical evidentiary information for nine years, especially from the DOJ. The news was absolutely shocking. John Walsh advised, "The letters were written in cryptographic style, threatening to kill me, saying this would be the ultimate, the crown jewel of all his killings, to kill the famous John Walsh."

If true, and we have no reason to doubt Mr. Walsh's fantastic story, and as the letters are threatening in nature, the FBI would now have the legal and official authority to open their own case on the Zodiac.

Subsequently, they, too, would rightfully maintain custody of the letters. A great deal of new evidence is now available, and has been for a long time: postmarks, handwriting, and possibly millions of cells to test and classify for the DNA. We can only assume this wealth of information was being shared with the Riverside, Vallejo, Benicia, Napa, San Francisco, Sonoma, Sacramento, and Stockton PDs.

"NEW EVIDENCE IN THE ZODIAC CASE"—NOT!—Nada, never happen, zip, zilch, and "no way, José."

We must ask, "He's had these for nine years, and nobody ever heard one word about the letters signed in blood by the Zodiac?"

Are these people really serious? I know, for a fact, they sold a bunch of magazines because I ordered ten.

Everyone was going to tape-record Walsh's television program. Pamela Huckaby called me two or three times telling me, "One of my Zodiac experts told me John Walsh knows you very well."

I told Pam, "I am sorry to disappoint you, but I have never talked to the man in my life."

Pam also said, "I received a very nice phone call from Mr. Walsh, and he was telling me all about the program, to be sure and watch. Mr. Walsh wants to invite my husband and me to his son's in Oregon for Thanksgiving dinner."

I recorded the *America's Most Wanted* show, and it was another boring and redundant program, whose substance had been aired before on many stations. If it contained anything new, neither Jerry nor I saw it. A total bust.

Two days later, my grandson, Ryan, and I met Jerry to help him move some furniture from his little theatre in Castro Valley, one of several occasions. (There is nothing Ryan does not know about the Zodiac case.)

I told Jerry, "I was very surprised at Walsh's program because he never mentioned the letters he received from the Zodiac."

Nor did he mention the DNA examinations currently in progress at San Francisco PD. And Walsh had promised to reveal four new suspects, but only three were mentioned.

A thorough page-by-page review of the FBI's Zodiac file was conducted at least twice. There is no mention of Mr. Walsh in the entire file, and no reference to any letters signed in blood, mailed to anyone.

"Even the best things are
not equal to their fame."

Henry David Thoreau

(1817–1862)

XXXII

THE MANDAMUS SEVEN

Mandamus:

A writ, issued by a superior court, commanding the performance of a specified official act or duty.

‹ CHP Officer Lyndon Lafferty ›

Mandamus Seven is the moniker I gave to those special people who contributed a great deal to this investigation. I regarded them as fine and superior people, all professionals in their respective fields. For years, some of them met with me every week or every month; some of the survivors still do. The title represents the inspiration they gave to me, and the admiration I felt for each and every one of them. To me, they represented a Superior Court, and their opinions and suggestions resembled a writ commanding an official act or duty. These people shared one thing in common—they all believed our suspect, Tucker, was the insane killer Zodiac.

≺ Investigator Sgt. Leslie Lundblad, Sr. ≻

Les was a homicide investigator for the Solano County Sheriff's Dept. He had an excellent law enforcement record and reputation. He was friendly, outgoing, a devoted father and husband, also a dedicated Christian, living his life with honor and integrity. He loved justice, and proudly respected the badge he wore. Les died when he was only 61 years of age, in October 1977. The last five years were filled with dismay, disgust, and shame, for he had been ordered to destroy his files on our suspect, and never mention the man's name again.

Les told me, time and again, "Lyndon, do not quit—ever. You have a very strong case."

I will never forget Les or his words.

≺ *District Attorney Neal McCaslin* ≻

Neal McCaslin, Solano County District Attorney, was one of law enforcement's greatest friends. Neal attended the CHP parties and other events without fail, and on occasion, would spend the entire night working the graveyard shift with two CHP officers. Every law enforcement department in Solano county had the highest regard for Neal. My partner, Jerry, and I would have lunch with him frequently, always exchanging information on our progress in the investigation. Neal was in a position to give us valuable feedback about our case, and he, too, was convinced we had the right man. He served as District Attorney from 1973 to 1982, and passed away in April 1997, at the age of 76. Neal had advised me that as a sworn peace officer in the State of California, I had the legal authority to conduct my investigation in the Zodiac case.

≺ ***CHP Officer Dave Fister*** ≻

Dave was a good friend of mine on the California Highway Patrol. He had an outstanding record with the CHP, including many commendations. Dave is a devoted father, husband, and a devout Christian. He has a college degree, has his teaching credential, and is a very intelligent individual. Dave has been very active in our field investigations, and has been an avid supporter for many years, never missing a meeting. Now living in Idaho, he will still drive down for a meeting, if at all possible. Dave also has personal knowledge of our suspect, and has always believed he is the Zodiac.

≺ ***Naval Intelligence Agent Chuck Forrest*** ≻

Chuck was one of the nicest men I have ever known. Chuck worked with my principal partner, Jerry, and they, too, were very close. Chuck, Jerry, and I spent many hours together planning and developing strategies for surveillance and other activities. Chuck was very aggressive and most insightful. He had excellent contacts in high places of the government, and was a key player in most everything we did. Chuck got very sick, though, and was still a young man when he died in August 1985. We lost a good friend and a great partner. There was absolutely no doubt at all in Chuck's mind that our suspect was the Zodiac.

≺ United Methodist Minister Ernie Bringas ≻

Ernie, author of two scholarly books, served as a United Methodist Minister for almost twenty years. Currently, he teaches religious studies at a community college and previously taught at Arizona State University.

In his younger days he was one of the two original members of the Rip Chords. Then, Terry Melcher and Bruce Johnston joined the group, and they recorded from 1962 to 1965 for Columbia Records in Hollywood, CA. The Rip Chords made 33 recordings placing five singles in the "Top 100." Their mega-hit was "Hey, Little Cobra."

Ernie has been a dear and close friend for many years, and on occasion, would spend time with me on patrol. Ernie volunteered his services in our investigation, and he soon became a member of the Mandamus Seven. His dedication and commitment was exceeded only by his bold courage and calculated risk-taking. Very few men would have faced the challenge or the danger as Ernie did. Ernie's a person the poet Lisa Pelzer Vetter wrote about, when she said:

> As we walk the path of life, we meet people everyday.
> Most are simply met by chance, but some are sent our way.

Everyone who meets Ernie feels the same way. The information he provided on the case was invaluable. He had been walking a razor's edge for a long time when his secret identity was revealed.

When Ernie's safety was compromised by Robert Graysmith's first book in 1986, he decided to leave the state. Had I been in his shoes, I would have done the same. Ernie is convinced, without a shadow of a doubt, our suspect was, and is the Zodiac.

Ernie Bringas Lyndon Lafferty Jerry Johnson

≺ Naval Intelligence Agent Jerry Johnson ≻

The best, I saved for last because Jerry Johnson (Double J) is truly one of a kind. If we ever make a movie about all this, I would want Pierce Brosnan to play Jerry. Debonair, convincing, and conniving, Jerry is a man with an agenda. Jerry is very bright. His military schooling may have instilled a sense of focus almost akin to tunnel vision at times.

There were occasions when we had differences of opinion, but we were always able to work them out, that is, most of the time. Jerry and I came from totally disparate backgrounds and being the typical "Virgo," predisposed to perfection, Jerry could be both difficult and impossible. Yet, he was a brilliant innovator and motivator in the entire investigation.

After 39 years, I can say this:

Jerry is one of the finest men I have ever known, and it has been an honor to have him for my dedicated partner.

"Double L" and "Double J"— leaving our favorite restaurant

ADDITIONS:

« *Superior Court Judge Eric R. Uldall* »

In the later years of our investigation, we were most fortunate when the brilliant and affable Superior Court Judge Eric R. Uldall joined our small task force. It was approximately 1994 when Rick came on board full-time. With his insightful views of the Zodiac case, his legal expertise and broad knowledge of thc police function, Judge Uldall became a valuable ally. Much like Neal McCaslin, Rick was law enforcement's best friend. When McCaslin retired from his district attorney position in 1982, and having a great deal of respect for Eric Uldall, I considered having a long talk with the distinguished judge. On June 11, 1985, I met with Rick in his chambers and handed him a brief summary of our case. We met there again on June 19.

While appearing interested in our investigation, Rick was very constrained and cautious. He knew a great deal about the Zodiac case, but very little about our suspect. After a few years Jerry and I agreed to invite him for lunch, and this was the first time the two of them had been formally introduced. The lunches continued for several years, and Rick attended them all. He became the pivotal force in our efforts to have San Francisco PD begin their DNA analysis. Rick was very convincing and persuasive in our discussions with Deputy District Attorney, Jim Lang, who was working with the Vallejo PD in their Zodiac investigation. It was Jim Lang who told the Vallejo police they should be investigating our suspect, George Tucker, and to leave Arthur Leigh Allen alone.

We all went to Rick Uldall's funeral on March 13, 2006.

« ***Detective James Dean*** »

James Dean, retired Detective from the Vallejo PD has joined the remaining members of the Mandamus Seven, and has attended nearly every meeting since 2002. Affable, extremely bright and outgoing, James Dean is a truly welcome addition to our group. On more than one occasion James has related a remarkable story about working with Lt. James Husted on the Zodiac case. He said that as they were reviewing the files of all the Zodiac suspects there was only one which was most outstanding, and it was our suspect, George Tucker. They compiled a summary resumé on Tucker and then walked in to see their Chief, Roland Dart. A short time later, when Chief Dart finally realized who they were talking about he went through the roof. He emphatically told them—*"Don't go there—you can't go there—leave that man alone and do not contact him."*

To stress the point with a final note, Chief Dart said with gusto, *"End of story."*

Dean and Husted were shocked and bewildered, but said nothing as they walked out of his office.

Dean also told us, "We ran a Soundex on your man Tucker (driver's license check, entire state of California), and we discovered he had obtained driver's licenses from different DMV offices on the same day. He was wearing different clothing and apparently a wig in a couple of photos. It was really weird, and this was one reason we got so hot on the guy."

Jerry and I looked at each other: *Say what?* We had never heard that story before and we were shocked.

I asked James, "Did you and Lt. Husted have Jerry's original report entitled, 'What, Another Zodiac Suspect?'"

Dean had no idea what I was talking about; he had never seen such a report. Another piece to this enormous puzzle had just been put in place.

The Vallejo PD (someone in charge of the Zodiac case) realized that Jerry's report contained a considerable amount of important information, and came to the conclusion they could not destroy it and could not make incriminating copies. What they did was transfer the responsibility and the liability to another agency with an ongoing investigation. So they mailed Jerry's report to the San Francisco PD, and this is exactly how the author Robert Graysmith got his unauthorized hands on our, really Jerry's, report.

We knew, for a fact, Graysmith had the original report as Jerry's red-ink highlights were plainly visible, proving they were not photocopies. Graysmith, a complete novice and using poor judgment, went on to disseminate sensitive investigative findings to the entire world—thanks to the unprincipled Vallejo PD, who were afraid to do their job.

« *Historian Robert Jernigan* »

When the *Contra Costa Times* newspaper interviewed my partner, Jerry Johnson, on June 30, 2002, on our Zodiac investigation, they published a front-page story entitled "Zodiac Killer Still Fascinates Sleuths." Bob Jernigan made contact with Jerry and has been a member of our diminishing task force ever since, attending every meeting and conference with us and the DOJ authorities. Bob provided new perspectives and his investigative research into the history of our country is quite remarkable. His unique genius, however, is the methodical and detailed presentation of his exhaustive work on Zodiac's Mt. Diablo Code. His explanation of the intersecting radians referenced by the Zodiac is brilliant and fascinating. The author's decryption combined with Bob's intersecting radians reveals the general location of Zodiac's alleged school bus bomb, a chilling discovery. There is also the possibility of a separate bomb location.

Bob's theory gained the interest of David Canter, Director of the Centre for Investigative Psychology at the University of Liverpool in Britain, for the analysis of its geographical profile.

Dr. Canter is the author of *Mapping Murder*, a book on the secrets of geographical profiling. Bob's work was forwarded to Dr. Canter by John Minderman, a former FBI agent and a staff member of the Behavioral Science Unit (BSU) in the 1970s.

Dr. Canter's assistant, Laura, visited the San Francisco Bay Area, in early October 2007, in order to see the actual Zodiac attack sites, and was hosted by the Mindermans. Bob was on one of those field trips to Lake Berryessa, along with John, Laura, and retired Capt. Ken Narlow. At one point Laura made the impromptu comment,

"Our work shows that the Zodiac lived in Vallejo."

(Tucker lived in Vallejo prior to 1968.)

In short, Bob has been an active participant in the pursuit of new evidence and is a valued member of our small group.

Before leaving this chapter, I must pay tribute to another fine man, ***Lewis Richey***. After resigning from the Solano County Sheriff's Dept., Lewis became a special agent with the National Auto Theft Bureau. He was a frequent visitor to the local CHP office in Vallejo and Fairfield, and in time we became good friends. Lew had a reputation of honesty and integrity. His word was his bond and whatever he told you, you could take it to the bank.

Lew was a close personal friend of our suspect's wife, and

a good friend of Judge Winston, as well. Lew told me one day, "I know, for a fact, it was your suspect—Tucker, who pummeled Judge Winston and put him in the hospital—she told me."

Lew offered to assist us in our investigation, and was always willing to do whatever he could.

LEWIS RICHEY
. . . Investigator Quits

LESLIE B. LUNDBLAD
. . . Named by Sheriff

Richey Resigns His Sheriff Post Here

Lewis Richey, member of the Solano County sheriff's department since 1948, has resigned to take a post as special agent with the National Auto Theft Bureau. Richey has been an investigator in the Vallejo branch sheriff's office.

In announcing the resignation, Sheriff Thomas C. Joyce disclosed he had appointed Deputy Sheriff Leslie B. Lundblad, of Vallejo, to succeed Richey.

Richey, who resided at 101 Dillon Dr., already has taken up his new duties in Los Angeles.

"I am always sorry to lose valued employes to other agencies," Joyce said in commenting on Richey's resignation.

Lundblad, who resides at 1016 Ohio St., has been a deputy sheriff since 1953. He began his law enforcement career with the Vallejo Police Department in 1940.

"Les is an experienced and capable man," Joyce said. "I know he'll make a fine investigator."

Vallejo Times-Herald: [print date unknown]

OCTOBER 2008

ZODIAC TEAM

L to R:

Robert E. Jernigan

Lyndon E. Lafferty

Jerry Johnson

James Dean

Not pictured: Ernie Bringas, Dave Fister

XXXIII

CODE WORK

Mary, Queen of Scots, was put to death by her cousin, Queen Elizabeth, for the high crime of treason after spymaster Sir Francis Walsingham cracked the secret code she used to communicate with her conspirators. The Navajo "Code Talkers" of World War II contributed a great deal to our ability to communicate with a high degree of security.

Today, our sophisticated codes are written in mathematical equations, intelligible to those with advanced degrees in mathematics and physics. Others open a worldwide "Pandora's box," like Michael Drosnin and his book *The Bible Code*.

His theory claims that equidistant letter sequences (EDLSes) are prophetic in nature, much like the work of Nostradamus (b. 1503), whose prophetic quatrains were also written in a type of code. The hieroglyphics of ancient Egypt were a pictorial code known only to the priests and other dignitaries.

The award-winning movie, *A Beautiful Mind*, with Russell Crowe portraying John Nash, was based on a true story. The mathematical genius became delusional, believing the government had taken over his life for his code-breaking talents.

In 1844 Samuel Morse demonstrated his famous code, a system of dots and dashes propogated electrically. The Morse Code became a common language around the world, extensively used in World War II and the wars in Korea and Vietnam.

A $30 million treasure is still buried somewhere in Bedford County, Virginia. Thomas J. Beale, a cowboy, amassed a huge fortune; and after burying it, he wrote three separate codes explaining how to find it. The code consists of a combination of numbers—71, 194, 38, 1701, and so on. The first code was broken, and the numbers correspond to the first letter of each word represented by the number. The first code is based entirely on the exact wording of *The Declaration of Independence*. These are referred to as "book ciphers."

However, in Zodiac's day, Morse Code was the universal language. The confidential and secret messages were generally based on letter substitutions, which were changed daily. Every radio operator in the field, on planes, and on ships at sea, had to refer to their daily codebooks for encryptions. These messages were a simple design because the operators could not carry the more sophisticated code-breaking machines. The more complicated messages between Washington and major military commands were based on groupings of letters, usually in four- or five-letter groups. Many of these messages employed a variety of techniques, and some were nulls, completely bogus. Combinations of letters would transpose into another single letter. For example, RJ would be M.

Letter frequency and repetitious use is the key to solving most codes and ciphers. The point of unicity is the number of letters, which must be used before it is possible to solve any code. Anything less would mean the code is something other than a substitution-type code. It is important for the reader to keep this fact in mind because the Zodiac knows it very well.

Very early in the Zodiac investigation, Jack Stiltz was the Chief of Police in Vallejo. Perhaps because of a recommendation from the FBI, he dispatched a letter to Henry Ephron, President of the American Cryptogram Association. Mr. and Mrs. Harden, schoolteachers in Marin County, had solved Zodiac's three-part cipher-code, all but the last 18 letters.

Chief Stiltz asked Mr. Ephron, "Could you or anyone in

your association decipher these 18 letters and symbols?"

Mr. Ephron replied in a couple of months, and his encryptions were shocking. The only thing he felt certain about was a last name and two letters of the first name, and they just happened to match our suspect exactly.

About two years later I, too, sent Mr. Ephron my own work, asking for his opinion, for I had obtained the same name. In a few weeks I received a very nice letter from him, but I was confused about his remarks. I put his letter away, and never thought of it again for several years.

Then one day, I read his letter again, still very confused, and suddenly the light went on. Mr. Ephron was responding as if he thought I was working with Chief Stiltz and had read the report he had mailed to Chief Stiltz. In fact, I had never seen his report, not until he sent me a copy of it years after our phone conversation. I had no knowledge that he and Chief Stiltz had ever communicated.

When I called him, he found the whole scenario fascinating and laughable. Then he said, "It is amazing we got the same name."

His original reply to me, which I did not understand at the time, was: "Surely, if such a man by that name actually existed, the police would have him by now."

(The best is yet to come.)

We had yet another match, one from the National Security Agency.

When Zodiac mailed another short code, "MY NAME IS," I was immediately struck by the arrangement and the pattern. Yet, it seemed impossible to decipher. Before long, however, the solution just jumped off the page, it was so obvious. The code is almost self-explanatory.

Ed Steinke, the newly appointed president of the American Cryptogram Association, was critical about certain aspects of my work, but he liked it and thought it was most likely a correct decryption.

When I explained the solution to Jerry, he just smiled and shook his head. He never did understand it until a few years later, when I showed him again, and this time he nearly fell out of his chair. I never saw Jerry so excited about anything.

He said, "Hey, Double L! You just solved the Zodiac case." He could not sit down.

Jerry was so enthused he called Ken Narlow at home and scheduled an appointment for the next day so I could explain the encryption to him. At our meeting Narlow, too, became very excited and said he would send it in immediately, requesting either the FBI or the NSA to appraise my work. Month after month, Jerry and I waited for the news. Jerry was already making plans for the ultimate arrest and the news release about our solving the most famous serial-killer case since Jack The Ripper.

One year later Narlow admitted he never sent it.

Lt. Husted of the Vallejo PD told Jerry, "God, did you see how Lafferty worked this out? This is really good."

Jerry said, "Yes, I know it is."

(I never asked Jerry how the Vallejo PD had a copy of my code work, as I had not shared this with anyone except him.)

The very first time I tried to explain the work to Jerry, he had Dave Peterson place the code on the front page of the *Vallejo Times-Herald*, asking the public to try and solve it. He even included a subtle clue to assist would-be code-breakers. As I had given Jerry very specific instructions not to share my work with another living soul without my permission, I was outraged by his actions. But nobody could solve the code.

Our man never believed in a thousand years he would become a Zodiac suspect. He, therefore, made a fatal mistake. While not technically correct, I like to refer to the evidence he gave us as fingerprints. Actually, it would be more accurate to say he left his "letterprints."

In a logical, straightforward analysis, you discover the remarkable evidence in the pattern.

This pattern, in my opinion, is absolute proof our suspect is, in fact, the Zodiac.

In his—"MY NAME IS" code he used a precise pattern and he had to add a null symbol to give him 13 characters so he had a equal-distant center. Thusly, he had 7 characters from both directions. He did not have this luxury with the 18 characters but he also employed a specific and precise arrangement with the 18 letters.

Unfortunately, as long as he lives, or until he is arrested, I cannot reveal his true name.

Sgt. Les Lundblad believed the "Top Secret" document he gave me was a copy of the FBI's decryption of the unsolved 18 characters. He immediately swore me to secrecy, advising in the same breath that he was not supposed to have it. Lundblad was very excited, and when I read the results, I could not believe my eyes. I was holding in my sweating hands a document, which proved beyond a doubt our suspect was the Zodiac. It was a moment in time I shall never forget. My mind was reeling and my legs were shaking. Can you just imagine, holding an official government document from the FBI, which tends to prove your suspect is the Zodiac?

Secret or not, I knew I could not live the next ten years wondering if this work was authentic. The agency name and address, the letterhead, had been removed from the eight-page summation.

Within a few days, I paid a visit to our local FBI office and had a long talk with Special Agents John Marchi and Floyd B. Barrus. Without any hesitation they both agreed the encryption was the work of the National Security Agency. Agent Barrus was also amazed, as he was the one who had conducted a background check on our suspect as a personal favor to me. Both Marchi and Barrus told me, "We have never seen this eight-page document." Zodiac had said,

> "IN THIS LETTER IS MY IDENTITY."

But in the body of the cipher itself Zodiac said,

> "I WILL NOT GIVE YOU MY NAME BECAUSE YOU WILL TRY TO STOP OR SLOW DOWN MY COLLECTION OF SLAVES."

This in itself is very cryptic, is it not? How is this possible? Quite simple. Considering how the Zodiac loves to play with words, he took a great deal of pride in his implied double meaning. It is possible to reveal one's identity without giving the name. Zodiac did not "give" us his name, but what he did give us revealed his identity. Like a riddle! However, Zodiac failed to realize, clever as he is, that he left his fatal "letterprints."

Fingerprints cannot be matched if there is nothing on file to match them with. We can apply the same logic by attempting to match the known with the unknown. While some may argue one cannot force or manipulate known letters to an unknown code, trying to make a match. I would argue that my methods and applications are identical to a fingerprint match. I believe this is a sound approach, but it means absolutely nothing unless, by coincidence or design, the cryptic matches are discovered.

Digraphs, trigraphs, letter formations and combinations: This was the approach of the Hardens who solved Zodiac's three-part cipher-code. They first assumed they would find letter combinations of "l"—will, kill, willing, etc.—and they were most successful.

Zodiac's own "Celebrity Cypher" mailed to the *Vallejo Times-Herald* on September 26, 1990, was never made public either by the newspaper or the Vallejo PD.

Was Zodiac commemorating the anniversary date of his murder at Lake Berryessa on September 27, 1969, or his Sierra

Club card of September 26, 1970? While several reasons exist to believe this was, in fact, sent by the Zodiac, the most important is the nature of the message—cryptic and vague, it appears to be illogical, with little or no meaning. An amateur, or someone playing a hoax, would have devised a logical, if not threatening, type of message, something most people would expect of the Zodiac.

Zodiac is always dropping clues, keeping us informed of the fact he is still here. Much like the time interval between his "Red Phantom" letter of July 8, 1974, and his last letter "I am back with you," of April 24, 1978. Nearly three years passed from the Terry's Restaurant note ("Bates Had to Die") to this "Celebrity Cypher." Zodiac wanted to keep it simple, and the police wanted it quiet.

The Vallejo detectives who gave us a copy of the "Celebrity Cypher" seemed to imply they thought it was a joke. In my opinion, it actually is from the Zodiac and an important clue because it tells us Zodiac is still around, still very close. The card was postmarked in Oakland. The fact that this was mailed to the *Vallejo Times-Herald* and not the *San Francisco Chronicle* tells us he resides closer to Vallejo, and has more ties murder-wise, so to speak.

If someone were playing a joke, why would they duplicate two lines? The top two lines on the left side of the card match the bottom two lines on the right side of the card. They are identical. Why? A prankster would not make such a simple mistake; therefore, I conclude it is not a mistake. A prankster, by utilizing the same symbols as in the first three-part code, could have invented or created a much spookier or nastier message.

Such a message might read, "I will keep killing, you will never catch me." Or, "My slaves need more friends"—or whatever, anything, something more chilling.

But the deciphered symbols give us a strange and almost incomprehensible array of jumbled words and vague messages:

LONGED HUNT LATE SLEUTH
INVITE U TO A SLUT YUTH HOTEL HIDE or,
LONG HUNTED LATE SLEUTH, etc.

The only investigator who called in our suspect died. He is indeed a LATE SLEUTH who HUNTED LONG. Does such a hotel as Hotel Hide exist, perhaps in the city? The message is bizarre and seemingly composed in a brief moment, just to tease the public and the police.

CYPHER is a British spelling for cipher, another clue. His misspelled HEROLD for Herald, another. If a prankster did all of this, he is very clever indeed. Even the hand printing is very similar to some of Zodiac's.

Zodiac is still here because Zodiac lives here.

He was married till recently, owns a nice home, and is active and well-established in the community.

The encryption of the suspect's name in the last undeciphered 18 letters of the first lengthy three-part cipher was discovered very early in this investigation. My work was directly confirmed by an eight-page analysis by the National Security Agency, which has never been disclosed before now. I use the term "confirmed" rather loosely since the NSA was confirming their own work that resulted in a match of one name in three possible. Sgt. Lundblad and I were very excited, and we both considered this very compelling evidence.

When I attempted to explain my own decryption work to Lundblad, he gave me a blank look and said, "Oh." I got the same reaction from my partner when I showed him a couple of years later.

Giving my work a "possible" status, it was placed in limbo for nearly 28 years. While it is confusing, let me try to set the record straight. Finding his name is one thing and finding the pattern is quite another. Finding the name is interesting, but it falls into the category of subjective speculation. Finding the pattern removes the speculation.

Year after year, I attempted to validate my work by examining the undeciphered 18 letters and symbols with a patient and determined dedication. Then, much like with his other plain-text transposition code "MY NAME IS," someone turned on the light. The date of this remarkable discovery was November 23, 1998. I arranged a meeting with my entire family, and I told them,

"I have just solved the Zodiac case."

Literally, I could not sleep for days, and was so excited I was nearly numb.

The discovery revealed a pattern, and the pattern confirmed the letters, each and every letter of the 18 letters in his entire name—first, middle, and last. In addition, the encryption verified the truth of Zodiac's puzzling statements when he said,

"IN THIS CIPHER IS MY IDENTITY" and

"I WILL NOT GIVE YOU MY NAME."

In the entire case, the "smoking gun" evidence, the code encryptions of the suspect's name, is without a doubt the most important evidence now existing. In the absence of a DNA analysis with a positive match, the name is the second critical option. An interesting aspect of the code solution is the fact—*Zodiac made two fatal mistakes.*

The first mistake was his presumption he would never become a suspect. The second was leaving his "fingerprints" in the form of the letters in his name. Much like the lands, whorls, and loops in a common fingerprint, letters in a name fit a similar profile. This is certainly not a conventional concept. Criminals never intentionally leave their fingerprints at the scene of a crime, even though there is some speculation Zodiac left some fake prints on Paul Stine's taxicab.

Zodiac, with his brazen ego, was certain it would be nearly impossible to decipher his name from the few letters he gave us and was very wrong. However, to prove his cipher could be solved Zodiac stated in a much later letter,

"WHEN YOU CRACK IT, YOU WILL HAVE ME."

Zodiac is definitely telling us his name is contained in the cipher. His original statements with the cipher are profoundly perfect. When he said,

"IN THIS CIPHER IS MY IDENTITY," this is totally correct. When he said,

"I WILL NOT GIVE YOU MY NAME," this is also correct.

He did not give us his name, only part of it. Yet, his complete identity and his full name were contained in the cipher. Zodiac loves a play on words.

When the sequential pattern was discovered, it shocked my senses. It was like a dream—unreal, and most incredible. While the word "pattern" may sound abstract, it is very real indeed. The pattern can only work with certain letters, and therefore proves the letters.

Within a few days, my partners and I had our monthly meeting. I had to temper myself due to my excited emotional state, and in a relaxed, calm tone I told my group,

"I have just solved the case."

One of them said, "Oh, jolly good! Now we can get on with the rest of our lives." They all laughed.

I gave my three buddies a large brown envelope containing a summary of my work telling them they were not to share this or show it to anyone, it was for their eyes only. I requested their assistance in a search for a retired cryptoanalyst to examine and evaluate my work. The group was in a heated debate over the John Walsh program, and we were trying to figure out who the fourth suspect was that was never mentioned. We speculated it was our man, and wondered if the San Francisco PD had anything to do with it, preventing the disclosure of our suspect's name. At this moment, the contents in the large brown envelope were not a priority, and feeling somewhat rejected, I did not say any more about my discovery.

For the next *four years* I tried to have an official agency review and appraise my code work, but all my pleadings were in vain. I could not and would not trust the police departments to handle my material with any degree of integrity. I could just imagine someone like Robert Graysmith getting his hands on it, like with Jerry's earlier report. Jerry and I were still on their "blackball list," as far as I knew. In all these years, they have never called us. Honor, integrity, and trust have been major issues in our sensitive and confidential investigation.

Unless you have devoted several years to law enforcement, packing a gun and a badge, you can never understand the power, the huge egomania, which controls the brain and blurs reality. The macho cop is proud, defiant, arrogant, and even obnoxious; he can do whatever the hell he wants to do because on the street he is the enforcer, the judge, jury, and at times the executioner. Sad but true, many actually believe it. They live for their "day of glory" when they make an exciting felony arrest, or get involved in a shoot-out, or solve a difficult crime. When an outsider starts probing and asking questions, they are defensive and protective. If you ask again, they get hostile and soon become your enemy.

Sensitive and confidential information must be handled with discretion at all times. When a lead homicide detective has to hide files in his own garage, you know something is seriously flawed in the system. Frankly, it is a matter of trust, and many cops cannot trust one another. So it was, apparently, with Inspectors Armstrong and Toschi of the San Francisco PD. We learned from their associates and other sources that before long, neither one would even speak to the other. Personally, I can attest to a false accusation made against me by my own CHP captain.

After I had arrested two young men from the center of the Carquinez Bridge in Vallejo, several phone calls from a former governor from back East and a Napa County judge were jamming the lines.

Under the particular section of law I elected to use in this arrest, I had the option of either releasing the two men or taking them into custody. They were not your routine "pedestrians" strolling down the freeway. Neatly dressed in expensive clothing, and their high-priced Nikon 35-MM cameras hanging around their necks, it did not appear they were taking typical tourist pictures.

I had received a call from dispatch that two men were literally climbing on the steel girders of the bridge. I ordered them to walk in front of the patrol car to the toll plaza, where their nice van was parked. I called for backup and obtained a second pair of handcuffs from another CHP officer. While I was booking the two men at the Solano County Jail, my partner had their vehicle towed away.

When I finished my reports and turned in my paperwork, my shift was over. The scene in the CHP rear parking lot was a sight to behold. FBI agents, and several of my CHP officers had stripped the van to pieces. Seats, floor mats, side-panelings, tires and rims, were neatly placed on one side of the van. I, of course, walked over to see all the action and one of my buddies told me, "Lyndon, you just arrested two terrorists from the notorious Weathermen organization, and we have found material you would not believe."

They photographed and photocopied everything, and the

FBI agents were "on Cloud Nine." Concealed behind the paneling they found books, records, maps, code names, and safe houses all over the world, a true bonanza. They even removed the film from the 35-MM cameras.

The next day was my day off, but at 6:00 AM I received a surprise phone call from Capt. Frank Bates, and he was furious. He told me, "Get your butt down to Flaky Cream Donut Shop, like right now."

When I walked in Capt. Bates handed me the morning newspaper, and plastered on the front page was some sensational headline about the CHP arresting some underground terrorists. The article contained word-for-word excerpts from the material found in the van. Madder than hell, he told me, "The FBI went ballistic, demanding to know how this sensitive material was leaked to the press."

"I never even saw the stuff at all, and I sure as hell never touched it." (I had absolutely no idea what was even found until a day or two later.)

"You better find out what the hell you're talking about before you accuse me of releasing information to our newspaper." I was totally pissed.

Two days later Capt. Bates called me into his office, and in front of his lieutenant, the second-in-command, profusely apologized.

"We discovered the night-shift CHP sergeant, at the request of the Vallejo PD, photocopied every single document and page of the privileged and confidential material." ("Top Secret" to the Weatherman group.)

The Vallejo police officer then placed the material in the "nightly activity" box. It was routine for the newswriters of the *Vallejo Times-Herald* to review the day's activity for their next edition. The journalists had free access to the police reports and any other material in the night-box. This procedure was changed immediately, but the damage was done. Priceless information on the infamous Weathermen was made useless by the act of one CHP sergeant, who had trust in a Vallejo police officer to handle the material with integrity.

Within a couple of days, I was advised by the FBI, "The rolls of film we confiscated were detailed photos of the San Francisco-Oakland Bay Bridge, plus the Golden Gate and Carquinez Bridges."

I also learned from the deputy booking officer, the father of one of the young men was a former governor of a state back East. The county jail took the call from a judge in Napa County demanding the immediate release of the two young men. They were in fact, released in quick order, and their van, completely returned to normal, arrived at the storage yard just fifteen minutes before the two men arrived. Days or weeks later, they would wonder how they lost their rolls of film. Unfortunately, the bust was busted. The entire world had read the newspaper.

The deputy booking officer said to me, "The judge from Napa told me, 'I'm acting on behalf of my good friend, the former governor.'"

On June 8, 1976, Larry Gratwohl autographed one of his books for me, *Bringing Down America*. Gratwohl was an FBI informant, going underground with the Weathermen in 1970. Gratwohl states,

> Of the 2,000 bombings every year since 1970, most are traceable to the Weathermen and their allies.

During the Vietnam War protests, the Weathermen were very active. Only the FBI would know their current status. Who do you trust? This has been my major concern.

In the Zodiac matter, here is a possible, if not likely, scenario:

Jerry and I reveal the sensitive details of our suspect, including his wife and the judge. I reveal the National Security Agency's code decryptions and the precise details of my own code work. We reveal the names and identities of our confidants and sources. During the next year, we hear absolutely nothing.

Our phone calls are not returned, we are stonewalled when we attempt to talk to the detectives, and the chief is never in. We are concerned, frustrated, and angry—in fact, furious.

Then, suddenly a spectacular and amazing headline hits the newspapers all over the Bay Area—"ZODIAC ARREST PENDING." "A major breakthrough," the article reads.

"Captain Allbright's brilliant code work is verified by the National Security Agency, the crucial piece of evidence leading to an intensive investigation coordinated by the DOJ. An anonymous source reported a search warrant had been issued for the suspect's home and two separate storage facilities. One weapon has been positively matched by ballistics, along with other evidence the authorities will not reveal. One detective advised an arrest is imminent. He reported that a task force of six detectives had been assigned to the investigation, based on a hot tip about one year ago." "There is no doubt this is the mad-dog killer, Zodiac," he stated.

The scenario would continue like this:

A prominent and distinguished Superior Court judge, recently retired, has assembled a "Dream Team" of powerful attorneys to represent the suspect. They tell the cops to get screwed, in legalese, of course, and file dozens of discovery motions to ascertain the true sources of the information. Jerry and I are soon discovered and revealed—in essence, busted.

The suspect is still running around free, and has now developed an uncontrollable fit of rage against me, my wife, and my children. Civil lawsuits are threatened and filed for defamation, illegal search and seizure, and a host of other "human rights" violations. Additionally, as a critical piece of evidence pertains to another jurisdiction, separate and apart from the search warrant authority, it is totally inadmissible under *U.S. vs. Hathaway*, 317 U.S. 91, 90 S.Ct. 2190, 43 L.Ed. 2d (a fictitious citation). Sorry, 40 years of our lives?

If you think these are unreasonable assertions, *then you do not know how easily things can get screwed up*. The police cannot afford to acknowledge us because then they would open the door to severe indictments. They would be charged with accusations of serious wrongdoing and failing to investigate a suspect brought to their attention so many years previously.

Consider the facts. It was 1991 when the Vallejo PD executed a search warrant on Arthur Leigh Allen's home at 32 Fresno Street, Vallejo, only twenty years too late. And these are the people who are trying to solve the Zodiac serial-killer case?

This story cannot reach its ultimate conclusion until one of two things take place:

1. The suspect is arrested.
2. The suspect dies.

Both events are directly related to the official results on the authoritative assessment of my code and cipher decryptions. Since discovering the systematic pattern on November 23, 1998, I have attempted every strategy, written every letter possible, with negative and agonizing results.

However, in an act of desperation, born from a conviction, which could not rest, I wrote my last letter of appeal in 2002 to the President of the United States, George W. Bush. With the war looming in Iraq and continuous terrorist threats playing the airwaves, I had little hope, from zero-to-none, that my letter would even be read. But it would be amazing, and I know miracles can happen.

On February 25, 2003, only fifteen weeks after I mailed my letter to the president I received a phone call from Mr. Dan Olson. The conversation went as follows:

"Lyndon, my name is Dan Olson, and I am in charge of the cryptoanalysis unit for the FBI in Quantico. We received a letter from the President, directing us to contact you, and make arrangements to examine your Zodiac code work."

I could barely talk and truly, I thought I was actually dreaming. I was still in bed and sound asleep when my wife called me to the phone. It was either my brain or my voice, but I was having trouble trying to put them together.

Finally, I said, "What, who is this?"

Dan Olson repeated his message and I told him, "I don't believe my ears."

He was very friendly, direct and outgoing; asking me about my code work in the Security Service.

"Lyndon," he said, "there are not many of us left."

He asked, "What security detachment were you with and where were you stationed?"

I told Mr. Olson, "I have discussed my work with your Northern California Special Agent Ken Heitmeier, and he told me he was going to submit my work. But when I checked one year later, he told me he had been too busy and had not sent it."

Olson said, "Well, you are talking to the right person now, and as soon as I examine your work, I will call you—you will be the first to know after I advise my supervisor." He then asked,

"Do you have Agent Heitmeier's phone number? I'll call and have him send me your code work."

"He's already returned my work in its entirety, so I'll send it to you by express mail tomorrow." I sent my entire package next-day service.

On February 27, 2003, I called Dan Olson advising, "You will receive my material today or tomorrow."

"I'm very anxious to look at your work."

On March 28, 2003, I received a letter from Mr. Dwight E. Adams, Director of the FBI Laboratory, saying they had my material. He commended me for my dedication, etc. His letter stated, "If your work provides additional leads in this matter, the appropriate FBI Field Offices will be notified."

Yes, I was excited, thrilled by the prospective potential in their official participation. Yet, I could not help noticing the date of Mr. Adams's letter was March 10. *This must be a very busy office*, I thought, *as the letter is postmarked March 25*. It is curious that my letter was in limbo for two weeks. The average person could understand my code decryptions with ease.

I told my wife, "If Dan Olson and his people do not agree with my work, if they say it is not plausible or is pure garbage, I am likely to receive a phone call within a week or two." He promised he would call.

But if they did, in fact, agree with my work, if they said it was correct, they would be in a major dilemma. They would have no way of knowing how I would react to a positive assessment. They would have no control over any public announcements I might make, or the newspapers I might contact. No, they would have to be very careful, very judicious, in revealing such a shocking story.

While Mr. Olson said he would call, the decision might not be his to make. So, as I told my wife, "The longer it takes, the better I feel."

This would explain the wording in Mr. Adams's letter, and the fact they held it for two weeks before mailing it.

Three months flew by and the suspense was too great to bear. I called Dan Olson on June 2, and caught him on his way to lunch. When he called back, about an hour later, we talked for nearly thirty minutes. In his straightforward way he said, "We haven't been able to spend much time on your code work."

Without elaborating on the details, Mr. Olson stated, "The work is most definitely plausible and credible, but I am not at the point I could raise my hand and swear before a court your work is absolutely correct."

"Please be patient because it is all there."

Two days later, I mailed Mr. Olson a one-page letter attempting to clarify a question he had on the pattern. While totally consistent for 99 percent of the "letterprints," Zodiac had literally (and mathematically) run out of options in his sophisticated pattern. The single inconsistency was unavoidable.

Mr. Olson mentioned two points of the work he believed to be very strong affirmations. He said, “I like it.”

Additionally, if requested by his department, I offered to give them a detailed, personal presentation. And I would be there tomorrow, if they asked. It would be nice to believe he was actually serious when he made the comment, “We would like to hire you,” but it was just his congenial manner of speaking.

If my work is confirmed, as I feel certain it will be, there is an excellent possibility I will never be informed. (Most recently, a retired FBI agent told me this is most likely.)

If the classical perspective falls into play, the situation could remain dormant for many more years. Thus, the critical importance of telling my story to the public-at-large.

Remember, we are dealing with a mass murderer the authorities were ordered not to investigate.

After waiting several more months, not hearing one word from Dan Olson, I called him again asking, “Have you found an opportunity to study my work.”

“Your work is most definitely in the ballpark,” repeating what he had said before, “it is plausible and credible.”

Before our conversation ended he asked me, “Have you ever looked at Zodiac’s Mt. Diablo Code, the one pertaining to the buried bomb?”

“Yes, I have, and on the face of it, it appears to be unsolvable.”

“Lyndon, will you take another look at it and let me know?”

“Certainly, I’ll give it another shot.”

Again I was dismayed and I could not believe my ears. Olson told me he teaches code to agents at the National Security Agency, and even told me he was going to discuss my work with them. The senior cryptologist for the FBI is asking me to render my opinion on one of Zodiac’s codes, one they cannot solve? So I did.

I studied it, night after night, for about two weeks, and suddenly the solution was very obvious. Every letter fell into place sequentially and most logically, absolutely nothing contrived and every letter utilized. Most chilling, but not too surprising, the location of the "bomb" appears to be at the intersection of Interstate 680 and Lake Herman Road (Vista Point), near where they found Shiri-Dine's body. And there are designated rural school bus stops in this area. (Zodiac said a passing school bus would trigger the bomb.)

I mailed my solution to Dan Olson, certified return receipt, and he received it in a couple of days. Mr. Olson never responded, and he never replied to my work in any manner whatsoever. And he is the one who asked me to do it.

The last phone call I made to him was when I began rewriting this manuscript in the fall of 2007. The conversation was somewhat strange, and he did not sound like the affable person I was used to dealing with.

"Is it OK for one of my female assistants to listen in on our conversation?"

"No problem here, fine with me."

"Dan, I am getting ready to submit my story and I am calling to ask you for your final assessment of my work."

"Lyndon, I told you that we cannot prove your work is wrong."

"That's it! You told me my work was in the ballpark, that it was plausible and credible. This is very important, and I need to know."

"No, I told you that since we could not prove your work was wrong, it could be correct."

Yet, an issue they will not address, or find convenient to ignore, is the fact that—*both codes reveal the same name precisely*.

Considering the mathematical probabilities, finding 18 exact letters in a sequential pattern spelling the suspect's 18-

letter name is astounding. Finding his name again, in a sequential pattern in the second code, is nearly unbelievable. *When the names match in both codes, the odds are beyond infinity.*

Lacking other physical evidence, the names revealed in the decryptions are the best evidence existing in the entire Zodiac investigation—two distinctively different codes with the same name. The detailed explanation and analysis, including the unbelievable and undeniable pattern, will be offered for sale at the first opportunity. The man is quite elderly but he is still driving around the countryside, even to Jenner, and Bodega Bay, California.

ILIKEKILLINGPEOPL
EBECAUSEITISSOMUC
HFUNITISMOREFUNTH
ANKILLINGWILDGAME
INTHEFORRESTBECAU
SEMANISTHEMOSTDAN
GEROUEANAMALOFALL
TOKILLSOMETHINGGI

TO THE VALLEJO TIMES-HERALD

VESMETHEMOSTTHRIL
LINGEXPERENCEITIS
EVENBETTERTHANGET
TINGYOURROCKSOFFW
ITHAGIRLTHEBESTPA
RTOFITISTHATWHENI
DIEIWILLBEREBORNI
NPARADICEANDALLTH

TO THE SAN FRANCISCO EXAMINER

EIHAVEKILLEDWILLB
ECOMEMYSLAVESIWIL
LNOTGIVEYOUMYNAME
BECAUSEYOUWILLTRY
TOSLOIDOWNORSTOPM
YCOLLECTINGOFSLAV
ESFORMYAFTERLIFEE
BEORIETEMETHHPITI

TO THE SAN FRANCISCO CHRONICLE

The solution to the three-part cipher as decoded by the Hardens

The *Celebrity Cypher*, mailed to the *Vallejo Times Herald* on 9-25-90, was never made public by the newspaper or the police department. The sergeant who gave this to us got his ass chewed out royally because they were trying to keep it very quiet. Perhaps they believed it was just another crank.

In my opinion it is not a hoax and it was mailed to the Vallejo newspaper and not San Francisco, and the wording is most curious. If someone was playing a joke why would two lines be duplicated? Cypher is a British spelling for cipher and he misspelled Herald, writing Herold. If a prankster did all of this he is very clever indeed—even the handprinting is very similar to some of Zodiac's.

This postcard was mailed on	9-25-90.	
Donna Lass (Sierra Club)	9-26-70	Are these dates just another coincidence?
Lake Berryessa	9-27-69	

<u>DECIPHERED:</u>

DGNLEOTNHULAETEUESLTIVEN (IAOE) UT (IAOE) UYTH TSLAUTETLHODIHE:

DGNLEO TNHU LAET EUESLT IVAN (IAOE) UT (IAOE) T SLAUT WYTH ETLHO DIHE:

LONGED HUNT LATE SLEUTH INVITE U TO A SLUT YUTH HOTEL HIDE (IQ = TM)?

The code writer utilized the same symbol and letter substitutions from Zodiac's first 3-part cipher. The only investigator who called in our suspect died—a "late sleuth," etc.

Another curiosity is that the reverse side of this postcard is "driftwood on an ocean beach," matching the card in the 1963 beach shooting of a young couple in a driftwood hut. The intent of the Zodiac is not the message contained in his code, but rather a tease to tell us—"Hey jerks, I'm still here." Also as the majority of the letters utilized are symbols his message would be limited in content—and the symbols look good anyhow—mysterious. From the Zodiac? Of course!

CELEBRITY CYPHER

I solved this March 9, 1995, at least my opinion:

.ilized same substitutions from ZODIACS first, - 3 part cipher: Remember, ZODIAC has used cards before, --Sierra Club; FLT 555 etc. etc. I had assumed that Z might have used another "plain text usage", just as he did in his code, - MY NAME IS, and it appears to be a correct guess.

DECIPHERED AS: DGNLEOTNHULAETEUESLTIVEN (IAOE) UT (IAOE) TSLAUTETLHODIHE: (UYTH)

DGNLEO TNHU LAET EUESLT IVAN (IAOE) UT (IAOE)T SLAUT (UYTH) ETLHO DIHE

LONGED HUNT LATE SLEUTH INVITE U TO A SLUT YUTH HOTEL HIDE (add IQ = TM) ??

Note the design used on the card, the first two letters appear to be, - "TO"

Note repeat of two lines: Are actually only 49 letters used, another clue to fact it was possibly a scrambled text.

The hand writing is very similar to our suspects. This was probably written by ZODIACS RIGHT HAND. Also, there exists strong relationships to two letters which are considered not to be ZODIACS writing, - but these were done with the right hand also, - my opinion. Check these questioned Zodiac letters with our suspects writing and you will say they were all written by the same man.

I believe my work above is valid for a couple of different reasons. Cryptic and short, like "birds fly south" etc., the tone, the character etc. it just sounds like something the ZODIAC would say. I think the profile shows that the ZODIAC very likely regards all women as SLUTS, and he likes to kill young girls, -- the YUTH. Again, we have the common misspelling, which many authorities believe is deliberate.

He has not hunted in a long time so, -- he LONGS TO HUNT:

Only two letters not used, -- the IQ and they would be TM if he followed same usage of substitution, and as you can see it may be at the beginning or the end of the message, hard to tell.

Lyndon

CELEBRITY CYPHER
VALLEJO TIMES HERALD
VALLEJO CA.

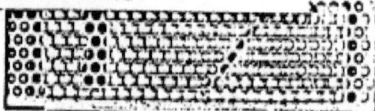

(POSTMARK IS OAKLAND 9-25-90

(LAKE BERRYESSA ANNIVERSARY) (OF 9-26-69) ?

Lyndon
3-9-95

REVERSE OF CARD - DRIFTWOOD ON OCEAN BEACH

(the Vallejo P.D. Officer that gave this to us later was chewed out when his supervisor found out) (woopee, love it, -- what a bunch of B.S.)

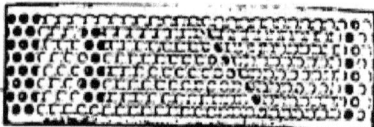

Zodiac's Mt. Diablo Bomb Code: Letter of June 26, 1970. He said:

"The map coupled with this code will tell you where the bomb is set. You have until next fall to dig it up."

C∆J I■O ꓘ ⫫ A M⊣▲ΩO R T G X ʘ F D V L◪ H C E L ⊕ P W∆

This is the code the senior cryptographer for the FBI asked me to "Take another look at it Lyndon, if you will." I had initially told him I thought it was unsolvable as I had already spent hours working on it years before. However, I examined it every night for about two weeks and suddenly the entire message just jumped off the page. Plain, simple, in sequence, and every letter is utilized precisely as intended by the Zodiac. I mailed my solution to the senior analyst, the one who teaches code to agents of the National Security Agency.

ZODIAC'S HALLOWEEN CARD

Mailed to Paul Avery, Investigative Reporter, for the *San Francisco Chronicle*

October 28, 1970

The letter was threatening in nature. Paul Avery obtained a concealed weapons permit.

The strange "spider-like" symbol was never regarded for what it was in fact—the sender's name.

It is in fact the Zodiac's initials. The three letters are very apparent if one is aware and knowledgeable of the "Freemason's Cipher" re: David Kahn's, *The Codebreakers*, page 772.

While a few other letters might also be construed our suspect's initials are most conspicuous.

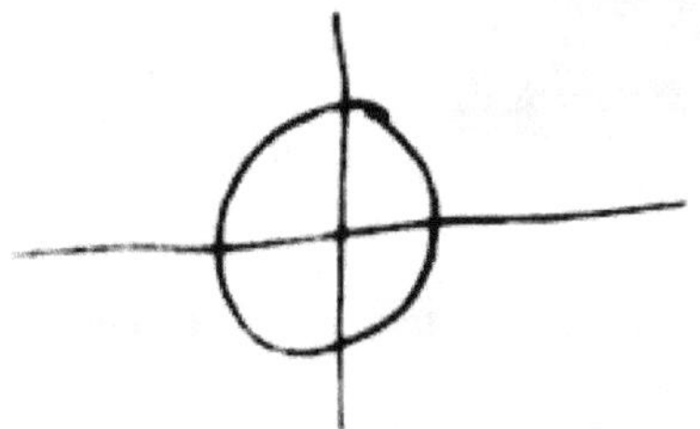

Zodiac's famous 340 character cipher-code remains unsolved. The leading authorities in cryptoanalysis cannot find the key to unlock its mystery.

Solving FBI's 2008 Code Cracking Challenge

- Home
- Contact
- Top Posts
- Subscribe

Root777

Computer Security & Technology

Solving FBI's 2008 Code Cracking Challenge

by Ajit Gaddam on December 29, 2008

The Federal Bureau of Investigation (FBI) has issued a code cracking challenge today. This was in response to a similar challenge the FBI issued last year, which proved to be hugely popular with many thousands responding to the crypto challenge.

The FBI Code Cracking Challenge

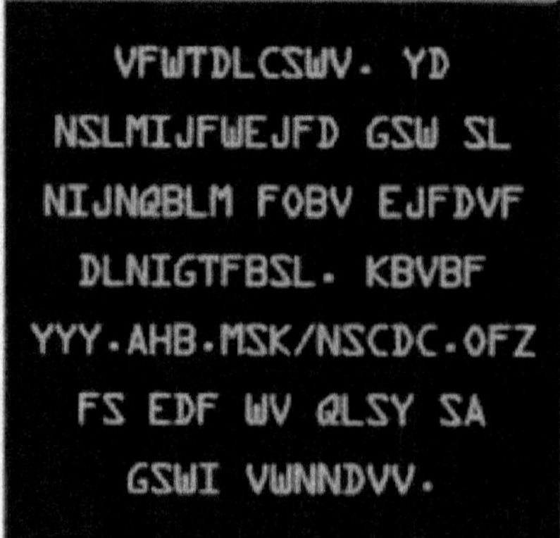

FBI

The FBI embedded the above code as a flash file. The code for all you cryptanalysts

> VFWTDLCSWV. YD NSLMIJFWEJFD GSW SL NIJNQBLM FOBV EJFDVF DLNIGTFBSL.KBVBF YYY.AHB.MSK/NSCDC.OFZ FS EDF WV QLSY SA GSWI VWNNDVV.

Federal Bureau of Investigation

Contact Us

- Your Local FBI Office
- Overseas Offices
- Submit a Crime Tip
- Report Internet Crime
- More Contacts

Headline Archives

CAN YOU CRACK A CODE?
Try Your Hand at Cryptanalysis

Congratulations, you did it! Thanks for participating, and happy holidays.

Deciphered;

STUPENDOUS. WE CONGRATULATE YOU ON CRACKING THIS LATEST ENCRYPTION. VISIT WWW. FBI GOV CODED. HTM TO LET US KNOW OF YOUR SUCCESS.

This is one example of a code the FBI issued on their web-site, challenging people to solve it. They had stated this code was more difficult than the one in prior years. Knowing the basics, this code is relatively simple and required only a short time to solve.

Thanks to my son Curtis, the Solano County Board of Realtors allowed me the use of their very nice facility on Springs Road in Vallejo, CA.

It became obvious that in order to preserve the precise methodology utilized in my Zodiac code decryptions it would be necessary to make a permanent record for posterity. When I am no longer here it would be very difficult for anyone to understand the nature of this complicated process, much less explain it to someone else.

So, my good friend James Dean offered to make a video recording of the entire presentation. After weeks of preparation, charts, and graphs, etc., on November 7, 2008, I attempted to explain the intricate details of my work.

Attending this meeting were my wife Yvonne, daughter Lisa, son Curtis, partners Jerry Johnson, James Dean, Bob Jernigan, our wonderful psychologist Kate Riley, and our distinguished guest from the California Department of Justice, Jim Selby.

The entire presentation lasted approximately one hour and the video turned out quite well. A buffet luncheon was provided by my wonderful wife and everyone seemed to enjoy the event.

We had the entire conference room for my display—confidential and undisturbed, a "closed door session."

Thank you Solano County Board of Realtors.

As stated previously, **I consider this code work as Zodiac's undoing, the best evidence in the entire case absent any DNA matches.**

XXXIV

PSYCHOLOGICAL PROFILE

The Psychological Profile

By

Kate Riley, PhD

~•~

Clinical Psychologist
Over 20 years experience
Specialty in Addiction Medicine
Private Practice and
Kaiser Permanente, San Francisco Bay Area

What kind of person could kill 37 or more complete strangers? What type of person would kill without the usual human motives—jealousy, greed, gluttony, lust, envy, sloth, or vengeance? The Zodiac claimed that he killed to "collect slaves for Paradise." He used popular idioms/literature/movies and music to publicize his depravity. His grandiose, narcissistic character and cunning intelligence made him front-page news in the early 1970s.

Although no accurate psychological profile of the Zodiac can be created until he is captured and interrogated, some generalities can be gleaned from the case based on current psychological theory. The Zodiac is a predatory serial killer motivated by power, envy, and devaluation. Fitting the diagnostic criteria for psychopathic and narcissistic personality character disorders, the Zodiac is an emotionally defective human incapable of forming expected empathic caring bonds. Individuals with these character structures have emotional deficits, which render them unable to experience tender emotional feelings derived from genuine human interactions. Psychopathic individuals have abnormal neuropsychological and biological processes, which impair the internal sense of balance/contentment. Consequently, their emotional and mental homeostasis is easily disturbed by perceived external threats to their fragile, but grandiose, self-esteem.

The Zodiac is exceptionally disturbed psychiatrically, but is not clinically "insane" by legal definition. When he plans to kill or send a threatening letter, he is maniacally calculated and psychopathic in his thinking and actions. During these periods, he can become intermittently psychotic, losing contact with reality. He blurred his own intra-psychic perceptions with actual events. All his immoral actions were carefully and methodically calculated to provide the exhilaration he craves. He is aware of the consequences associated with stalking, threatening, and murder. Zodiac received immense pleasure from taunting and sadistically teasing police, as well as inflicting terror on the public. Like most serial killers, he felt no guilt or remorse, just complete disdain for his victims and those who cared about them.

For a successful serial killer to remain undetected, he must be able to compartmentalize his feelings, and disassociate himself from the gruesome actions he executes. The suspect described in this case was capable of maintaining extremely morally discrepant behaviors without apparent cognitive dissonance. Psychopathic characters, such as the Zodiac, have an intense need to feel superior to other people, and thrive on the emotional weaknesses of others. In order to maintain balance in his turbulent internal world, he formulates maniacal delusions of his powers to control others.

Never having interviewed or met the suspected Zodiac killer, the following is a speculative comparison of the personality and psychological characteristics of the suspect with details particularly relative to this case. This character comparison is derived from discussions between parties who know the suspect and the suspect's wife, and those who were directly involved in the investigation.

The suspect is profoundly and emotionally disturbed and is a callous social deviant. He likely has some degree of a genetic/biological component of bipolar or schizophrenic illness; perhaps a schizoaffective type of imbalance influenced by both vulnerable brain chemistry and highly disturbed characterological factors. Because of early experiences of emotional misalignment with others, he has maintained a lifelong sensitivity or perceived rejection, especially from women. This likely incited intense feelings of anger and hatred, which defensively was displayed as superiority and disdain. He probably grew up as an only child with an absent or distant father and a detached, preoccupied mother who did little to care for his developmental emotional needs. It is likely that the suspect despises vulnerability and innocence in others because his own innocence was deeply violated/wounded in a callous manner. Perhaps a grandmother, or aunt was especially *sadistically cruel* to him. He may have been a victim of humiliating sexual abuse, which caused deep shame, scarred his emerging sexuality, and further damaged his self-image. He developed a strong defense against emotional vulnerability by creating an elaborate grandiose fantasy of himself as especially superior and in control, unconsciously defending an inadequate self-identity by destroying that which he lacks. When he feels threatened or scared, he imagines himself to be in a position of omnipotent power over the destiny/fate of others.

Throughout his life, he has felt little sense of connection to humanity nor has the capacity to care about the plight of other human beings. He selects people in his life in the same manner he selects his victims—*carefully*—in a calculated fashion to enhance his feelings of potency and grandiosity. He interacts solely with people who are able to serve his needs. He feels extremely competitive with other men, and can easily become aggressive and bullying. He is compulsively driven to engage in behavior that brings him intoxicating or sadistic pleasure. He enjoyed the police and media attention as much as the sensations he received from killing his victims. He had a disturbing ability to see others as non-humans who were without separate meaningful lives. He was indifferent about how his actions caused grief to the families of his victims. He slept peacefully without conflict, remorse, or guilt. Unlike most humans, he does not experience upsetting memories or flashbacks of the brutality he inflicted. Suffering and fear may actually excite him. For example, should he observe a child being abused, he would lack the expected altruistic protective anger other empathetic people experience. In other words, he does not have the ability to respond with genuine emotional responses. Publicly, the Zodiac killer can be composed, bright, and adaptive to his surroundings, while privately, he is depraved, heinous, and cruel, with a chilling capacity to shut off fear, and fear of consequences. He is a highly intelligent, well organized, methodical serial killer who is exhilarated by inciting terror and panic in innocent people.

The suspect was very duplicitous. He publicly identified himself as a recovering alcoholic, and was active in Alcoholics Anonymous for over 40 years. It is likely he developed a serious substance addiction during the military, which endured throughout his first marriage. The AA fellowship encourages members to develop humility, spirituality, forgiveness, and gratitude, through self-examination of character. For several decades the suspect attended weekly support groups and participated in the AA service organization on a national level. He was seen as an emotionally supportive role model for other people who wanted to recover from alcoholism. Coexisting with this persona of a spiritually awakened, recovering alcoholic, the suspect was repeatedly hostile, vindictive, self-serving, dishonest, and amoral.

The Zodiac claimed the righteousness to judge, punish, and even kill women who he felt were unacceptable. The suspect was repeatedly violent, condescending, and controlling with his female co-workers, acquaintances, and his first wife. The suspect was narcissistically entitled and self-aggrandizing in his relationships with employers, co-workers, and AA members. While employed at a major bank, he victimized a female co-worker by falsifying a loan for $20,000 in her name. When working in another business he embezzled $25,000 and used the funds to buy into a title company, which was closed down after a short period of time. This unscrupulous, illegal behavior occurred while he was promoting the principles of the AA 12-Step program, which encourages members to conduct themselves with honesty and integrity.

In psychopathic fashion, the suspect skillfully cultivated personal connections that were strategically beneficial to him. He affiliated with other narcissistically ill people who were in positions of power and notoriety. He used the connections and knowledge gleaned from the interpersonal relationships to his advantage. In 1964 the suspect met his future wife, an ambitious, intelligent woman, who worked at the courthouse as a legal secretary for a prominent, well-connected Superior Court judge. This judge also had severely narcissistic features as well as a habit of sexual indiscretions. When the suspect learned that his wife had been seen having sex with the judge in the courthouse, the suspect became enraged and later assaulted the judge in a public parking lot outside a bar, beating him severely. The judge did not dare identify his assailant and told investigators to stop looking at the suspect in connection to the Zodiac case. The suspect's wife also established a personal and professional relationship with the wife of the Highway Patrol officer who is the key witness/investigator in the case. It is likely that the suspect experienced immense excitement from having social contact and playing psychological roulette with the patrol officer.

The suspect was a gambler literally and figuratively, always trying to beat the odds and stack the deck in his favor. During the years 1966–1971 the suspect was unemployed and had large blocks of *unaccounted time* to prepare his codes, letters, and plot details of his murders. At the height of the Zodiac killings the suspect and his wife lived in a rural house, isolated from neighbors and away from town. This was also the height of the hippie era with the "free love" movement, anti-war protests, race riots, and the first landing on the moon. It was a time of rapid societal reconfiguration of racial and gender norms. Psychedelic drugs were glamorized and promoted. He would have been charismatic and engaging, encouraging his wife to be a "cool cat," a swinger and freethinker, unbound by stereotyped conventions. He likely came to know other sexual deviants in the area who were feeding off vulnerable societal outliers.

With his AA involvement, he had freedom to be out all hours of the night. He drove all around the nearby cities on the back roads and freeways in fast cars, having sex with men in motels and rest areas, tailing waitresses, and affiliating with unscrupulous business partners. He engaged in numerous illicit sexual connections involving wayward young men, misguided young females, and other lost souls. He may have deepened his involvement in the subculture by becoming a drug-dealer or pimp. He associated with youth on society's rebellious fringe and victimized the disenfranchised. During this period, his private psychotic fantasies leaked out into his interpersonal interactions.

After experiencing several blows to his self-esteem—being fired from a couple of jobs, losing a business, and having his associates go to prison, his wife's affair with the judge may have been the breaking point. The suspect's fragile narcissistic personality may have been so injured and humiliated at being cuckolded and displaced by the powerful judge, that he was triggered into a psychopathic killing spree. The suspect may have become the Zodiac killer to intimidate his wife and the judge, terrorize the public, and embarrass law enforcement. Psychopathic killers have a higher threshold for excitement, and the ability to remain calm and calculating while executing their plans. They also tend to be extremely self-confident and condescending. With each killing, he perceived himself as more superior, even omnipotent.

I think a good case can be made that the suspect is the Zodiac killer. The suspect has atypical behaviors, which are similar to those of the Zodiac killer. The suspect displayed overt hostility, arrogance and disrespect for police in car chases and while being interviewed, and repeatedly took bold, calculated risks (driving 100 MPH, threatening the Highway Patrol). The suspect is prone to abrupt violent outbursts with people whom he could bully without repercussions. Arrogant, vindictive, and overflowing with contempt for women, the suspect was physically and emotionally threatening to judges, legal authorities, and female acquaintances. From what was observed by people involved with the suspect, his vengeance was aimed at both men and women, but particularly at male authority figures and pretty young women.

Earlier in his life, his abuse of alcohol likely disinherited and fueled his aggression, which caused his first wife to divorce him with charges of cruelty and domestic violence. Assuming that he did have connections with homosexual and subculture fringes, it is likely that he had experiences with mind-altering substances besides alcohol (LSD, Speed, Cannabis), which may have interacted with a preexisting abnormal brain chemistry and narcissistic personality structure. It was even possible that our suspect was associated with the subgroup of AA members, such as Bill W., the co-founder of AA, who were experimenting with LSD during the late 1960s and early 1970s. Unfortunate interactions between expanding (or altering) substances and brain chemistry do occur more frequently and profoundly if there is genetic predisposition for mental illness. His wife's affair with the judge may have disrupted an underlying neurobiological imbalance, pushing him over the edge and triggering maniacal fantasies of vengeful psychopathic superiority and psychotic entitlement.

The characterological and behavioral patterns of the killer and our suspect are quite similar. The suspect had opportunity, means, and motive. He lived near the majority of the murder sites, had code and firearm training, and was psychologically unbalanced with a lifelong pattern of hypocritical, unethical, and amoral behaviors. Both the suspect and the Zodiac had mastered the ability to anticipate others' intentions and probable reactions. Exhilarated by danger and confidently cocky, the Zodiac reveled in his own cleverness in success over the police. During the past 40 years of investigation, the suspect was brilliantly perceptive and skillfully evasive. He consistently outsmarted and outmaneuvered investigators who were trying to link him to the case. The suspect acted with defensive hyper-vigilance, constantly calculating optimal strategies to maintain his advantage. Both the suspect and the Zodiac enjoyed inciting abject terror in innocent people and observing their fearful reactions.

If the suspect described within this book is the Zodiac killer, he has been a highly functioning psychopath who eluded discovery and capture for the past five decades. He was incredibly brilliant in his ability to predict and plan criminal and murderous acts yet, unable to use that same intelligence to secure wealth or legitimate fame. He is now 91, living alone, and without an observable avenue for power over others; and he sits on the biggest secret in Northern California.

Dr. Kate Riley:

Our brilliant and charming clinical psychologist, who gave us new insights and perspectives, a true luminary, who exudes a profundity of excellence. Kate wrote the psychological profile of the Zodiac, expressly for my book. Her treatise will be regarded as a masterpiece not only by her peers, but by students of the criminal mind for many, many years. I do not believe our meeting was just a random coincidence.

Kate Riley, with members of the Zodiac Team:

L to R:

Jerry Johnson
Kate Riley
Your Author
James (Jimmy) Dean

XXXV

CURRENT EVENTS

Since writing my final chapter, a great deal has taken place. Warner Brothers and Paramount Studios spent $81 million to produce *Zodiac*, which I think was a flawed movie that could have been spectacular.

Their first mistake was to base the movie on Robert Graysmith's second book, *Zodiac Unmasked*. Unfortunately for them, Graysmith was never aware of the behind-the-scenes investigation, and in his widely acclaimed two books he never knew the true details of the Zodiac case. He was regarded as the expert, but was privy to practically nothing.

Second, for some unexplained reason, the movie began with the shooting of Darlene (Suennen) Ferrin and Michael Mageau. This failure, whether technical or not, was a gross injustice to the young couple who sacrificed their lives to the insane Zodiac, Betty Lou Jensen and David Faraday, and their loving family members. Additionally, the director and/or producer missed the phenomenal opportunity to describe a major clue throughout the entire investigation—the white 61/62 white Chevrolet, a four-door sedan.

The true and chilling essence of the Zodiac mystique began on a lonely and remote road, a lovers' hideaway, on the dark and chilly night of December 20, 1968. Six-and-a-half months later, July 4, 1969, the second shooting took place at Blue Rock Springs Park, in the same geographic location as the first double-killing. Tall groves of eucalyptus trees stand like shadowy guards at both sides, and a lone Century cactus looms over the narrow twisting snake called Lake Herman Road. An old wooden guard shack nearby bears testimony to a Japanese compound used in World War II—obscure, out of sight, out of mind. The US Navy "ghost fleet" still haunts the gloomy area of Lake Herman Road. This is where the Zodiac truly begins.

The third attack on another young couple occurred at the desolate shores of Lake Berryessa on September 27, 1969, nearly three months after his attack at Blue Rock Springs Park. In this killing, Zodiac reinforced his infamous name and became a homicidal legend by wearing a black hood emblazoned with a large white cross-hair symbol that hung across his chest.

In my opinion, the movie failed to capture the chilling, menacing fear that came from the psychosis of the Zodiac.

In January 2008, Warner Brothers and Paramount released their two-disc Editor's Cut of the movie, which contained many personal witnesses and investigator testimonials. Author Graysmith had to laugh when Capt. Ken Narlow took the film crew to the wrong location at Lake Berryessa, but the mistake was soon discovered. (Years before, Narlow had given Jerry and I the wrong directions, also.)

Michael Mageau, the young man shot at Blue Rock Springs Park with Darlene Ferrin, told a fascinating story that deviated considerably from his original statements to the police. Now he's stating, "Darlene and I were being chased by an older man. She had a fight with him earlier at Terry's Restaurant."

He repeated this more than once, "Boy, were we ever chased. When he pulled up behind us at Blue Rock, I asked Darlene, Who is this guy? She said, 'Oh never mind, but if he knew I was talking to you about him killing someone in Mexico, he would kill me, too.'"

Mageau said the man drove off, then came back in just a few minutes.

"I rolled down my window and got out my wallet to show my ID, and he walked up with a blinding flashlight. I was certain it was a cop. Then he started shooting. He was a white male, about six feet tall, 180 to 185 pounds, and had jet-black, wavy, curly hair. I think he was driving a light-tan Chevrolet. He drove off so slow you could barely hear the engine.... I was wearing a lot of clothes to beef myself up because I always looked skinny."

Vallejo Police Officer Richard Hoffman was the first to arrive at the scene, and he stated, "Darlene was trying to say something, but was unable to do so."

Hoffman said, "There was no talking to Darlene under CPR in the ambulance, and she expired en route to the hospital."

Robert Graysmith stated in his book that Officer Hoffman also knew Darlene, but, in truth, he had never seen her before, and certainly did not know her.

One other anomaly in this Editor's Cut should be addressed. After Arthur Leigh Allen's nationwide television interviews, and his photo appearing in every crime magazine and newspaper in the country for many years, Michael Mageau's photo lineup identification was totally absurd. Officer George Bawart located Mageau in mid-1992 showing him Allen at about 220 pounds, 6'2", very round face and virtually bald.

Staring into a blinding light and a blazing gun only added doubt to his "positive" identification, especially after 23 years. I personally believe that Mageau recognized Allen from all the publicity Allen had received, and was, in fact, thinking, *Yeah, this is the guy they say shot me.* Mageau's revised statements are extremely important, as they tend to confirm with a high degree of certainty that Darlene Ferrin knew her killer.

[Officer George F. Bawart passed away on January 25, 2010.]
[9-3-39 / 1-25-10]

In early 2007, we found a phone message from our suspect, George Tucker, that said, "I had just returned from my AA meeting, and I called Travis Air Force Base hospital and they told me Lia had died."

He left his phone number for us to call. We knew she had been very sick.

Eventually, after about two weeks, a short notice appeared in the newspaper giving her name and the date of her death. It was not even in the obituary column. The article was most unusual, short, and almost callous.

It read, "Those who knew her will miss her."

We called to check on the time and date of the service, and he said, "There is none. I will spread her ashes in the ocean at Jenner."

We asked if he needed any assistance, perhaps someone to drive, and he said, "I am very capable of driving and I need no help whatsoever." His voice was stern and very emphatic.

He said, "A relative from back East had flown out, and I drove him to Hooters in Sacramento."

My wife in a shocked tone said, "Hooters?" And he said defensively, *"Yeh, Hooters."*

Catherine Aurelia Maldonado Tucker, a beautiful woman who lived an exciting, fabulous, and dangerous life filled with suspense, a woman dedicated to her sick and tormented husband, passed away in obscurity. It was like she never existed. She was his rock, and now she is gone.

Will the bingeing and killing start again? Has a sociopathic killer been released from his cage like Hannibal Lecter in *The Silence of the Lambs*? Since the psychiatric counseling in 1976 and the AA confessions, there have been few strange murders, no killing sprees, no clusters of young unsolved female homicides, whatsoever, in an area stretching from Stockton to San Francisco, from Santa Rosa to Vallejo, Napa to Fairfield, and from Sacramento to Lake Tahoe—the geographic purview of the Zodiac.

However, stretching the point to a perhaps unlikely scenario, one the authorities will ridicule forever (while they solve nothing), is the Jenner connection and the AA meetings held around a campfire at Fishhead Beach. This beach is only five-and-a-half miles from the beach where a young couple was found shot to death on August 18, 2004. Jason Allen and

Lindsay Cutshall, Christian camp counselors, could not find motel accommodations and made camp in a driftwood shelter right on the beach. Just like the young couple in Santa Barbara in 1963, they were shot to death in their sleeping bags. The sheriff in Santa Barbara was convinced that Zodiac was responsible for that double-homicide in 1963.

A bizarre note was found at the murder site on the Jenner beach. It read, "At the Driftwood Inn, alone again, outside of myself and placid as hell."

The possibility that the Zodiac shot this young couple in Jenner is remote, but the authorities have been informed of a possible connection. One must ask, "What kind of person has a reason to be in the area and has the psychotic capacity to commit such a vicious and inhuman act?" We do know that the ocean at Jenner now holds the remains of Catherine Maldonado Tucker.

A similar killing of two unwed Christian activists occurred on Vancouver Island, British Columbia in 1972. Leis Carlsson and Ann Durrant were in their sleeping bags on a beach and shot in the head with a .22-caliber rifle. A Joseph Henry Burgess had moved to Canada from New Jersey in the 1960s to avoid the draft, and was described as a religious fanatic. His fingerprints were later matched to the killings on Vancouver Island.

For the past ten years, the Albuquerque, New Mexico authorities were staking out cabins in the Jemez mountains attempting to catch the "Cookie Bandit" who was stealing items and clothing from the mountain homes. A Sgt. Joe Harris and Deputy Theresa Moriarty attempted to arrest Burgess, who began shooting at the officers. Officer Harris was fatally wounded and Burgess was killed in the exchange of gunfire on July 18, 2009.

Lt. Eric Garcia of the New Mexico State Police and Sgt. Tim Duke of the Sonoma County Sheriff's Department were continuing the investigation. Burgess was a leading suspect in the Jenner killings as he had "links" in Northern California. It was not reported whether or not a .45-caliber Marlin rifle was found in Burgess's possessions. The authorities in Sonoma County must have had information that Burgess was in the Jenner, CA area in August 2004.

Other possible connections to the unaccounted and non-credited Zodiac murders are the cases of Judith Gail Williamson, and Linda Edwards and Robert Domingos. Edwards and Domingos were found on an isolated sandy beach north of Santa Barbara, CA. The possible connection is another white car and an unusual cryptic-coded letter mailed to the *Times Union* newspaper in Albany, NY—similar, if not identical, writing of the Zodiac's, phraseology, transitional writing from block to script, and the fact that Judy was abducted from her home town, Albany, CA. Her remains were found 29 months later in a deep ravine about 15 miles northwest of Santa Cruz, CA. Obviously, the killer transported her body from Albany, situated in the east Bay Area of San Francisco, to the Santa Cruz area.

Judy, a pre-med student at UC Berkeley was observed getting into a white car on San Pablo Avenue in Berkeley on October 29, 1963. An hour later she was observed in a white car in the Berkeley foothills, above the university on Fish Ranch Road, fighting off a man who was stabbing her to death. Two of her blood-splattered textbooks were found a few days later in a university garbage can. A three-inch paring knife was found with her remains.

We must ask, "Was this the same white car Tucker was driving on Lake Herman Road the night of December 20, 1968?"

Linda Edwards and Robert Domingos were found shot to death in June 1963, still laying in their sleeping bags in a driftwood shelter. After a nine-year investigation and after the Cheri Jo Bates murder on October 30, 1966, on the Riverside UC campus, and after the surfacing of the Zodiac in December 1968 in Vallejo/Benicia, CA, Detective William Baker and Sheriff

John Carpenter revealed that their evidence strongly suggested their killer was, in fact, the Zodiac.

While refusing to release sensitive details they did state they had information, which placed the Zodiac in the Santa Cruz area in 1963. Sheriff Carpenter said: "Although the anticipated response of this statement would be one of skepticism, let me say that we do not make this assertion frivolously."

Is this what Zodiac meant when he said, "I have to give you credit—you are only finding the easy ones—there are a hell of a lot more down there"?

So now we must ask, "What was George Tucker doing in 1963?" We know that in 1962 his wife divorced him after nearly 17 years of marriage, and after 16 years of dedicated employment with Wells Fargo Bank, they also fired him. To pour salt into a festering wound he lost the money he had obtained fraudulently when his new venture collapsed in the title company in Vallejo, CA in 1963. Had his cup of hatred "runneth over"? Did he drive to the home office of the title company in Southern California to plea for financial mediation, or to see the woman the bank officials thought he had married—the one who was the victim of his $20,000 fraudulent loan—with the corpse of Judy Williamson in the trunk of his car? A frivolous assertion perhaps, but not necessarily so.

In January of 1964, he married a woman he had recently met in the Fairfield, CA courthouse. With George Tucker, the coincidences are at least compelling, if not convincing.

Compare the Albany, NY letter of August 1, 1973, to Zodiac's other writings. The E's, D's, F's, G's, H's, and R's, all lower case, are not similar—they are identical, perfect matches. The authorities in California regarded this letter with contempt calling it: "A pure hoax from another "wanna-be" Zodiac copycat."

He also said, "Vallejo is a nice town." And which Albany did he mean—Albany, CA or Albany, NY?

On August 1, 2007, I called the DOJ in Sacramento asking if they had an agent who was the contact person on the Zodiac case. In a few days, I received a phone call from Agent Bill Ahern with the Attorney General's Office. After a brief conversation he advised he would like to meet our Zodiac task force, and we scheduled an appointment for August 27, 2007, at their office, 2720 Taylor Street, down on the wharf, San Francisco.

Our group consisted of Jerry Johnson, James Dean, Robert Jernigan, and me. The Special Agent in charge was Bob Castillo, California DOJ, and his two associates Bill Ahern, Attorney General's Office, and Jim Selby, Special Agent with the DOJ.

I made the initial presentation attempting to convey the most pertinent points of our 35-plus years of investigation. In this meeting, I withheld absolutely nothing, disclosing for the very first time every sordid detail of the case, from top to bottom. I included everything. This was the first time I had the freedom to reveal everything because Catherine Tucker was now deceased. That was the primary reason I called the DOJ. The Tuckers had been married 43 years.

Bill Ahern informed us they had ten suspects and our man, Tucker, was number one on their list and they were preparing to interview him. I am not certain if it was Ahern or Bob Castillo, but one of them stated that the Attorney General had a genuine interest in the Zodiac case, and the DOJ, State of California, had just officially opened a Zodiac case. Our meeting lasted nearly three-and-a-half hours, without a coffee break.

Within the next few days Jerry had prepared a list of questions he wanted their task force to ask our suspect and Jerry wanted us to have another meeting right away.

After Dr. Kate Riley wrote her psychological profile on our man, Tucker, I invited her to attend this meeting. When I read Jerry's eleven-page list of questions, my skin began to crawl. They were all designed to put our suspect between a rock and a hard spot, and I disagreed with his approach entirely. Not surprisingly, Dr. Riley agreed with me, advising the session should be so designed to let Tucker control the interview. After all, *he* has to be the one in control.

I told Jerry, "If he says yes to every question, you have nothing; if he says no to every question, you still have nothing. And if he failed a polygraph, we would still have nothing."

"I disagree with you completely. Either way, he will implicate himself," Jerry replied.

"Jerry, he is already implicated, we would have nothing more than we already have."

Jerry mailed his list of questions to Agent Ahern, including a letter of recommendations I had also prepared.

The weeks went by, and we heard nothing. Eventually Jerry tried to contact Ahern to ask if they had concluded their interview with our suspect. Jerry left a message for Ahern, and Agent Ahern replied by e-mail as his phone number was not working for some reason.

He wrote: "We asked him a couple of your questions, but the interview was uneventful." Not one other word.

After 35-plus years his response was "uneventful." Hello, anybody home? "Uneventful?"

I asked Jerry, "And you want me to believe they actually interviewed our suspect, 'El Psycho Grande,' *uneventfully*?"

A postscript, the *coup de grâce* in general terms: Suddenly and mysteriously, a document hiding in obscurity for 17 years and 2 months is revealed.

On September 28, 2008, our psychologist Kate Riley, Jimmy Dean, Bob Jernigan, Jerry Johnson, and I met for lunch in Concord. Jerry, my partner of almost four decades, passed out several pages of Zodiac material, explaining that he would like us to complete his test and mail our results to him in the stamped, addressed envelopes he provided. Two days later, I was reviewing his test and found two pages of a personal interview Jerry had conducted with a person on July 29, 1991, and I was dumbfounded.

I could not believe what I was reading: A female real estate agent worked for George Tucker for two-and-a-half years. When she could no longer handle his abuse, she left his office in July 1980, and was considering taking legal action against him for the theft of commissions of approximately $4,000.

She said, "He would tell me, to tell his wife, he was out showing property when he would, in fact, be playing cards in Benicia. He had three or four hundred-dollar bills on him at all times. A very unusual and inexplicable individual. He could be most charming, funny, and personable, and within seconds, with no compelling reason, become cruel verbally, at times physically a true Jekyll and Hyde. He would harangue, criticize, belittle, and verbally torment agents in his office, men and women alike. He tore up the real-estate license of one of his agents and told the young man he had misplaced it. He would give me angry stares, but I would always stand my ground."

On one occasion, she saw him in a raging fit grab a woman agent by the arm and yank her out of her chair. Yet, he was always fastidiously attired and groomed, taking great pride in his appearance; he had a Catholic upbringing on the East Coast and he was very involved in AA; he was open about playing cards and appeared to be in good physical health.

I immediately called Jerry for an explanation asking him, "Why in 17 years had you never mentioned this interview or the incriminating evidence it contained?"

Jerry relayed he could not recall the interview nor could he recall the name of the person he interviewed.

Amassing volumes of records, notes, dozens of reports from many different sources for 39 years, names and phone numbers of detectives, witnesses and other sources, things mysteriously disappear into tattered, dusty cardboard boxes. It has happened to me many times.

Gross deception or honest mistake?

In the final stages of the author's book review, it was remarkably discovered that the military identification number given by the suspect to Sgt. Leslie Lundblad was, in fact, his correct serial number. When advised initially by an official investigative agency that the number was entirely bogus, this author believed and trusted his source. Additionally, when attempting to confirm the information, as recommended by the FBI with Naval Intelligence, and being advised they had the suspect's *real identification number*, the author assumed the number given to them was *not* the same number.

Therefore, to set the record straight, the suspect did not lie to Sgt. Lundblad in an attempt to conceal his code experience.

In retrospect, the misunderstanding was not unusual considering the serious nature of the information contained in the files of Naval Intelligence.

Thanks to his due diligence, this matter was discovered quite by accident when my partner, Jerry, casually mentioned a note to FBI Agent Floyd Barrus from Sgt. Lundblad. The note contained the suspect's correct military ID number, which was dated March 16, 1971, the day after the suspect was interviewed.

Looming through the haze like a silent witness, Mt. Diablo strains to reveal the Zodiac's code. The compass to "magnetic North" points to his house,... "North West" to the buried bus bomb in the Lake Herman Road and Vista Point. The US Navy "ghost fleet" still haunts the gloomy area of Lake Herman Road. This is where the Zodiac truly begins.

Stamp date 8-1-73

THE TIMES-UNION
ALBANY, NEW YORK
12201

YOU Were WRONG I AM NOT DEAD
OR IN THE HOSPITAL I AM ALIVE
AND WELL AND IM GOING TO
START KILLING AGAIN
Below is the NAME AND
LOCATION OF MY NEXT VICTIM
But you had Better hurry be
cause I'm going to kill Her August
10th at 5:00 P.M. when the shift
change. ALBANY IS A NICE TOWN

XXXVI

CONCLUSION

If the theory is true that Zodiac was a manic moral crusader, we can speculate that his perverted rationale helped justify his killings. At Lake Berryessa, the two victims failed his test. In their maybe 30-minute conversation, he was actually probing their views on life in general, concepts of morality, and most likely God.

Being Seventh-Day Adventists, Shepard and Hartnell would fail by most Catholic standards and traditions. Seventh-Day Adventists teach salvation is given by faith alone. No one can "work his way" into the kingdom of God; no degree of obedience, works of penance, or money entitles anyone to any divine favor. Plus, their hard line against alcohol and tobacco can create contention with so many in our liberal society, especially alcoholics.

Zodiac regarded this young couple as suitable candidates for his revengeful lust. He was already anticipating his call to the police when he reached the town of Napa. Most important, he thought, *I must have absolute proof that I am the killer*.

He wrote a short note on the door of their Karmann Ghia in which he claimed the previous murders in Vallejo. He needed to give us the evidence to continue his crusade of superiority.

One thing seems clear in the Zodiac profile: His victims were at the wrong place at the wrong time, and all of them were doing the wrong thing.

If Zodiac can save a young girl hitchhiker from committing other acts of mortal sin, he becomes the right arm of

God, smiting evildoers and saving their souls ("collecting souls for my afterlife"). This is why our suspect said, "Nicole Brown Simpson 'stepped over the line,' she got exactly what she deserved," and my spine quivered as I gazed into his dark, reptilian eyes. (Yes, he was very, very serious.)

Considering the young ages of both Hartnell and Shepard, they were no match for Zodiac's worldliness. In one interview with a news journalist, Bryan Hartnell stated, "I offered to help the insane man standing before us, in a black hood of death, holding a gun and a large knife strapped to his belt. I offered to take the man home with me—give him a check or whatever he needed. I was trying to do anything I could do to defuse the situation."

In hindsight, the Zodiac might have resented Hartnell's take-charge attitude, seen it as a holier-than-thou demeanor on someone who might need killing. While calm, cool, and collected for 30 minutes or longer, Zodiac became weak and began to shiver and shake.

He made the statement, "I'm getting nervous."

He became nervous because he is not a hardened, vicious killer. Make no mistake about it, he had to kill the girl—dead. This is why he stabbed her repeatedly, 24 or 25 times. His first blow was so forceful he cracked her ribs. He administered single stab wounds to each breast, and one to the groin, revealing his intent to punish her sexually, to accentuate the evil of the female body and his violent hatred of all women. Bryan Hartnell survived (as did Michael Mageau).

There are overtones here of the quasi-religious beliefs contained in the precepts of AA, which itself has striking similarities with Freemasonry. Aside from the oaths of anonymity and secrecy, most members, if not all, have sponsors.

The primary point of comparison is the symbol itself. In its purest form, the triangle is drawn within the confines of a circle, just like the primary symbol of AA. While Zodiac did not use this exact symbol in his codes and ciphers, he used the triangle and circle profusely.

In the Zodiac case, I have been bewildered by the cavalier attitudes of certain officials. "How," I ask, "is it possible, legally and morally, to terminate a serial-killer investigation before it ever begins?" Blackmail of course, but was there something more?

Over the years, assimilating the evidence in its totality, the facts are truly real, and nearly normal when you consider the man is a sick, sociopathic maniac. Many people, not so inclined or endowed with his genes, might still be pushed to the brink if they, too, suffered his unbearable indignations, humiliation, and pain.

His hatred of women, and perhaps of the power they had over his weak ego, engendered his murderous vengeance. The outward hostilities toward the female associates he worked with and his uncontrollable fits of anger nearly got him fired on several occasions. When his first marriage ended in a bitter divorce he became a committed alcoholic. His lifestyle of bingeing and withdrawal continued for many years, and it is entirely possible he became a "maintenance drinker," maintaining a blood-sugar level for safe and maximum performance. As they say in AA, "There is never a problem that one drink doesn't make worse."

The maintenance drinker is always progressively worse, and they know it better than anyone.

Walking a tightrope of self-destruction and trying to retain his sanity, he was a typical, but serious alcoholic. However, as fragile as he was at this stage of his life, he had not yet encountered the devastating event that turned him into a mad-dog killer, the mother of all triggers. Yes, knowing and understanding the circumstances creates a most believable story, as the evidence, like a gigantic puzzle, all comes together. So, in its proper perspective, it is all, some might say, quite normal for a man with a huge ego and no conscience. This is the true mark of the serial killer or mass murderer—they know the difference between right and wrong, but they simply don't care.

Never having any children, he was neither blessed with their love nor charged with the responsibility of being a moral compass or guiding light. He was a free agent, living for himself only. Yet, Zodiac is not the typical serial killer. His letters are filled with pleas for help, afraid if he doesn't get any, he will lose control. He said,

"SOME OF THEM FOUGHT, IT WAS HORRIBLE."

The primary element, the principal causative factor in Zodiac's killings is—REVENGE. Adultery, the unpardonable sin, is terrible.

Adultery committed by your wife, with a person you already despise, is a pain, which cannot be endured. To kill the powerful judge would be too simple, for the blame lay at both their feet. He would beat up the judge, just to let him know he knew what had transpired, just to set the record straight. It was a brutal beating that knocked the judge unconscious, and put him in the hospital for two days.

Simultaneously, he involved himself in a subtle strategy to drive his wife insane, waiting for the day he would reveal his identity to her. Tucker was known for his prankster-like attitudes, always joking around. As indicated by the psychiatrist's pleading in the *San Francisco Chronicle*, asking the Zodiac to turn himself in to the "Grand Wizard," Tucker succeeded by forcing his wife to the brink and over.

The pivotal piece of evidence in the case was the extraordinary situation of the attractive young schoolteacher, Kimberly Lawrence, in 1974. She had no idea how she was turning herself into another victim. Driving in front of Tucker's house twice a day, Zodiac's "Sleepy Hollow," she was teasing him, forcing him to lose control. The positive identifications of the apartment manager, and the near-perfect identification by the grandmother, are both absolutely critical information, which cannot be ignored or dismissed. Did our fateful intervention save her life? We would like to think so.

In Michael D. Kelleher and David Van Nuys book, *This Is The Zodiac Speaking* (Westport, CT: Praeger Publications, 2002), they quote Zodiac on page 209:

> I want you to print this cipher on the front page of your paper. In this cipher is my identity.

The authors say,

> When the complete cryptogram was published, and quickly broken by a husband-and-wife team who were amateur cryptographers, it became immediately apparent Zodiac had lied... There was no clue to his identity in the coded message. As Zodiac himself said in the coded message, 'I will not give you my name because you will try to slow down or stop my collecting of slaves for my afterlife.'

The above assumption of a lie is false. As bright and well-intentioned as these two authors might be, they make it much easier for us to understand why so many of our children are put on Ritalin and other mind-altering drugs. The alleged professionals are often wrong. (Jerry and I met Kelleher with his television crew at Pam Huckaby's house in Antioch, years prior.)

Since discovering, in November 1998, the meticulous fashion in which Zodiac arranged the heretofore undeciphered 18 letters in his name, and thereby confirming Zodiac's identity, I have made a concerted effort to document every letter asking for a review and evaluation of my work. Sometime after I made my discovery, the FBI in Washington referred me to Special Agent Ken Heitmeier in their Sacramento office. Heitmeier was the FBI's Zodiac contact for Northern California. I again erroneously assumed something positive could finally be achieved. In fact, much to my surprise, Agent Heitmeier called me and we scheduled an appointment.

In a blinding rainstorm, my wife and I drove to Heitmeier's FBI office, at 4500 Orange Grove Avenue in Sacramento. The date was January 23, 2001. During our meeting, I had the distinct feeling I was at long last talking to a concerned and intelligent person. Agent Heitmeier appeared to take a genuine interest in my detailed explanations, but his remarks—like stating he was not a code expert—and his failure to ask more questions, gave me pause. It is a strange phenomenon, which we all experience. We are often intimidated by simplicity and become embarrassed to ask obvious questions. We are trained to believe that if something sounds "too good to be true," it is false. I have prepared a scroll, approximately eight feet long, wherein I detailed every single step of my decryption. Additionally, I had prepared a binder with a folded miniature version of the scroll, a detailed explanation of one other code, and other personal information concerning our suspect. Also included was an analysis of the similarities of the two codes, one with the other, a definite pattern.

I waited one year before I gave Special Agent Heitmeier a call. I was not going to pester him with phone calls, as I assumed the code authorities were in the process of evaluating my work. He had initially told me, "Your work appears to be very credible, and I will send it to our crypto-section in Washington, DC."

Now, after a year of anxious anticipation, Heitmeier advised me, "I have not mailed your material due to my excessive workload with the 9-11 disaster, plus the fact I have been reviewing other people's code work as well." (Right!)

I was not shocked when Heitmeier did not submit my code work. This entire quest has been either an obscene joke, a bad dream, or another page out of *The Twilight Zone*. His response was the typical and classical kiss-off. Disgusted and offended? Yes! Surprised? No!

The non-productive trail of certified return-receipt letters to Attorneys General state and federal, as well as to Louis Freeh and Robert Mueller, Directors of the FBI, does attest to the futility of my pleadings. It's like trying to report an imminent attack by a cell of Jihadian terrorists, while you listen to a recording telling you to punch number 9 to repeat the menu, or 8 if you want to hear it in some other language—and if you need to talk to a real person, call back Monday morning. So, upon calling Monday, you are advised the number is no longer in service and there is no referral. However disappointing, their refusals to assist could not begin to compare to the real day of infamy yet to come.

After being libeled and maligned by Inspector Toschi in the early 1970s, I had promised myself and my partners I would never again talk to him, or ever discuss our case with the San Francisco PD, after Toschi accused me of creating my suspect. As clearly as possible, I made my partners understand this completely, and asked them to do the same. Yet, after the San Francisco PD finally and officially cleared their favorite suspect, Arthur Leigh Allen, through their DNA examinations, I relented. I was told by Inspector Michael Maloney, "We had no jurisdiction and could not step into your case." He stated, "As your suspect does not live within our area, we lack the authority."

I was shocked beyond belief. Obviously, Inspector Maloney is unaware of Arthur Leigh Allen's previous address in Vallejo, or that San Francisco PD had executed a search warrant for Allen's trailer in Santa Rosa.

So now, I tell the world there is no justice, there is no integrity, and there are no existing laws that morality can supersede. There is no agency, and not one individual, who will step forward to intervene in this noble cause of justice. These "authorities" do not know the identity of Zodiac, and unless he is a resident of their city, *they do not want to know*. These are a few reasons why it seems the Zodiac case will never be resolved. The Mandamus Seven has known his name for many years, but we may never see him tried in a court of law.

If I am no longer here, my heirs will have the opportunity to publish my copyrighted code decryptions upon the death of our suspect. This special book will also include the eight-page code analysis of the National Security Agency, and those personal solutions of Edward Steinke and Henry Ephron, both past presidents of the American Cryptogram Association.

William Sutton was the last president of the American Cryptogram Association I communicated with, by letter and phone. He was very ill during this period of time, and I had not yet discovered the pattern in the unsolved 18 letters of Zodiac's first three-part cipher.

However, without the benefit of the pattern Mr. Sutton told me on at least two occasions: "I have examined a great deal of Zodiac decipherments from several authorities and police agencies, and yours is absolutely the best I've ever reviewed."

Henry Ephron said, "I am very surprised you have obtained the same last name in two different codes." He further remarked, "If a person with that name actually existed, he would be a prime suspect."

As there exist a great number of circumstantial facts in this case (*156 and still counting*), based on our liberal standards, most juries would find our suspect guilty, solely with these factors. As in the Juan Corona trial, when his attorney Richard Hawk could not prove the machete in question "was not the murder weapon." The prosecutor, District Attorney Teja, told Corona's jury, "Richard Hawk cannot prove Juan Corona is not the killer of 25 men." (And this is justice?)

While there might have been a total miscarriage in Corona's case, he was nonetheless convicted of 25 counts of first-degree murder, and all the evidence was circumstantial.

There is yet one other pivotal point in our investigation, perhaps not so dramatic as the schoolteacher incident. An unexpected meeting with the Tuckers at a local restaurant, which revealed a great deal.

While the conversation turned to eating places in the Vallejo area, I mentioned Terry's Restaurant. Terry's was notorious in the Zodiac case, this being where Darlene Ferrin worked at the time of her tragic death. The restaurant was owned by a former mayor of Vallejo, Terry Curtola. Whenever the locals mentioned the Zodiac case, Terry's would immediately come to mind—the names became synonymous.

When I mentioned Terry's, Lia instantly began talking about something totally different. At that moment I thought, *She is shifting in her seat*. The fact she changed the conversation to another subject was not so unusual in itself, but we were still in the middle of discussing restaurants.

When lunch was over, we said our goodbyes, and the Tuckers left before we did. Halfway to our car, my wife said in a surprised and emotional tone, "Did you see that? I could not believe my eyes! Did you see it?"

"I have absolutely no idea what you are talking about. I didn't see anything."

My wife stood with her mouth half-open, shaking her head, repeating, "I don't believe it! You really didn't see her kick him under the table?"

"What?"

"As soon as you mentioned Terry's Restaurant, she leaned over, I saw her, and she kicked him under the table."

Later the same evening and again the next day, I was trying to convince my wife she imagined the entire kicking episode.

I asked her, "On a scale of one to ten, how certain are you about the incident?"

She did not hesitate in saying, "It's an absolute ten because *I know what I saw*. Sit down at the table and I will show you." When my wife leaned, ever so slightly, I immediately recalled the very moment when I saw Lia shifting her weight in the chair.

There are, perhaps, several ways to read her action. Even

my wife, the ambivalent skeptic, was stunned by Lia's strange behavior. My partners and I agree that the only reason she kicked her husband under the table was to prevent him from saying something he should not say. She was afraid for him—afraid he might say something about Darlene Ferrin, the waitress killed by the Zodiac. Whatever he might have said, *she did not want him to open his mouth.* The only reason she would react in this bizarre manner was if she knew the truth about her husband. Based on other facts and information, we were nearly positive he had confessed to his wife. The kicking incident confirms what we have believed for many years—his wife knew everything and would protect her sick husband till her dying day.

Throughout the story, I have attempted to stress the fact that our small task force had no official authority whatsoever. Our primary objective was to convince or persuade a department, with jurisdiction, to review our case in detail.

We were certain they would take action when they comprehended the 156 factors of circumstantial evidence and the entire chain of events.

However, we were very cautious about revealing some of the more intimate details in the case, and we were prohibited from using other critical information provided by government agencies. For seven years, I honored my sworn oaths of secrecy with Sgt. Lundblad, never mentioning one word to my partner or anyone else.

My real nightmare began when the suspect's wife, Aurelia, initiated a strategy to develop a social relationship with my wife. The timing and motives behind her clandestine behavior seemed obvious and very transparent. She wanted to develop a friendship with us, to get cozy and close. At this time she had no idea why her husband had been called in for questioning, but she knew I had something to do with it. She was determined to find out what the hell was going on.

When my partner told his friends about the unbelievable social connections my wife and I had with the Zodiac, I was shocked, hurt, and stunned by his lack of discretion. We have had other problems and differences of opinion over the years, but the most egregious was when Jerry allowed sensitive information about our "fish bowl" caper to be published in Robert Graysmith's first book. My dear friend and I were mortified. Ernie—the calm, cool minister—was extremely angry. The release of this information placed Ernie in great jeopardy, which quite possibly could reach me and my family members.

Other crucial details revealed by Naval Intelligence cannot be discussed. Highly classified, the information fits the profile of perhaps a criminal genius. I mentioned this briefly in an earlier chapter, and I mention it now because it tragically demonstrates the flaws now inherent in our entire scope of criminal investigations. The dedicated marshal in the days of the Old West would take off his badge, cross the border, and either perform justice on the spot or bring the villain back for trial. Today, if a detective refuses to reveal his informant's identity, he stands the risk of losing his job. If he does, he stands the risk of losing his life.

Plea bargaining, due to the crowded courts, is a national disgrace. The "Three Strikes" law, recently upheld by the Supreme Court, is a crime against humanity. I recently observed a young black male running through the parking lot of a local restaurant, throwing a small green box away, trying to hide it behind a parking berm. Two police cars raced in, blocking both exits. Within seconds, two more cops pulled in, and one walked over and picked up the small green box. It was a TV dinner. If by chance, this is a poor guy's third strike, he could spend the rest of his life in prison. We are living in a modern version of the Dark Ages.

This investigation was doomed to fail when blackmail and politically correct, good-old-boy favoritism prevailed, giving Zodiac immunity from the eyes of the law. While the notes in my diary confirm this allegation as absolute fact, nothing has been so dynamic as the personal testimony of the Lundblad family.

They stated, "He was ordered to destroy his file and notes on your suspect, and never mention the man's name again. As God is our witness."

Of the suspected and possible 37 victims, 22 were murdered after March 15, 1971, the day he was called in for questioning. The arrogance of the badge is a bitter and outrageous legacy, shared by more than a few members of law enforcement. Fortunately, the vast majority of cops take pride in their personal integrity, and feel good at the end of the day.

The true irony in the entire Zodiac case is—

*The **last** remaining suspect, after thousands of eliminations, is still the absolute **first** suspect.*

The last investigator and the only investigator in law enforcement to write about the Zodiac was the very first to report the suspect in December 1970. It is essential to show whether the suspect is guilty or not, that the detectives directly involved in the investigation were made impotent—forbidden to investigate our suspect.

We should ask, "Which is worse, the Zodiac himself or the corrupt and nefarious officials who gave him a free pass to continue his killings?"

In retrospect, there are many things, which could have been done better and mistakes, which can never be erased. Yet, thanks to a powerful and intelligent support group, the Mandamus Seven, I did my best to keep our case alive. Without their active participation, their encouragement, and words of wisdom, this case would have died and withered away to nothing many years ago.

When I became depressed, emotionally and physically

exhausted, frustrated, and defeated, I told my partners, “I am dropping out.” But then once again, I heard the voice of my strongest advocate, Sgt. Leslie Lundblad telling me,

> *“Lyndon, do not ever quit. You have a strong suspect. Do not stop your investigation until you have cleared him completely and absolutely, or proven, for a fact, that he is the Zodiac.”*

On Lundblad’s heels was Double J. Jerry would never allow me to resign either, and there were several times his dogged persistence nearly drove me crazy.

Every person reading this book is now a juror by proxy.

It is my solemn wish the Zodiac will now confess.

He has proven himself a superior intellect, bold and creative, perhaps a genius. In his old age and failing health, he can receive the notoriety of the world, the fame he has so long desired. And, most likely, he would never spend a day in prison after his attorneys pled his insanity defense.

ZODIAC,

You know, we know, who you are.

This act of redemption will be your salvation.

You always wanted the last word.

It is the final curtain call.

It is the right thing to do!

BILL LOCKYER
Attorney General

State of California
DEPARTMENT OF JUSTICE

3046 PROSPECT PARK DRIVE, SUITE 1
RANCHO CORDOVA, CA 95670
Public: (916) 464-2001

Facsimile: (916) 464-0889
(916) 464-2001

February 8, 1998

Mr. Lyndon E. Lafferty

Dear Mr. Lafferty:

Your letter dated December 2, 1998, concerning the Zodiac case was referred to the Bureau of Investigation for response. Many of the concerns discussed in your correspondence were either investigatory or evidentiary in nature. The Department of Justice cannot respond to your questions, as this is an active investigation.

The Zodiac investigation is currently being handled by the local law enforcement agencies who have jurisdiction in the geographical areas where the crimes were committed. The local authorities have fully cooperated with this Bureau in sharing information and we continue to provide whatever investigative support is requested. We also continue to provide investigative strategies through our criminal investigative profiler.

The primary role of the Bureau of Investigation is to provide investigative support as requested by the investigating agency(s). This department is confident that the local agencies are appropriately investigating this case and, therefore, there is no basis for the Department to take over responsibility for this investigation.

Any pertinent information you may have regarding this case should be directed to one or more of the local law enforcement agencies who have jurisdiction. We appreciate your interest and concern, and can assure you the Bureau of Investigation considers this case to be very important.

Sincerely,

BILL LOCKYER
Attorney General

ALLEN BENITEZ
Special Agent in Charge
Bureau of Investigation

Lyndon E. Lafferty

January 7, 2002

Robert S. Mueller, Director
Federal Bureau ofInvestigation
Department of Justice
935 Pennsylvania Avenue
Washington, DC NW 20535

Re: ZODIAC
Serial Killer
FBI File number
9-HQ-49911

Dear Director Mueller:

It has become painfully apparent that my pleadings over the past few years will not change anything. I have been naive to think that my twenty eight years of law enforcement gave me a favored status. That I was offered a position with the esteemed National Security Agency upon my honorable discharge; That I worked in code for three years with the United States Air Force Security Service; That I was the first person in the history of the security service code school to pass the final examination with a perfect score, enabling them to make eight corrections to their own tapes, means absolutely nothing. It was never known if this academic achievement earned me the privilege of a personal interview with the base commander. In any event, Major General Powell offered me a teaching position in their code department. To this day I have never considered myself to be an expert as my knowledge is admittedly very limited. However, I do have some background on the subject which I suspect most of your agents do not. I am hoping you and your new administration will consider my request in a more positive manner.

Stalemated and bewildered for thirty three years, the local police agencies will most likely never resolve the ZODIAC investigation. If the FBI could render a probable or even a possible opinion in my code work, new doors of investigation couldbe opened. The current DNA controversy in this case is nothing more than a shadowy pretext to do nothing. Personally, I sincerely believe the systematic pattern employed proves the suspect's name to an absolute certainty.

Attached is a copy of my six page letter dated December 3, 2000 to Director Louis J. Freeh. This letter explains my thirty one year involvement in detail.

My meeting with your agent Ken Hittmeier in the Sacramento office on January 23, 2001 was very cordial. However, it is my opinion that my work has not and will not be submitted for your expert and professional analysis, -- and that is all I have ever asked. I gave my entire and detailed explanation of both name encryptions to agent Hittmeier on the day of our meeting, and I trust he still has them.

New information recently discovered in your own ZODIAC Killer File Number 9HQ-49911, Section 4 is most relevant. Please refer to page #43 and page #45. The Qc36 envelope postmarked DEC 16 PM 1969 was mailed in Fairfield, CA. The Qc 34 envelope of December 7, 1969 was also mailed in Fairfield, CA. To my knowledge these Fairfield mailings and letters have never been disclosed. We consider this critical evidence as our Suspect lives in Fairfield. Your analyst on page 45 states, --- "HOWEVER, CHARACTERISTICS INDICATE QC 34 and QC 35 MAY HAVE BEEN PREPARED BY WRITER OF OTHER LETTERS THIS CASE". In this regard I am also enclosing a separate file containing a few samples of our Suspects handwriting and printing. Also enclosed with these specimens is a large desk calendar which your staff will find extremely interesting.

The ZODIAC has claimed thirty seven victims and the record of unsolved female homicides maintained by the Department of Justice here in Sacramento is a very close match. My six page letter reveals that there are several knowledgeable and credible persons who also believe we have the right man, and they have never known the truly hard facts in the case. Our Suspect also has one other thing that no other has ever had, motive. Trust me when I tell you, the investigation of our Suspect was ordered to a close before it ever began, and on this statement I will swear under oath.

Yours truly,

Lyndon E. Lafferty
CHP #3511, retired.

Enclosed:

1) copy of six page letter dated December 3, 2000
2) 12 pages of specimen writing
3) 1 desk calendar
4) cover page -- question marks

Lyndon E. Lafferty

November 11, 2002

President of the United States
George Bush
1600 Pennsylvania Ave, NW
Washington D.C. 20500

Dear Mr. President:

When I am on my death bed, hopefully years from now, I never want to look into the eyes of my wonderful grandchildren and confess to them I should have written my last letter of appeal to President Bush. True, I had faith and trust in him, ----- and we voted for him. So, after a devoted and dedicated 32 years of investigation into the infamous ZODIAC killer case I am in fact writing my last letter of appeal.

Stonewalled and rebuffed by FBI Director Robert Mueller and the former Director Louis Freeh, the California State Attorney General and now the San Francisco Police Department, you are in fact the only living person who could intervene and you are my last hope. My request is not really about me, it is about solving the notorious ZODIAC case. My request is very simple and one I have made repeatedly for several years. I have discovered ZODIAC's name in two of his codes, --- the same name in two separate codes (ciphers), the only two in which he boasts his name is to be found. As this is critical evidence in the totality of the case, to help resolve this case, it is extremely valuable. Our Suspect never believed he would ever be a Suspect so in his flagrant ego he made a fatal mistake of actually giving us the hidden letters of his name. Like a fingerprint which is left by mistake, he did the same thing with his name.

At long last the San Francisco Police Department announced to the world about one month ago that they had now discovered enough cells to replicate ZODIAC's DNA, and their favorite and chosen Suspect, Arthur Leigh Allen had been officially eliminated. We have known for many years the true identity of ZODIAC but nobody seems to care. They have never asked us for the details of our investigation. Now however, as they had just cleared Allen and assigned two new homicide investigators to the case I naturally assumed they would be excited and elated to receive the results of our 32 year investigation and make the official request to have my code work reviewed and evaluated by either the FBI or the NSA. How wrong I was. I was informed they, San Francisco, could not get involved in "OUR CASE". My attempts to explain our situation fell on deaf ears.

I am a 69 year old retired law enforcement officer, devoting 28 years to the noble cause of justice. I am also a Korean veteran giving 4 years of my life to our great country from 1952 to 1956. One might think that under our bureaucratic red tape the cause of justice will prevail.

With the terrible burden and stress of our global threat of war and terrorism I feel somewhat embarassed to bother you. But I can assure you that if I truly did not believe our Suspect was and is the ZODIAC killer, still alive, I would never be sitting here writing this letter.

If an agency my tax dollars support cannot or will not help, where do I go from here?

Enclose: copy of letter to FBI
Director Robert Mueller

Yours truly,
Lyndon E. Lafferty

Lyndon E. Lafferty

February 26, 2003

Re: ZODIAC CODES

FBI Laboratory
Racketeering & Records Analysis Unit
Attention: Dan Olson - Room 2106
2500 Investigation Parkway
Quantico, VA 22135

Dear Dan:

When I received your call yesterday I thought I was still dreaming, and I am still in a state of shock and disbelief. Considering the pending war with Iraq and the terrorist alerts, I truly did not believe my letter to the President would even be noticed. It proves that from time to time, good things can and do happen.

I am enclosing the brown envelope that your agent Ken Hietmier used to return my code work. You will find everything intact, just as he sent it.

In the very back portion of the binder I did enclose a three page explanation for the 18 character solution. The prior pages are basically the same.

So, enclosed you will find the "MY NAME IS" code work, and the "18 character code work".

I hope you find my work self explanatory and I am hoping you can give my work a favorable and positive assessment/

Years ago, when I explained the "MY NAME IS" code encryption to my dedicated partner of thirty years, former Naval Intelligence agent, he nodded and smiled. Years later I showed him again and he nearly fell out of his chair. I told him Duh, I showed you years ago. He made an appointment with Captain Kenneth Narlowe, in charge of the Lake Berryessa, ZODIAC killing. So, in a couple of days we drive up to Napa and show Narlowe my work and he too became very excited. He said he was going to send my work into the Federal authorities for examination. A year later he told us he had NEVER sent it in.

If you can render a positive opinion this could open the doors for a continued investigation by the proper local authorities. If I had a choice between the various departments, San Francisco, Vallejo or Napa, I would prefer Napa. I have thought for several years the jurisdiction dispute would best be handled by the Attorney Generals Office.

I cannot thank you enough. Good luck - please call .

Enclosed: Binder with two encryptions of
TWO ZODIAC CODES, other
related material, Palm Prints
photos, etc.

Sincerely yours,

Lyndon E. Lafferty

U.S. Department of Justice

Federal Bureau of Investigation

Washington, D. C. 20535-0001

March 10, 2003

Mr. Lyndon E. Lafferty

Dear Mr. Lafferty:

First and foremost I would like to thank you for your years of service to our country and commend you for your continued efforts to support law enforcement.

In your letter to the President, dated November 11, 2002, you stated that you have in your possession information that may assist in resolving portions of the unsolved Zodiac cipher. Like you, I share the same desire to see a final closure to the decades long investigation into the horrific string of Zodiac murders. I have directed the Racketeering Records Analysis Unit of the FBI Laboratory to review your materials. Supervisory Forensic Examiner Daniel Olson has reported that he contacted you on February 25, 2003, and made arrangements for your materials to be shipped to the FBI Laboratory in Quantico, Virginia. We are now in receipt of your materials. If they provide additional leads in this matter, the appropriate FBI Field Offices will be notified.

Again, let me express my gratitude to you for your years of dedicated work and willingness to share your findings with the FBI.

Sincerely,

Dwight E. Adams
Director
FBI Laboratory

AUTHOR'S FINAL NOTE

In the past 40 years our suspect's name has never been spoken in public. We refer to him by a letter of one of his names. Whenever we discuss our case over the telephone we always adhere to the same practice, never mentioning his name, whether we are talking to one of our partners or another investigator.

However, there are a few careless and ignorant people who flaunt his name without thinking, and this has created serious problems in the scope of this investigation, not to mention the element of danger to those directly involved.

These people continue to make false assumptions about things they cannot and do not understand. Therefore, the author asks for your understanding in this very serious matter, and hereby requests that you avoid the temptation to mention the suspect's real name.

The proper authorities are fully aware of every detail in this complicated case and will proceed as the circumstances and evidence dictate. This investigation is still in progress and if it is ever resolved, leading to a successful prosecution, will depend on strict guidelines of non-interference by the public.

DIARY NOTES

To help establish the validity of this incredible story, I have selected a few pages from my first diary. During the first several years, I maintained a detailed summary of everything that transpired in this investigation with a religious dedication. The last entry in my second diary was made on September 12, 2000.

On three of the pages, the reader will find three references made by two Vallejo PD detectives, which say, in essence, they would have to talk to the powerful judge first before they began an investigation of our suspect.

They would not investigate our suspect until they received permission to do so from the judge—the same judge who created the mad-dog killer Zodiac in the first place.

The proper legal protocol required them to discuss the matter with the highest-ranking member of law enforcement, the District Attorney. As the district attorney was a member of our select Mandamus Seven, the covert Zodiac task force, we know he was never contacted by any police detective or any other person in law enforcement within Solano County.

The diary speaks for itself, and every word is totally true.

LYNDON E. LAFFERTY

14 MARCH 1972

1 of 2 Diaries

-ZODIAC-

THE

STANDARD*

DIARY

for Any Year

* Reg. U. S. Pat. Office

Published in U. S. A. by

THE STANDARD DIARY COMPANY

DIVISION OF

WILSON JONES COMPANY

The number of this diary is stamped on the outer binding edge of cover.

~~January 5~~

30 NOV. 1970

My First Disclosure

F.B.I. – Mr Barris.

Barris said–"strong suspect," that I should definetely follow through.

Barris made retail credit check and called me the next day and said– "this guy looks like a real phony"! ('ere – phony operation & folded."

employed by –
Ssbotaged train in 66-67? –
behind – Suisun ?
Barris said – F.B.I. interested.

~~January 7~~

1 DEC. 1970

My Second Disclosure

My C.H.P. Captain —
Frank Bates

Bates excited —
He called Inspector Walker at 9:30 A.M. in my presence. Bates asked if I could be relieved of patrol duty to investigate. Walker had to check — called right back and said —
"NO FIELD INVESTIGATION"
"NO INTERROGATION"
but I could —
"ACT AS ADVISOR" and
"INTERPRET"

Walker asked me "HIS" name and I told him I felt

~~January 12~~

Note: Capt. Bates - C.H.P.
Floyd Barris - F.B.I.
Mel Nicoli - C.I.I.
Les Lundblad - SHER. DEPT.

All agreed that [redacted] appeared to be a good suspect, after evaluating my work.

C.I.I. "C" ST., SACTO.
3301 "C"
445-7458

3-December 1970 ~~January 13~~

C.I.I. - Criminal Identification & Investigation. Sacramento

Today Mr. Mel Nicoli of C.I.I. came down & reviewed my work He said - "looks good". Together we met with Sgt. Les Lundblad of the Vallejo Sherriffs Office. Lundblad in charge - ZODIAC. I revealed my information and Lundblad was also excited.

(C.I.I. is the control center of all ZODIAC files and investigation.)

✡ IMPORTANT ~~January 19~~

During the week of 3-15-71
Sgt. Lundblad called
in - on a pretense of HOMO -
activity on Hunter Hill - Rt 80.
The purpose: to obtain his
Social Security number and his
Military I.D. number.
asked - "whats wrong
with homo - sexuality?"

was terribly upset and
went home & told his wife.
His wife was furious and she
told her
alled the Sherruff -
and they called
Lundblad up to Fairfield.
Judge , Judge
and
verbally reprimanded Lundbla
and Lundblad was told —
"HANDS OFF

January 20

Note:
If Lundblad had permission to pursue the investigation of ■. there would have been no reason for him to say - "if he ZODIAC - I'll resign."

This indicates that Lundblad was given an order - "Lay Off"

Lundblad showed me how he removed file and placed it in the rear.

~~January 21~~

Also told to-"destroy" any file on [redacted]

Lundblad later, had to reveal to [redacted] that [redacted] was a ZODIAC suspect and [redacted] told Lundblad — "good, you handled it real well — but - cool it"

Lundblad told [redacted] — "if this guy turns out to be ZODIAC, I'll resign".

(SOC. SEC. # [redacted]
A.F.
MILITARY # [redacted])

[redacted] told Lundblad - he developes Real Estate Deals!

NEW AREA
SIERRA CLUB - "TAHOE LAND DEVELOPMENT

3 January 1976

~~October 8 2~~

A few months ago, Jerry met another V.P.D. cop - (Hustead? or?) Jerry said this detective was really excited about our case & told Jerry he would do all he could. Jerry had made a couple of appointments with him, but for some reason the cop broke these appointments. Jerry became aggravated - angry, and eventually met with him. At this time, the detective told Jerry the following: -

1. - He had been busy!
2. - There are "restraining orders" about releasing information to both of us!
3. - That Mulanax hates Jerry's guts!
4. - He did not want to upset Judge - to get permission to work on this!

Jerry was flabbergasted - this is almost unbelievable!

?

~~October 9~~

WHY

It would appear that [redacted] is calling the shots! Does [redacted] have that much lever on [redacted]? This is absolutely amazing. Why, if its true (the past tends to confirm it as true) is [redacted] protesting [redacted]? Why does Mulanax hate Jerry's guts? Jerry hasn't really had much dealing with him at all and I am certain Mulanax doesn't even know Jerry very well! I have always been of the opinion that Mulanax is a big stupid ass, and now I am convinced. This detective also told Jerry that Mulanax has most of the police file on Z in his garage. HA - I believe it!

I told Jerry -- here we are, trying to work on a difficult matter and with ass holes like this to contend with makes it practically impossible.

September 28

Note: Very important ↓

Sue was very friendly with [redacted] mother ([redacted] abortion—same time as Mageu in hospital-- [redacted]) & told her that Darlene had an arguement with a man of Terry's an hour or so before they shot-- & that Mageu told [redacted] that this man followed them to Blue Rock Spgs. & that she & the man argued again out there, & verified by the caretaker's daughter who had to get out of her car to unlock the chain on the road to caretakers house. She told her Dad-- there are two 2 cars out there & they are in an arguement--later—they heard shots, believed to be firecracker (4th of July)

Mageu then told [redacted] that after this arguement the man left & about 10" later returned & shot both of them!!!

November 13

Inspite of our differences, we plod ahead!

NOTE: At another of the meetings, Mr. said- "IF I WERE TO TELL YOU ALL THE HORRIBLE THINGS I HAVE DONE, YOU WOULD ALL GO OUT AND GET STONED, RIGHT NOW"!

Can you conceive of this? Think about it. Here is a dedicated group of A.A. members, whose salvation is in A.A., and he tells them this! Unreal! - Unless - - - !!!! he is Z!

Also, he apologized to the members for not knowing their names! After all these years! knows them by name, better than

Does this say anything - mean anything?

Getting the fish bowls and all of the other items, and arrangements, has truly been exasperating. Transporting, preserving, photography, lights,

Today 5-10-77

November 23

H.B. missed a few meetings — while hand healing -- Jerry stumbled onto a girl - that lived with Darlene, shortly before she was killed -- "older, middle aged man - white car, setting in front of Dee's house couple of hours & heard he also at Terry's etc. -- Darlene supposedly told this girl that "she saw him kill somebody, that he been out of State & now he back keeping tabs on her."

Girl said she has never told the police because she didn't really believe Darlene, but now, she not so sure. Also that Dee told her his name -- but girl has not as yet been able to think of it. Jerry showed list & photos to no avail. Jerry seriously — asked girl & her husband if she would consent to be hypnotized! (Bad idea) ✡

Today - 23 July 1976 - I off duty
from back sprain - (Bus) ~~October 19~~

Yesterday, had lunch with Jerry at One Mile House. We discussed case & luncheon Jerry had set up with Capt. Ken Narlow - Napa S.O. for today.

☆☆ Note: Jerry was *finally* able to understand my code work on Z's "MY NAME IS"! Incredible, after all these years! Jerry said - "*Lynn, I think you have just broken the case*"! I said - "I tried to tell you several years ago"! I typed a letter to Narlow & explained my work. I made copy (in files) Jerry hand carried to Narlow. Jerry was truly excited. Jerry phoned me tonight & advised he spent about 3½ hours with Narlow, and that Narlow was enthused about my code work. He remarked - "It looks credible - consistent"

7-7-77

~~November 28~~

Jerry's notes - last meeting with Husted

Karen (hypnotized) is cooling off - refused to help make sketch - believe her husband is becoming upset -- she spooked.

Toschi, Narlow & Husted think Z will start writing again because of "MR. 44" in N.Y."

Prime Suspects

Toschi = Lee Allen (schoolmate of mine)

Narlow = Thompson

Husted = Zane

Narlow + Husted = Mr. [redacted]

☆ Husted wants to talk to me. He also wants to go talk to Judge. so he will not interfere when Husted calls for a palm print & search warrant. ☆

Husted is likely to blow my 7 years of exhaustive work right out the window. Husted asked Jerry - "DID YOU SEE HOW LAFFERTY WORKED THIS CODE? THIS IS REALLY GOOD"! Jerry said - "Yes - - it is good!

www.ingramcontent.com/pod-product-compliance
Lightning Source LLC
Chambersburg PA
CBHW060837100426
42814CB00016B/410/J

* 9 7 8 0 9 8 2 9 3 6 3 0 6 *